Lessons for Little Ones

Mathematics

Cooperative Learning Lessons

Lorna Curran
In consultation with Dr. Spencer Kagan

Kagan

Kagan Publishing
981 Calle Amanecer
San Clemente, CA 92673
1(800) 933-2667
www.KaganOnline.com

ISBN: 978-1-879097-19-3

Table of Contents

Foreword
Acknowledgements
Preface
Overview
Table of Social Skills
Table of Structures
Table of Literature

Chapter
1 Cooperative Learning in Primary Math Instruction
2 Organizing and Managing Cooperative Learning
3 Social Skills in the Primary Classroom
4 Cooperative Learning Structures

Lessons
1 - 36

Bibliography
Resources

Lessons

Counting
1 Twenty-Two Bears
  1a Can't Sleep, Count Sheep
  1b Ten Balancing
  1c Count Down
2 On My Way Counting Books
  2a Black Dots Counting Books

Patterning
3 Sensational Sweaters
  3a Favorite Flavor
4 Patterned Shoes
  4a One Fish, Two Fish
  4b Frog and Toad
5 Hippo and Lion Up
  5a Several Shapes

Geometry
6 Rainbow Shapes
  6a Framing the Rainbow Circle
7 Beautiful Balanced Butterflies
8 Buddy Builders
9 Shape Specialists

Classifying
10 Shape Search
11 Big Button, Small Button: Two Holes Or More
  11a Sort and Sweet

Graphing
12 Finding Favorite Apples
13 Plenty Of Pockets

Numerical Order
14 Coin Collection
15 Apples On Top
16 Numbers Line Up
17 Batches Of Bunnies
  17a Ten Rabbits
18 Number Search 2's, 3's, & 4's
19 Favorite Number

Table of Contents

Addition

20 More Mittens
  20a More Mice
  20b Plenty of Plants
  20c Cat Collection
21 Mosaic Math
22 Lots Of Ladybugs
  22a Adding Acorns
  22b Both Bug Jars
23 Animal Addition
  23a Cock & Hen
  23b Double Dogs

Subtraction

24 Minus Mittens
  24a Minus Mice
25 Changing Cherries
  25a Five Little Monkeys
  25b Ten Bears
26 Chickens Here & Chickens There
  26a Rabbits & Carrots
  26b Bears & Fish
27 Share A Problem: It Makes Cents
  27a Share A Problem: It's Just Ducky

Fractions/Proportions

28 Fraction Feast
  28a Cookie Swap

Measurement

29 Coin Characteristics
  29a Dollar Detectives
  29b Double the Data Detectives
30 Inchworm Exploration
  30a Finding Feet
31 Big, Bigger, Biggest Bear
32 Heavy Or Light

Time

33 A Couple Of Clocks
34 Roll And Write the Right Time
35 Changeable Clock
  35a Favorite Times
36 Time Around

Bibliography
Resources

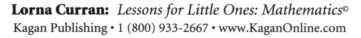

Lorna Curran: *Lessons for Little Ones: Mathematics*©
Kagan Publishing • 1 (800) 933-2667 • www.KaganOnline.com

by Spencer Kagan

Foreword

When *Kagan Cooperative Learning* first published Lorna Curran's original *Cooperative Learning Lessons for Little Ones* I did not imagine the response it was about to receive. It quickly became a best seller and has remained extraordinarily popular ever since. Ever since publishing *Lessons for Little Ones,* as I have traveled the United States and Canada to give workshops, in each city teachers come up to tell me how that book has changed their teaching.

Teachers Say

Teachers all over tell me how useful *Lessons for Little Ones* has been for them. They say things like,

> "I had tried and tried, but until I found Lorna's book, I really couldn't make cooperative learning work in my kindergarten class. Now we do cooperative learning every day."

> "*Lessons for Little Ones* makes it easy. Please let Lorna know how much I use her book."

> "My student's just love her lessons. They are always successful."

> "Lorna really knows my kindergarten kids."

Lorna Does It Again

The first volume of *Lessons for Little Ones* put it all together for the primary teacher wishing to incorporate cooperative learning: Lorna provided concrete management tips; a down-to-earth social skills program; cooperative learning structures adapted to the primary classroom, and three dozen easy, successful language arts lessons.

And now Lorna has done it again! But this time she has added another ingredient to her successful blend. As Lorna worked with districts, schools, and individual teachers who were using her book, she found a need for a new set of lessons - lessons which integrate math into her already successful blend of cooperative learning, social skills, and literature. The result is another volume of *Lessons for Little Ones,* - this time with a focus on integrating literature and math. Once again Lorna provides a ton of practical, proven lessons. Like the first volume, this new book of *Lessons for Little Ones* structures for success among both teachers and students. The new book is not dependent on the original book; it stands alone: Lorna has included even more of her successful primary management tips along with the social skills curriculum, and cooperative structures.

Tons of Tips

Lorna makes cooperative learning easy for teachers and students through her practical strategies. She tells us to take the time to have students learn signals - lots of signals: Speak Louder, The Tap, Active Listening, Team Questions and many more. This investment in learning signals has great payoff. It makes the difference between the classroom which wastes time with difficult transitions and the classroom which quickly and smoothly moves from task to task; it makes the difference between the classroom with diffuse attention and the classroom in which each student gives full attention to the teacher's instructions on content and management.

Lorna gives practical answers to key questions:

How do you assign roles? Lorna tells us to use a "Task Designator:" Pass four different colored slips of paper to each team. After students on each team each have their own color, use the Task Designator to reveal the roles associated with each color.

How do you make sure students acquire the social skill and the cognitive skill? Lorna explains that every lesson has two objectives, social skills and cognitive skills. So, if the cognitive skill is new or difficult, make the social skill easy or familiar; if the social skill is new or difficult, make the cognitive skill easy or familiar.

How do you make sure the primary students understand complex instructions? Lorna reminds us of the power of modeling. But she takes it a step further, suggesting we select the weakest team to become our "Demonstration Team." After working with the Demonstration Team to get them up on the skill to be modeled, they become the models for the whole class. By having the weaker teams serve as models we increase their pride and confidence as well as picking up the pace of the class because they do not slow down the rest of the class.

Integrated Lessons

Lorna's integrated lessons do not integrate all curriculum areas. They integrate three curriculum areas only: literature, math, and social skills. Lorna's integrated lessons also do not pretend to be a complete math curriculum. A full primary math curriculum would be far broader, including free explorations and a wide range of real-life problems. The lessons should be viewed as supplemental, a wonderful resource of great literature-based math activities to complement existing literature and math curriculum.

The lessons allow students to acquire and strengthen primary math skills. Students reinforce math skills as they play with manipulatives they love because of their link to literature. At the same time students work in carefully structured cooperative groups designed to ensure they acquire a range of specific social skills such as active listening, making polite suggestions, and taking turns. What more could we ask? - Cooperative learning, social skills, literature, and math all rolled into an easy-to-implement set of lessons any teacher can pick up and use.

Reflecting now, I realize I should not have been surprised at the tremendous popularity of the first volume of Lorna's *Lessons for Little Ones*. In one book she provided practical answers to some of the most difficult problems facing the primary teacher. And now with this new book, Lorna provides an answer to another important set of questions: How can we fit Literature, Math, Social Skills, and Cooperative Learning in one success-oriented lesson? How can we make sure students get the content and still get the social skills? In short, how can we integrate math, social skills, literature, and cooperative learning?

(By the way, Lorna is busy with her next book. Soon we will see *Lessons for Little Ones Volume 3: Literature-Based Science Lessons*.)

Spencer Kagan
March 1994

**by
Lorna
Curran**

Acknowledgements

When my first book *Cooperative Learning Lessons for Little Ones: Literature-Based Language Arts And Social Skills* was complete, I thought that book would be my only contribution to the field of cooperative learning. But as I did workshops across the United States and Canada, many of the teachers asked when they could get books which addressed cooperative learning in other content areas. So thanks to their persistence and encouragement, this book which connects math, literature and cooperative learning has evolved.

The lessons in this book are a collection of lessons that come from several sources. They have been used in my classroom, in the classrooms of other teachers in the ABC School District, suggested by teachers I have met while working with different school districts, or tailored to the specific needs of districts that have requested inservice sessions for their teachers. As districts have requested inservices focusing on math, I have been prodded to continually document the latest cooperative math lessons to use with literature.

Again I would like to give thanks to the teachers at Aloha Elementary School for collaborating on cooperative lesson ideas. A special thanks to my teaching partner Jean Chee for being willing to try many new cooperative learning lessons with me. Planning lessons with her has made it especially easy for me to try either a new lesson, a new lesson structure or a new social skill.

Just as I appreciated the many opportunities to acquire knowledge about the many facets of teaching language arts during my years as a language arts men-

Acknowledgements

tor for the ABC School District, I now appreciate the opportunities I have as a math mentor to acquire the latest information and strategies for teaching math. I appreciate the hours our Math Facilitator, Nancy Rach Fisher, has spent finding and pointing out the most important information from materials such as the *Mathematics Framework for California Public Schools*, the *National Council of Teachers of Mathematics* (NCTM), *Professional Standards for Teaching Mathematics*, and the National Research Council's *Everybody Counts.*

The knowledge of these math strategies, combined with effective use of cooperative learning structures, has resulted in lessons that address many of the necessary changes stated in the NCTM's *Professional Standards For Teaching Mathematics.*

- Use of manipulatives
- Cooperative work
- Discussion of mathematics
- Questioning
- Justification of thinking
- Writing about mathematics
- Problem-solving approach to instruction
- Content integration

Fran Kammel, who through her company The Reader's Clubhouse, found much of the literature used in these math lessons. She has spent much time either hunting for a specific book I have heard about or she has introduced me to new literature that teaches specific math concepts or makes connections between math and other curricular areas.

A specific thanks goes to Spencer Kagan who has taught me so much about the variety of cooperative learning structures and continues to expand and update those structures to find what works best for all learners. His book *Cooperative Learning* is a gold mine of information as I hunt for additional structures that are perfect for primary students or, that with simple modifications, will work effectively with young learners. I also appreciate his suggestions and support through the various stages necessary to complete this book.

Many thanks to Catherine Hurlbert, Celso Rodriguez, Benjamin Taylor and Michael Cifranic of **Kagan Cooperative Learning** who formatted, edited, and illustrated the book.

Again a loving thanks to my husband, Tim, who has spent many hours by himself while I communed with my computer.

Because this book was composed on the computer instead of the typewriter, I must thank my son, Steve, for being my technology teacher. If it weren't for his help I would still be on page one gazing in confusion at the computer screen wondering where to have that mouse go next. After his help I can look proudly at that computer screen and say, "I've come a long way baby."

Lorna Curran

Lorna Curran
September, 1993

Preface
&
Overview

Preface

When I first became a mentor teacher my area of focus was cooperative learning. I was asked to teach teachers of all grade levels the fundamentals of cooperative learning structures and to model cooperative lessons in their classrooms. I soon had a collection of lessons using many of the cooperative learning structures. Teachers would ask when I was going to put the lessons together into a book. There never seemed to be the time to format the lessons into a publishable form.

Then I started to teach kindergarten. I went looking for help on how to make cooperative learning work just as effectively in primary grades as it does in upper grade levels. I went to cooperative learning conferences seeking information to help me work with young students. I found instead that I would come back with many wonderful ideas that I could have used when I was teaching the upper grades but the content and format of the lessons wasn't workable for primary students. I wasn't alone. There were many primary teachers feeling the same frustration. It was the frustration of being told that most cooperative learning lessons could be used across the grade levels, and all we had to do was adapt them to our own grade levels. But it takes time to think of how to transfer the lessons to primary curriculum and it takes some degree of trial and error to change the format of the lessons so primary students will be successful.

I was convinced that cooperative learning had a positive effect in the classroom. I knew that it was important to have that positive feeling in my kinder-

Lorna Curran: *Lessons for Little Ones: Mathematics*©
Kagan Publishing • 1 (800) 933-2667 • www.KaganOnline.com

garten classroom. I wanted my students to receive positive statements from everyone in the class, rather than just from me. I wanted the students to care about each other and help take responsibility for their own behavior and the completion of academic work. I didn't want to become the sole disciplinarian again. So I began to explore ways to use the same cooperative learning standards and lesson structures for younger students.

Suddenly there was a need to revise my collection of lessons so they could be done by students who could do little or no writing, children who lack the wealth of background information that older students have acquired, and students who have short attention spans. Most important, these students were still in that egocentric "me, not we" stage. The younger students needed more structure, more variety of ideas, and more frequent praise and rewards. They also needed a lot of guidance in knowing how to share materials and ideas. They needed suggestions on how to ask for help, give suggestions, and give praise.

I saved my revised lesson plans and created lessons specifically for kindergarten students. Other lessons were created for other primary classrooms. These lessons most frequently used the structures of Community Circle, Pair Work, Cooperative Projects, Corners, Line-Ups, Corners and Formations. Many management techniques were also incorporated in the lessons to assure success for these young learners. I started to incorporate these lessons into hefty handbooks for cooperative learning workshops and conferences. Realizing these handbooks were still the only source teachers had for

cooperative learning lessons geared specifically the primary grades, I heeded my friends' advice to incorporate the lessons into a book. The result was the book *Cooperative Learning Lesson For Little Ones: Literature-Based Language Arts And Social Skills.*

As teachers started using the book or attending my workshops and conferences, they started asking for lessons geared toward specific content areas. My growing interest in math and science, the strong emphasis on group work in the new math framework, my decision to change from a language arts mentor to a math mentor, and my growing collection of math lessons connected to literature were among the many reasons I decided to write this book.

I hope that by trying some of the lessons in this book, you and your class will become hooked on cooperative learning and will want to use a variety of cooperative structures within your math lessons. I hope the connection to literature will motivate the students to turn math into an eagerly anticipated experience, that will make both math and literature more meaningful for them.

Overview

This book has been designed so that classroom teachers find it easy to use. First of all, the literature used in each of the lessons is listed in the Table of Literature so teachers know of the math connections that are available when they use a particular piece of literature in their classrooms. Additional literature is suggested for most of the lessons. This literature can be used in addition to the main piece of literature or can be used as an alternate piece of literature. A bibliography is included at the back of the book to facilitate reserving the books at the library or purchasing the books.

Chapter 1 provides a glimpse at primary students who are using cooperative learning as they manipulate materials to learn math concepts. It provides rationale for using cooperative learning lessons to enrich the teaching of mathematics and to make the necessary changes stated in the *Curriculum and Evaluation Standards For School Mathematics* which is published by The National Council of Teachers of Mathematics. It explains how use of cooperative lessons helps students be more successful on state and national tests. It points out the special advantages of using cooperative learning for young students and the value of connecting math lessons to literature.

Chapter 2 includes ideas for organizing and managing cooperative learning. It provides suggestions about what size group to use for cooperative learning lessons. It provides a definition of the cooperative learning standards that are used to develop a risk free environment where students enjoy sharing ideas in their cooperative groups. A section describes all the components of a cooperative learning lessons and reasons for leaving out certain components. Also provided are classroom management suggestions and ideas for moving smoothly through cooperative lessons. It addresses the importance of signals and commands which help the lesson flow with minimal interruption. It gives ideas on using praise and rewards to encourage increased quantity and quality of the social skills. There are additional teaching tips on creating positive interdependence, assigning tasks, forming teams, length of time teams stay together, assisting teams and assisting students who have difficulty working with others.

Chapter 3 explains the wide variety of social skills used in the book and the importance of each social skill. There are suggestions on how to incorporate the social skills within the lesson. Lessons which use each of the social skill are listed along with the definition of the social skills. If a teacher wants to focus on a certain social skill for a series of lessons, it is easy to find the lessons that use that skill. Or if a teacher wants to see what the skill looks like in a lesson, it is easy to find several samples of how to incorporate that social skill into a lesson.

The structures used in the lessons are presented in alphabetical order in Chapter 4. Each structure is defined so that the information is specific to using that structure with young students. The definition includes the advantages of using that particular structure and the procedures for using the structure. The definition may also include suggestions for adapting the structure to the needs of different age and ability levels, examples of how to use the structure, and management tips to assure student success.

The rest of the book, Lessons 1 through 36, contains lessons that address specific math concepts. Although all concepts are taught at all grade levels, there are some concepts that tend to be taught with more frequency to young students to develop a basic vocabulary and mathematical background. These chapters are arranged in a order of teaching progression. They start with the concepts that tend to be taught first or with more frequency with young students. The lessons then progress to those concepts that usually are introduced in kindergarten but are dealt with in more depth with first, second, and third grade students. The concepts addressed are:

Lessons 1-2: Counting
Lessons 3-5: Patterning
Lessons 6-9: Geometry
Lessons 10-11: Classifying
Lessons 12-13: Graphing
Lessons 14-19: Numerical Order
Lessons 20-23: Addition
Lessons 24-28: Subtraction
Lesson 29: Fractions
Lessons 30-32: Measurement
Lessons 33-36: Time

The lessons provide a variety of structures for teaching each math concept. This allows teachers the flexibility of choosing those structures they are most comfortable with or finding the structure that best meets the needs of the students. It also provides samples of how the same concept can be taught again in a different format to make a review of math concepts fun and exciting.

The lessons in this book differ in format from the lessons in my previous book. The lessons in the literature-based language arts book focused on a single cooperative learning structure. The lessons in this book use a series of structures in each lesson. Using a different structure for each part of the lesson adds interest to the lesson. Different structures can be used for each of the lesson parts: gathering ideas or "gambits" for using the social skill, gathering ideas for the team product, making the team product, sharing the team product, evaluating the use of the social skill, and debriefing the lesson.

Also there is attempt to make a balance between lessons that use the old "tried and true" literature and brand new literature books that have been published within the past couple of years. Some of the older books are out of print but are readily available in libraries. The new literature may not yet be available in school libraries but is available through book stores so that teachers can have their own copy in the classroom.

The lessons included in this book incorporate structures I learned while receiving cooperative learning training from Spencer Kagan. This book gives sample lessons from his Cooperative Learning structures that I found to be effective with young students. My description of the structures provides information specific to primary teachers. For further information on each structure, and other structures that you might find effective for your students, I refer you to Spencer Kagan's book *Cooperative Learning*. His book will provide in-depth information and rationale for using certain structures, procedures for using the structures and ideas of how to apply each structure in a variety of content areas.

LESSONS

19	Active Listening
32	Agree/ Disagree Politely
1, 3, 7, 8	Encouraging Statements
2, 4, 9, 10, 12, 15, 16, 20, 23, 24, 26, 28, 33, 35	Happy Talk/ Praising Students

LESSONS

9, 29	Helpful Teacher
11	Paraphrasing
13b, 31	Please and Thank You
34	Polite Passer

LESSONS

12, 21, 30, 35	Polite Suggestions
16	Polite Waiter
17, 25	Positive Suggestions
5, 13a, 13d, 22, 30	Quiet Voices/ Inside Voices

Table of Social Skills

LESSONS

6, 36	Ready For Your Turn
8, 18	Speak Clearly/ Strong Voice
13c	Stay in Position / Place
27	Team Praisers
6, 21, 36	Work Quickly

Table of Structures

LESSONS

8	Build-What-I-Build
5, 17, 18, 19	Class Discussion
5	Class Evaluation
3, 19, 24, 26	Community Circle
6, 13a, 20	Corners
13b	Find Someone Who...
14	Formations

LESSONS

7, 15	Gallery Tour
2	Group Project
3, 10, 22, 24, 26	Inside-Outside Circle
9	Jigsaw
1, 5, 13c, 14, 16, 17, 31, 32	Line-Ups
20	Make-A-Match
2, 8, 10, 11, 18, 28	Mix-Freeze-Share

LESSONS

1, 13d, 15	Numbered Heads Together
4, 7, 13b, 20, 22, 23, 24, 26, 30, 33	Pair Discussion
4, 7, 20, 23, 26, 30, 31, 32, 33	Pair Project
10, 17, 23, 28, 35	Pairs Check
29, 30	Partner Switch
32	Partners Consult
1, 17	Rallyrobin

LESSONS

34	Roll and Write
12, 18, 24, 25, 29	Rotating Reporter
2, 9, 10, 16, 17, 18, 28, 29	Roundrobin
2, 6, 9, 10, 12, 21, 27, 36	Roundtable
2	Send-A-Problem
7, 16, 21, 25	Stand and Share

LESSONS

10, 11	Structured Sorts
35	Talking Chips
1	Team Card
21, 34	Team Praise
2, 3, 6, 8, 13a, 15, 16, 17, 18, 21, 23, 24, 25, 27, 28, 29, 31, 34, 35	Team Discussion
3, 15, 24, 25, 35	Team Projects

LESSONS

5, 17, 21, 28, 32	Teams Check
4, 6, 7, 8, 9, 12, 16, 18, 25, 30, 32, 33, 35	Teams Compare
1, 2, 3, 7, 9, 11, 12, 13c, 15, 17, 19, 20, 23, 26, 29, 33	Think-Pair-Share
17, 27, 29	Think-And-Praise
7	Think-Pair-Square
9, 10, 17, 21, 28, 31	Two Stray

The list of books below is comprised of those books used in the Lessons, and also those which are suggested for Lesson Adaptations. This list is helpful as a reference to the literature used in the lessons, not as a list of required materials. The numbers in the parantheses correspond to the Lessons each book is used in.

Table of Literature

A

Alexander, Who Used to Be Rich Last Sunday by Judith Viorst (27)

All My Shoes Come In Twos by Mary Ann and Norman Hoberman (4)

An Apple is Red by Nancy Curry (12)

Anno's Counting Book by Mitsumasa Anno (16)

Apple Wars, The by Myers (12)

Applebet by Watson (12)

April Rabbits, The by David Cleveland (17, 23)

Are You Square? by Ethel and Leonard Kessler (5, 6)

B

Baby Bunny Book, The by Margaret Hillert (23)

Baby Grizzly by Beth Spanjian (26)

Bear Child's Book of Hours by Anne Rockwell (34)

Bears In Pairs by Niki Yektai (1, 31)

Biggest Bear, The by Lynd Ward (31)

Brown Bear, Brown Bear, What Do You See? by Bill Martin Jr. (1)

Bugs by Nancy Winslow Parker and Joan Richards Wright (22)

Bunny Book, The by Richard Scarry (23)

Butterflies And Moths by Henry Pluckrose (7)

Button Box, The by Margaret Reid (13)

C

A Cake For Barney by Joyce Dunbar (25)

Calico Cat Looks At Shapes by Donald Charles (10)

Carrot Seed, The by Ruth Krauss (26)

A Chair For My Mother by Vera Williams (29)

Changes, Changes by Pat Hutchins (8)

Chicken Little by Steven Kellog (22, 26)

A Children's Zoo by Tana Hoban (5)

Chipmunk Song by Joanne Ryder (22)

Circles, Squares And Triangles by Tana Hoban (6)

Clifford's Pals by Norman Bridwell (23)

A Clock For Beany by Lisa Bassett (35)

Cock, The Mouse, And The Little Red Hen, The by Lorinda Bryan Cauley (23, 26)

Corduroy by Don Freeman (13d)

D

Dandelion by Don Freeman (5)

Deep In The Forest by Brinton Turkle (31)

Don't Count Your Chickens by Ingri D'Aulaire (26)

Don't Forget The Lion by H.A. Rey (5)

Doorbell Rang, The by Pat Hutchins (28)

Table of Literature

E

Each Orange Has Eight Slices by Paul Giganti Jr. (2)
Eating Fractions by Bruce McMillan (28)

F

Finding Out About Shapes by Mae Freeman (6)
A Fishy Shape Story by Joanne and David Wylie (6, 9, 10)
Five Little Ducks by Jose Aruego and Ariane Dewey (27)
Five Little Monkeys (25)
Frog And Toad Are Friends by Arnold Lobel (11)
Frog and Toad Together by Arnold Lobel (4)
Fun With Shapes by Joanne Wylie (6)

G

Go-A-Round Dollar, The by Barbara Johnson Adams (29)
Grouchy Ladybug, The by Eric Carle (22, 33, 34, 36)

H

Happy Hippopotami by Bill Martin Jr. (5)
Harriet's Halloween Candy by Nancy Carlson (11)
Harry By The Sea by Gene Zion (3)
Harry The Dirty Dog by Gene Zion (3)
Heavy Is A Hippopotamus by Miriam Schlein (32)
How Big Is A Foot? by Rolf Myller (31)

I

Ice Cream Soup by Gail Herman (3)
If I Had A Lion by Liesel Moak Skorpen (5)
Inch by Inch by Leo Lionni (30)
Is It Large? Is It Small? by Tana Hoban (11, 31)

J

Jesse Bear, What Will You Wear? by Nancy Carlstrom (31)
Jim And The Beanstalk by Raymond Briggs (30)
Jump, Frog, Jump by Robert Kalin (4)

K

Katy No Pockets by Emmy Payne (13b, 13d)
A Kiss For Little Bear by Else H. Minarik (31)

L

Ladybug by Emery Bernhard (22)
Ladybug, Ladybug by Ruth Brown (22)
Leroy and the Clock by Juanita Havill (35)
Life of the Ladybug by Heiderose and Andreas Fischer-Nagel (22)
Little Circle, The by Ann Atwood (6)
Little Dog Laughed and Other Nursery Rhymes, The by Lucy Cousins (35)
Little Rabbit, The by Judy Dunn (23, 26)
Little Rabbit's Loose Tooth by Lucy Bate (26)
Little Red Hen, The by Paul Galdone (26)
Look...A Butterfly by David Cutts (7)
Look Around! A Book About Shapes by Leonard Everett Fisher (6)
Look At A Tree by Eillen Curran (22)
Look At Trees by Rena K. Kirkpatrick (22)

M

Marshmallow by Clare Turlay Newberry (23)
Millions of Cats by Wanda Zag (20)
Mitten, The by Jan Brett (20, 24)
Mouse Count by Ellen Stoll Walsh (20, 24)
My First Look At Shapes by Toni Rann (6, 10)

N

No Roses For Harry by Gene Zion (3)

O

One Crow A Counting Rhyme by Jim Aylesworth (16)
One Fish, Two Fish, Red Fish, Blue Fish by Dr. Seuss (4)

One Little Elephant Balancing by Edith Fowke (1)

One Red Rooster by Kathleen Sullivan Carroll (16)

One Was Johnny: A Counting Book by Maurice Sendak (16)

Out For The Count by Kathryn Cave (1, 20)

P

Pezzettino by Leo Lionni (21)

Plant Sitter, The by Gene Zion (20)

A Pocket For Corduroy by Don Freeman (13)

Puppy Who Wanted A Boy, The by Jane Thayers (3)

R

Rain Makes Applesauce by Julian Scheer (12)

Remember The Butterflies by Anna Grossnickle Hines (7)

Richard Scarry's Big And Little Book Of Opposites by Richard Scarry (31)

Rooster, The Mouse, and The Little Red Hen, The by Nova Nestrick (26)

Round and Round and Round by Tana Hoban (6)

Runaway Bunny, The by Margaret Wise Brown (23)

Run Away Mittens by Jean Rogers (20, 24)

S

Sam, Who Never Forgets by Eve Rice (5)

Season Of Arnold's Apple Tree, The by Gail Gibbons (12)

Shapes by John Reiss (9, 10)

Shoes by Elizabeth Winthrop (4)

Small Rabbit by Miska Miles (23)

Some Dogs Don't by Marlene and Robert McCracken (3)

T

Tale of Peter Rabbit, The by Beatrix Potter (23, 26)

Ten, Nine, Eight by Molly Bang (1)

Ten Apples On Top by Theo Le Sieg (15)

10 Bears In My Bed, A Goodnight Countdown by Stan Mack (25)

Ten Black Dots by Donald Crews (2)

Ten Little Rabbits by Virginia Grossman and Sylvia Long (16, 17)

The Three Bears by Paul Galdone (31)

Three Baby Chicks by Ruth Jaynes (26)

Tomie dePaola's Mother Goose by Tomie dePaola (35)

Too Many Mittens by Florence and Louis Slobodkin (20, 24)

Twenty-Two Bears by Claire Huchet Bishop (1)

26 Letters and 99 Cents by Tana Hoban (14, 29)

Two Bad Ants by Chris Van Allsburg (22)

V

Venn Diagrams by Robert Froman (11)

Very Busy Spider, The by Eric Carle (22)

Very Hungry Caterpillar, The by Eric Carle (7)

W

What Comes In 2's, 3's, and 4's? by Suzanne Aker (18)

What Do Bunnies Do All Day? by Judy Mastrangelo (23)

What Time Is It Jeanne-Marie? by Francoice Seignobosc (34)

Where Does the Butterfly Go When It Rains by May Garelick (7)

Who Stole the Apples? by Sigrid Heuck (12)

Who Wants Arthur? by Amanda Graham (3)

Who Wants One? by Mary Serfozo (16)

Wildlife 1.2.3. A Nature Counting Book, The by Jan Thornhill (16, 19)

Wing On A Flea, The by Ed Emberley (6)

Why Frogs Are Wet by Judy Hawes (4)

Y

Yellow Button, The by Anne Mayer (11, 13d)

Chapter 1

Cooperative Learning in Primary Math Instruction

A Picture of Primary Cooperative Learning in Math

Math in action. There is plenty of action in an integrated, whole language, cooperative learning classroom. Groups of students motivate, encourage, and challenge each other to create, complete, and improve upon math activities. They are anxious to create products that elaborate on the literature they enjoy or that reinforce key concepts they are studying. Let's take a look at students who are involved in three literature-based, high interest math lessons.

Making a Pattern

There is an air of excitement as teams of students decide what pattern their team will make. Positive comments abound as team members encourage each other to complete their patterns. There is almost that "field trip" feeling as teams tour the room to view the patterns made by other teams. They anxiously return to their own team's work space to read the symbols left by visiting teams, symbols that let them know if other teams could read their pattern or had difficulty reading their pattern. They intently analyze the pattern to find out why teams could easily read it or why teams had difficulty reading their pattern. Many teams find their pattern can be read and discuss the reasons why the pattern was easy to read. Some teams through group investigation easily correct their pattern by rearranging a couple of pieces. They are now satisfied that their team displays a perfect pattern. Other teams are excited to find that visiting teams couldn't read their pattern because they had created a new pattern that can be taught to the class.

Lorna Curran: *Lessons for Little Ones: Mathematics©*
Kagan Publishing • 1 (800) 933-2667 • www.KaganOnline.com

Writing Addition Problems

Partners have heads together deciding how many dogs they would like to color brown and how many dogs they would like to color black. As they color, cut, manipulate the dogs, and discuss how to write the addition problem, the students are enjoying an activity about a story they love. They are not aware that they are learning addition facts and also developing an understanding of mathematical concepts.

Creating a Math Problem

Groups of four are eager to complete their own version of *An Orange Has Eight Sections*, so they can send it on to other teams to solve. Through writing the problems, they learn to recognize necessary components of a math problem, learn strategies for problem solving as they make answer keys for their problems, solve other teams problems and then correct and give positive feedback to teams that solved their problem. What could have been an agonizing drill and practice has become high interest "thrill and practice." The fun of working with story characters they enjoy and the challenge of creating and solving problems for their peers, makes math activities a highlight of the day,— if they even realize they are doing math.

Need For Cooperative Learning in Math Instruction

The National Council of Teachers of Mathematics states several instructional practices that need to be in place for students to develop an understanding of math concepts. They say that students should use manipulatives more often so they will have a concrete basis of understanding for using abstract numbers and equations. They also say that there should be an increase in cooperative work.

Through cooperative ventures the students have more opportunity for discussion to gather ideas, think of many possibilities, question, analyze, and justify their procedures and results. They can use the problem solving approach as they use the expertise of all team members to arrive at solutions. What they discover for themselves through experience will be remembered.

The NCTM says that students should write about mathematics. After developing the skills needed to work together, cooperatively gathering data, and acquiring multiple strategies for solving problems, the students have many meaningful experiences to write about. It works best for young students to continue to work in groups to record their ideas. They then have help in deciding how to record the information and group support when it is time to report their information to others.

The NCTM also advocates content integration. Real life situations encountered daily incorporate all we have learned about solving problems. Students need that integration so that what they learn in school prepares them for life beyond the classroom.

The lessons in this book will enhance those recommended changes. In all the lessons the students focus on the improvement of their interpersonal skills, and thus improve in their ability to work cooperatively. Through evaluation and debriefing they share problem solving strategies so they learn many ways to tackle a problem. Information gathering and sharing structures are used in the lessons, so students benefit from the ideas of all their team members. The lessons integrate content because each lesson is connected to piece of literature. This literature connects to many content areas.

Preparation for State and National Tests

National tests on mathematics are changing to a more authentic assessment which focuses on problems that test the student's ability to consider many possibilities and multiple solutions for situations. The students are also asked to recall their thinking processes and be able to analyze and justify their answers. Increasingly, students are being asked to work with other students to create, observe, gather data, or solve problems and situations together. Then, independently, they are asked to analyze, justify, describe, and explain the work they did in their group. If students have had a lot of experience working in groups throughout the year, their social skills will be well developed. They will find it easy to work together during the testing. If students have had opportunities to share solutions and strategies within their groups and between groups, they will be ready to do the independent analysis of the group functions. Their experiences working in cooperative groups will give them the skills they need to use metacognition and divergent thinking that is necessary to be comfortable and successful in the testing situation.

Need For Cooperative Learning For Young Students

Young students are very egocentric. They think of the world as revolving around them. Our job as primary teachers is to broaden the "I" perspective into a "We" perspective. The classroom functions so much better when we are working together as a unit or family. Cooperative learning helps the students focus on one social skill at a time. This makes caring about and working with others a manageable and enjoyable task.

Another difference in primary students is that they can not read and write fluently. The lessons in the book are built around activities that can be done with pictures or with few written words. Keeping in mind that young students find it hard to concentrate for long periods of time, the lessons are made up of several structures. Changing the structure changes the form and pace of the lesson, thereby keeping the students interest throughout the lesson.

Managing Cooperative Learning For Young Students

The lessons also include special management tips that help young students be successful. There are suggestions for developing comprehensible directions, for modeling the lesson, deciding on group size, for developing the social skills, and for using praise and rewards to increase use of social skills. There are ideas on how to form teams and how long teams should stay together.

There are many signals that students and teachers can give during cooperative learning lessons that help the lessons flow smoothly with minimal interruptions. There are suggestions for positive interruptions that focus students on the social skills and increase the learning they acquire from the lesson.

Finally there are ideas on how to help those students who have a difficult time working with others. Ideas on how to help them acquire the necessary social skills. Ideas on what to do when they can't use the social skill. Ideas on how the teams can help these students.

Use Of Literature In Math

The math lessons in this book capture the students interest because they are based on ideas of characters from stories they love. The students don't realize they are learning math facts and concepts. They think they are doing a fun game or activity about a favorite story.

Using ideas from literature also helps connect the math to other content areas. The story *Chair For My Mother*, which focuses on caring for others, and *10 Little Rabbits*, which gives insight into other cultures, would fit into social studies units. *Ice Cream Soup* addresses change in form, *Jesse Bear What Will You Wear* addresses change in time of day and *The Seasons of Arnold's Apple Tree* addresses seasonal changes and value of living things; all concepts addressed in science.

Lesson Format Makes Cooperative Learning Easy

The lessons in this book are easy for students because the lessons provide the students with an overview of the lesson and then break the lesson down into short, easy-to-understand sections. The students are also provided with samples of what to say and do.

The lessons make cooperative learning easy for the teacher because everything the students need to do is listed step-by-step in the lessons. Much of the dialogue the teacher uses with the students is also included. A box, Curran's Comments, provides rationale or suggestions that apply to that lesson.

Suggestions on how to extend the lessons to do more lessons using the same theme are included in some lessons. Variations tell how to adapt the lessons to different grade or ability levels. Variations also may refer to use of different materials.

Extensions give ideas on other math activities that fit the lesson topic. Some extension ideas provide activities connected to other content areas.

Many of the lessons also have adaptations in which the same math concept and format are used with another piece of literature. These lesson adaptations can be used instead of the main lesson. Or the lesson adaptations can be used to reinforce the math concept.

Chapter 2

Organizing and Managing Cooperative Learning

This Chapter provides information on how to plan cooperative learning lessons to assure they will be successful and enjoyable for both students and teacher. It gives management tips that will help the lesson run smoothly from beginning to end. First are suggestions on using different sized groups for cooperative learning, and some suggestions of structures that work well for each size group. Second is a description of the three cooperative learning standards that need to be in place so the students feel they have a safe, risk-free environment in which to work. The next section includes a description of all the components of a cooperative learning lesson. A section on the use of praise and rewards gives suggestions on how group members can give each other special recognition or how the whole class can be rewarded for completing the task and using the social skills. A list of signals and commands that can help the lessons flow smoothly are included in the final section.

This chapter begins with additional teaching tips that answer questions teachers often ask.

❧ *How can you make sure all group members participate?*
Answer: Make sure the students in the group are really interdependent and really need each other. Types of interdependence are listed and described. *See page 2:14.*

❧ *How do group members know what tasks to do so all do a fair share?*
Answer: Think through the lesson, note all the jobs to be done, choose the best

way for your students to find out their responsibilities. Suggestions for beginning and more advanced students are given.

❧ What is the best way to form teams?
Answer: Because primary students seldom know the criteria for forming well balanced teams, the teacher should form the teams. If the teams are meeting for a short term activity, the teams could be formed by random selection. Tips are provided for both types of team selections. *See page 2:15.*

❧ What do you do with the students who have a difficult time working with other students?
Answer: Check the team formation, provide composure time, have conferences with students and/or parents about social skills, and promote team support for students needing help. Suggestions for using these remediation techniques are described. *See page 2:16-17.*

Progression of Group Size

Each teacher will introduce new groupings, practice them until the students feel comfortable using them, and then move on to new groupings that fit the needs of the students and the content and type of lessons that are being taught. I will share the progression of groupings I generally use. These can be used as a general guide for how you might like to progress with your students.

Whole Class

Whole class structures are used at the beginning of the year so the students in the class can learn information about each other. As they learn about each

other, their names, facts about their lives, or their likes and dislikes, it becomes easier for them to really care about each other as they work together. Several of the cooperative learning structures such as Community Circle, Eight Square, Corners, and Line-Ups, are especially useful for helping students learn about each other.

Community Circle (see Chapter 4) is the structure I start with because students learn something about each other and at the same time they are provided with excellent opportunities to practice Active Listening. Active Listening, in my opinion, is the most important of the cooperative learning standards. Until students know how to be good active listeners, it is difficult for them to work effectively together in cooperative activities. Community Circle also makes the students aware of the necessity for being good speakers.

Eight Square is another whole class structure that is used for information gathering. Students have an opportunity to wander around the room and meet up with new people to obtain interesting facts about a topic of common interest. They find new friends with similar interests and also gather information to use for future class activities.

Corners and Line-Ups are two more structures that help the students learn about each other as the students group themselves either in corner groups or along a line according to facts about themselves or their feelings about a certain issue. Students feel comfortable as they have a chance to talk along the Line-Up first with students with similar interests and feelings, and then they become very curious as they do a Split and Slide or The Wrap and talk to students who have experienced different situations or have different ideas and feelings.

Pairs

Pairs is the next grouping I use because it is easiest for the students to work with just one other person when they are deciding on an answer to a question, or agreeing on and producing a product.

During discussions, Pairs are always involved as either listeners or speakers. Turns come frequently and there is minimal wait time. Materials need to be shared with only one other person. That there are only two people, is the weakness of Pairs. If there are students who have poorly developed social skills, they need to be placed with the most caring students in class. However, in fairness to these caring students, the partnerships should be rotated quite frequently so they don't always have to put forth that extra effort of working with students who have exceptional social needs.

Triads

The next group size I usually use is Triads. This configuration is used for group projects that have three parts and each team member is responsible for completing a part, such as, reporting on the beginning, middle, and end of a story.

When students work in triads, they have to wait a little longer. During discussions, they may have to wait for two other students to speak before they can speak, but more ideas are generated. There are more students to share the equipment, but there are also more hands to complete

the job. Having tasks assigned by either the students or the teacher becomes important so everyone knows who is accountable for each portion of the team project.

Groups of Four

Groups of four are generally used after the students have had successful experiences with pairs and triads. Groups of four work well with large group projects in which there are four parts to be completed, or where it is important to gather many ideas, such as in Sequential or Simultaneous Roundtable. Groups of four also can be used as sharing groups for two pairs to share their answers or products with each other.

Groups of 5 or 6

Groups of this size are usually used in the primary grades for group projects that have five or six distinct sections or topics. Each person agrees to do a section. Then all sections are combined into a group product. A story may have five characters and each group member draws or writes about an incident, a point of view, or a quote from that particular character. If there were six characters, I might move to groups of six.

Simplifying Cooperative Learning Standards
Standards

Primary teachers find it is easy for students to remember the cooperative learning standards if they are written in simple phrases and include pictures to help convey the message. In the primary classroom the standards could be written as they are in the box on next page.

There are three social skills which are so central to the primary classroom that I call them Standards. To create the environment for cooperative learning, students learn the standards of Active Listening, Happy Talk, and Everyone Participates. Consistent use of these Standards provides a comfortable, positive atmosphere, in which students are willing to share ideas and work together.

Standards

Active Listening
Look at the speaker.
Listen to what is said.
Have your hands
in your lap.

Happy Talk
I like your coloring.
Nice job.
Pretty Coloring.
Super duper job.
I like how you stay in the lines.
That's a very good job.

Everyone Participates
Right to pass.

2. Happy Talk
Happy Talk involves development of a repertoire of positive statements that students say to each other as they work together. Use of these statements is called Happy Talk because it recognizes the positive contributions each individual makes toward the team effort. Sample Happy Talk statements from my kindergarten class are included on the standards chart. Your class could compose and post their own statements which are appropriate for their team projects.

1. Active Listening
The most important of the cooperative learning standards, and the one to teach the students first, is Active Listening. Until the class is really ready to listen to the students as they speak, they will not be very willing to share their ideas. The class needs to show that they are interested in listening by looking at the speaker, listening to what they say, and by keeping distracting objects put away.

As the chart is presented to the students they are given the following definition for each of the symbols: "The eyes remind you to look at the person who is supposed to be speaking. The ears remind you to listen to the words that are said and think about what they mean. The hands remind you to keep your hands in your lap (or on your desk) so they won't bother you or anybody else."

3. Everyone Participates
This standard makes everyone willing to work hard for the team because they know that everyone will be responsible for completing their fair share. The tasks necessary to complete the project are identified and then assigned in various ways. The trick is to have the tasks assigned in such a way that the students feel the tasks have been fairly distributed. Then the teams start their work in a positive way.

As the students first start doing the cooperative lesson, it seems to work best to have the tasks assigned. The fairest and easiest way to assign tasks is for the students to number themselves within the team, and then a chart of numbered tasks is posted. The students do the task that matches their number. A similar way of assigning tasks is to have a colored card as a task designator for each team member. After the cards have been selected by the team members, a color coded chart is displayed which lists the tasks to be completed. To keep the assignment of tasks fair, the students need to select their task designator card before they know which tasks are associated with that card. If they know what each number or color stands for, they could argue about who has which task designator card.

When they are familiar with sharing the jobs, they are ready to make team decisions about who should do each of the tasks. When those decisions are made, they sign up for their task on the team task sheet. Everyone then knows who is responsible for each of the jobs on the team. This is especially important when each person has more that one job to do for the team. Also, observers can tell if everyone is on target.

For some cooperative lessons everyone just pitches in to complete the job. There are no distinct jobs, so everyone pitches in, completes the job and then signs the product to show that they contributed to the completion of the job and agree with the final product.

The students use the right to pass when they are not able to participate in the group activity. These are two reasons students need to use the right to pass. If English is their second language, they may not be able to contribute to the group discussion in Roundrobin or Community Circle, but active listening would be expected. The second reason for

the right to pass is emotional. If the topic were emotionally upsetting, the student might need to "pass" from the discussion or project. An example would be a child who just lost a pet and the group activity was focused on pets. The student would inform the group and or teacher of their need to pass. The rest of the group would then continue the activity minus that group member's input or participation.

Components of a Cooperative Learning Lesson
Two Objectives
All cooperative learning lessons have two objectives: the cognitive objective and the social skills objective. To keep the students from having to focus on too many things at once in the lesson, we make sure that only one of the objectives is new or difficult for the students. If the cognitive objective is covering new materials, the social skill objective is one the students know very well. If the social skill is new or one that is still difficult for the students, then the cognitive objective covers material that is easy for the students to handle.

Instruction/Review of the Social Skill
Before the students do the cooperative lesson they need to think about how they can use the social skill effectively. The teacher could make a chart that lists their ideas on how to use the social skill. This is what Spencer Kagan calls "gambits." Making a *Does* and *Says* Chart helps students know how to act and what to say as they use the social skill. This chart can be used as the criteria for their evaluation of

Direction Chart:

A Place for Pair Work

Talk about places to go.

Both draw the picture.

Use Happy Talk.

Practice sharing:

One holds.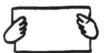

One talks.

the social skill at the end of the lesson. These "gambit" charts can be made either before or after the lesson is modeled for the students.

Clear Directions

Primary students need lessons that are explained with clear, step-by-step directions they can follow from the beginning to the end of the lesson. It helps if the directions are given in a written, as well as an oral form. The wording of the directions needs to be simple enough so the students will be able to read and understand them. Often as groups are working, I see them pause a minute, read the direction chart just to be sure they are doing the activity correctly, and then proceed through the lesson. Directions written for kindergarten and first grade students should contain a few simple words for each step of the procedure accompanied by pictures that illustrate the directions for them. See the sample direction chart on the previous page.

The teacher reads the words written on the chart, but for the kindergarten student it is the pictorial clues that help them as they work their way through the lesson. First grade students begin to focus more on the written part of the directions.

For students at the end of first grade and beyond, charts can be completely written, but they still should be written in short easy phrases and sentences. To help students at this level understand which tasks they are responsible for, the charts can be color coded. Before the directions are read, each team is given a pack of colored cards.

In the pack are enough cards so each team member will be able to select a different colored card. If there are four members on each team, there would be four different colors in each pack. Directions for all of them to follow, would be written on white paper. Any job that is for a specific team member, would be written on paper that is the same color as one of the colored cards that a member of each team is holding.

Third grade students should be able to follow directions without pictures or color coding. It helps, though, at all grade levels to keep the wording and or picture symbols as consistent as possible from lesson to lesson.

Modeling Lessons

All students remember a procedure better if they have a chance to see it before they need to do it themselves. This is especially true for the primary students, who find it more difficult than older students to follow written directions. The teacher can model the lesson or students can be part of a demonstration. If it is a short, easy activity, the students remember it well by watching the teacher's demonstration. If the activity is more involved, the students remember better by watching a team made up of their teacher and peers go through a sample activity.

Another advantage of having students involved in the demonstration is that the students who were involved in the demonstration have extra practice and are now experts in doing that particular lesson. Often, I will ask students who I feel might have some difficulty doing the lesson to be part of the demonstration lesson. This extra practice with me as part of the demonstration team, gives them extra self confidence before they do the activity with their team.

Another reason I like to have students help me demonstrate the lesson, is that as a member of a demonstration team, I can help model the social skill for that lesson. If the social skill is using Happy Talk, I use a lot of Happy Talk statements while our team works, such as: "That is a good idea," "I like your coloring," "What a terrific house you made." If the social skill were to do paraphrasing, I would be sure to restate what had been said in different words. Because I start doing the social skill, the team usually starts to do it too. Then the class sees and hears examples of what the social skill looks and sounds like.

If the class has already brainstormed a list of phrases to use while they work together, they have an idea of how to use those phrases as they progress through the lesson. If the lesson is demonstrated before the chart is made, having seen the lesson and having heard the demonstration team's comments, the class has a better idea of what kind of statements to suggest. No matter what the social skill is, seeing the teacher and the demonstration students helps show behaviors that develop positive interaction within the teams.

The Cooperative Lesson or Activity

While the students are doing the cooperative lesson or activity, the teacher has several responsibilities. These responsibilities are:

🖎 **Be a facilitator and…**

… have procedure charts on display so the students can remember what tasks need to be done.

… have gambit charts on display so the students can get help on what to say and do as they use the social skills.

… set time limits so teams know how long they have to complete the tasks.

… insert sponge activities so teams will have constructive activities to do when they finish.

… direct the evaluation, validation, debriefing, and sharing.

🖎 **Observe, take notes, and…**

… watch for effective use of social skills.

… notice individual strengths that can be used when forming new groups.

… look for any improvements that can be made in the lesson design or directions.

… notice any difficulties in social interactions, these can be the social skills to focus on for the next few lessons.

🖎 **Praise and…**

… give signals or verbal praise to groups who are using the social skills.

… give points or rewards to groups who are following the procedure and social skills.

🖎 **Give guidance by …**

… answering team questions if all team members have their hands raised.

… frequently visiting groups where students have a potential for having difficulties.

… helping groups find solutions to their problems by having them review what they have already done and think of other things they could do.

… leading groups on to the next step of the procedure.

Evaluation Techniques
A. When To Evaluate

Students often need to be reminded of the social skill several times during the lesson. There are three times during the lesson where it is common to focus on the social skills.

Before the lesson starts. After a demonstration team, made up of the teacher and some students, models how to do the lesson, students discuss what they saw and heard that were examples of the social skill being used in the lesson.

During the lesson. The teacher can stop the lesson to focus on the social skill for several reasons.

… to compliment and/or reward teams for using the social skill

… to review with the students what the social skill looks and sounds like if the social skill has not been used yet

… to add variety to the gambits (positive phrases) the students are using

After the lesson. Time should be taken at the end of a lesson to allow students to reflect on what they said and did when using the social skill and to decide what else they could have said or done while using the social skill.

B. How To Evaluate

The students have an easy time with the evaluation if they know at the beginning of the lesson how they will be evaluating the social skill. Then as the lesson progresses they remember specific information they want to share during the evaluation. These following tips help make the evaluation positive and meaningful.

Introduce Evaluation. Explain the method of reporting the evaluation. The reporting methods are given in an order of difficulty from easiest to hardest, so it is advisable to start with the easier types of evaluation at the top of the list and progress to the more difficult types as the students have some experience with cooperative learning.

Types of Signals.
Signs
- Thumb signals
  - thumbs up = we did it
  - thumbs sideways = we need to fix it
- Finger signals
  - five fingers = we all did the social skill
  - three fingers = most of us did the social skill
  - one finger = we tried but need more practice

Oral Statements
- "You made it easy for me today by…"

Written Feedback
- Written symbol (happy face or star)
- Written number which can be done by counting up the finger signals
- Written comment about what worked best and what could be better next time

Reflection Time. Give the students reflection time to remember how the team used the social skill.

Student Evaluations. Call on students to give their evaluation and validate (give reasons) for the evaluation.

Generalize. Use the words someone, somebody, or some of us, instead of names during the validation.

Rewards. Teams can receive praise or certificates for use of the social skill.

Debriefing the Lesson
A. Reasons for Debriefing
At the completion of every new type of cooperative learning lesson, or after the introduction of a new social skill, the students should have a chance to let you

know how they felt about doing the lesson. It is a great feeling at the end of a successful lesson to discuss the factors that made it turn out so well.

B. Types of Debriefing

At the end of the lesson, time should be provided for the students to analyze how they felt about the lesson. The teacher can have a class discussion and call on some students to find out how each of them felt about the lesson. Or the teacher can have team discussions to find out how the team members felt about the content, the structure, and the interactions.

1. Total Class Debriefing

A class discussion can be used to do the debriefing. Usually in this case just a few of the students share their ideas. If the students do a Think-Pair-Share to discuss and share the debriefing questions, then all the students have a chance to discuss ideas with each other even though only a few of the students may share the ideas with the whole class. The following are a sampling of the questions that can be used when debriefing is done with a class discussion.

* What made this easy/difficult for you?
* How did it feel when it was your turn to share? Explain.
* How did it feel while it was your turn? Explain.
* How did it feel when the group used Happy Talk? Explain.
* How did it feel when you used Happy Talk? Explain.
* For you, what was the best thing about this lesson? Why?
* What would make a lesson like this better for you next time?

2. Team Debriefing

By having a team discussion for the debriefing, everyone has a chance to par-

ticipate in the discussion. Everyone becomes more involved in the analysis of the procedures and interactions that occurred in the lesson. Everyone has more interest in planning improvements for the next time the teams work together. These are a few questions that could be used for a debriefing that uses team discussion.

* What did the team do best today? Why did it turn out so well?
* What did the team do that made the job easy?
* What did your team do that helped you?
* Why was this easier to do as a team than to do alone?
* What could the team do to make it easier to do the job next time?

Sponge Activities

Not all teams work at the same rate. To assure that teams who finish the lesson more quickly are busy doing a meaningful activity, a sponge activity can be assigned. Teams know they automatically start the sponge activity when their lesson is complete. The sponge activity is a challenging, fun project usually closely related to the lesson just completed. For example, in Lesson 36: Time Around, the team does a sponge activity by having a Roundrobin discussion about their favorite times of day and why they like that time of day.

Signal and Commands

Teaching the students several commands and signals that trigger recall of specific directions helps the lessons flow smoothly. By saying a few words or by giving various hand signals, students can change from one type of activity to another both quickly and quietly.

Active Listening

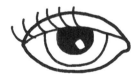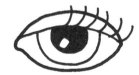

Look!

Look at the speaker.

Listen!

Listen to what is said.

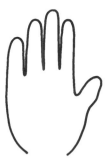

Quiet Hands!

Have your hands in
your lap.

Active Listening Signal

The Active Listening signal is used to help primary students give full attention to a designated speaker. When the command "Show Active Listening!" is given, the students signal back by folding their hands together and looking at the speaker. The students are taught that Active Listening consists of the three following components:

Look. Use your eyes and look at the person who is supposed to be talking.

Listen. Use your ears to listen to and think about what the speaker is saying.

Quiet Hands. Fold your hands together so you know what they are doing and they won't bother you or anyone else.

Students can discuss these rules, and how the rules help them to be good listeners. It is easier for the primary students to remember the components of Active Listening if they are given visual representations for each one. Teachers have made charts with simple written directions using visual clues similar to those on the chart on the previous page so the students can check to see that they are doing all parts of Active Listening when the command is given.

Finished Signal

A quick way to find out when teams have their job done, is to ask them to give the Finished Signal when they have completed the lesson. To do the finished signal, all team members rest one hand on top their heads. This quickly and quietly gives you the message without bothering other teams or gives you a quiet answer from all teams if you are checking with the whole class.

Silent Signal

The Silent Signal is used when the teams are doing any activity which involves a lot of discussion, and all the teams might not hear when the teacher asks for Active Listening. For the Silent Signal, the teacher puts up one hand with the index finger raised and says, "Show the Silent Signal, please." Students are to raise one hand, have the other hand empty, and look at the teacher. As soon as team members see the Silent Signal, they are to remind the other team members to give the signal by raising their hands too.

Combination Silent Signal and Active Listening

When students are using manipulatives, writing tools, or art supplies, they often give the silent signal with one hand and keep on working with the other hand. They will be quiet, but they will still be concentrating on their work rather than listening. If the students are asked to give the silent signal and change it to active listening, the students now have their hands together and all their supplies are put down. They are now ready to concentrate on the message being given.

The Tap

When teams are deeply involved in a lesson or activity, it is sometimes difficult for them to see or hear the Active Listening or Silent Signal. The teacher, as the facilitator of the cooperative learning activity, goes to those groups who have not seen or heard the signal. The teacher lightly touches the shoulder of one of the team members. This person then has the job of showing the rest of the team members which signal is being given, so they can all respond.

Ten Second Signal

To motivate the teams to give quick responses to the signals, the teacher can use the Ten Second Signal. To do the Ten Second Signal, the teacher gives a command such as "Show Active Listening" or "Silent Signal, please" and then, using a whisper, counts to ten, at the speed of about a count a second. If the teams all return the signal before the teacher reaches the count of ten, the class is praised and/or rewarded.

Speak Louder Signal

In order for the students to be active listeners, they must be able to hear what the speaker is saying. So the students need to learn an easy way to let the speakers know that they can't be heard. Anyone who is having a hard time hearing, simply raises a hand. If the speaker sees several hands raised, he/she knows to start using a louder voice. By using the signal, the speaker isn't interrupted, yet knows how to modify his or her voice to accommodate the needs of the audience.

Team Question Signal

If a team member has a question, it is that member's responsibility to ask each of the team members if they have the necessary information before the teacher can be asked to help. This makes the team members reliant on each other as a valuable source of information. If between them they cannot solve their problem, all team members raise their hands and that is a signal to the teacher that there is a real need for help.

Two Tiered Timing

The last piece of information that is given to the students as part of their directions, is the amount of time the lesson should take. This helps even kindergarten students, who do not have a well developed sense of time, have a general idea whether they will have a long or short amount of time to do the lesson. If the students are told the total amount of time they will have to complete the lesson, many teams will finish, but some teams will not be done and have to turn in an incomplete project which can deflate the team's esteem. Other teams will work very quickly and have nothing constructive to do. A solution to the problem is to use Two Tiered Timing.

To use Two Tiered Timing, the teacher breaks the working time he/she would like the students to use, into two sections. The first section of time lets the students know how much time the lesson might take. The second time stated lets the students know the maximum amount of time allotted for the lesson. The directions for a 15 minutes lesson would sound like this: "We might finish this lesson in 10 minutes, we must be done in 15 minutes. I will give you the Silent Signal in 10 minutes to see if you are done."

If Two Tiered Timing is used to tell them how much time they have, the teams work at their own pace during the first time period, taking as much time as they need to gather ideas and plan. They know they will still have the second period of time. The students are asked to give the Silent Signal and change it to Active Listening. They are asked to give the Finished Signal if their team is done. During the second time period, teams that got the job done quickly, will be ready to find out about the sponge activity. Other teams that are almost done will be ready to start the sponge activity as soon as they finish the lesson. Teams that still had a lot to complete, will speed up so they can complete the job.

Additional Teaching Tips

Use of Lesson Components

All the components of a cooperative learning lesson should be used when the students are learning a new structure or when they are learning a new social skill. The necessary components are:

* Cognitive and social skills objectives.

* An overview or modeling of the lesson and instruction on use of the social skills.

* Using the social skills while doing the lesson or activity.

* Evaluation of the social skill.

* Validation of the evaluation to find out the reasons for that particular evaluation.

* Debrief the lesson to find out how the students felt about the lesson.

There are reasons that a teacher might want to leave out a component of a cooperative learning lesson. One of the components that can be left out is the modeling of the lesson when students are familiar with the structure, the social skill, and the type of lesson or activity. Evaluation of the social skill can be left out after it has been successfully used several times. However, remember that a social skill that isn't thought about for a while, tends to disappear. Debriefing a lesson isn't necessary after a structure has been used several times and everyone knows how they feel about using that structure.

Positive Interdependence

In a cooperative learning lesson if all the students in the group really need each other to complete the project, they are truly interdependent. If the students don't need each other to complete the

tasks, they will begin to work independently within the team, and then the sharing of information and the development of social skills will not occur. Each cooperative learning lesson should contain one or more of these types of interdependence.

* All students work to make one product.

* The resources are limited.

* Each member is responsible for doing a specific portion of the lesson. A task sheet is signed so everyone knows who is responsible for each portion of the lesson.

* Tasks are assigned within the group where each team member can complete his/her task only if all previous tasks are done.

* Awards or praise are given only when there is evidence that all team members contributed to the product or used the social skills.

* Random selection is used when evaluating the team so the team needs to be sure that all members perform up to the criteria.

* A group progress chart is kept and the teams earn credit for products that are equal to or better that their previous work.

* Individual tasks can not be accepted from the team until all team members complete have their assignment.

Assigning Tasks

Tasks can either be assigned to group members, or they can choose what tasks they would like to do. For young students and students who are just starting to do cooperative learning, I like to have their tasks assigned to they won't argue about who will do which job. If they argue about their jobs, their group will start off with bad feelings and this makes it difficult for them to work harmoniously together for the rest of the lesson. After teams are working well and the students understand that everyone must do their share for the team, then the team members can begin to assign jobs for their team. Tasks can be assigned in the following ways:

* Have a team member sign a task sheet. The person who signs for the job is responsible to complete it.

* Team members number themselves. Then the tasks are numbered. Each person does the task that has his/her number.

* Each team member draws a slip of paper out of an envelope which indicates his/her task.

* Teams assign tasks based on the talents or interests of their team members.

Forming Teams

When forming teams that will work together for several days or longer, I construct the teams carefully to help assure success. I make certain each team has someone who can be a leader and someone who could use some help developing their social skills. I also look at the talents so there will be a person who is comfortable doing each of these tasks: reader, writer, speaker, and illustrator. I try for equal numbers of girls and boys. Finally, I try to have students from different ethnic groups on each team so they can make their own unique contributions to the team.

If teams are meeting for just one activity, they could successfully be formed using random selection. Some methods of random selection are:

* Students with the same colored strips of paper form a team.

* Students who have the same shape are a team.

* Students match numbers and dots to form partners.

* Students match upper case and lower case letters to form partners.

Duration of Groups

Teachers often ask how long groups should stay together? The answer is there is no definite period of time that is best for groups to work together. Groups can work together for just one activity. They can be together for several days, several weeks or for most of the year. At the beginning of the year, I construct different groups for each activity so I have a chance to observe a variety of student interactions. As the year progresses I want groups to remain together for longer periods of time. At this point, they become a team that concentrates on strategies that enable them to do their best work, and on procedures that help them improve their social skills as they work through the lessons.

There are several factors that determine how long groups work together. One is of the activity being done. If it is a difficult task, they could need several days to complete the job. The content being covered could determine how long groups meet together. An example would be groups who are writing math problems and sending them on to other groups to be solved, they might need to meet several times to develop the problems, make an answer key, solve other groups problems, get their problems back to be checked, and then decide how to write better problems for another group to solve and so the cycle continues. If they are making a pattern together they might meet just once to make the pattern, or they may continue to meet together, to see how many different types of patterns they can make. If several of the students have difficulty with their social skills, groups might be changed often so those students would have the advantage of learning from many different people and so all groups get a chance to experience students with different levels of social development.

A procedure that works well for determining how long groups should work together is this. Have the students do some inclusion lessons and observe their interactions. If the group interactions were difficult, form new groups, trying to get group members that are more compatible. When you have groups that function well together, those groups could be kept together for quite awhile. Do what works best with the students, you, and the material that is being taught.

Assisting Teams

Sometimes students have questions while they are working. They will raise their hands as they have always done before and hope to get an answer from the teacher so they can continue their work. When they are working in groups, I want to make them depend upon each other and not on me, so I use some of the strategies listed below to make them seek help from each other instead of the teacher.

- All team members must have their hands raised before the teacher comes to help.
- Find out what the team has already done to solve the problem.
- If many teams have similar questions, stop the lesson and do some instruction or go through the directions again.

- Have an observer from the team go to visit other teams to see how they are solving the problem.
- Have the teams share their successful strategies for problem solving so teams can learn problem solving techniques from each other.

Assisting Students with Special Needs Using Social Skills

One of the most frequent questions asked during workshops and conferences is, "What do you do with the students who have a hard time working with groups ?" This question refers to student with various problems that interfere with other students in the groups. Following are some of these problems and some suggested solutions.

Domination of Conversation: Talking Chips

There are some students who want to control the conversation when teams are planning together. A solution is to use Talking Chips. When using talking chips, each student in the group is given an equal number of tokens (I use construction paper circles that say "Talking Chips"). Each time a team member makes a contribution to the conversation, that person must put one of his/her talking chips on a pile in the center of the group. When a person has used all his/her talking chips, that person may not talk again until all team members have used all their talking chips. This assures equal access to the conversation by all team members.

Domination or Avoidance of the Activity: Task Sheets

Some students want to try to do the whole activity for the group; other students would like to take a free ride. If either of these happens then real cooperation is not happening. Students who are pushed out of the planning and constructing of the group activity feel useless, frustrated, or bored. Students who are left with the bulk of the work to do, feel put upon and upset that the group gets credit when one person had to do most of the work. If, before they start working, the students sign up for the same number of jobs on team task sheets, which lists all the tasks needed to complete the activity , then all team members will be responsible for an equal amount of the work. Also they can remember during the project who is to do which job. It makes it easier for the team to facilitate the lesson because a quick look at the task sheet lets the teacher know if everyone is focused on their particular part of the lesson.

Disruptive Behavior: Several Suggestions

A student with disruptive behavior makes it very difficult for a team to complete their job because one portion of the job is not getting done and the others may be distracted as they try to do their parts of the team project. More than one disruptive student on a team makes it almost impossible for the team to function.

1. Teacher Form Teams

As teams are formed, the teacher should make sure that there is no more that one student per team who has weak interpersonal skills. Also, there should be a student on each team who has well developed social skills and can be a role model for the other students on the team. Also, check personalities to assure that the students on the team can work well together.

2. Conference on Social Skills.

For a student who is having difficulty using the social skills, that student can be taken aside before the cooperative lesson. Have a short discussion about the social skill for the upcoming lesson and what the student needs to work on to do well with that social skill. This sometimes helps these students be more successful with the social skills. Time spent with this student after the lesson helps to reinforce the things that worked well so they can be used again.

3. Change Groups

Sometimes just providing a different environment, helps students have an easier time using the social skills. Try to put that student in a group that has very strong social skills and nurturing personalities.

4. Composure Time

If a student is having a difficult time using the social skills, it often helps if they have a time out so they can take time to gain control of their attitudes or emotions. It can just be a time out to start thinking about the correct behavior or there can be an assignment waiting that needs to be done. However, these are the students who need the cooperative experience the most so they can develop their interpersonal skills. So allow them the opportunity to return to the group as soon as possible.

5. Conference and Contract

If the student continues to have a difficult time using the social skills, it is time to have a conference with the parent and child. Develop a contract that has the student focus on one aspect of a particular social skill that he/she will work on for the next week. Parent, student, and teacher sign the contract and decide on rewards and consequences that go with the contract. Meet weekly to discuss progress, rewards, and the new contract that adds another social skill. It usually helps to have the student move to another group to start working on the contract. A new group may be found by:

- Asking a group with good social skills and nurturing personalities if they would work for a week with this student and help the student develop the social skill that is on the contract.
- Present the contract to the class and ask if there is a group who would work with the students with their contracts.

Use of Praise and Rewards

Part of what makes cooperative learning successful is the rewards the students receive for having been successful with the social skill the lesson addresses. Just as students enjoy an excellent grade or a positive comment written on an assignment when they have shown that they mastered the cognitive objective of a lesson, they also feel good if they are given praise or a tangible reward for having successfully demonstrated their ability to do the social skill. Rewards have the most effect if they are given immediately after the social skill has been performed. Also, rewards given frequently when a social skill is first introduced helps students focus on that skill. They often over use it as they are first learning how to improve their interpersonal skills. Types of rewards that can be given are praise, points, certificates, and cumulative rewards.

Praise

Praise comes from the teacher, but also is given by students as they learn to use Happy Talk and Praising Statements. Students make Praising Statements as they work together to let each other know what they like about the work they are doing or what they like about how they are doing their work.

Rewards

There are many different types of rewards that can be given to team members or the team members can give to each other.

Points

Points may be given for teams who show evidence of following the social skills or for teams who have improved the quantity or quality of their work because they used the social skill. Points can be given to individuals who encourage the rest of the team to do the social skill.

The Silent Cheer. All the team members can shake their hands in the air energetically to give the silent cheer which will not disturb other teams who still are working. Also, the silent cheer can be given by the whole class without disturbing the class next door.

Round of Applause. All the team members can applaud in a circle to give the team members a round of applause for their effort in using the social skill.

Inside High Five. Once the students know what an inside voice is, they can start giving an inside high five to their team members. A high five is when all teammates slap one hand together at once; an inside high five is when they do so silently. The inside high five is gentle so it makes no noise to disturb others.

Happy Face From The Group. The team

has a discussion to recall how each team member used the social skill. When they remember what a team member did, a happy face is drawn on the group project by that person's name.

Praise and Encouraging words from the team. Team members think of praising statements to give each other to tell each person the things he/she did to help get the team job done.

Certificates and Awards. The team validates that they used the social skill by sharing with the class or with another group the specific ways they used the social skill. Then either a certificate is given to the team as a whole and is fastened to their team product, or a certificate is given to each of the team members.

Extra Credit. Teams that use the social skill can earn extra credit either in points for the product or in points for the reward chart.

Cumulative Point Rewards

Cumulative points which are earned by teams, individuals, or the whole class can lead to a reward. When the class reaches a designated number of points, which they should be able to accomplish every two or three weeks, there is some special event for the class.

Primary students especially enjoy the following rewards:
- An extra recess on their playground.
- A recess on the older students playground.
- A popcorn or cookie party.
- Toys from home for special play time.
- A free choice art time.
- A movie shown both forwards and backwards.

Kiddie Recognition Certificates

These are two of the four Kiddie Recognition Certificates available in packet of 40, on 5" x 8" assorted colored paper. See order form at back of book.

Recognition Certificates

Terrific Triad

Perfect Partners

Chapter 3

Social Skills in the Primary Classroom

Active Listening

❧ See Lesson 19

Active Listening is the most important of the social skills. With this skill in place all students gain information from the speaker. In turn the speaker enjoys sharing the information because he/she knows all students are processing what has been said. Active Listening is divided into three parts to aid the primary student. These parts, Look, Listen, and Quiet Hands, are described in detail in Chapter 2.

Agree/Disagree Politely

❧ See Lesson 32

Often students have a difficult time letting others on the team know that they like their ideas. They find it difficult to express appreciation for others ideas and contributions. It is even more difficult for them to tell others that they disagree with their ideas in a positive manner. They need modeling and suggestions on how to express agreement or disagreement in such a way that others appreciate their suggestions. The modeling is done with a group, which includes the teacher as one of the members. The group demonstrates the lesson and the teacher models agreeing and disagreeing in a positive manner. As the students analyze the demonstration lesson they can recall the statements they heard. They make a chart of these positive phrases to use when they want to express agreement or disagreement in their teams. These charts are used as the criteria for evaluating their use of polite agreement and disagreement.

Ask For Help/ Assist Politely

✻ See Lesson 10

As students work on projects where each team member is completing part of the work, or where team members are helping all members to complete individual assignments, there is a need for them to ask for and receive assistance. The class makes gambit charts that list phrases that can be used to politely ask for help or polite phrases to use while giving assistance. For example:

> Could you help me please?
> I will try to help you.
> How do you do this?
> This is how I would do it.
> I'm stuck. Help me please.
> Maybe we can do it together.

Encouraging Statements

✻ See Lessons 1, 3, 7, 8

When teams use encouraging statements they gently and politely entice team members to produce more for the team. Sometimes everyone on the team has the job of making encouraging statements to all the team members. At other times one member takes the responsibility of being the Encourager. Before the lesson starts, the students take a couple of minutes to think of statements such as: "Let's all think of one more idea." or "You listened to all our ideas; now we would like an idea from you."

Happy Talk/ Praising Statements

✻ See Lessons 2, 4, 9, 10, 12, 16, 20, 23, 24, 26, 28, 33, 35

A very positive tone quickly develops in a classroom if students are complimenting each other while they work. This is a social skill that most students need help to develop. Happy Talk, as these compliments are called, promotes a close knit team, a wealth of ideas, and brings out the best effort from all team members. Students are given a few minutes after they have heard an overview of the lesson, to brainstorm nice things they can say to each other. The teacher compiles a list from the suggestions. The Happy Talk suggestion list is added to as they complete the lesson or do additional lessons which focus on Happy Talk. The Standards Chart in Chapter 2 contains some sample Happy Talk Statements.

Helpful Teacher

✻ See Lessons 9, 29

When students do a Jigsaw/Expert Groups lesson, they need to teach their team members the information that they learned in the expert group. If the students are doing a pair worksheet, drill and practice, or experiment, they need to be sure both of them know the answer and understand why their answer is best or correct. To use this social skill effectively, the students need to be aware of simple teaching techniques. They focus on any one of these techniques each time they teach a lesson.

- learn and practice the information to be taught
- include illustrations of examples to make the information more understandable
- speak clearly and answer any questions

Paraphrasing

✻ See Lesson 11

As the students refine their speaking and listening skills, it is important that students are able to paraphrase each other so they are sure their ideas are understood. After they understand the concepts of Active Listening, second grade students are able to move into a lesson where pairs of students take turns, one stating an opinion and their partner restating it in words that have the same meaning. Kindergarten and first grade students simply repeat what their partner said until they are capable of true paraphrasing.

Please and Thank You

❧ See Lessons 13b, 31

When students are using any of the structures to gather information from each other saying "Please" and "Thank You" are appropriate social skills. Interview and Eight Square are especially appropriate structures for practicing these social skills.

Polite Passer

❧ See Lesson 34

A Polite Passer checks to see that the person he/she should pass a paper to is ready to receive the paper before the paper is passed. This keeps papers from accumulating in front of some team members, while other team members have none. This skill is especially important during Roundtable (See Chapter 4). It helps reduce pressure on a particular team member because papers are piling up in front of him/her. It also keeps the papers rotating in the correct order.

Polite Suggestions

❧ See Lessons 12, 21, 30, 35

When students accept each others suggestions and opinions in a polite way, everyone is much more willing to take a risk and offer an abundance of ideas, some of which are unique and unusual. Offbeat and different ideas often are those which help the team create a superior answer or product.

Some polite ways students accept suggestions and opinions are by using statements such as these.
"That's a neat idea!"
"Great idea!"
"Here is another idea."

Polite Waiter

❧ See Lesson 16

Young students have difficulty waiting, and that is one reason why cooperative groups of four or less work well with young students. Even with these small groups, their is some wait time. When the teacher notices some of the students are having difficulty waiting for their turn, then this is an appropriate social skill to use for several lessons.

When total class structures such as Line-Up, Corners, or Inside-Outside Circle are used, it is especially important that they wait in their correct position so information is shared with the correct group of students.

After the students have heard an overview of the lesson or have seen it modeled, the class can make a list of appropriate things to do while waiting for a turn. Examples of ideas they contribute are:
• Think of an answer you would give.
• Think of compliments for your team mates answers.
• Do the sponge activity for that lesson.

Positive Suggestions

☙ See Lessons 17, 25

The teacher and a few students model the lesson and use Polite Suggestions as they work together. The class identifies the polite suggestions used. These suggestions, and others the students think of, are recorded to make a class gambits chart. See the sample gambit chart on page 3:6. The chart is used as a reference by the students as they work together so they know what to say to each other. It is also used at the end of the lesson as the criteria for evaluating use of the social skill. For beginning students, the teacher reads the list of suggestions before the lesson starts and possibly mid-way through the lesson to refresh the students memories as to positive things they should be saying.

Quiet Voices/ Inside Voices

☙ See Lessons 5, 13a, 13d, 22, 30

Teams can easily do their work in an environment where the discussion of one team does not interfere with that of another team. Quiet Voices is the skill that enables this to happen.

Quiet Voice, or Six Inch Voice as it is sometimes called, is easier to accomplish if several room environment features are in place. The team members need to be seated in such a way that they can get their work and heads close together. For example, students could be seated across a narrow table, around a single student desk, or around a piece of tagboard on the floor. The teams should have at least 3 to 4 feet of space between them so it is possible to keep their own team's ideas to themselves. When a team first starts using Quiet Voices, the team can have a prompter who listens and reminds any members who need to use a softer voice.

Ready For Your Turn

☙ See Lessons 6, 36

Being ready for their turn is especially important for kindergarten and first grade students so they have positive experiences sharing materials. They need to grow in their ability to let others use materials or express ideas before they have a turn. They also need to focus on the team activity or project so they are ready to contribute when it is their turn.

Speak Clearly/Strong Voice

☙ See Lessons 8, 18

This skill is the counter part of Active Listening. It is hard for students to be active listeners if they have a hard time hearing the messages being sent to them. Some skills to teach students about speaking clearly are: voice projection, enunciation, and body language. The Speak Louder hand signal described in Chapter 2 lets members of the class notify the speaker that he/she needs improvement in the Strong Voice Skills.

Stay In Position/Place

☙ See Lesson 13c

For structures to succeed, all the students need to be in their designated or chosen place doing their part of the team task. In structures such as Corners or Line-Ups, the students need to find the place that correctly represents their choice or point of view. If their team is changing locations as in Two Stray or in Share and Compare, it is important for them to stay with their team. In Inside-Outside Circle, they need to move to a new location with the group and stay in the correct order as they move around the circle. The class or teams discuss how they could help each other remember their place or position.

At the end of the lesson they evaluate how well the class or team did in staying in the correct place. They discuss what they did to help each other and how well each idea worked.

Team Praisers

✒ See Lesson 27

The team members decide on something they can say or do to compliment themselves for a job well done. Sample team praisers are a team handshake or a team cheer. They could give their team praiser each time they give a correct answer in a structure such as Numbered Heads Together or they could give the praiser as they complete each section of a lesson that has several steps.

Work Neatly

✒ See Lessons 1, 3

After the students have heard an overview of the lesson, either teams, or the whole class, decide how to help their team members do their neatest work so they will end up with a quality product. These ideas can be discussed and listed to use as the criteria for their evaluation.

Work Quickly

✒ See Lessons 6, 21, 36

Working Quickly is a skill that is important for any activities where parts made by all team members must fit together for the project to be complete. It is important in a Roundtable or Roundrobin lesson where one person must complete an answer before the others can contribute their ideas. One effective way to help teams work more quickly is to have the teams analyze and share the things they did that helped them work quickly. Be sure that the fastest teams share their ideas.

Work With the Group
(pay attention to the group)

✒ See Lesson 21

If some students are being distracted by other groups, first check out the class environmental issues. Are the groups spread out so each team has their own private work space? Are the teams seated close enough together so they are able to use inside or six inch voices? If some students still are distracted, have the teams focus on how well their members concentrated on team tasks. They discuss what they would see if their team members were concentrating on their task. List these ideas and use them as they evaluate at the end of the lesson how well they concentrated on their task.

How Social Skills Work In A Lesson

To help students understand how a social skill works within a lesson, the students, after hearing an overview of the lesson, are given an opportunity to brainstorm some things to say or do to achieve the social skill in that particular lesson. Their ideas are recorded and used as a basis for evaluating their success in having accomplished that social skill. For example, before using the social skill of Active Listening, the teacher lists student suggestions of what the students should do and say to be good active listeners. Some examples of ideas they offer are provided in the box on next page.

Social Skills Phrases Chart

If accomplishing the social skill would be enhanced by using specific phrases or behaviors, the class makes a chart of those "gambits" before they start the lesson. If the social skill is to encourage others, the class makes a list of phrases that remind their team members to do their best, such as:

- "You look like you have an idea, what is it?"
- "Everyone started right away."
- "That's terrific that you are making your pictures so neat."

Review of the Social Skills Chart

In lessons that use a social skill from previous lessons, the chart of phrases from the previous lesson is reviewed after the students have heard an overview of the new lesson. They decide which phrases on the chart are applicable to this lesson.

Additions to the Social Skills Chart

At the end of each lesson, time is provided for students to add new phrases that they used in the lesson. Soon the students have a variety of phrases to use for each of the social skills.

Continued Focus on Social Skills

Another factor that leads to successful use of the social skill is to keep the students aware of the skill as they work through the lesson. As the lesson starts and the students hear the directions for doing the lesson, they receive a quick reminder of the social skill. "Remember, as you discuss with your partners today, you will be paraphrasing each other so you will know you understand what each other is saying." After the students have been involved in the lesson for a couple of minutes, they can be reminded of the social skill in several ways.

Teacher Quotes

The teacher interrupts the lesson and quotes phrases heard, then praises and reward the teams or class for using them.

Reflection Time

During the lesson, the teacher gives teams an opportunity to reflect and see if they have used any of the gambits from the chart. They volunteer to share those they used.

Refer to Gambits Chart

The teacher rereads the gambit chart, such as the example below, so the teams can decide which phrases from the chart they would like to try to use.

Active Listening
Student Responses

Do
Look at the speaker.
Nod your head.
Smile.
Lean toward the speaker.

Say
"That's great."
"I like that."
"Good idea."
"Yes, I like that too."

Reminders

The teacher reminds the students that they will be evaluating their use of the social skill at the end of the lesson. So, they should be sure to use at least two of the phrases while they work together.

Record and Praise Phrases

The teacher should make a point of recording phrases used and purposely stand near teams that need encouragement to use the social skill.

Evaluation & Debriefing of Social Skills

At the end of the lesson, the social skill is evaluated. The students need a way to signal or record their score. See Debriefing in Chapter 3 and Evaluation Structures in Chapter 4.

Evaluation Structures

Finger Evaluations. The scores are signaled by giving a certain number of fingers a particular value. Five fingers means everyone did the social skill. Three fingers means most people did the social skill. One finger means everyone was so busy with the activity that they forgot to do the social skill.

Evaluation Slips. Scores are written down on small pieces of paper and shared with the team or the class.

Team Evaluations. The skill is evaluated either by individual students, or by teams who agree on a score, or by taking an average of the individual scores on their team.

Teacher Evaluations. The teacher arrives at a score or validates student's scores by giving specific examples of what was observed while the teams worked.

Think Time. Students are also given time to think of reasons for their scores. Then students are called on to validate their score to the class, or students share reasons within their teams, or students pair up to share their reasons.

Another useful method in the evaluation process is the use of Team Cards. The team fills out a Team Card that records the following types of information:

- The card contains an agreed upon answer that is shared with other teams or the teacher.

- The card is used for recording the team assessment of how well they used the social skills.

- The card is displayed along with a group project so that the visiting teams leave an assessment mark or a positive statement.

Chapter 4

Cooperative Learning Structures

The structures in this section are the "How" of cooperative learning. They can be used over and over with different content to create fresh, new activities. This section is intended primarily as a reference section, to turn back to as you prepare your lessons. It gives the steps of each structure.

If you have read about the structures elsewhere, you may want to review this section because I have included a number of original management tips which make cooperative learning successful with primary students, such as the use of tape and yarn to direct students where to stand or how to move.

Most of the structures in this section were originally designed by Spencer Kagan, although I have created variations and new structures for primary such as Double Line-Up, Partner Think and Praise, Partner Switch, and Make-A-Match.

Build-What-I-Build

Build-What-I-Build is an excellent structure for helping young students, who cannot write, have opportunities to think through a process and organize their thoughts as they give oral directions to someone else. They enjoy the chance to be teachers as they give directions to their partners. It also develops their spatial awareness and strengthens their vocabularies as they describe positions on the building boards.

Partners are provided with bags which contain matching sets of building materials; pattern blocks, legos, unifix cubes, colored pieces of paper. The partners also receive building boards and a folding divider, called the Secret Screen. They determine who builds first, Partner #1, and who builds second, Partner #2.

Partner #1 sets up the secret screen between the partners. He/she has a set number of minutes to use the materials in the bag to build a design or object on the building board. The number of minutes is determined by how quickly the students work and by how many materials are in the bag. The time is usually three to five minutes.

Partner #2, during this time, is turned around with his/her back to the partner. This time is used to do free exploration with the materials in his/her bag.

When time is called, Partner #1 covers the item that was built with a piece of paper. Partner #2 turns around with his/her building board and materials. Partner #1 makes sure the secret screen is in place. He/she uncovers the design or object that was built, and one piece at a time, gives directions to Partner #2 on how to build a matching design or object.

When the building is complete, they compare what is on the two boards and discuss how the directions could have been changed to make it easier for Partner #2 to make a matching design or pattern.

Now they repeat the process with Partner #2 making the design or pattern while Partner #1 does free exploration. Then

Partner #2 gives directions to Partner #1 for building a matching design or object.

When students are able to write clearly enough that others can understand their directions, they can do Build-What-I-Write, where the students build, write directions for building the same item, cover what they have built, and trade places with a partner to follow the written directions to make an item that matches. The partners get together to decide how the written directions could be improved so the building matches exactly.

Color-Coded Co-op Cards

This structure is best done in the primary grades first with partners, and then with groups of four. When doing Color-Coded Co-op Cards with partners, each partner is given a set of 5 or 6 colored cards, a different color for each partner. The cards are either pre-printed or the students print the information on the cards. Types of information that is printed on the cards to help reinforce math are: a) numbers, b) shapes, c) addition or subtraction facts. After the cards are made, Partner #1 hands his cards to Partner #2. Partner #2 shows the cards one by one to Partner #1. All the cards

Color-Coded Co-op Cards

that are said correctly are marked with a happy face and placed in a pile on the floor. When a card is answered incorrectly, Partner #2 teaches the number name or addition or subtraction fact to Partner #1 and returns the card to his hand to show again. If neither of the partners can remember the information on the card, they both raise their hands. The teacher can give them the information they need.

After Partner #1 has learned all his cards, the partners reverse roles so Partner #1 shows the cards and teaches the information to Partner #2. Doing Color-Coded Co-op Cards with teams of 4 is very similar. While Partners #1 and #2 are paired up studying, Partners #3 and #4 are following the same procedure. When both sets of partners finish their studying, the teams form new study partners. Partners #1 and #4 work together and Partners #2 and #3 work together to review the material and check that they remember all the information.

Community Circle

During Community Circle students sit with their legs crossed in a large circle, so that each student is able to see all the other students. One person, usually the teacher, is the leader and starts the Community Circle by stating an open ended sentence. Everyone answers

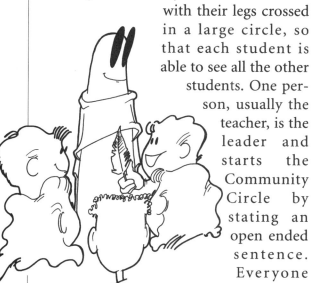

Community Circle

by completing the sentence with an answer that expresses his/her own likes, dislikes, feelings, or knowledge of the topic. For example, the teacher might use the sentence, "My favorite number is…. because…" Everyone is given a minute to think of the ending they will use for the sentence. The teacher states the social skill, such as "active listening" or "speaking so others can hear you." The leader completes the sentence and the turn passes to the right until all students have had their turn. If they can't think of an answer, when it is their turn they say "Pass." After all the other students have had their turn, they are expected to have their answer ready to share. After everyone has shared, the students evaluate how well they used the social skill.

Corners

Corners

The students find out about themselves and others by selecting which of four choices would be their favorite. They choose shapes they would like to illustrate. A sign labeling each shape is hung in the room. The students write down their choice. They go to the sign for that choice. They share reasons for selecting that choice.

Find Someone Who...

Students search for people who have certain characteristics. Possible characteristics: Favorite television program, type of family car, favorite food.

In one version students fill out a form describing themselves and then go on a people hunt to find others with the same characteristics.

Find Someone Who...

Formations

The students use their bodies to form simple shapes such as geometric shapes, numbers, or letters. The teacher draws the shapes the teams should make or tells them the shape they are to make. Then the teams or class discuss how to make the formation. They discuss which students will become which part of that for-

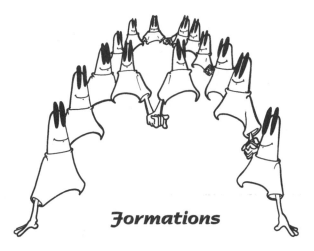

Formations

mation. They then take their places to make the assigned formation. The teacher or teammates may assign one team member to be a Checker to see if their team has created the right shape, or if it needs some modifications.

Gallery Tour

To do the Gallery Tour, the students move about the room as a team to look over, discuss, and give feedback on the products of other teams. The products may be posted if they are pictures or posters. Or they may be displayed at the team work space, especially if they have movable parts such as a pattern made of manipulatives. Often a blank feedback sheet is posted so teams can give feedback to the team members who made the product. It helps facilitate the flow of the Gallery Tour if the products are displayed in a circular fashion. The teams move to the next product in the circle every time a signal to move is given.

Inside-Outside Circle
Individual Inside-Outside Circle

Inside-Outside Circle is an excellent structure for simultaneous sharing of information. Half the students form an inner circle that faces outward. Half the students form an outer circle that faces inward. Students stand or sit facing a partner from the opposite circle. Students share with their partner. The partner from the inner circle shares first. Next, the partner in the outer circle shares. Then, the students in the inner circle stay in place while the students in the outer circle move an indicated number of spaces to their right to find a new partner.

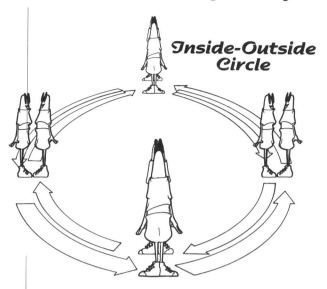

Inside-Outside Circle

For kindergarten students I have 12" x 18" carpet scraps the students sit on that clearly mark the spaces. They count the carpet scraps as they move. They continue sharing and moving on signal.

Team Inside-Outside Circle

Teams stand together in an Inside-Outside Circle. This means that four teams are in a circle facing in. Four teams are in another circle facing out. This creates a double circle with each team facing another team. Teams do a presentation for each other. They then take planning time to evaluate and improve their presentation. Next the outside circle rotates to their right to the next team. Teams present again. With successive rotations, teams improve their presentations considerably. The outer circle teams keep sharing and moving until they return to their original position. So the primary students have an easy time knowing which direction to move, it helps to tape cards with direction arrows on the floor.

Jigsaw

Jigsaw can be a very difficult structure for primary students if it is done too soon; before the students have had some opportunities to develop strategies for working together. It is an easy structure to use in primary grades, if the students have had several opportunities to successfully participate in team building, communication building, and mastery structures. The team building structures, such as Roundtable or Team Interview, develop accountability and a sense of trust, which is necessary if team members are depending upon each other to learn information that the team needs to complete their project. The communication building structures, such as Line-Ups and Think-Pair-

Share, give them the skills they need in order to be able to share the information they learned with their team. The mastery structures give the teams the strategies they need to be effective students and teachers as each team member teaches the rest of the team the information which was learned in his expert group. The structure Corners is good preparation for Jigsaw because the students become familiar with going to interest or topic groups to share information with each other.

If Jigsaw is done before the students are comfortable doing the structures mentioned above, the lesson could easily fail because the students don't possess the interpersonal skills necessary to work with two different groups, gather information, learn that information, and teach that information all within one lesson. If the structure is used in the primary classroom later in the year, when the students have the necessary skills, it is a fun way for them to learn a lot of information in a short time.

Expert Groups

To do Jigsaw each team member is assigned to an expert group. An effective way of assigning students to expert groups is to give each team an envelop of pictures. Each picture in the envelop represents one of the expert groups. Each team member takes out a picture and takes it to the expert group. Each expert group learns one part of the information that the class is accountable to learn. The expert group members then take their portion of this information back to their teams. Each team member teaches the team the information learned in the expert group. Kindergarten and first grade students learn the information in oral or pictorial form. The team then uses the information gained from each of their team members to complete the team activity.

Double Expert Groups

Double Expert Groups are the same as Expert Groups except that each of the groups that meets to become experts are divided into two sub-groups. If Expert Groups are used for a class of 32 students, there would be eight students in each expert group. If Double Expert Groups were used instead, the sub-groups are kept to three or four students. This increases student interest and participation within the expert groups. Also the two sub-groups from each Expert Group can do a Teams Compare to share information and teaching techniques before they go back to their teams to teach the information.

Line-Ups
Characteristic Class Line-Up

In a characteristic Line-Up the teacher lays tape or yarn on the floor and labels sections along the line with answer choices. The teacher reads the labels that are on the line. The students decide which choice is the best one for them. They write down that choice on a Post-it or small paper. The students take the paper with them to the Line-Up. They stand in the section that has the same label that is on their small papers. The students count how many are in each section of the line up. Then they discuss why they chose their answer or the

Line-Ups

advantages or disadvantages of their answer. For example they discuss the advantages and disadvantages of having a large or small family.

In a characteristic Line-Up, students choose from answers that are arranged in an established order. The line could be labeled so the students line up by the month of their birthday, by the number that shows how many members there are in their family, to show the time they got up in the morning, or by their height or weight. Characteristics can be assigned to students to practice numbers, letters or other content. For example, students can be given number or letter cards and then be asked to Line-Up in numerical or alphabetical order.

Value Line-Up

The Value Line-Up shows how students feel about something or it shows their opinion. Once the line is labeled, students line up according to how much they like or dislike something, or they line up as to whether they agree or disagree with something.

Students stand closer to the ends or closer to the middle according to how much they liked or disliked the idea or object being discussed. Ideas for Line-Ups are: happy/sad; agree/disagree; a lot/some/none; yes/maybe/no. Students in a Value Line-Up can number from 1 to 4 along the Line-Up to talk to other students with similar opinions. The #1 and #2 students talk with each other. The #3 and #4 students talk with each other. In order to have students talk to others with different opinions, they do the Split And Slide or The Wrap.

Split And Slide

To discover reasons given for a different view point, students do the Split And Slide. For the Split And Slide, count the students to establish equal halves of the line. Have one half of the line stay standing on the line. The other half of the Line-Up takes two steps forward to create two separate lines. Have the students in each of the lines number themselves in order along the line, having the numbering go in the same direction in each of the lines. Then have the new line move in front of the established line until the students are standing face to face with the person who has their same number. Kindergarten and first grade students actually need to hold the number card or need to be carefully directed to their partner. Now the students are facing someone who has a different view point and they are ready for a discussion.

The Wrap

To have certain students with extreme opposite ideas talk to each other, have the students do The Wrap. To do The Wrap (Folded Value Line), one end of the line comes down to meet the other end of the line. This makes partners of the first person and the last person in the Line-Up. The end partners talk about extreme opposite opinions, but the students who were in the middle of the Line-Up are discussing with someone who has a very similar opinion.

Double Line-Up

Sometimes I have half the class make one Line-Up, and the other half of the class stands in another Line-Up. This is particularly useful in primary grades, because there are not so many students in each line. It makes it easier for the students to find their place. Also when it is time to discuss with a partner, the two lines just move toward each other and automatically the students have their partners.

Team Line-Ups

Team Line-Ups are done just like Class Line-Ups except teammates stand together in the Line-Up.

Make-A-Match

Make-A-Match is a fun way to have students find a partner. The teacher makes up some cards about a topic or concept that would be good for the class to review. Each student is given one of the cards and must find the student or students that have the cards that match up with his/her card. An example would be that the person holding the card with the numeral three must find the person with the card that has three dots. Groups of four would be formed when the students with these cards found each other; 4+2=, 3+3=, 5+1= and the number 6. They then become a group to have a discussion or to do an activity.

Mix-Freeze-Group

In this structure, the students are asked to move about the classroom making quick changes to the right, to the left, or reversing their direction. When directed to "freeze," the teacher gives a cue how to group. For example, the teacher claps his hands twice the student would form pairs; with four claps the students form groups of four. Students exchange ideas with this partners. Then, on signal they move again, stop on signal, and meet up with a new partner or partners to again share ideas. This continues until they

have met with several groups and gained several ideas. The last person or group they meet can be their partner or team, to do an activity, or everyone goes back to an established group to act on the information they gained.

Think-Mix-Freeze-Group

If students need reflection time to organize their own answers, adding think time allows the students time to collect their thoughts in the peace and quiet of their own work place before they get up on their feet and feel pressure of having an idea to share as soon as they meet a partner.

If the students are to share the best ideas only, they need time to think about the ideas they shared, and the ideas they received, to evaluate which was the best. Each time they share they need think time so they can evaluate which of the two ideas is the best one to tell the next time.

Numbered Heads Together

Numbered Heads Together is a structure that encourages a team to consider many ideas and then share the most appropriate answer. Numbered Heads Together has the following components. The students in each team are numbered. The teacher asks a question. The teammates put their heads together to discuss possible answers. The team agrees which is the correct or best answer. They make sure each team member knows that answer. The teacher says a number. The person on each team that has that number raises their hand, ready to answer the question.

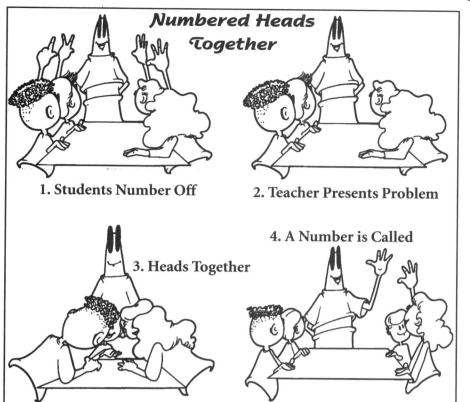

Numbered Heads Together

1. Students Number Off

2. Teacher Presents Problem

3. Heads Together

4. A Number is Called

This makes coming to agreement easier because first of all it limits the number of answer choices. Also, no one feels attachment to a particular answer because it was an answer provided by the teacher rather than by one of them. Some students become very attached to an answer when it was their idea and have a hard time accepting the fact that it was not the answer chosen by the team. Finally, sharing the answers becomes very quick and easy because all teams can show the answer at the same time.

Pair Discussion

Pair Discussion is the simplest of all cooperative learning structures. Students pair up with a person who is sitting next to them on the rug, with a desk partner, or with a partner for a cooperative project. The teacher says, "Discuss with your partner........" The two students discuss that topic until time is called.

In Sequential Numbered Heads Together, only one person at a time is called upon.

In Simultaneous Numbered Heads Together, all the students with the number have the opportunity to respond at once using answer cards or checkboards.

Forms of Simultaneous Numbered Heads Together

When primary students first start using Numbered Heads Together, I use information that could be answered with a limited number of predetermined alternatives which can easily be signaled by showing the correct number of fingers, or I provide the team with a set of answer cards. The team decides what would be the best solution or answer and then signals the answer by holding up a card or by showing the number of fingers that represents the best answer.

There are several advantages of Pair Discussion for primary students. One advantage of Pair Discussion is that it keeps the young students focused on the discussion by involving all the students all the time as either a listener or a speaker. Also each person does not have to wait long for a turn to speak. Another advantage of Pair Discussion for the young student is that the speaker has the smallest audience possible. This helps develop confidence for a speaker who is developing the ability to share ideas focused on a specific topic.

Pairs Check

1. Individual Work 2. Coach Checks 3. Coach Praises

4. Individual Work 5. Coach Checks 6. Coach Praises

7. Pairs Check 8. Team Celebrates

Pairs Check

Pairs Check is used to divide teams into small groups so they can peer coach while they work. It allows for better communication and concentration as they complete their tasks. The steps for Pairs Check are as follows:

1. Teams of four or six, divide into partners. These pairs do the worksheet or project. Partner #1 does the first problem or part of the project while Partner #2 is the coach.

2. The coach watches and either signals approval of the answer or offers a positive suggestion to correct the problem.

3. When they both agree on the answer, the coach praises his/her partner for the work that was done.

4,5,6. Partners reverse jobs with Partner #2 working the problem and Partner #1 being the coach. They continue reversing jobs until the worksheet or project is completed.

7,8. The pair checks their answer with the other pair and celebrate if they agree. If they don't agree on the answer, they try to solve the problem as a team. If the whole team does not know the answer, they all raise their hands and the teacher comes to assist them.

Pairs Compare

Pairs Compare is a simple structure used following a pair discussion. After a pair has discussed a topic, the pair compares their thoughts with another pair. The teacher asks them to discover what ideas both pairs discussed and what ideas only pair one had.

Partner Switch

Partner Switch is an easy form of interviewing to use when the students have been working in Pairs. People in the Pairs are numbered so they know who is Partner #1 and who is Partner #2. Two sets of partners meet together. They switch partners so that both partners who are #1 are together and both partners who are #2 are together. Then they are ready to ask each other questions, to find out how each of them feels about the issue at hand. The information now is shared with the original partner, with several students by doing an Inside-Outside Circle, or with the class during a class discussion.

Partner Switch works very effectively for the debriefing at the end of a lesson. It gives the students a chance to quietly talk with a new person about how they felt sharing the tasks required to complete an assignment or working on a particular social skill. They also gain insights into cognitive and social strategies used by other partners.

Partners Consult

Two students discuss to come to agreement on an answer. In this structure students are always involved, as a listener, speaker, or a recorder. For the younger students, it is easier to do Partners Consult successfully before attempting Teammates Consult.

Teammates Consult

Teammates Consult gives all students an opportunity to give input, hear other opinions, explore alternative possibilities, and form a better understanding of an issue before writing an answer.

The recommended number of team members for primary students would be from three or four.

For the structure Teammates Consult, all team members must agree to an answer before anyone writes the answer on their own paper. The procedure is as follows.

1. All pencils and crayons down.

2. Student #1 reads the first question. Team discusses possible answers or may use manipulatives or books to find the answer.

3. The students come to agreement and give the thumbs up signal when they agree on the correct answer.

4. The students then pick up their own pencil or crayon and write the answer on their own paper.

5. Again all writing tools are down and Student #2 reads the question.

For kindergarten and first grade students, this structure usually works best if the answer can be written with a simple number, letter, word or quick sketch.

Rallyrobin

Students form pairs within the team and take turns with their partner sharing ideas back and forth. Afterwards, the pairs share ideas with each other. This structure has the advantage of having the highest level of interaction by keeping the original conversation between two students, and yet providing for a variety of ideas when they combine the ideas of all four people on the team. For young students there is a real comfort in being able to organize and share ideas with only one other person. After the practice of discussing the ideas with one person, it is easier to continue the discussion with more people.

Roll-and-Write

In this structure, which is perfect for drill and practice, the teams tasks are determined by rolling one or two dice. Two, three, or four students are grouped together. They number themselves to determine the order in which they roll the dice. Each team member has a paper and pencil to practice the skill for the day. Each dot on the dice stands for a particular item to be practiced and/or the number of times the practice is done.

Roll-and-Write starts as the first person rolls the dice and counts up the dots.

Rallyrobin

The team members give a thumbs up if they agree with the count. Then everyone practices the items which are represented by that number of dots. Next, the second person rolls the dice, counts the dice, gets team agreement and again everyone practices the items represented by the dots. They continue taking turns rolling. The whole team practices until time is called or until they have finished their team practice sheets.

Dice can be made by sticking dots on a wooden cube. This allows control over the numbers being used. This is necessary at the beginning of kindergarten when the students are just working with the numbers 1 through 3, or 1 through 5. By writing numerals on the cubes, larger numbers can be used in the Roll and Write problems.

Examples of the meaning of the dot in One Dice Roll-and-Write:

· Look at the numbered illustrations of shapes. Draw the shape with that number.

· Count the number of dots. Write the number. Check the team numbers for accuracy.

· Draw a shape with that many angles. Tell what shape you made. [Make dice with 0,3,4.]

Examples of the meaning of the dots in Two Dice Roll-and-Write:

· The first die tells the number to practice writing. The second die tells how many times to practice it.

· Write the addition problem for the dots on the two dice.

- Write problems from the two numbers on the dice.

- Write a subtraction problem by subtracting the smaller number from the larger number.

- Write a two digit number from the dots. Share and compare the numbers written.

- Write two digit numbers by writing the number on the blue die first and then writing the number on the green die.

- The first die has numbers on it and determines which letter of the alphabet to practice. The second die has dots and determines how many times to practice the letter.

Rotating Reporter

Rotating Reporter is used to have one team member move as directed to the other groups to share the team information or product. They can choose a person to be their reporter. This works well early in the year or for the first few times the students are reporters. But if this is the way reporters are always selected, the students could have little interest in internalizing the group information.

If on the other hand, the team members number themselves, and know that the teacher will select a number, and that person will be the team reporter, all students will be interested in learning the team information. This interest can be increased by changing the number of the reporter several times as the reporters move around the class to share with all the teams.

Roundrobin

The students use Roundrobin to orally collect ideas without recording them. The team members take turns around the team sharing ideas about the topic being discussed. Sometimes it is easier for the students to take turns if the team members number themselves so everyone knows the speaking order. When it is a team members turn and he/she does not have an idea, that team member says, "pass." That keeps the flow of conversation going. If a team member says pass more that once, the team members encourage that person with a suggestion or a question that would trigger an idea.

Roundtable

Sequential Roundtable

During Sequential Roundtable, the students all contribute ideas on one sheet of paper. The team members need to know the order or direction in which the paper and pencil will be passed. Primary students usually need a minute or so to practice the passing order before they begin the Roundtable. When the signal to begin is given, a team member quickly writes or draws an idea. Then the paper and pencil are passed to the next person so they can add an answer. The students continue adding answers and passing the paper until the time to stop is announced. Usually in primary grades, there are no more than 4 students per team. The teammates need to sit close together so it is easy for them to pass the paper. Also, teammates are sometimes allowed to suggest answers to each other if they need help. Because they are seated close together, teams can converse without disturbing the teams around them.

Signaled Sequential Roundtable

Signaled Sequential Roundtable is done exactly like Sequential Roundtable except for one change. Before a group member draws or writes an answer, the answer is told to the team members. If they agree that it would be an acceptable answer for the topic, they give the thumbs up signal. If any team member thinks the answer is not correct, he/she gives a thumb sideways signal which means talk it over. If, after talking it over, the team decides the original answer is right, that answer is recorded. Many times after the person who suggested the answer explains their reason for choosing that answer, the team agrees that the answer is correct. If the team feels another answer is needed, then the person contributes another answer or asks for suggestions for an alternative answer from the team. When agreement is reached and all team members have thumbs up, then the answer is recorded.

An advantage of Signaled Sequential Roundtable is that all the team members know immediately what all the answers on the recording sheet mean. Also, because each person needs to give the signal before an answer can be recorded, it keeps all team members focused on the lesson even if it is not their turn to draw or write.

Simultaneous Roundtable

This structure is the same as Sequential Roundtable except that each student has a paper. Each team member writes an answer at the same time and then passes the paper to the next person on the team. Primary students need to focus both on working quickly themselves, but also on waiting politely until the next person is ready. Sometimes only two or three papers are passed in a group of four.

Send-A-Problem

The structure Send-A-Problem and its variation Trade-A-Problem are fun and exciting ways for the students to have drill and practice or review of facts. The students are more interested in doing the problems because they have been created by their peers rather than by the teacher.

Send-A-Problem

Each team member makes one or more problems that will be sent to another team to solve. Each team member is given a card. The team member writes a problem on his/her card. Each team member reads their problem to the team. If all the members agree upon the answer, the answer is written on the back of the card. If there is duplication of problems a new problem may be written. If time allows each team member may create more cards. To build in accountability, each team member has their own color card or writing tool. The stack can be checked to see that there is an equal number of each color.

The stack of cards are sent on to another team. Team member #1 reads the problem from the first card. They think of an answer for the problem. If the team agrees, they turn the card over to see if they agree with the answer of the sending team. If they don't agree, they write an alternative answer. The team members take turns reading the problems until all the problems have been solved. Then cards go back to the original team or they move on to more teams.

Trade-A-Problem

Each team makes a problem that is to be solved by another team. The team does not write down the answer for the problem but must agree on the answer and remember that answer. After the teams have made their problems, two teams are paired up and they exchange problems. The team who received the problem agrees upon an answer and writes the answer down. When both teams have solved the problems, the problems are returned. The teams check to see if the answer given on the paper is the same as the answer they remembered.

Stand and Share

Stand and Share is used to involve everyone in the sharing of team answers. In preparation for Stand and Share, the teams should have discussed until they agreed upon an answer or set of answers for their team. There are several different versions of Stand and Share to have students share their answers.

Numbered Stand and Share

This type of sharing is valuable when each team has several different answers that can be shared. The team members number off so each team member has a different number. The teacher calls out a number. The person from each team with this number stands up. The students standing are responsible for sharing one of their team's answers when their team is called on. They are seated as soon as they have shared an answer. Call out another number and a different person from each team stands to share another answer the team had agreed upon. Continue this process until all the teams have shared all their answers. A variation of the Numbered Stand and Share is to call on only one or two teams each time a number is called. This way not every person shares when their number is called but they must be ready to answer which keeps them focused on the answers. This variation is good when there are not many possible answers to be shared.

Class Stand and Share

A second way to do Stand and Share is to have the whole class stand up when it is time to share. A person from each team is called on to share an answer. When that answer is shared, that team and any other team that has the same answer, sit down. Continue sharing answers until all teams sit down. This type of Stand and Share is best used when each team agrees on just one or two possible answers to be shared.

Individual Stand and Share

Sometimes you may want the whole class to know the best ideas of every individual. In Individual Stand and Share each student thinks of his or her best idea to share with the class. When students are ready to share they stand. After all students are standing, one is called upon to share. That student and all the other students with that idea then sit. The process is repeated until all students are seated. When all the students are seated, not every student has stated his or her best idea, but all best ideas have been shared.

Stray and Stay
One Stray

One team member goes to another team to share the team's information. Three students stay to gather information from all the speakers who come to their team. This structure is good for confident speakers and when there are small amounts of information to share.

Two Stray

Two Stray is a structure that is used for teams to share their products or information with other teams or the class. Two team members are selected from each team to go to another team to share the information from their team. Pair a confident speaker with an insecure speaker. The two team members can share their information with just one other team or can follow a rotation pattern to share the information with several or all the other teams. The two team members who share can be chosen by the team or can be determined by having the team members number themselves. The two numbers called by the teacher decide which two are selected to share. Having two students work together to share the information has several advantages for the young learners:

- They feel more confident going to another group when they can go with someone. As confidence builds, they then share the information alone.

- The more confident person tells about the team product and the other person holds the product or picture, but will hear how to do an oral presentation by the more confident speaker. Part way through a series of presentations, the two change jobs so the less confident speaker has a chance to develop his/her presentation skills.

- It is easier for them to remember the information to be shared or to share more that one idea when each of them takes responsibility for sharing a portion of the information. Part way through a round of presentations, two team members go replace the two team members

who have been sharing. That gives the whole team some experience sharing the information and gives the whole team a chance to hear the ideas from other teams.

Three Stray

Three of the team members go to the next team's work space, while one team member stays behind to share the team information. This structure is best if there is a product to share that could fall apart or be cumbersome to carry from group to group.

Structured Sorts

The students are to place items using a system. The systems most often used with primary students are the Two Column Sort, the Four Square (2x2 Matrix), the Graph and The Venn Diagram. See the sample frameworks on the next page.

The students are given the sorting framework and the materials to be sorted. They then take turns selecting an item to go on the sort. They tell where they think the item should go and give reasons. They get agreement from their partners or the team and then put the item on the sorting frame. If there is disagreement, the item is set aside to be dealt with at the end. At this time if they still can not agree, they all raise their hands and the teacher can assist them.

Two Stray

Two Column Sort

This is the easiest sort in that the students sort objects by one characteristic. In this sort the students put all the objects that are circular in one section and all the objects that

Structured Sorts

Circles	Not Circles

Two Column Sort

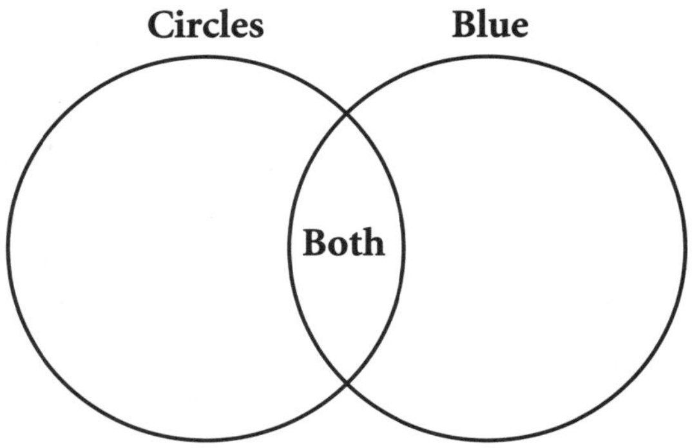

Circles   Blue

Both

Venn Diagram

	2 Holes	Not 2 Holes
White		
Not White		

The Four Square (2x2 Matrix)

Red	Green	Yellow	Red & Yellow

Graph

are not circular in the other section. Objects, pictures of objects, or words for the objects can be put in the sections depending upon the ability level of the students.

Venn Diagram

In the Venn Diagram the students are comparing two sets of objects or ideas for differences and similarities. For the Venn Diagram example the partners have a few minutes to draw shapes of different colors. They cut out their shapes. If they made a blue circle, it is glued in the center section. A blue square is glued in the blue section. An orange square is glued outside (belonging in none of the sets). An orange circle is glued in the circle section. Objects, pictures or words can be placed on the Venn Diagram depending upon the ability level of the students.

The Four Square (2x2 Matrix)

The students sort objects by one characteristic and then sort the objects by one more characteristic. For example, partners would take turns sorting buttons first by two holes and not two holes. Then they would sort each of those groups into buttons which are white and buttons which are not white.

Graphs

The students use objects to make graphs and then change those graphs to pictorial graphs by exchanging the objects for pictures. An example of this graph is where the students brought their favorite type of apple to school and then the apples were replaced with pictures they drew of their apples.

Talking Chips

Talking Chips are tokens or paper markers distributed equally to all team members, usually three or four per member. Every time a team member contributes a comment or idea, he must put one of his talking chips into a team pile. When he has spent all his chips he cannot offer any more ideas until all the other team members have spent all their chips. Then the chips can be redistributed so more ideas can be gathered. If students are limited to one chip each and there is a rule that students place their chips in the center as they speak and can only gather them back when all the chips have been used, the structure forces all students to participate each round.

Talking Chips

Team Discussion

Team Discussion is used when each team needs to have time to gather information or to come to consensus on an idea. The team members are seated close together so it is easy for them to share ideas with each other. If the conversation is dominated by a few of the team members or if some of the team members are reluctant to contribute, the structure Talking Chips is used along with Team Discussion to assure equal opportunity for contributing ideas.

Team Interview

Team Interview

One teammate is selected to be interviewed by the rest of the team. Team Interviews are good ways to have one team member share their thoughts, accomplishments, and plans for a project. A Team Interview in which a team member role plays a character from the story, allows the students to gain detailed information about that character.

Team Projects

Students are put together to work in groups or teams of three to six students. The number of students usually depends upon the number of tasks necessary to complete the project. Some projects are short, such as finding the answer to a story problem or lining up by birth date. Other projects may be more involved, such as surveying class interests and making a graph to record the information. When teams are making a product, it helps assure success for each team if they have the talents within the team that are necessary to complete the product.

Pairs Project

Partners work together to complete a project. Their projects have tasks that are in multiples of two so they can each do half of the jobs. Pair Project works well with primary students whose attention span is short.

The partners decide how they will share the task, or the tasks are assigned. After completing the task and deciding how to share, the partners group with other partners and all participate in sharing their products. Pairs seem to be the best grouping to start with in primary grades. It is easy for the young students whose attention span is short. When students need to take turns giving ideas or using equipment, their turn comes quickly and often, helping to keep them focused on the lesson. Also it helps their attention during discussions because they are both continually involved either as a speaker or a listener. Finally, it is easy because the students only have to deal with one other personality besides their own. A caution to consider, though, is that pairs need to be put together carefully so that two abrasive personalities are not put together to do a pair project. Also, if there are students in the class with poorly developed interpersonal skills, pairs need to be changed frequently. Then several people will have the job of working

Team Projects

Lorna Curran: *Lessons for Little Ones: Mathematics©*
Kagan Publishing • 1 (800) 933-2667 • www.KaganOnline.com

with and being those students role models, showing how students should work together.

Teams Check

Teams Check provides the opportunity for two teams to give each other feedback on their team products. It is used when the class, because of time or maturity, can handle only one checking of their product or when the product has pieces that can get misplaced or rearranged if several groups come to visit the team's work space. After all teams have completed their projects, let the teams know who their partner team is. This is the team that they will pair up with for Teams Check. Each team member signs a feedback paper which they leave beneath or beside their project. Then they designate one person as team recorder. The teams switch places with their partner teams and the team recorder takes a pencil.

When the team arrives at the partner team's work place, they look at the team project. If it is easy for the team to figure out and they agree that it is correct, the reporter puts a happy face on the feedback paper or the team agrees on a praising statement. The recorder writes that statement for the team. If the team thinks that the project is incorrect, the recorder puts a plus sign. The plus sign lets the partner team know that they did do the job, and it might be correct, but the partner team had difficulty understanding the project.

When the signal is given to return, the two teams switch back to their own working places. The team looks at the assessment mark. They decide why the partner team would have given them that mark. The recorder then writes down a sentence on the feedback paper that tells why the team thought they got that mark. Young students have the recorder, or a reporter they choose, come tell the teacher the reason for the mark. The teams work on a sponge activity while the oral reporting is done.

Teams Compare

Designate which teams will pair up to share their best answers with each other. If it is a problem that has one correct answer, they compare answers to see if they are the same. If it is a problem that has multiple correct answers, they can compare their answers and decide how their answers are the same and how they are different. The teams also explain to each other why they chose their answer. If it is a project that results in a variety of products, each team explains why and how they produced their product.

For the first few times primary students do Team Compare together, I pass out sets of Team Compare identification cards so each team gets a visual message as to which teams meet together. One team gets a red card marked #1, another team gets a red card marked #2. These two teams meet together with the first team sharing first while the second team is the audience. Then the second team shares and the first team is the audience. The same procedure is happening with the two blue teams, green teams, etc. If there are uneven numbers of teams, I either group three teams together to share or I become the audience for one of the teams.

Think-Pair-Share

Think-Pair-Share is one of the most frequently used cooperative learning structures for two reasons. One, it is so easy to use. Two, it immediately involves everyone in a class discussion. The procedure for Think-Pair-Share is as follows: Remind the students who their established partner is or have them quickly find a partner by making eye contact or touching someone next to them. Then the teacher asks a question. The students are given a minute or two to think of their own answer. The students pair up and discuss their answers with their partners. The teacher gives the silent signal.

Think-Pair-Share

1. **Problem Posed**
2. **Think** Time
3. **Pair** Work
4. **Share** with Class

The students are then given an opportunity to share with the class any ideas they heard or said. Directions to the students might sound like this:

"Think about this question inside your head."

"Turn to your partner and pair up to tell each other your ideas."

"Would anyone like to share an idea they heard or said?"

Think-And-Praise

The structure Think-And-Praise is a modification of Think-Pair-Share that is used to give team members time to reflect on the task they just completed and to think about praise they can give the other team members. The praise could be for use of the social skills, for contribution of good ideas, or for think-ing of a procedure that helped the team successfully complete their job. There are several versions of Think-And-Praise.

Partner-Think-And-Praise

The partners think about the project they worked on together. Provide time for each to person think of some praise to give to their partner for something helpful he/she did. When the signal to share is given, first one person and then the other person praises his/her partner.

Roundrobin Think-And-Praise

The students think about the project they just finished. Provide time for each person to think of something special or helpful that the person on their right did. When the signal to share is given, they take turns around the circle praising the person on their right for his/her special contribution.

Think-Pair-Square

1. **Problem Posed**
2. **Think** Time
3. **Pair** Work
4. **Square** Work

Team Think-And-Praise

The students think about the project they just completed. Provide time for each person to think of something each of the team members did to help get the job done. When the signal to share is given, the first person praises each of the team members. Then the second person praises each team member. This continues until every team member has told each of the team members about something they did to help the team.

Share-Think-And-Praise

After listening to another team's presentation or seeing their group product, the team members put their heads together to agree on praising statements they would like to give that team about the quality of the product and presentation.

Sometimes I have teams put their heads together to agree on a praising statement that their own group deserves for the work they have done. They share this compliment about their work or product with other groups.

Think-Pair-Square

Think-Pair-Square is very similar to Think -Pair-Share. The students meet in teams of four or maybe six. They make partners within the team. Just like in Think-Pair-Share, the students are given think time inside their heads, to organize their thoughts. They discuss their ideas with their partners, to further organize and revise their ideas. The difference is that now, instead of sharing their ideas with the class, they share them with their team instead. This allows for more participation during the sharing and the smaller audience makes some students feel more comfortable.

twenty-two bears

K-1 Counting

Literature

- **Twenty-Two Bears** by Claire Huchet Bishop
- **Brown Bear, Brown Bear, What Do You See?** by Bill Martin Jr.
- **Bears In Pairs** by Niki Yektai

materials

Adding machine tape
(1 per team)
Glue
Scissors
Crayons

Groups Line-Up to arrange bears in numerical order.

The students have heard a counting story such as *Twenty-Two Bears*. They have practiced counting and recognize numbers through twenty-two.

1 Provide lesson overview using *Teacher Talk*

"We have been reading stories about bears. Today we are going to work in groups to make a bear Line-Up. Each of the bears in our Line-Up is wearing a number and we will be sure they are standing in numerical order in the Line-Up."

2 Share ideas for quick, neat work using *Think-Pair-Share*

"Think for a moment of things you could say to your team members that encourage them to work quickly and neatly. Reach out and touch your share partner on the shoulder. Tell the statements you thought of to your partner." After they discuss for a couple of minutes, ask if anyone can share a statement to encourage quick or neat work. Encourage the students to use the statements as they worked together.

3 Place bears in order using *Team Product Line-Up*

Structures
Think-Pair-Share
Line-Up
Numbered Heads
    Together
Rallyrobin
Team Card

Social Skills
Encourage each other to work quickly and neatly.

Cognitive Skills
Sequence numbers 1-22.

Lorna Curran: *Lessons for Little Ones: Mathematics*©
Kagan Publishing • 1 (800) 933-2667 • www.KaganOnline.com

Preparation For Team Product
Line-Up. Students meet in teams of four and number themselves from 1 to 4. Each team is given a strip of adding machine tape, a Twenty-Two Bears Handout, crayons, scissors, and glue.

Make the Team Product *Line-Up.*
"Person #2, take the Twenty-Two Bears Handout. Cut off sections of five bears and give a section to each student on your team. There will be two extra bears that you can put in the center of your work space. Each of you will color and cut out your five bears. When you finish take an extra bear to color and cut out. After all the bears are cut out, put them in the center of your table and mix them all up. Then take turns, each one taking one until you have showed them all. Now you are ready. Each of you will help make the Line-Up by setting your bears in the right spot on the adding machine tape. Read the Line-Up together to be sure the bears are in numerical order. Then each of you will glue on the bears that you cut out. Again read the Line-Up to be sure the bears are still in numerical order."

4 **Evaluate use of encouraging statements using *Numbered Heads Together***
"Put your heads together and think of an encouraging statement your team used." After the teams discuss for a couple of minutes, say, "Person #3 from each team stand up. When you are called on, share the encouraging statement from your team." The teams can put their heads together again, discuss another encouraging statement they used, and team members with a different number can again be called on to Stand and Share the team statement.

5 **Debrief the lesson using *Rallyrobin/Team Card***
"Team member #1 and #2 are talking partners and team members #3 and #4 are talking partners. Take a couple minutes to discuss how you felt about doing the bear number Line-Up together." Give the silent signal. "Now both sets of partners share your ideas with each other. Agree what the best thing was about your team making the bear number Line-Up together. Have person #4 write down that idea on your team card." Collect the team cards and read them to the class.

Lesson 1a Adaptation

can't sleep
count sheep
K-2

L i t e r a t u r e

Out for the Count
by Kathryn Cave

Students follow the same lesson sequence from Twenty-Two Bears.

Preparation:
Teams of six students meet to make the bears.

Team Product *Line-Up:*
Each person makes ten bears with one bear left over that could be done by a person who finishes early. They color, cut and lay the bears in the Line-Up. Check and glue the bears.

Procedure for the Sheep Preparation:
Partners meet to make the sheep.

Team Product *Line-Up:*
Each partner does three sheep, with one left over that can be done by the person who finishes first. They color, cut out and lay the sheep in the Line-Up, and check and glue the sheep.

Evaluate and debrief.

Lesson 1b Adaptation

ten balancing
K-1

L i t e r a t u r e

One Little Elephant Balancing
by Edith Fowke

This is an easy version of the Team Product Line-Up because it involves only ten elephants. The students use the same lesson sequence as in the lesson Twenty-Two Bears, to put the ten elephants from the story in the correct numerical order.

Preparation:
Students meet in teams of four.

Team Product *Line-Up:*
Each student receives two elephants, with two left over for those who finish early to work on. They color, cut out and lay the elephants in the Line-Up. Then they check the order and glue the elephants.

Evaluate and debrief.

count down
Lesson 1c Adaptation
K-1

L i t e r a t u r e

Ten, Nine, Eight
by Molly Bang

The students use the same lesson sequence from Twenty-Two Bears to arrange the numbers in reverse order, from highest to lowest.

Preparation:
The students work in teams of five.

Team Product *Line-Up:*
There are two pictures for each team member. They color, cut out and lay the pictures in the Line-Up. Then they check the order and glue the pictures.

Evaluate and debrief.

Twenty-Two Bears

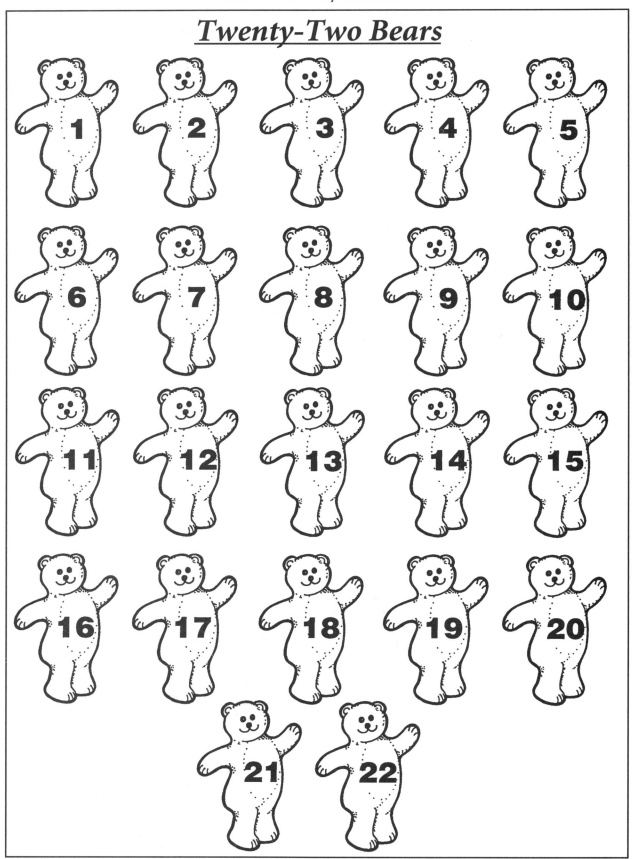

Lorna Curran: *Lessons for Little Ones: Mathematics©*
Kagan Publishing • 1 (800) 933-2667 • www.KaganOnline.com

Can't Sleep Sheep Handout

Ten Elephants Handout

Lorna Curran: *Lessons for Little Ones: Mathematics©*
Kagan Publishing • 1 (800) 933-2667 • www.KaganOnline.com

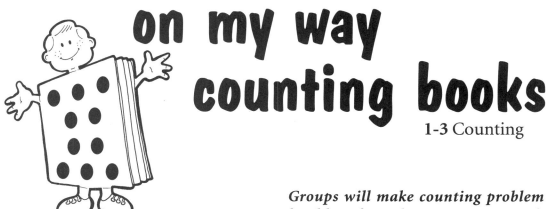

on my way counting books

1-3 Counting

L i t e r a t u r e

• *Each Orange Has Eight Slices*
by Paul Giganti Jr.

materials

On My Way booklet pages
  (1 per team)
Task and Answer sheet
  (1 per team)
Pencils
Crayons

Groups will make counting problem booklets for other groups to read.

The students have heard the story *Each Orange Has 8 Slices*. The class uses Think-Pair-Share to solve the problems as the story is read. The students then write some of the problems from the book on the board or do a Think-Pair-Answer-Check-Share. Everyone takes a minute to think if an answer a student or teacher has given that is correct. The first partner tells the second partner if he/she agrees with the answer that was given. The Partner signals "agree" or "lets talk about it." Then agreed upon answers are shared with the class.

1 Provide lesson overview using *Teacher Talk*

"Today, teams are going to make counting books that will be sent to other teams to read. As we work on the books, we will use Happy Talk to let the team know that we like how they are working and helping us work together."

2 Create ideas for happy talk using *Think-Pair-Share*

"Inside your head think of some Happy Talk you could use as you make the math books with your team. Now turn to a person next to you and share your Happy Talk ideas." After they share ideas for a few minutes, ask if there is

Structures
Think-Pair-Share
Group Project
Roundrobin
Team Discussion
Roundtable
Send-A-Problem
Mix-Freeze-Pair

Social Skills
Use happy talk.

Cognitive Skills
Create a booklet of math problems.

anyone who would like to share a statement they made or heard.

3 Make math book pages using *Group Project*

Teacher Talk: Instruction For Book Making. "So it will be easy for us to make a page for our class counting book, let's take a look at several problems in the book *Each Orange Has 8 Slices*, to see how the problems are written. Notice that each problem has three sentences that tells how much there is of three different objects that go together. Then there are three questions, one question that asks about each object."

Curran's Comments

Kindergarten students would have a difficult time writing the sentences and questions. They could just make an illustration that shows the three types of objects that fit together. The students would read the single words that label the illustrations instead of reading sentences. See the variations section at the end of this lesson.

Preparation for book making. The students meet in teams of three and number themselves from 1 to 3. The team needs two pages for the On My Way Addition Book. One is for the rough draft, and the other is for the final copy.

Roundrobin: **ideas for math book page.** "Take turns around your team to discuss possible ideas for your team math book page. After you agree on an idea, decide who is going to do each sentence of the problem and who is going to do each question of the problem. Remember, each problem has three sentences and three questions, so to divide the job fair-

ly, each person should do one sentence and one question." Sign the task sheet by the number of your sentence and your question. This will help you remember who is responsible for each job as you make your problem.

Team Discussion/Roundtable: **writing the math problem.** "The person who is writing the first sentence will take an On My Way Book Page. Put your heads together and decide what the first sentence should say. When the team agrees, the person responsible writes down the sentence. The paper is passed to the person who does the second sentence. Discuss, agree, and write. Pass the paper to the person who does the third sentence and repeat. Use this same procedure to write the questions. Check the problem and see if there are any changes that would make the problem easier to understand. When you finish, put the problem paper at the end of your table so I can see it as I come by."

Team Discussion: **ideas for the illustration.** "Decide what will be in your illustration. Remember the number of things in the picture must match the numbers in your problem. Then share the job so each of you is doing part of the illustration. While you work on the illustrations, I will come around and check your problems to see if I can solve it. After I have checked the problem, you can take turns writing your part of the problem very neatly so it is ready to be put in the class book."

Team Discussion. Assemble the pages. Make the Answer Key when the illustration is done and the problem has been checked and written neatly. Glue the problem sheet on to the bottom of the illustration. Then fill in the answer key section of your task sheet.

4 Share and solve math pages using *Send-A-Problem*

Let the teams know which direction the problems will be sent. "In a minute one person from your team will give your math page to the team next to you. At the same time your team will receive another team's problem. As soon as the problem arrives, put your heads together and decide what the answers to the questions are. Take turns so each team member writes one of the answers on the answer sheet that I will bring to your team. Check the answers on the answer sheet to be sure all of you agree with all the answers. When you do agree, sign your names on the bottom of the answer sheet."

5 Check answers and problem using *Team Discussion*

"Return the problem and answer sheet to the team that wrote the problem. When you get the problem and answer sheet back, compare the answer sheet to your team's answer key. If they are the same answer, your team problem was easy to understand and is ready for the book. Your team is ready to do the sponge activity. If the answers don't agree, discuss why you think the team did the problem differently than your team did. Did they just do the problem wrong or do you need to change something in your problem to make it easier to understand? I will come around to check with each team."

Sponge Activity

"Think of a problem you could make about something at your house and share the ideas with the team."

6 Evaluate happy talk using *Roundrobin*

"Take turns around the circle sharing a Happy Talk Statement that the team used. If Everyone in the team remembered a Happy Talk Statement, send someone to get a Happy Talk Card for each team member."

7 Debrief the lesson using *Mix-Freeze-Pair*

"Think about how working as a team helped with the job of making the math book. Move about the room until you hear the signal to stop. Then pair up with the nearest person who is not a member of your team. Share ideas about how working as a team helped get the math page done." Have the students move several times to gather several ideas.

8 Share ideas using *Roundrobin*

"Take turns around the team to share an idea that was heard during the Mix-Freeze-Pair. Continue around the circle until all ideas are heard. Decide if your team found the same ideas to be important."

Extensions
- For homework the students now write a problem about something at their house. The sponge activity ideas will have helped them get ideas about objects to use in the problem.
- Do Send-A-Problem several times until all teams have worked all the problems.
- The class book of problems can be sent to another class so they can solve the problems.

Variations

- Kindergarten students would just make an illustration with pictures of the objects that go together. In each illustration they would draw three objects that go together and the teacher could come around to the groups while they are working and give the team a slip of paper with the names of their objects. They could copy these words on to their illustration. If the class is familiar with the format of the story, they would use the illustrations and the labels to tell the story in sentence form. They would "read the words into the picture" as they read the book.
- The students could write an addition book by adding an addition problem to each page (3+3+3=9).
- The students could write a multiplication book by adding a multiplication problem to each page (3X3=9).

Lesson 2a Adaptation

black dots counting books
K-2

L i t e r a t u r e

——— *Ten Black Dots* ———
by Donald Crews

To have an easier format for making team counting books, use the book *Ten Black Dots* (3 per team). The students would use basically the same lesson sequence as in the lesson On My Way Counting Books, to make team books instead of a page for a class book. The lesson sequence for team books is as follows:

Teacher Talk:
Show the student the book and point out that the object in each picture has to have the correct number of dots.

Preparation:
Students would be in teams of five and need two book pages per person.

Roundrobin:
Each person signs up for two numbers on the task sheet. They decide as a team what ten things that have circles could be in the book.

Team Discussion/Roundtable:
Decide what objects will be used for each page. Then each person would make two pages for the team book.

Team Discussion:
All the pages are put in order. The team reads the book to be sure it is correct.

Send- A-Problem:
The books and evaluation cards are sent to the next team to be read. The teams read the books and put an evaluation mark on the card.
- Happy Face = The book was in the correct order.
- Plus sign = The book is interesting but check the order.

Team Discussion:
The team decides why they think they got a happy face or a plus sign. If there is correcting to do, they do it at this time.

Sponge Activity:
The team thinks of objects that could be drawn for the numbers from 11 to 20.

Evaluate and debrief.

On My Way Task Sheet

Sentence 1 _____

_____

Sentence 2 _____

_____

Sentence 3 _____

_____

Question 1 _____

_____

Question 2 _____

_____

Question 3 _____

_____

On My Way Answer Key

Question 1 _____

_____

Question 2 _____

_____

Question 3 _____

_____

On My Way Answer Sheet

Answer 1 _____

Answer 2 _____

Answer 3 _____

Names _____

_____

_____

On My Way Answer Sheet

Answer 1 _____

Answer 2 _____

Answer 3 _____

Names _____

_____

_____

Lorna Curran: *Lessons for Little Ones: Mathematics©*
Kagan Publishing • 1 (800) 933-2667 • www.KaganOnline.com

On My Way Book

On my way to _____

I _____

Each _____

Each _____

On My Way Book

On my way to _____

I _____

Each _____

Each _____

Dots Handout

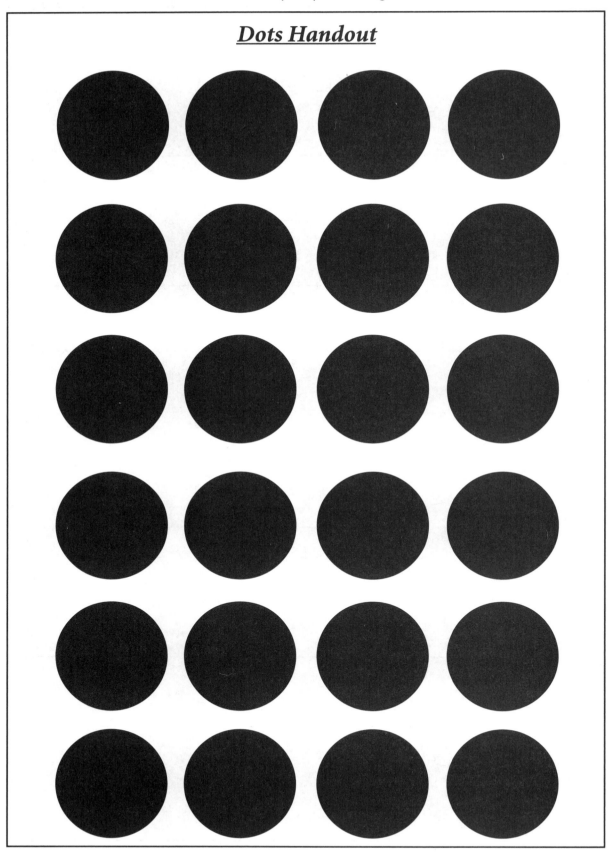

Lorna Curran: *Lessons for Little Ones: Mathematics©*
Kagan Publishing • 1 (800) 933-2667 • www.KaganOnline.com

sensational sweaters

K-1 Patterning

L i t e r a t u r e

- **The Puppy Who Wanted A Boy**
  by Jane Thayers
- **Harry the Dirty Dog** *by Gene Zion*
- **No Roses for Harry** *by Gene Zion*
- **Harry by the Sea** *by Gene Zion*
- **Who Wants Arthur?**
  by Amanda Graham
- **Some Dogs Don't**
  by Marlene and Robert McCracken

materials

Sensational sweaters handout
  (1 per student)
Sensational small sweaters handout
  (2 per team)
Direction chart
Background strip of paper
Glue, Scissors, Crayons

Triads work together to develop a pattern to read to other students.

Students have heard the story *No Roses For Harry*. They have looked at and discussed various sweater designs such as cable, striped, floral, polk-a-dot, etc. They have used active listening many times.

1 Provide lesson overview using *Teacher Talk*

"Now that you have heard the story *No Roses For Harry* you will make a picture of a sweater you think Harry might like. We will use active listening while we share those pictures in a Community Circle. Then you will work in groups of three to make a pattern using three different kinds of sweaters. You will help each other remember to work quickly and neatly so the team pattern will be done on time."

2 Design a sweater for Harry using *Independent Activity*

"We have looked at and talked about many kinds of sweaters that Harry could have. Now you will decide what sweater to draw on the handout of Harry that I give to you. Be ready to tell us what kind of a sweater you made for Harry and why you think Harry will like that sweater. When you finish making Harry's sweater, draw a background that shows where Harry is while he wears his sweater."

Structures
Community Circle
Think-Pair-Share
Team Project
Team Discussion
Inside-Outside
  Circle

Social Skills
Encourage each other to work quickly and neatly.

Cognitive Skills
Create a pattern, verbalize a pattern.

Lorna Curran: *Lessons for Little Ones: Mathematics*©
Kagan Publishing • 1 (800) 933-2667 • www.KaganOnline.com

3 Share sweaters using
Community Circle

"Bring your picture. Come sit in a Community Circle. Remember to put your picture on the floor in front of you so you can do all three parts of active listening." See the active listening chart on page 4 of chapter 2. "We will use our active listening while each person in order around the circle shows us their picture and tells us what kind of sweater they made for Harry and why Harry would like that sweater."

4 Evaluate active listening using
Finger Evaluation

"In a few minutes we will signal an answer to show how well we did in using active listening. Remember, five fingers means everyone used all parts of active listening. Three fingers means most people used active listening. One finger means that a few people used active listening. Take a minute to think what your signal will be and your reason for having that signal. One, two, three, show." Ask several students to state their reasons. Praise or reward according to how many fingers you see.

5 Think of statements using
Think-Pair-Share

"We will be encouraging each other to work quietly and neatly during the next part of the lesson, so let's think about some nice ways to remind each other to do neat work and also to work quickly. Turn to your partner. Tell each other any statements you can think of to encourage us to work quietly and neatly. Who would like to share an idea they heard or said?" Write down the students suggestions which may be similar to these: "Great,

Tom got started right away." "Everyone have your ideas for the sweaters ready to share." "That's neat coloring."

6 Make the pattern using
Team Project

Preparations for the pattern. Students meet in triads. Each triad is given a page of small sweaters and a pair of scissors for each team member. The team is given glue and a long strip of construction paper for the pattern background.

Team Discussion: **plan the pattern.** The triad discusses the type of sweaters they saw during the class sharing. They choose three different types of sweaters to use in their team pattern. Each team member chooses one of the types of sweaters to make.

Make the sweaters. Each team member colors and cuts out six sweaters of the type they chose to make. For example if the team decided that the three types of sweaters in their pattern are floral, striped, and plaid, one team member makes 6 floral sweaters, another team member makes 6 striped sweaters, and the final team member makes 6 plaid sweaters.

Team Discussion: **check for encouraging statements.** Part way through their work time ask for active listening. Give the students a minute to recall which encouraging statements their triad used. Ask triads to share any encouraging statements they used. The teacher also shares any statements she heard. Add any new statements to the list. Reread the statements on the list to refresh the student's memories. Discuss some new encouraging statements you can use because we will evaluate how well we are using encouraging statements later on in the lesson."

Make the pattern. The triad decides how to arrange the sweaters into a pattern. The pattern is laid out on the background paper, (extra papers are available if needed). They read the pattern to make sure it is correct. Each person then glues the sweaters he/she made on to the background paper.

Practice the pattern. The triad practices reading the pattern so they are ready to read it to other students. Everyone must participate in the reading of the pattern.

7 Evaluate encouraging statements using *Team Discussion*

Again, give the teams a couple of minutes to remember the encouraging statements they used. "Choose two of your team members to share an encouraging statement your team used."

8 Share patterns/ two tell encouraging statements using *Teams Share*

Teams take turns reading their patterns to the class. The designated people on each team tell the two encouraging statements the team used. At this time, points or praise can be given both for the completion of the cognitive objective and for use of the social skills.

9 Debrief the lesson using *Inside-Outside Circle*

Half the students form an inside circle. The other half of the class forms an outside circle, thereby forming partners. Have partners discuss any of the questions below to find out how the students felt about doing the lesson together. The outside circle moves one person to the right to a new partner to answer each of the questions. Answers can be shared with the whole class.

- How did you feel about sharing your picture of Harry's sweater with the class during Community Circle?
- What made it easy or hard for your triad to decide which sweater designs to use for the pattern?
- How did each person know which type of sweater to make?
- How did you feel about working together to make the pattern? Explain.
- How did you feel about using encouraging statements while both of you made the pattern? Explain.
- How did it feel when someone gave you an encouraging statement? Explain.
- How did it feel to share the pattern with the rest of the class?

Extensions

- The students graph the different types of sweaters the class made for Harry.
- Celebrate "Sweater Day" where each student wears a sweater. Graph the types of sweaters the class is wearing.
- Partners make patterns of the sweaters they are wearing on "Sweater Day"
- The students make a picture of their favorite sweater and compare it to the favorite sweater they made for Harry.
- The partners are each responsible for making two different types of sweaters for the pattern so there would be four different types of sweaters in each pattern.
- Students work in groups of three or four so there will be more types of sweaters in the pattern.
- Teams think of several descriptive words for each sweater in the pattern. They use the descriptive words as they share the pattern.

Lesson 3a Adaptation

favorite flavor

K-2

Literature

— Ice Cream Soup —
by Gail Herman

Students use the same lesson sequence from Sensational Sweaters to make a pattern using their favorite flavors of ice cream.

Community Circle:
Students color a picture (1 per student) of an ice cream cone to match their favorite flavor. They share these cones in Community Circle.

Preparation:
Each triad member is given a handout of small ice cream cones (2 per team) and a background paper.

Team Discussion:
They decide on three different flavors of ice cream for their pattern.

Group Project Pattern:
Each partner colors a page of ice cream cones with the right color for his/her flavor. Then Triads make a pattern using three flavors of ice cream.

Evaluate and debrief.

Share the patterns with the class.

Sensational Sweaters

Sensational Sweaters Small Sweaters

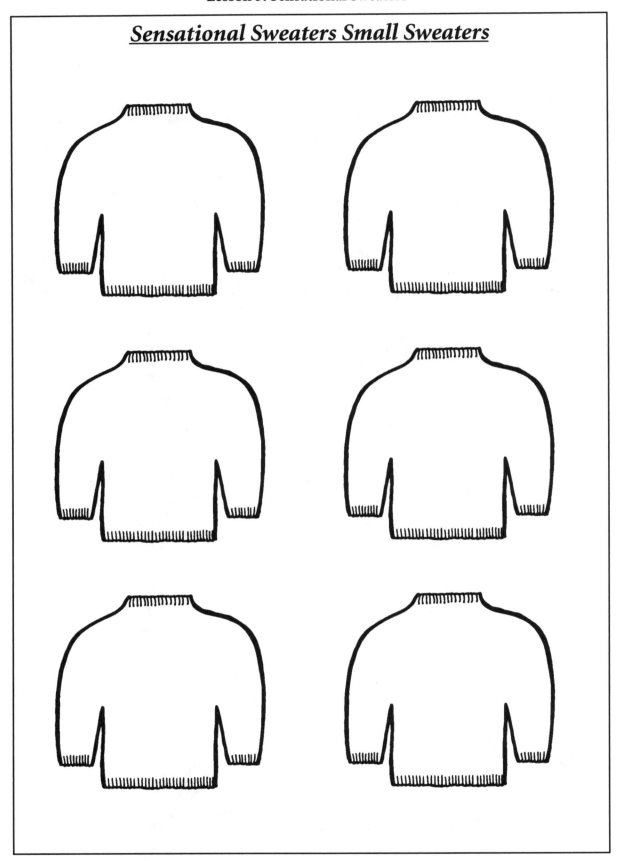

Lorna Curran: *Lessons for Little Ones: Mathematics©*
Kagan Publishing • 1 (800) 933-2667 • www.KaganOnline.com

Direction Chart for Sensational Sweaters

Plan the sweaters.

Color the sweaters.

Cut out the sweaters.

Plan the pattern.

Check the pattern.

Glue the pattern.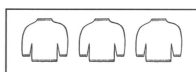

Read the pattern.

Lorna Curran: *Lessons for Little Ones: Mathematics*©
Kagan Publishing • 1 (800) 933-2667 • www.KaganOnline.com

Favorite Flavor Large Ice Cream Cone

Lorna Curran: *Lessons for Little Ones: Mathematics*©
Kagan Publishing • 1 (800) 933-2667 • www.KaganOnline.com

Favorite Flavor Small Ice Cream Cones

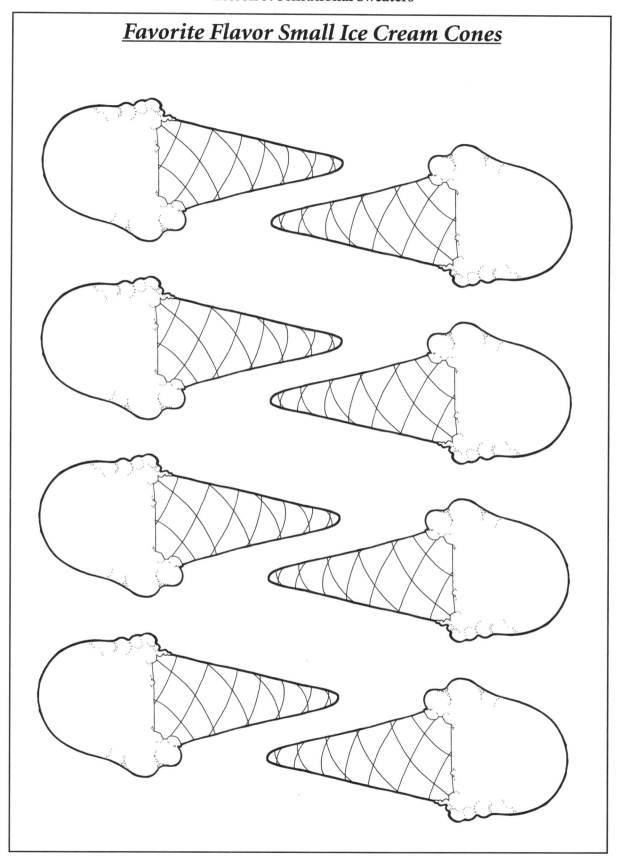

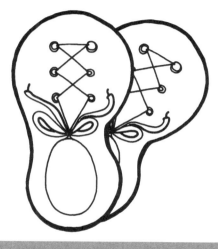

patterned shoes

K-2 Patterns

- *All My Shoes Come In Twos*
  by Mary Ann and Norman Hoberman
- *Shoes* *by Elizabeth Winthrop*

Partners create a pattern to read to other students.

This is a good follow up lesson for the story *Shoes* by Elizabeth Winthrop. Students have manipulated concrete objects, such as their shoes, to make patterns. They have seen demonstrations of patterning with pictures or objects.

1 Provide lesson overview using *Teacher Talk*

"Today we are going to make shoe patterns. You will think of a pattern to make from the shoe pictures I give you. Both of you will practice reading the pattern so it can be read to other students. While you work together, you will use Happy Talk."

2 Read or create ideas for happy talk using *Class Discussion*

Either read phrases from a Happy Talk Chart that was made from previous lessons or create a Happy Talk Chart as the students tell you nice things they say to each other as they work together. Some of the ideas they might contribute are:

"I like your work."
"That's a neat shoe."
"Great coloring."

materials

Patterned shoes handout
  (3 half-sheets per team)
Background paper strips
Glue
Scissors
Crayons

Structures
Pair Project
Pair Discussion
Teams Compare

Social Skills
Use happy talk.

Cognitive Skills
Create a pattern,
verbalize a pattern.

Lorna Curran: *Lessons for Little Ones: Mathematics©*
Kagan Publishing • 1 (800) 933-2667 • www.KaganOnline.com

3 Make a pattern using *Model*

Before the students start working with their partners, choose a student to work with you to model for the class how to make several different types of patterns with shoes. The pattern types you demonstrate could be: A, B, A, B, or AA, BB, AA, BB, or B, A, B, A, or BB, AA, BB, AA.

4 Shoe patterns using *Pair Project*

Preparation for patterning. Pair up the students. Give each pair 2 half sheets of the shoe handout so the partners only work with two different styles of shoes. They also need 2 pairs of scissors, a glue bottle, and a long narrow strip of paper as a background for their pattern.

Making the pattern. "Students, there are two kinds of shoes on your shoe picture strips. One of you colors and cuts out one type of shoe. The other partner colors and cuts out the other type of shoe. When all the shoes are colored and cut out, both of you plan together as you arrange the shoes in a pattern on the background paper."

Pair Discussion: use of happy talk. As the students work, walk around and record the happy talk statements you hear. After you hear a couple of happy talk statements, ask the students to show the silent signal. They will stop raise their hands, and listen. Then change the silent signal to active listening. Share with them the Happy Talk statements you have heard so far. "I am glad these students used Happy Talk. I'm adding a point to our reward chart because they helped us get started using Happy Talk today. Get

your heads together and decide on some Happy Talk statements that you will use as you continue your work."

Check the pattern. "Check to be sure that you both agree you have made a pattern that repeats itself over and over again."

Finish the pattern. "When the pattern is correct, each of you glues the shoes that you colored and cut out onto the background. Each of you writes your name on the bottom of the pattern sheet to show that you helped work on the pattern. Practice saying the pattern together so you are ready to read it to other students."

Curran's Comments

Some partners finish their patterns more quickly than others. When they finish cleaning up, I either have the students look at books at the library center or do selected free time activities such as: patterning with unifix cubes, patterning with art scraps, or drawing their favorite part of the story *Shoes*.

5 Evaluate happy talk using *Pair Discussion*

When the students finish their patterns, have the partners remember Happy Talk they used. As they tell their partner a Happy Talk statement they made, they draw a happy face by their partner's name at the bottom of the pattern strip.

6 Share patterns using *Teams Compare*

Put two sets of partners together to make groups of four. "First one pair will read their pattern. Then the other pair will read their pattern. Decide if the patterns are the same or different." Refer back to the types of patterns that were modeled at the beginning of the lesson: A, B, A, B or AA, BB, AA, BB. When you finish sharing, think of Happy Talk statements you can give to each other."

7 Compare patterns using *Class Signal*

"Let's find out how many sets of partners found out that they had the same type of pattern and how many found out that they had different types of patterns. Sets of partners that had the same type of pattern show thumbs up." A person from each group is asked to tell what type of pattern the two sets of partners had. Now the sets of partners who had different patterns share. The data is gathered just for appreciation or is used as material for graphs.

8 Debrief the lesson using *Class Discussion*

Find out how the students felt about the lesson by discussing some of the following questions:
* How did it feel to make the pattern together? Explain.

* How did you like having a partner to help read the pattern? Explain.
* How did it feel when your partner used Happy Talk?
* How did it feel when you used Happy Talk?

Extensions

* Students use the position of the shoe to create a pattern (sideways/up and down)
* The partners use all four types of shoes in their pattern.
* Instead of providing a shoe handout, have the students draw their own shoes to use in the pattern.
* As students read the shoe pattern, have them add a descriptive word for their shoes.
* Each partner has a turn to tell about an interesting place that their shoes have been. Then two sets of partners get together as sharing groups. Each person tells the sharing group about the place where his/her partner's shoes have been.
* The class makes a shoe graph that shows what kinds of shoes the students are wearing.
* Groups of students form a team to make a pattern out of their own shoes.

Lesson 4: Patterned Shoes

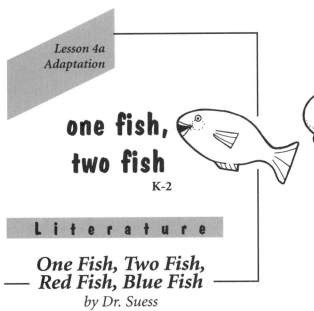

Lesson 4a Adaptation

one fish, two fish
K-2

L i t e r a t u r e

One Fish, Two Fish, Red Fish, Blue Fish
by Dr. Suess

Partners use the same lesson sequence from Patterned Shoes as they make a fish pattern using different colors of fish.

Preparation:
Partners are given a long background paper. Each team receives a fish hand-out.

***Pair Project* Pattern:**
One Partner colors all the fish red. The other partner colors all the fish blue. After the fish are cut out, the partners lay out the pattern, check the pattern and glue the fish on to the background paper.

Teams Compare:
Partners share their pattern with another team.

Evaluate And Debrief.

Teams Compare:
Two teams meet to share their patterns.

Lesson 4b Adaptation

frog & toad
K-2

L i t e r a t u r e

Frog and Toad Together
by Arnold Lobel

Jump, Frog, Jump
by Robert Kalin

Why Frogs are Wet
by Judy Hawes

Students use the same lesson sequence from Patterned Shoes to make a pattern about Frog and Toad.

Preparation:
Partners are given a long background paper. Each team receives one or two Frog and Toad handouts.

***Pair Project* Pattern:**
One partner makes a page of frogs by coloring with the green crayon. The other partner colors with the brown crayon to make toads. After the frogs and toads are cut out, the partners lay out the pattern, check the pattern and then glue the frogs and toads on to the background paper.

Teams Compare:
Partners share their pattern with another team.

Evaluate and debrief.

Teams Compare:
Two teams meet to share patterns.

Lorna Curran: *Lessons for Little Ones: Mathematics©*
Kagan Publishing • 1 (800) 933-2667 • www.KaganOnline.com

Patterned Shoes

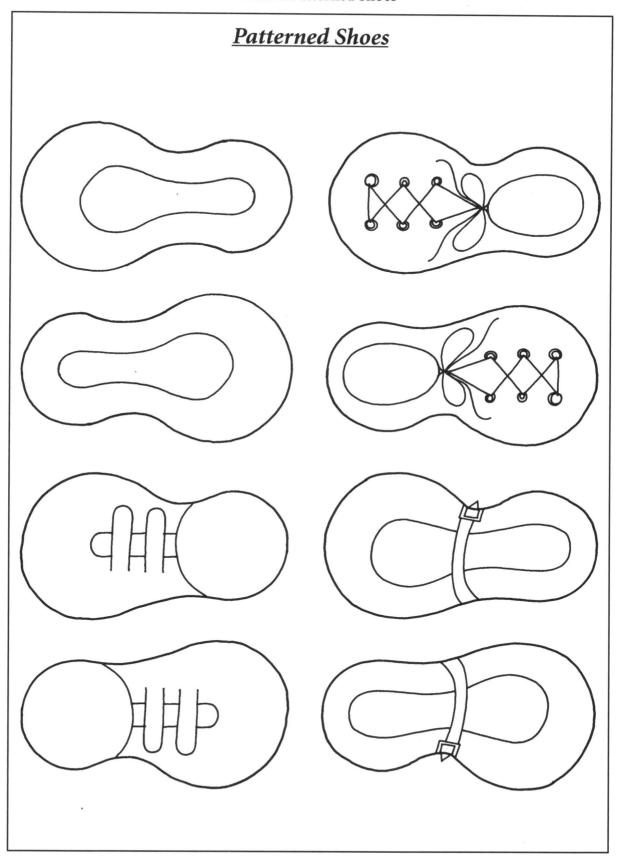

One Fish, Two Fish

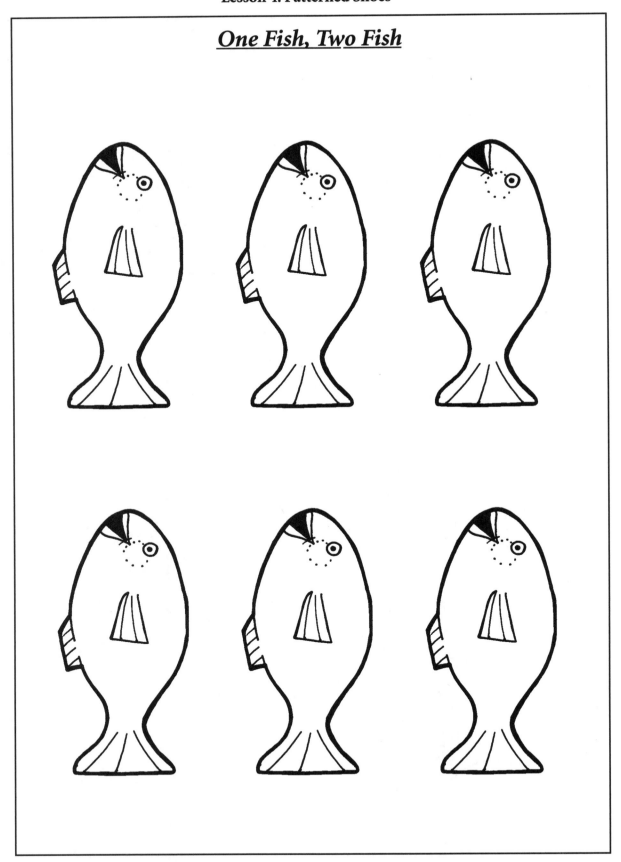

Lorna Curran: *Lessons for Little Ones: Mathematics©*
Kagan Publishing • 1 (800) 933-2667 • www.KaganOnline.com

Frog and Toad

hippo and lion up

K-1 Patterning

- *Happy Hippopatami* by Bill Martin Jr.
- *If I Had A Lion* by Liesel Moak Skorpen
- *A Children's Zoo* by Tana Hoban
- *Sam, Who Never Forgets* by Eve Rice
- *Dandelion* by Don Freeman
- *Don't Forget the Lion* by H.A. Rey

materials

Hippo and lion cards
(lion cards for half the class,
hippo cards for the other half)
Two colors of yarn
Tape

The class or groups Line-Up to form a repeating pattern.

Students have heard some stories about zoo animals so they recognize lions and hippos. Review how to make patterns.

1 Provide lesson overview using *Teacher Talk*

"Today we are going to work together as a class to make a pattern using the animal pictures that I pass out to you. While we form the Line-Up, you will use your inside voices. Help each other so we will end up with a pattern."

2 Line up using *Model*

Choose four or five students to work with you to make a pattern. Have the class notice how everyone uses inside voices as they help each other find the right place in the Line-Up so the pattern is correct.

3 Lion & hippo pattern using *Double Line-Up*

Preparation for the *Line-Up.* "So we will be ready to do our Line-Up, let's think about the kinds of patterns we know how to make." Write down the suggestions they make. Divide the class into two equal groups. "I am now going to pass out slips of paper to each of you. On your paper you will see either a picture of a lion or a picture of a hippo.

Structures
Double Line-Up
Teams Check
Class Evaluation
Class Discussion

Social Skills
Use inside voices.

Cognitive Skills
Create a pattern.

After I have told you which type of pattern we will make, you are to take your animal picture and stand on the yarn line that is designated for your group so we make a pattern that continues across the line."

Do the group *Line-Ups.* "We will make an A, B, A, B pattern. Take the picture of your animal and go to your Line-Up. If your animal is yellow, go to the yellow line. If you animal is brown, go to the brown line. Remember to use inside voices as you help each other. Watch for my silent signal after you get to the Line-Up."

Check the pattern. "Have the last two people in your Line-Up read the pattern. All of you listen to see if it sounds like the pattern is correct. When it is correct give the thumbs up signal."

Curran's Comments

To make the Line-Up even easier or faster, the class can be divided into three or four equal groups. Each group makes its own pattern and each group has its own color of animals and yarn for the Line-Up. Having fewer students in the line and having one color group at a time go to the Line-Up makes it easier for everyone to find their place on the line.

4 Read the patterns using *Teams Check*

The yellow group reads the brown group's pattern. The brown group reads the yellow group's pattern. Students vote thumbs up if they think the pattern is correct. They vote thumbs sideways if they think the pattern needs to be corrected.

5 Evaluate inside voices using *Class Evaluation*

"In just a moment when I say, 'One, two, three, show.' you will show how you feel about our use of inside voices. If you feel we used inside voices, give the thumbs up signal. If you feel we need to improve in using our inside voices, show thumbs sideways. One, two, three, show." Call on several students to tell why they gave the thumbs up or thumbs sideways signal.

6 Debrief the lesson using *Class Discussion*

Find out how the students felt about the lesson by asking some of the following questions.
- How did you feel about finding your place in the Line-Up?
- What did the students do that made it easy for you?
- What would make it easier next time?

Extensions
- Do the same lesson using three or four animals.
- Groups of students have a pile of the animal picture. They arrange the cards in order along a piece of string. When they agree the pattern is correct, they tape the pattern to the string. Two groups get together to read their patterns to each other.
- Partners are given a stack of animal cards and several strings. They make as many different patterns as they can within a given time limit.

Other Applications

• Students do a boy and girl pattern.
• Students do a position pattern. Examples: stand and squat, forwards and backwards.
• Students do a classroom object pattern. Example: book and paper.

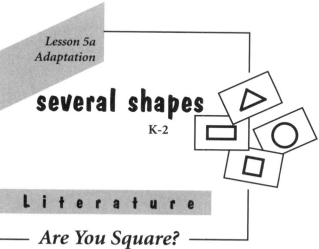

*Lesson 5a
Adaptation*

several shapes

K-2

L i t e r a t u r e

—— *Are You Square?* ——
by Ethel and Leonard Kessler

Students use the lesson sequence from Hippo and Lion Up to make a shape Line-Up.

Preparation:

Choose two shapes and two different colors. Half of the students are given one of the shapes, half of one color and half of another color. The other half of the students are given the second shape, again half in one color and half in the other color.

Group *Line-Ups:*

They take their shape card to the Line-Up that is the same color as their shape card to make a pattern. Use three or four shapes when the students are ready for the challenge.

Hippo and Lion Cards

Several Shapes Cards

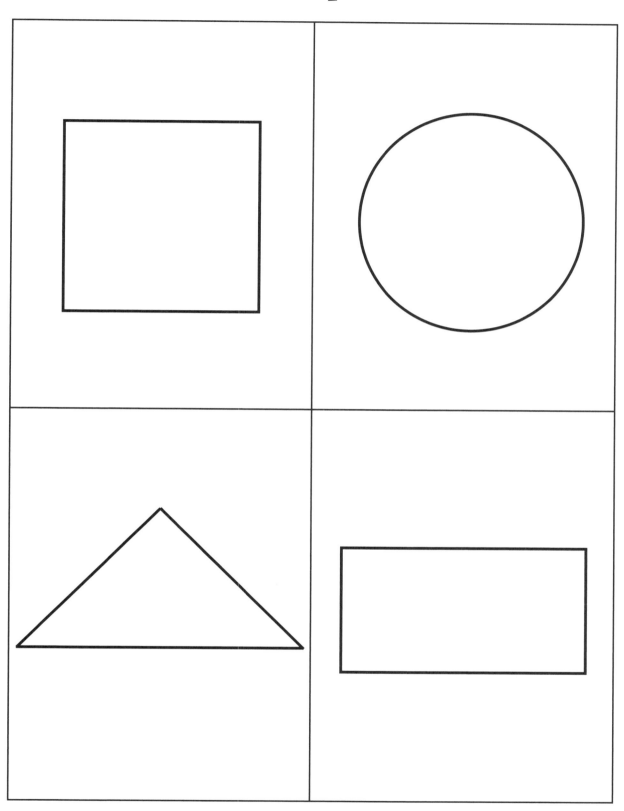

rainbow shapes

K-2 Shapes

- *Are You Square?* by Ethel and Leonard Kessler
- *Look Around! A Book About Shapes* by Leonard Everett Fisher
- *My First Look At Shapes* by Toni Rann
- *The Wing On A Flea* by Ed Emberley
- *Round and Round and Round* by Tana Hoban
- *Circles, Squares and Triangles* by Tana Hoban
- *Fun With Shapes* by Joanne Wylie
- *The Little Circle* by Ann Atwood
- *Finding Out About Shapes* by Mae Freeman
- *A Fishy Shape Story* by Joanne and David Wylie

materials

Rainbow Circle handout
(1 per team)
Crayons (4 colors per group)

Students practice drawing a particular shape.

The students have talked about the characteristics of the shapes they use for this Roundtable lesson. They also have drawn the shapes independently. They know what a rainbow is so they understand why their project is called a rainbow circle.

1 Provide lesson overview using *Teacher Talk*

"Today, in groups of three, you will take turns drawing circles to make a beautiful rainbow circle picture. These pictures will decorate our classroom. We want to make a colorful rainbow that has many circles, so it is important for us to be ready for our turn and to work quickly when it is our turn. When we finish making our Rainbow Circle, we will evaluate how well we did in being ready and working quickly."

2 Demonstrate rainbow circles using *Model*

Choose two students to join you in demonstrating how to make the rainbow circles. Emphasize how important it is to be ready for your turn and to work quickly when it is your turn.

3 Make Rainbow Circles using *Sequential Roundtable*

Structures
Sequential
    Roundtable
Team Discussion
Corners
Teams Compare

Social Skills
Being ready for
your turn, and
working quickly.

Cognitive Skills
Draw a particular
shape.

Lorna Curran: *Lessons for Little Ones: Mathematics*©
Kagan Publishing • 1 (800) 933-2667 • www.KaganOnline.com

Preparation for the _Roundtable_. Each group is given a Rainbow Circle Sheet and three different colors of crayons. "Each group member is to choose one of the crayons and write his/her name on one of the lines at the bottom of the Rainbow Circle Sheet. Now we know who uses which color crayon and who draws the circles first, second and third."

Make rainbow circles. Students use these directions to make the rainbow circle.

- Person #1 uses his or her crayon to draw a small circle around the circle in the center of the paper.
- The paper is passed to person #2 who draws a circle around the circle that person #1 made.
- The paper is passed to person #3 who makes a circle around the circle made by person #2.
- Person #3 passes the paper back to person #1.
- The team keeps passing the paper and drawing circles outside the last circle until time is called or until they run out of space.

"This is a suggestion. Make your circle right up close to the last circle so you will have room for many circles. When there are many circles on the paper it is colorful and beautiful."

4 Evaluate social skills using _Team Discussion_

"Were all the people in your group ready to take their turns and work quickly when it was their turn? If you feel they were ready and worked quickly, person #1 draws a happy face in a bottom corner of the paper." Validate their happy faces by sharing what you had observed while they worked. Give praise or points according to how well the students did in using the social skills.

5 Debrief the lesson using _Corners_

Group Discussion: _Corners_ sub groups answer questions. Label each of the corners of the room with a sign that is one of the colors that the students used for the rainbow circle. "Students, when I finish directions you are to go to the corner that has the same color sign as the crayon you used to draw the circles." Divide each corner group into two sub groups. Find out how the students felt about the lesson by giving the students in the corners groups a couple minutes to discuss answers for some or all of the following questions:

- What did your group do that made it easy to be ready for your turn?
- How did you feel when it was your turn to make a circle?
- What made it easy for your group to make the rainbow circle?

Teams Compare: sub groups compare reactions to the lesson. The two sub groups in each corner meet for a few minutes to compare their feelings about the lesson.

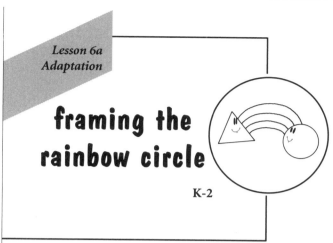

Lesson 6a Adaptation

framing the rainbow circle

K-2

Lesson Overview

1. Person #1 gets the background circle, scissors and glue.

2. Person # 2 cuts out the circle and takes care of the scraps.

3. Person #3 glues the rainbow circle to the background paper.

4. Each team member signs his/her name on the back of the rainbow circle.

Extensions

- Several rainbow shapes are made by each group to make a mobile. When the class is done with the mobiles, each group member takes home one of the shapes from the mobile.

- Each group member has a shape and the class does Simultaneous Roundtable. This way everyone is drawing and passing at the same time.

Other Applications

- Use the same procedure to practice making other shapes.

- Use this procedure to make decorations for the holidays.

- rainbow hearts for Valentine's Day

- rainbow shamrocks for St. Patrick's Day

- rainbow stars for Christmas, February, or the Fourth of July

Rainbow Circle Handout

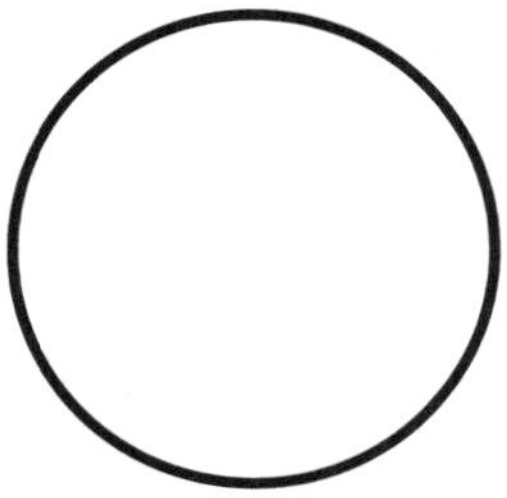

1._____

2._____

3._____

Lorna Curran: *Lessons for Little Ones: Mathematics©*
Kagan Publishing • 1 (800) 933-2667 • www.KaganOnline.com

beautiful balanced butterflies

K-2 Symmetry

L i t e r a t u r e

- *The Very Hungry Caterpillar* by Eric Carle
- *Butterflies and Moths* by Henry Pluckrose
- *Look ... A Butterfly* by David Cutts
- *Where Does the Butterfly Go When It Rains?* by May Garelick
- *Remember the Butterflies*
  by Anna Grossnickle Hines

materials

Beautiful butterfly wing pattern
    (1 per student)
Narrow paper strip for antenna
    (2 per team)
Glue, Crayons

Partners make a butterfly with symmetrical wings.

The students have seen many pictures of butterflies so they are familiar with the kinds of designs butterflies have on their wings. Also, they understand the term symmetrical.

1 Provide lesson overview using *Teacher Talk*

"We have seen pictures of many beautiful butterflies with many different designs on their wings. In the story *The Very Hungry Caterpillar*, the caterpillar became a beautiful butterfly. Eric Carle made that beautiful butterfly have symmetrical wings because the designs on both wings of a butterfly are the same. You and a partner will each make a wing of your symmetrical butterfly. First one partner draws a shape or line on one wing. Then the other partner copies the same shape or line on the other wing. Both of you take turns drawing and copying until your symmetrical butterfly is done. While you work together you give each other encouraging statements to help each of you do your best work."

2 Make symmetrical butterfly using *Model*

Choose a student to work with you to

Structures
Think-Pair-Share
Think-Pair-Square-
    Share
Pair Project
Pair Discussion
Teams Compare
Stand And Share
Gallery Tour

Social Skills
Encouraging
statements.

Cognitive Skills
Imitate a partner's
drawing.

Lorna Curran: *Lessons for Little Ones: Mathematics*©
Kagan Publishing • 1 (800) 933-2667 • www.KaganOnline.com

demonstrate how to make a symmetrical butterfly. Have the class listen for any encouraging statements that are used during the demonstration.

3 Think of encouraging statements using *Think-Pair-Share*

"Take a minute and think of any encouraging statements you heard during the demonstration. Talk to your partner about the encouraging statements you heard." After they discuss for a couple of minutes, invite students to share the statements that were discussed. List these statements on an "Encouraging Statements" chart. Then do a Think-Pair-Share to see if they can think of any additional encouraging statements that could be used.

4 Make butterfly using *Pair Project*

Preparations for making the butterfly. The students sit with their partners. Each set of partners is given a cut out butterfly, antenna, crayons and glue. They decide who is person #1 and who is person #2.

Make the butterfly. "Person #1 starts by drawing a shape or line on the wing that is on his/her side of the butterfly. Person #2 then makes the same shape or line with the same color, in the same place on the other wing. Person #2 makes the next shape or line on his/her wing and Person #1 copies that shape or line. Take turns drawing and copying lines and shapes until your butterfly has a beautiful symmetrical design. Person #1 colors the body of the butterfly. Person #2 glues the antenna on the butterfly's head.

5 Evaluate use of encouraging statements using *Think-Pair-Square-Share*

Pair Discussion: remember encouraging statements. "Discuss to remember what encouraging statements you and your partner used. Also, discuss what other encouraging statements you could have used."

Teams Compare: share encouraging statements. Have two sets of partners meet together and share the encouraging statements they used. "Share with each other the encouraging statements that the four of you used or could have used. Decide on one encouraging statement your group would like to share with the class."

Stand and Share: share the encouraging statements. "All groups please stand. I will call on a group to share their encouraging statement. If that was the statement your group agreed to share, you will sit down. If your group has a different statement to share, stay standing until someone says your group's statement." These statements can be identified on the class chart or can be added to the class chart.

6 Share the butterflies using *Gallery Tour*

Teams are given a rotation order. They move as a team from one butterfly to the next to admire the butterflies.

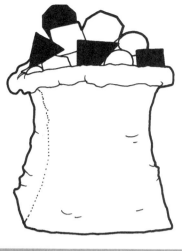

buddy builders

K-2 Shapes

Literature

• *Changes, Changes*
by *Pat Hutchins*

materials

Construction paper building
board (2 per team)
Secret screen (tri-sectioned railroad
board study corral-1 per team)
Pattern blocks or construction paper
Pattern block shapes (2 sets per team)
Paper bags (2 per team)
Block shapes (2 per team)

Students reinforce knowledge of shapes and colors as they build a design and describe to a partner how to build a matching design.

Students know the colors, shapes and the words to describe spatial concepts such as: beside, around, on top, above, below, etc. They also have done free exploration with the pattern blocks and have followed directions for creating simple designs with the pattern blocks.

1 Provide lesson overview using *Teacher Talk*

"We have had fun creating designs with the pattern blocks. Also you have learned to follow my directions for building designs. Today you will build a design. You will do the teacher's job as you give directions to your partners so they will be able to make the same design. Today we will speak clearly so it is easy for our partners to understand our directions."

2 Buddy building using *Model*

Choose a student who has an easy time speaking clearly to do Buddy Building with you. Have the students notice how it helps when you speak clearly and how partners can help each other remember to speak clearly.

Structures

Class Discussion
Build-What-I-Build
Team Discussion
Teams Compare
Mix-Freeze-Pair

Social Skills

Speak clearly,
encouraging
statements.

Cognitive Skills

Create a design with
shapes, describe the
design to a partner.

3 List clear speaking suggestions using *Class Discussion*

First, have the students make a list of things they need to do to be clear speakers. Then have them think of polite ways they can encourage each other to be clear speakers. Make a list of their ideas.

4 Make matching designs using *Build-What-I-Build*

Preparation for Building. Students meet with partners and decide who will be #1 and #2. Partners are given two bags of pattern blocks with matching sets of blocks in each of the bags, two building boards and a Secret Screen. "Each of you take a bag of pattern blocks and a building board."

Partner #1 Builds. "Partners, you will follow these directions to do the Buddy Building."

- Partner #2 turns around with his/her back to partner #1 and does free exploration with the blocks from one bag.
- Partner #1 sets up the building board and Secret Screen and makes a design using the ten blocks from the other bag.
- Partner #1 asks partner #2 to turn around.
- Partner #1 keeps the pattern hidden behind the Secret Screen. One block at a time he/she tells partner #2 where to put the blocks to build the pattern. Remind them to speak clearly so their partners will understand the directions. Examples:
  - Put a yellow hexagon in the middle where the lines cross each other.

  - Put a green triangle up against the yellow hexagon on top and on the bottom.
  - Put an orange square right up against the yellow hexagon on each side.
- When partner #2 has finished, remove the Secret Screen. Compare the two patterns.
- Now partner #1 turns around and does free exploration with the blocks. Partner #2 builds a pattern.
- Both partners put blocks in the bags. Partner #1 returns the bags to the table.

5 Evaluate speaking clearly using *Team Discussion/ Finger Evaluations*

"Talk it over and decide if both of you talked clearly and how your partner helped you remember to speak clearly as you gave directions. Show me how well we did with speaking clearly. Either give the 'we did it,' thumbs up signal or the 'fix it,' thumbs sideways signal." Praise or encourage the class according to the signals given.

6 Share clear speaking ideas using *Teams Compare*

"Meet with the partners next to you and share the ways you encouraged each other to be clear speakers." Ask the students to share any new ways they thought of to help each other.

7 Debrief the lesson using *Mix-Freeze-Pair*

"Partners stand. When I say go, start walking around the room turning this way and that until I say to stop. Make partners with someone near you. Each of you share how you felt about doing Buddy Building." While they talk for a couple of minutes, listen to get a sense of how they felt about the lesson. They can mix several more times to get new partners. Also they can share some of the best ideas with the class.

Extensions

- After a design has been build, they each draw it in their Buddy Builders Book so they remember what designs they have done. Building board pages are run off to use for the pages of the book. When they meet together again or with a new partner they create a design that neither of them has done yet.

- Kindergarten students would be more successful using five blocks to start the game. Keep increasing the number so it is a challenge to the partners.

Other Applications

- Use other materials such as unifix cubes, colored counters or building blocks.
- They use a certain number of rubber-bands and explain to their partner how to make the same design on the geoboard.
- The students make designs with pieces of yarn of three lengths(short, medium and long)on a piece of carpet. The partner makes a matching design on another piece of carpet.

shape specialists

K-2 Shapes

• *A Fishy Shape Story*
by Joanne and David Wylie

• *Shapes* by John Reiss

materials

Shape teaching poster
(1 set per team)
Shape posters
(1 per Corner sub-group)
Shape samples sheet
(1 set per team)
Construction paper
Scissors, Crayons, Glue

Students learn about a shape and teach that information to others.

The students have looked at shape books and are familiar with the names of the shapes. However, they might not yet be able to connect the correct name with the correct shape.

1 Provide lesson overview using *Teacher Talk*

"We have looked at books that show us different shapes. Today we are going to work in expert groups to find out how to recognize a particular shape and to try making that shape in several different ways. The group will come up with a definition for that shape to use when you teach your team about the shape you made. As you work in the Expert Groups to make the shapes, remember to use Happy Talk."

2 Discuss ideas for teaching using *Think-Pair-Share*

Students meet in teams of four. They form partners within the team. The partners discuss ideas for being a terrific teacher, someone who makes it easy to learn. Partners discuss for a couple of minutes. Signal that it is time for the whole team to discuss their ideas and come up with additional ideas if they can.

Structures
Think-Pair-Share
Jigsaw
Team Discussion
Roundtable
Teams Compare
Roundrobin
Two Stray

Social Skills
Use happy talk, be a terrific teacher.

Cognitive Skills
Recognize the properties of a shape, describe the properties of a shape.

Lorna Curran: *Lessons for Little Ones: Mathematics*©
Kagan Publishing • 1 (800) 933-2667 • www.KaganOnline.com

3 Teach shapes using *Jigsaw*
Preparation for *Double Expert Group.*

Each team is given a set of expert group shape papers. Each sheet has one of the shapes used in the lesson drawn at the top. Each person chooses a paper and writes his/ her name at the top. Hang the Shape Posters so the Expert Groups will know where to meet and yet in a place where the group members can write on the poster. Students take their Shape Samples Sheets and go the corner where their group meets. Form sub-groups so there are three or four students in each group. The sub-group members number themselves. Each sub-group has a Shape Poster and receives a crayon, scissors, glue, and construction paper.

Team Discussion: **characteristics of the shape.** "Take a look at your shape. Decide what makes your shape look like it does. How many corners does it have? How many sides does it have? A recorder is chosen who uses the crayon to write the information down on your poster." While they are discussing, visit each group to see if they have identified the proper characteristics for their shape or if they need any help recording the information.

Roundtable: **shape samples.** "Person #1 cuts out a triangle. The other team members cut out a triangle that is the same size and type. Everyone glues those shapes to his/her Shape Samples Chart. Then person #2 cuts out a triangle that is a different shape or type. Everyone again makes a triangle to match and glue to his/her samples chart. Continue until everyone has

made a different type of triangle and all group members have copied each of the triangles." If anyone has difficulty thinking of a way to make a different version of the shape, they can ask for suggestions from the group. While they are working you again check their posters to see if they have included all the critical elements for that shape.

Teams Compare: **evaluate use of happy talk.** "Put your heads together to think of some Happy Talk Statements your group used. Now meet with the other group in your corner. Share Happy Talk Statements that each of your groups used. Which statements were the same? Which were different?" Have the sub-groups move back to their work spaces.

Team Discussion: **plan teaching the team.** "Put your heads together and take a couple of minutes to remember the ideas you had for being a terrific teacher. Now think of the best way to teach your teams about your shape so they will be able to recognize and draw it."

Roundrobin: **practice teaching.** Everyone practices teaching about the shape. Tell each person what they did to be a terrific teacher.

Roundrobin: **teach the team.** Experts return to their teams and each member is given a Shape Illustrations Paper. "Team members take turns using their Shape Samples Charts to teach the team about the shapes. As each team member finishes teaching about his/her shape, the team members take a minute to draw an illustration of that shape on their Shape Illustrations Paper." One team member from each team turns in the Shape Illustration Papers.

4 Evaluate teaching using *Think-Pair-Share*

"Discuss with your partner, the best things your team members did as they taught today. See if there are any things that would have made the teaching and learning easier. Now both partners share your ideas with each other."

5 Debrief the lesson using *Team Discussion/ Two Stray*

"Take a couple of minutes to discuss what you think the best part of the lesson was today." After the discussion, give the silent signal, and tell them how they will rotate for Two Stray. Now one set of partners stands, moves to the next team and tells them what your group thought was best about the lesson." Have them move several times. Then the team discusses the ideas they heard.

Shape Poster Titles

Triangle

Circle

Square

Rectangle

Lorna Curran: *Lessons for Little Ones: Mathematics*©
Kagan Publishing • 1 (800) 933-2667 • www.KaganOnline.com

shape search

K-2 Classification & Shapes

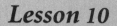

Literature

- *Calico Cat Looks at Shapes*
  by Donald Charles
- *My First Look at Shapes*
  by Toni Rann
- *A Fishy Shape Story*
  by Joanne and David Wylie
- *Shapes* *by John Reiss*

materials

Shape Hunt collection kit
(1 per team)
Magazines, Glue, Scissors
(1 per team)

Students categorize shapes by one characteristic.

The students are able to recognize and know the names of the shapes they use in the lesson. Good preparation for this lesson is Lesson 9: Shape Specialists where the students become experts in characteristics and recognition of shapes. If the same teams are used for both lessons, shape experts would already be on the team.

1 Provide lesson overview using *Teacher Talk*

"We have learned a lot about shapes. In fact, each of you are shape experts that taught your team about one of the shapes we will use in this lesson. Today, we are going to use our experts as we are detectives going on a shape search. The teams will look in magazines to find pictures of objects that fit the categories in our Shape Hunt Collection Kit. Each time an object is found for a particular shape, the team checks with the expert for that shape before the shape is put into the collection kit. While we work together we will use Happy Talk to compliment each other about the great work that is being done."

2 Think of ideas for happy talk using *Inside-Outside Circle*

Half the class forms an inner circle that

Structures
Inside-Outside
Circle
Structured Sort
Roundtable
Pairs Check
Roundrobin
Two Stray
Mix-Freeze-Pair

Social Skills
Happy talk.

Cognitive Skills
Sort shapes by one characteristic.

faces out. Half the class forms an outer circle facing in. They shake hands with their partner to be sure everyone has a partner. "Think for a minute of a Happy Talk Statement to make while the team is making the shape collection kit. Partners share your statements." Partners need a couple of minutes to share their ideas. "In a minute the people in the outer circle will move to the right. Please raise your right hand, move it out to the side. That is the direction you will move. Now, move to the next person on the right and each of you share your ideas for Happy Talk." Students move several times so they collect several phrases they can use.

3 Demonstrate the lesson using *Model*

Choose three students who will join you to model the lesson. Follow the steps in the next section to show the class how to do the shape sort. Each student should be an expert for a different shape.

4 Classify shapes using *Structured Sort*

Preparation for *Sorting*. The students meet in their teams. They number themselves around the team from one to four. Each team needs a Shape Search Collection Kit paper, a magazine, a pair of scissors and glue. Each team member signs his/her name on the line in one of the shape sections on the Shape Search Collection Kit paper.

***Roundtable*/teammates consult: hunt for shapes.** "In just a minute look in the magazine to find pictures that can fill your Shape Search Collection Kit." Before the teams start working, take a couple of minutes to go over the steps

that the demonstration team did to fill their kit."
- Person #1 turns pages. The team puts heads together looking for shapes for your kit.
- Signal that you found a shape by saying the name of the shape.
- All team members check to see if they agree.
- give thumbs up to show that you agree
- give thumbs sideways to show that you would like to talk about it
- Cut out the page and give it to the person in charge of that shape. Do not take time to cut out the object.
- Pass the magazine to person #2 and continue.
- Keep hunting until the team has found pictures of five objects for each shape.
- Remember to use Happy Talk.

Pairs Check: **glue pictures in collection kit.** "Team members #1 and #2 are partners and #3 and #4 are also partners that do the Pairs Check. Each person is responsible for cutting out the pictures of the objects for your shape. Before you glue on the object, double check with your partner. Be sure that you cut out the object from that page that is the correct shape."

Roundrobin: **read the collection kit paper.** "Prepare to share your collection kit paper by having each team member take turns reading the objects in each shape section. First everyone reads all the squares, then all the circles, then all the rectangles, and last all the triangles."

5 Share collections using *Two Stray*

Let the teams know the order for moving from one group to the other to share. "People #1 and #2 take the collection paper and move to the next group to share. Each of you tell about the objects in two of the sections." After they share a couple of times, have the other two team members do the sharing. "People #3 and #4 please go stand next to people #1 and #2 from your team. Now people #1 and #2 come back to your team's work space. People #3 and #4 move to the next team and share."

6 Evaluate happy talk using *Finger Evaluation*

"Put your heads together to talk about your team using Happy Talk. Decide how many fingers you should show for your team." Give them a couple minutes to discuss, "One, two, three, show."
   • Five fingers = great job.
   • Two fingers = good job
   • One finger = fair job, lets fix it.

7 Debrief the lesson using *Mix-Freeze-Pair*

"When I say to start, all team members head off in a different direction. Keep moving until I say to stop. Then pair up with the nearest person who was not one of your team members. Share with each other something that was fun or interesting about doing the shape search." Students are directed to move several times to hear several different ideas.

Extensions

• Teams make shape collections of shapes found on the playground or each contribute pictures of items from their homes that would fit into each of the collection categories.
• Teams make a shape chart to memorize and/or illustrate and present to other groups. Example:
   Square box, square window,
   Square things are everywhere.
   Round ball, round wheel,
   Round things are everywhere.

Other Applications

• Students do a number search to find pictures of things that are in sets of 2, 3, 4, etc.
• Students look in the newspaper, especially advertisements, for numbers in the tens, twenties, thirties or under $1.00, between $1.00 and $2.00, etc.

Shape Hunt Collection Kit

Name: _____
Shape:

Name: _____
Shape:

Name: _____
Shape:

Name: _____
Shape:

big button, small button: two holes or more

K-2 Classification

L i t e r a t u r e

- ***The Yellow Button*** *by Anne Mayer*
- ***The Button Box*** *by Margaret Reid*
- ***Frog and Toad are Friends***
  by Arnold Lobel
- ***Is It Large? Is It Small?***
  by Tana Hoban

m a t e r i a l s

Venn diagrams (1 per team)
Containers of buttons

Students sort objects by more than one characteristic.

The students have experienced watching someone use a Venn Diagram or have used them. They have had some instruction and practice in sorting by two characteristics.

1 Provide lesson overview using *Teacher Talk*

"We have heard some stories about buttons and have looked at some buttons on our clothes and from our button box. We found out that buttons have different characteristics. We can look for these characteristics to sort them. We used the characteristic of size to sort buttons and we used the characteristic of number of holes to sort buttons. Today you and a partner are going to think about both of these characteristics at the same time as you sort the buttons on to a Venn Diagram. Before you put a button on the diagram, you tell your partner the reason you decided to put the button in that section. Your partner repeats or paraphrases your reason and then signals that he/she agrees, or that you should discuss other possible answers."

2 Classify buttons using *Structured Sorts*

Preparation for *Team Sorts*.

Structures
Team Sorts
Think-Pair-Share
Think-Mix-Freeze-
    Pair

Social Skills
Repeating and
paraphrasing.

Cognitive Skills
Sort objects by
more than one
characteristic.

Lesson 11: Big Button, Small Button Two Holes or More

Students work in pairs. Each pair of partners is given a Venn Diagram and a container of buttons.

Pairs Check: **sort buttons.** "In just a minute partners follow these directions to sort the buttons."

Step 1: Person #1 will start the sorting by choosing a button and then saying one of the following statements:

- "The button goes in the center section because it is large and has two holes."
- "The button goes in the 'large' section because it is large but it does not have two holes."
- "The button goes in the section for two holed buttons because it has two holes but it is not large."

Step 2: Person #2 gives thumbs up and repeats or paraphrases the reason or gives thumbs sideways and gives the reason for a different answer.

Step 3: When they both agree that the button is in the correct section, person #2 praises person #1 for a job well done.

Step 4: If the partners cannot agree on an answer, they are to check with the other set of partners on their team.

Step 5: Person #2 now chooses a button and continues the sorting.

Step 6: The partners continue sorting until time is called.

Step 7: When time is called the team checks both of the Venn Diagrams.

3 Share the venn using *Teams Compare*

"In a few minutes, two pairs will meet to share Venn Diagrams. Put your heads together. Decide how both of you will explain your Venn Diagram to other pairs of students who come to visit." When the partners are ready, give the directions telling which pairs meet together.

4 Evaluate paraphrasing using *Think-Pair-Square*

"Talk with your partner about how easy or difficult it was to repeat or paraphrase what your partner said. When you see me give the four fingers up signal, both sets of partners meet together and all four of you share ideas."

5 Debrief the lesson using *Think-Mix-Freeze-Pair*

"Think what worked best for you and your partner as you made the Venn Diagram. Stand and move around the room until you are told to stop. Then become partners with the person nearest you and share answers." Have the students mix and share several times.

6 Share ideas from Mix-Freeze-Pair using *Class Discussion*

"Take a few minutes to share the ideas you heard from other students about what worked best for them."

Extensions:

- Teams record the information from their Venn Diagrams, take another batch of buttons and sort again. They begin to make some predictions about the number of buttons they would find for each type of button.
- Change the categories and do other sorts.

Other Applications:

- Sort shape tiles by two different characteristics.
- Sort cookies like Teddy Grahams by color and broken or not broken.

Lesson 11a Adaptation

sort and sweet

K-1

Literature

Harriet's Halloween Candy

by Nancy Carlson

For the first few experiences in sorting the students feel more confident if they are sorting by one characteristic. After hearing the story *Harriet's Halloween Candy*, they follow the lesson sequence from Big Button, Small Button: Two Holes Or More as they enjoy sorting jellybeans, gumdrops or colored miniature marshmallows by color. If clean hands have been part of the criteria for doing the lesson, then eating the sort after it is complete, could be the grand finale of the lesson.

Preparation:

Teams of four receive a Two Column Sort and a container of jellybeans.

Pairs Sort:

Partners within the team sort, paraphrase, check and praise.

Three Stray:

The reporter explains the sort to visiting teams.

Evaluate and debrief.

Other applications:

For a more healthy sort, the students could sort a mixture of raisins, golden raisins, currants, and muscat raisins.

The Venn Diagram can be used with this story by making a mixture of regular and peanut M&Ms.

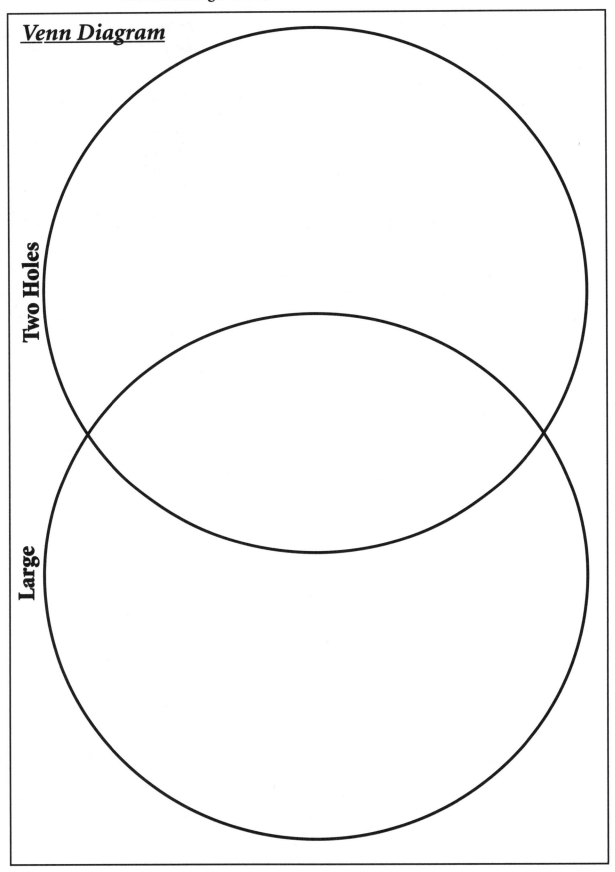

Venn Diagram

Two Holes

Large

Sweet Sorts
Two Column Sort

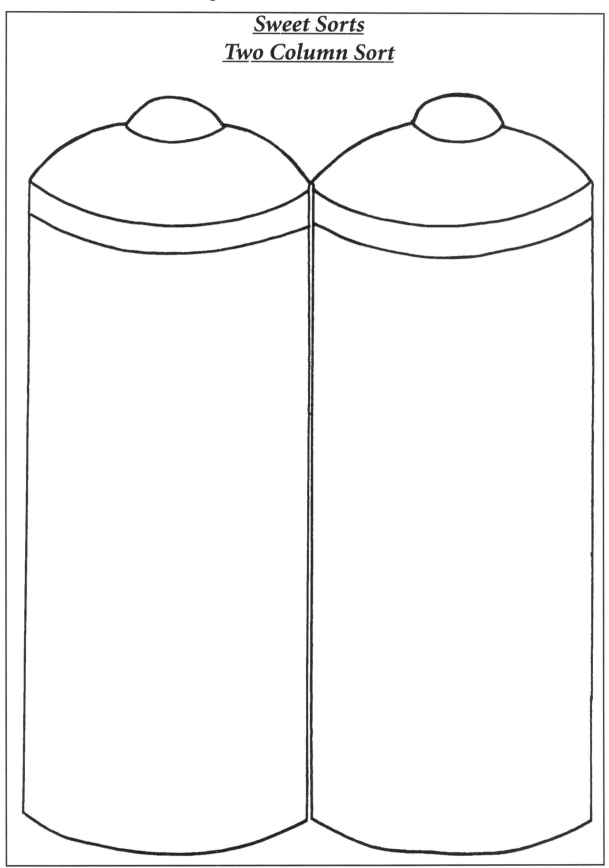

finding favorite apples

K-2 Graphing

materials

A graph sheet (for kindergartners use appropriate crayon to draw a circle around the color word)
Finding favorite apples handout (1 per team)
Finding favorite apples paper (1 per team)
Glue, Scissors, Crayons

Students make a picture graph that represents the favorite apples of the team members.

The students have heard stories about apples and have tasted red, green, and yellow apples. They have had enough experience putting graphs together as a class that each team will have some students who can assist while the graph is being assembled.

1 Provide lesson overview using *Teacher Talk*

"We have just finished tasting red, green and yellow apples. Now each of us will decide which color apple was your favorite. You are to color the apple I gave you so that it shows the color of your favorite apple. Then we will make team graphs that record which apples we liked best."

2 Make team apple graph using *Model*

Choose five students to join you to make a graph. As your team makes the graph, have the students notice how everyone participates by taking their turns in the correct order and by giving the thumb signals to each person as they lay their apple on the graph.

3 Think of polite statements using *Think-Pair-Share*

After the students have watched the

Structures
Think-Pair-Share
Signaled Sequential Roundtable
Rotating Reporter
Teams Compare

Social Skills
Happy talk, polite suggestions.

Cognitive Skills
Collect and organize information for a graph.

demonstration lesson, they do Think-Pair-Share with a partner to think of some polite things to say when they think an apple should be moved to a different column. Make a gambit chart for those statements.

4 Make apple graph using *Signaled Sequential Roundtable*

Preparation for the graph. Students take their apple pictures with them as they meet in their teams of six. Each team is given a graph paper (with the color words circled in crayon if your students need this visual clue), scissors, and glue. The team members number themselves from 1 to 6.

Signaled Roundtable: **making the graph.** "In a moment when I am done with directions, each of you glues your apple on the graph paper. Person #1 starts by placing his/her apple in the column that matches the color of the apple. The team gives a thumbs up signal if they agree that the apple is in the correct column. Then person #1 glues the apple in that spot. Continue with each team member taking his/her turn to lay the apple on the graph, get the thumbs signal from the team, and then glue the apple onto the graph. If some of the team give the thumbs sideways signal, discuss what might need to be done to get the apple in the correct place on the graph. Remember that each person is to participate by taking his or her turn to lay an apple on the graph, by giving the thumb signals when team members lay their apples on the graph, and by using Happy Talk.

5 Evaluate happy talk using *Team Cards*

The team puts their heads together to

see if they can remember if each team member used a Happy Talk Statement. They write down on a team card a Happy Talk Statement that each team member used. These cards are collected and any new statements are added to the class chart. Students who cannot yet write draw a happy face on the team card as they remember a Happy Talk statement that each team member used.

6 Debrief the lesson using *Rotating Reporter*

Team members discuss to find out what the team did that made it easy to make the graph. Choose a reporter who will rotate to all the groups to share the team's best ideas.

7 Share graphs using *Teams Compare*

"Class, in a moment, two teams will meet together to discover how the two graphs are same and how they are different. When the two teams decide how the graphs are the same and different, work together in partners to practice explaining these similarities and differences to the class. One partner tells the things that are the same about the two graphs. The other partner tells the things that are different about the graphs. After you have had a couple minutes to practice, I will call on some partners to tell about their graphs."

Extensions

- Second grade teams have the graph from their team and another team and compile the information from both graphs into one graph.

- Second grade teams survey the whole class about favorite colors, favorite pets, favorite playground equipment, etc. Then they each complete a graph that shows the information their group gathered.

Other Applications

- Make a graph that shows the favorite season of each person on the team.
- Make a graph that shows the favorite time of day for each person on the team.

Finding Favorite Apples

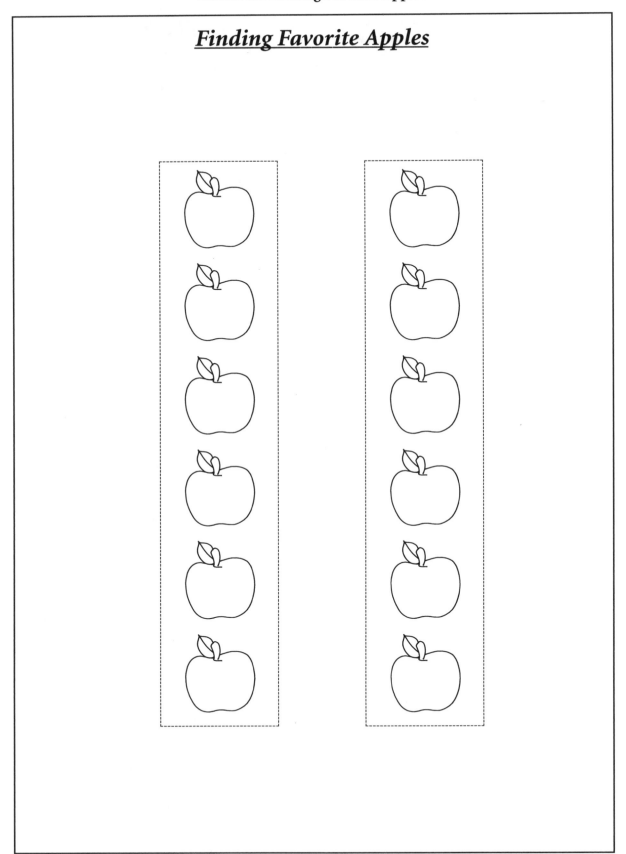

Lorna Curran: *Lessons for Little Ones: Mathematics©*
Kagan Publishing • 1 (800) 933-2667 • www.KaganOnline.com

Finding Favorite Apples Graph Paper

RED	YELLOW	GREEN

Lorna Curran: *Lessons for Little Ones: Mathematics©*
Kagan Publishing • 1 (800) 933-2667 • www.KaganOnline.com

plenty of pockets

• *A Pocket For Corduroy*
by Don Freeman

Students have enjoyed the story *A Pocket For Corduroy*. They will do several lessons about pockets. Students try to guess what is the most frequent number of pockets people in class are wearing today. They do a Pocket People Hunt. The class then does a Double Line-Up and graphs to find out exactly how many pockets there are in class. The information on the graphs can create some group addition problems.

pockets prediction

Estimation

• *A Pocket For Corduroy*
by Don Freeman

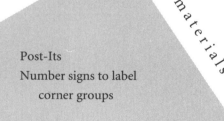

materials

Post-Its
Number signs to label
corner groups

Students estimate the number of pockets most students have on their clothes today.

The students have heard the story *A Pocket For Corduroy*. The students can count and write the numbers from one to ten.

1 Provide lesson overview using
Teacher Talk
"We enjoyed the story *A Pocket For Corduroy*. Today we are going to have fun doing some things with pockets. Just like Corduroy, you might not have pockets in your clothes today. That is fine. Pockets or no pockets, either is all right. We will find out the number of pockets most people in class have in

Structures
Corners
Team Discussion

Social Skills
Quiet voices

Cognitive Skills
Estimate the number
of pockets.

Lorna Curran: *Lessons for Little Ones: Mathematics©*
Kagan Publishing • 1 (800) 933-2667 • www.KaganOnline.com

their clothes today. When we talk in our groups, we will use quiet voices so all of us will be able to hear the discussions in our groups."

2 Number of pockets using *Corners*

Estimation of number of pockets. "Take a minute and think about this. How many pockets do you think most people in the room have? Write that number on a small Post-it."

Label the *Corners*. "In just a moment when I have finished hanging these number signs, you will put on your Post-it and do Corners by going to the number sign that is the same as the number on your post-it. People with #1 go here, People with #2 go here.. Go to the correct corner and watch for the silent signal."

Check *Corners* group numbers. After the students give the silent signal, ask them to check if everyone in their corner has the correct number. The corner

group gives a thumbs up signal when they agree that everyone has the same number.

Group signal: record most frequent number. "Stand so you can see all the groups. Take a minute to decide which corner group has the most students in it. Quietly talk it over. When I say "One, two, three, show,' put up the correct number of fingers to show which group has the most students in it." Record that number.

Team Discussion/finger evaluation: evaluate quiet voices. The corners groups decide how well they think the class did in using quiet voices. "Decide what finger signal the group will give: five fingers means everyone used quiet voices, three fingers means most people used quiet voices, one finger means the class needs to concentrate on using quiet voices. 'One, two, three, show." Ask some people to validate the scores their group members are giving.

pockets please

Number writing, Data collection, Following directions

• *A Pocket For Corduroy*
  by Don Freeman
• *Katy No Pockets*
  by Emmy Payne

materials

Paper folded in 8 sections
   (1 per student)
Drawing paper (1 per student)
Pencils

Students follow directions to play a game where they gain some information on how many pockets are in the clothes students are wearing.

The students know how to write the numbers 1 to 10 and how to write their names.

1 Provide lesson overview using *Community Circle*

"We are going on a People Hunt where we ask and find out how many pockets some of our classmates have. As we ask for and receive help, we will remember to use please and thank you."

2 Count pockets using *Partners Consult*

Make sure each person has a partner. "First count your own pockets. Then one partner counts his/her pockets while the other partner checks to see if all the pockets have been found. Then the partners switch jobs. Remember how many pockets you have for the game we will play next."

3 Fill out pockets eight square using *Find Someone Who...*

Preparation for eight square. Give each student a piece of paper folded into eight sections. This is their Find Someone Who... Recording Sheet. "Put your name on the top line so you are ready to use the Find Someone Who...

Structures
Pair Discussion
Find Someone Who...

Social Skills
Use please and thank you.

Cognitive Skills
Record information from another student.

Lorna Curran: *Lessons for Little Ones: Mathematics*©
Kagan Publishing • 1 (800) 933-2667 • www.KaganOnline.com

Recording Sheet to find out how many pockets people in our room are wearing. You will ask students in the room to please write their name and the number of pockets they have in the clothes they are wearing in one of the squares."

Use of please and thank you. " W h e n you ask them to fill in the square, remember to say please. When they finish filling in the square, remember to tell them thank you. You continue asking people to write on your recording sheet and saying please and thank you until all squares contain a name and number."

Sponge activity: picture of Corduroy

"When your sheet is full go to your seat and work on a picture of your favorite part of *A Pocket For Corduroy*."

4 Evaluate use of please & thank you using *Pair Discussion*

"Think if all the people who had you sign their sheet and said please and thank you. If the answer is yes, draw a happy face on the top of your paper because they made us feel good. If you think some people forgot to tell you please and thank you, put a plus that means we tried but still need to improve. Turn to your partner and show him/her the evaluation you gave and tell them why."

While the students are sharing, look at their evaluation and validate what they recorded by what you saw as they worked together.

5 Share Find Someone Who... Recording Sheets using *Class Sharing*

"I will call on a person and that person will look at one of the boxes, will read the name of the person and the number of pockets in the clothes they are wearing. The person we just heard about will be the new person to read information from one of the boxes on his/her paper. Watch carefully so when it is your turn to share, you will read about someone who has not shared yet. If all the people who signed your paper have shared already, you call on someone who has not shared yet to keep the game going."

a line of pockets
Graphs

- *A Pocket For Corduroy*
  by Don Freeman

materials

Red and blue yarn, tape for lines
Number cards
Post-Its
Red and blue crayons

Students use information from a Line-Up to make a graph recording numbers of pockets the students are wearing.

1 Provide lesson overview using *Teacher Talk*

"We now know that some of us have a few pockets and some of us have many pockets. We will do a couple of Line-Ups that will let us know exactly how many pockets there are on our clothes today. We also will find out which number happens most frequently. We need to stay quietly in our place in the Double Line-Ups so we can get an accurate count of the numbers of pockets we have today. We will use the information from our Double Line-Ups to make graphs."

2 Line-Up by Number of Pockets using *Double Line-Up*

Preparation for the *Line-Ups* and graph. Divide the students into two equal groups. One group uses a red crayon to write their numbers. The other group uses a blue crayon to write their numbers. "Count Your Pockets. Write that number on a Post-it. Put it on your chest." Lay out two pieces of yarn, one red and the other blue, for the Line-Ups. Put numbers along the lines to indicate where the students stand. "In just a moment you will find your number on the yarn that matches the color of your number. Stand in a line behind

Structures
Double Line-Up
Think-Pair-Share

Social Skills
Stay quietly in designated place.

Cognitive Skills
Collect and organize information for a graph.

Lorna Curran: *Lessons for Little Ones: Mathematics©*
Kagan Publishing • 1 (800) 933-2667 • www.KaganOnline.com

that number. Watch for the silent signal when you get to the Line-Up. Remember to wait quietly in your number group while we count along the Double Line-Up and make our graphs."

Curran's Comments

The first time a class does a Double Line-Up it is often easier for younger students to have one color at a time go to the line up. With fewer students moving in the room it is easier for the students to go to the correct Line-Up and find their correct number along the Line-Up.

Stand in the *Line-Ups.* "We will count how many students are by each number in the Line-Ups. People at each number count up how many are by that number in your Line-Up. Give a finger signal that shows how many are at your number." Have the Red Line-Up check the accuracy of the finger signals for the Blue Line-Up. Then they switch jobs with the Blue Line-Up counting and the Red Line-Up checking. Look for the number that has the most people by it. See if it is the same number that the students predicted in Lesson 1.

Make graphs. Hang up two graph papers, one for the red group and one for the blue group. "When I call your num-

ber, go to your color graph and put your Post-it in the correct number column. Then wait quietly at the rug while all the numbers are called."

Think-Pair-Share/ finger evaluation: evaluate quietly staying in place. "Think to your self how well all of us did in staying in place quietly while we counted up the Double Line-Up and made the graph. In a minute, give your partner a thumbs up signal, which means you think everyone stayed quietly in their place, or give a thumbs sideways signal, which means you think we need to do better. Be ready to share a reason for your signal. Turn to your partner. Share your signals and reasons." After the partners have a couple of minutes to share ideas, ask if there is anyone who would like to share information about a signal and reason that they shared.

Extensions

- The students do addition and subtraction problems by comparing the numbers in the two graphs. (See the lesson Pockets Plus Pockets).
- Students do the Line-Ups and graphs for several days to see if the number of pockets varies from day to day.
- Do Line-Ups and graphs that compare pockets in various types of clothing: shirts, pants, shorts, dresses, jackets.

Lorna Curran: *Lessons for Little Ones: Mathematics*©
Kagan Publishing • 1 (800) 933-2667 • www.KaganOnline.com

pockets plus pockets
Addition

Literature

- ***A Pocket For Corduroy***
  by Don Freeman
- ***Katy No Pockets***
  by Emmy Payne

materials

Numbered response
cards #1-10 for each group

Triads work addition problems using information from two class graphs.

The students understand how to read a graph and have had practice combining the information from two different graphs. A good time to have the class practice adding information from two graphs is while the students are still in the Double Line-Up in Lesson 13c.

1 Provide lesson overview using *Teacher Talk*

"We will work together in groups of three to do some addition from the two graphs we made. You quietly figure out the answer together. Then one person from each group shares the answer. Be ready, you never know who will be called next to give the answer. We need to use quiet, 6 inch voices so just your own group hears your voice."

2 Model using *Simultaneous Numbered Heads Together*

Ask two students to join you in doing section 3 to model how to do the addition using Simultaneous Numbered Heads.

3 Prepare for group addition
Students meet in triads. Each group is given a set of number response cards. They lay the cards in numerical order in

Structures
Simultaneous
   NumberedHeads
   Together
Numbered Heads
   Together

Social Skills
Quiet voices.

Cognitive Skills
Interpret information from a graph, add numbers.

---

front of them. "Number yourselves from 1 to 3." Asking first for person #1, have all students with that number raise their hands to be sure each person got a number in each group.

4 Group addition using *Simultaneous Numbered Heads Together*

"I will say a graph number. Your group puts their heads together. Look first at that number column on the Red Group Graph to see how many people had that number of pockets. Look at that number column on the Blue Group Graph to see how many people had that same number of pockets. Then add the two pocket numbers together. Show thumbs up when your group agrees how many people had that number of pockets, be ready to pick up the right number card for the answer if I call your number when you hear me say, 'Person #1, show the answer.' Remember these directions:

- Graph number ___. Means put your heads together. Look at that number column on both graphs. Add the pockets from both graphs together.
- Person # ___ show the answer. Means the person from your group with that number holds up correct number card.

Curran's Comments

If you would like to have the students practice writing their numbers, each group can have a chalkboard and the person whose number is called writes and shows the number. When students know how to write addition problems, the person called on writes and shows the addition problem.

5 Evaluate quiet voices using *Simultaneous Numbered Heads Together*

"Heads together and decide how well your group did in using quiet voices that could only be heard by your group. The number 5 means your group always used quiet voices. The number 3 means you used quiet voices most of the time. Number 1 means your group had a hard time using quiet voices today. "Person #3, show your number."

6 Validate the Score using *Numbered Heads Together*

"Heads together and think of reasons why your team decided on that score." Vary the numbers as you call on a person from each group to share a reason for their group's score.

Lesson 13D
Adaptation

bunches of buttons
K-1

Literature

Corduroy
by Don Freeman

The Yellow Button
by Anne Mayer

The students use this same procedure to find out the most frequent number of buttons.

- The students count their own buttons, and estimate what number of buttons are the most frequent number that students in class are wearing that day.

- They go to Corners according to the number of buttons they estimated.

- They do a People Hunt to find information on the number of buttons people are wearing.

- They do a Double Line-Up according to the number of buttons they are wearing.

- They do addition based on the information from the Line-Up.

coin collection

2-3 Numerical Order & Graphing

• *26 Letters and 99 Cents*
by Tana Hoban

Students Line-Up according to coin dates and make a graph of the number of coins in a century.

The students have been introduced to four digit numbers. They are ready to practice the numerical order of four digit numbers. They also understand the term "decade".

1 Provide lesson overview using *Teacher Talk*

"We have practiced reading and writing four digit numbers. Today we are going to do a fun game using four digit numbers. These numbers are found on a penny. We will make a Line-Up and graph based on pennies that we are given. For today's activities it is important that we use inside voices and stay in our position in the Line-Up as these are the social skills we are focusing on."

2 Sequence dates on pennies using *Class Line-Up*

Preparation for the *Line-Up*. The yarn line for the Line-Up is labeled with cards for the decades 1930 through 1990. Each student is given a penny. "Everyone cut out your penny circle. Write the date of your penny on your penny circle." Remind the students that their social skills for the lesson are to use quite voices and to stay in their correct position in the Line-Up.

Structures
Class Line-Up
Class Formations

Social Skills
Use quiet voices, stay in position.

Cognitive Skills
Sequence coins by year, organize information into graph form.

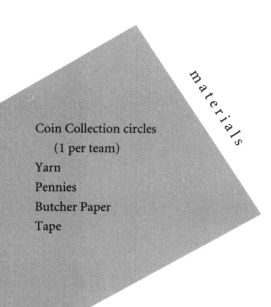

materials

Coin Collection circles
  (1 per team)
Yarn
Pennies
Butcher Paper
Tape

Lorna Curran: *Lessons for Little Ones: Mathematics©*
Kagan Publishing • 1 (800) 933-2667 • www.KaganOnline.com

Make the order *Line-Up*. "In just a moment, take your paper penny and stand between the correct decade cards which are along the yarn line. Check with the people on each side of you to be sure that everyone is in the correct numerical order along the Line-Up. Watch for my silent signal when you get to the Line-Up." Record which years are represented and how many coins there are for each year.

3 Evaluate quiet voices using *Class Line-Up*

"Students, think about the type of voices you heard as people helped each other find their places in the Line-Up. When I say '1,2,3, show,' give the thumbs up signal if you feel that everyone used quiet voices. '1,2,3, show.'" Validate their signals by sharing information about what you saw and heard.

4 Sequence by decades using *Formation*

"In just a moment when I finish with the directions, all students whose coins come from each decade, Line-Up behind the card for that decade. For example, students with pennies that have the dates 1952, 1956, and 1958 stand behind the card which is labeled 1950. Watch for the silent signal. "

5 Place pennies on a decade Graph using *Class Formations*

"Our formation now makes a human graph that shows how many coins we have from each century. We will record this information in a pictures graph. One decade at a time I will call you up

to the graph paper. Quickly glue/tape your penny in the correct decade column on the graph."

6 Evaluate staying in position using *Finger Evaluation*

"In just a moment you will give me a signal that shows how well you think we did at staying in our position along the Line-Up. If you feel we all stayed in our positions, you will show 5 fingers. If you feel most of us stayed in our position, show 3 fingers. If you feel only a few of us stayed in position, show 1 finger. Think how we did, 1,2,3, show." Praise or reward according to the signals you see.

Extensions

• Make two Line-Ups with one half of the students in each Line-Up. Compare the similarities and differences in the number of pennies for each date. Then both of the Line-Ups can merge together to make the graph.
• Make another Line-Up and Graph using another batch of pennies. Compare the results of both graphs.

Other Applications

• Students do a Line-Up and graph according to the number of pages in their library book.
• Students select a mathematical term and look it up in the dictionary. They do a Line-Up and graph according to the page number in the dictionary where they found the definition for their term.

Coin Collection

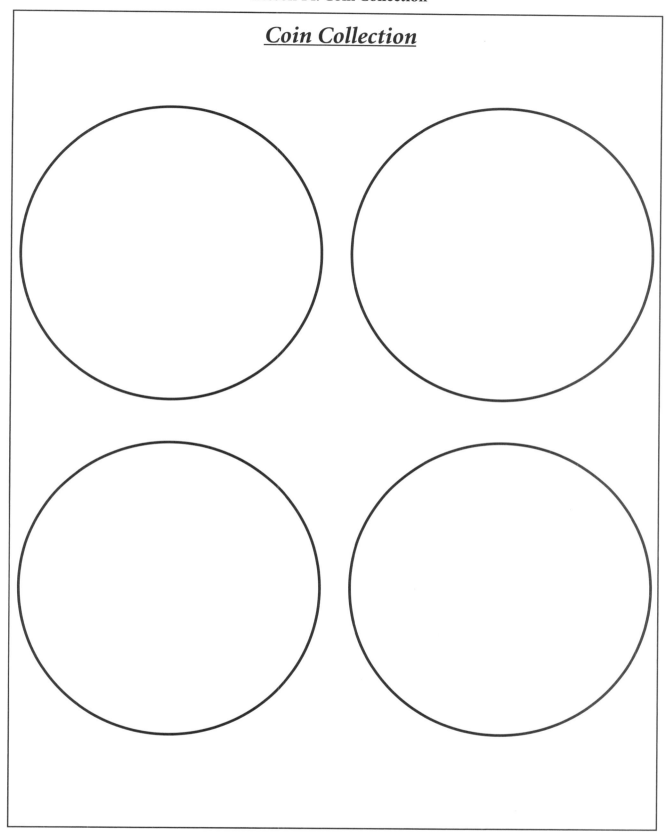

Lorna Curran: *Lessons for Little Ones: Mathematics©*

Kagan Publishing • 1 (800) 933-2667 • www.KaganOnline.com

apples on top

K-1 Classification

Literature

• *Ten Apples On Top*
by Theo Le Sieg

Students make the correct number of apples to match numbers and arrange them in numerical order.

Having heard the story *Ten Apples On Top*, the students counted the apples as the story progressed. Most of the students recognize the numbers 1-10 and can put them in numerical order.

1 Provide lesson overview using *Teacher Talk*

"You enjoyed the story Ten Apples On Top. Today you will make illustrations that show the numbers of apples in the story and then the group will arrange the apples in the correct order. We will remember to use Happy Talk as we work together."

2 Think of happy talk statements using *Think-Pair-Share*

"As I read the Happy Talk Chart, think of a couple of statements to use as we make our illustrations. Turn to your partner. Each share at least one of these statements with each other." Call on a few students to share a Happy Talk statement they heard or said.

3 Make the illustrations using *Team Project*

Preparations for group illustrations. Students are arranged in teams of five. The team members number themselves

materials

Apples On Top sheets
(1 per team)
Gallery Tour Recording sheet
(1 per team)
Envelopes, Glue, Scissors, Crayons
Strips of paper for team's
numerical order
Paper cut lengthways for each
person's characters

Structures
Gallery Tour
Numbered Heads
Together
Team Project
Team Discussion
Think-Pair-Share

Social Skills
Use happy talk.

Cognitive Skills
Count apples 1-10,
sequence numbers
1-10.

from 1-5. Each team is given an envelope containing two of each characters from the Apples On Top Character Handout, an Apples On Top Task Sheet and Gallery Tour Recording Sheet. "Find your numbers on the task sheet and sign your name by the correct number."

Make the illustrations. "Use the two characters you took from the envelope. Make illustrations for the two numbers by your name on the task sheet. You make the illustrations by coloring, cutting out, and gluing each character at the bottom of a background paper. Then you draw the correct number of apples on top of the character. When everyone has finished their characters, the team checks all the illustrations to see that the number of apples matches the numeral. Then the team arranges the illustrations in numerical order. Each person glues the illustrations he/she made to the long strip of paper."

4 Think of happy talk using *Team Discussion*

Do Think And Praise. "Everyone take a minute and think of Happy Talk that you heard the team use. Now share those Happy Talk statements with each other."

5 Evaluate happy talk using *Numbered Heads Together*

Use Numbered Heads Together to have the teams share with each other. "I will call a number and all team members with that number stand. Now I will call on a team. The person from that team who is standing shares one of the Happy Talk statement from his/her team." Call different numbers and team numbers until a

person or two from each team has shared.

6 Check the illustrations using *Gallery Tour*

Space the teams equally around the outside of the room. Each team puts their Gallery Tour Recording Sheet next to their illustration. "Every time I give the direction, 'Move to the next illustration,' the team moves clockwise to the next team's illustration. If your team thinks the illustrations and numerical order are correct, the team recorder marks a happy face on the recording sheet on the line for visit #1. If they don't feel the illustrations and numerical order are correct, the recorder makes a plus sign. Person #2 is the recorder and needs to take a pencil. Stay at that illustration until you hear me give the directions to move."

Curran's Comments

The first time the students do the Gallery Tour, it helps to have them practice moving so it will be easy for them. They won't be so likely to get lost when they are also concentrating on the correcting.

---

7 Validate the scores using *Team Discussion/ Team Card*

The team looks at the Gallery Tour Recording Sheet for their team they discuss reasons why they got happy faces and/or pluses. Person #3 uses the back side of the recording sheet as a Team Card and writes the team reasons on the recording sheet. Person #4 brings the recording sheet and illustrations to the teacher.

Curran's Comments

If the students are not capable of writing down the reasons, persons #3 and #4 orally report the reasons to the teacher as the teacher visits each team. The team members can do one of the lesson extensions while the teacher visits each team.

Extensions

- Make an apple collage. Provide a background paper and red, yellow and green paper for cutting out apples and leafs.
- Make numbers out of yarn and or strips of paper.
- Do Sequential Roundtable to cluster favorite things that are made of apples.
- Students draw themselves with ten things on top.

Apples On Top - Characters Handout

Lorna Curran: *Lessons for Little Ones: Mathematics©*
Kagan Publishing • 1 (800) 933-2667 • www.KaganOnline.com

Apples On Top - Characters Handout

Person #1 _____ Do numbers 1 and 10.

Person #2 _____ Do numbers 2 and 9.

Person #3 _____ Do numbers 3 and 8.

Person #4 _____ Do numbers 4 and 7.

Person #5 _____ Do numbers 5 and 6.

Gallery Tour Recording Sheet

Visit #1 _____

Visit #2 _____

Visit #3 _____

Visit #4 _____

Visit #5 _____

Visit #6 _____

numbers line up

K-2 Numerical Order

Literature

- **Anno's Counting Book** by *Mitsumasa Anno*
- **One Red Rooster** by *Kathleen Sullivan Carroll*
- **One Was Johnny: A Counting Book** by *Maurice Sendak*
- **One Crow A Counting Rhyme** by *Jim Aylesworth*
- **The Wildlife 1.2.3. A Nature Counting Book** by *Jan Thornhill*
- **Who Wants One?** by *Mary Serfozo*
- **Ten Little Rabbits** by *Virginia Grossman and Sylvia Long*

materials

Three colors of yarn
Three colors of 3x5 cards
Envelopes

Students arrange numbers in numerical order.

The students have heard and read many number stories. The students can easily count to 10 or 12 and are able to recognize those numbers.

1 **Provide lesson overview using Teacher Talk**

"In the past few days we have heard many stories where we count along with the story. Today, groups of us are going to count as we work together to line up in the correct numerical order. We will need to be polite waiters while all the groups are getting organized and checked in the Line-Up."

2 **Arrange in numerical order using Line-Up**

Preparation for Line-Ups. Make three sets of number cards. Each set is a different color. Each set contains enough cards for 1/3 of the class. Divide the class into three equal groups. Give each group an envelope of number cards. Make three lines for Line-Up, preferably in the same three colors as the number cards. Label one end of each line 'beginning' or 'lowest number' and the other end as 'end' or 'highest number'."

Groups: make the Line-Up. "In just a moment, each group member takes a

Structures
Group Line-Up
Team Discussion
Numbered Stand
   And Share
Roundrobin
Teams Compare

Social Skills
Polite waiting.

Cognitive Skills
Sequence numbers 1-12.

number card out of the envelope. Go to the yarn that matches your number card. Help each other get arranged from the lowest number to the highest number. Remember to be polite waiters as you finish your Line-Up. Watch for the Silent Signal so we can hear the directions for the next step of the Line-Up."

Group Discussion/signal: check *Line-Ups.* "Count along your Line-Up. Keep the thumbs up signal as long as you agree with the number order. Change to a thumbs sideways, fix-it signal, if the numbers do not match the count."

Finger Evaluation: class check of *Line-Ups.* Two of the color groups check the third color group by reading the numbers along their Line-Up. They give the thumbs up or fix-it signal. When the fix-it signal is given, make the corrections and continue reading the Line-Up. Continue the reading and correcting until all the Line-Ups have been checked.

3 Evaluate waiting politely using *Team Discussion*

Team Discussion: **agree on finger evaluations.** "Count off 1, 2, 3, 4, along the Line-Up. Each set of four people sits down in a small circle. Think inside your head for a moment about how your line up group waited during the Line-Up. Think whether your group waited — discuss why you would signal thumbs up or thumbs sideways for the people in your group Line-Up. Share your ideas with each other. "

Numbered Stand And Share: **reasons for finger evaluations.** "Person #3 from each group stand up." Call on a

few or all these students to show their finger signals and reasons for the signals.

4 Debrief the lesson using *Roundrobin*

Starting with person #1, groups of four discuss in order around the group how it felt to be a polite waiter. Also discuss how polite waiting helped the class do the Line-Ups.

5 Share debriefing information using *Teams Compare*

Pair two groups of four together to share. "Groups, share with each other how your group members felt about being polite waiters and how polite waiting helped the class do a good job with the Line-Ups."

Extensions:

• Using Double Line-Ups have one group use dot cards and the other team use number cards to do a line up. The members of each line up match with their equivalent in the other Line-Up.
• Do math problems while the students are in the Line-Up. The teacher states a problem. The person holding the number card that is correct for that answer stands forward. Sample problems are:
- Add together the number of fingers on one hand plus the number of eyes. The person with #7 stands forward.
- The number of months there are in a year. The person with #1 and the person with #2 stand forward.

Other Applications

• Use higher numbers to make Line-Ups.
• Make odd or even number Line-Ups.
• Make Line-Ups that are in 5 or 10 number increments.

batches of bunnies

1-2 Numerical Order & Number Value

Literature

• *The April Rabbits*
  by David Cleveland

Students make number value strips and arrange them in numerical order.

The students experience counting to 30. They know how to write the numbers 1 to 30. They also are fairly sure of the number value of the numbers from 1 to 30.

1 Provide lesson overview using *Think-Pair-Share*

"Every day in the story *The April Rabbits*, Robert discovered another rabbit. Today we are going to make a Line-Up that shows all the rabbits Robert saw during the month. In your group each of you is responsible for making the number of rabbits he saw on five of the days. You will show the rabbits he saw by writing the date on a strip of paper and then cutting out and gluing the correct number of rabbits on to the strip. You will give each other praising statements as you work together.

2 Think of praising statements using *Think-Pair-Share*

"Think of some praising statements to give each other as you work together. Tell each other the praisers you thought of. Is there anyone who heard or said a praising statement that we can use today."

materials

Rabbits handout
   (1 per team-print on card stock)
Envelopes of task cards
Perfect Praiser Badge
4 foot long heavy yarn
Long narrow strips of paper
Clothes pins or glue

Structures

Think-Pair-Share
Group Line-Up
Pairs Check
Rallyrobin
Teams Check
Think-And-Praise
Team Discussion
Two Stray
Roundrobin

Social Skills

Praising statements, encouraging suggestions.

Cognitive Skills

Count bunnies 1-30, sequence numbers 1-30.

Lorna Curran: *Lessons for Little Ones: Mathematics*©
Kagan Publishing • 1 (800) 933-2667 • www.KaganOnline.com

3 **Show the number value strips in numerical order using**

Group Line-Up

Preparation for the Line-Up. The students meet in groups of six. Each group is given a piece of yarn, 30 long strips of paper, rabbit handouts and either clothes pins or tape to fasten the strips of paper to the yarn. They also have crayons, scissors and glue available. Each student takes a task card from the envelop and signs his/her name on the card. On each person's task card are the five numbers he/she makes number strips for.

Pairs Check: make number strips. "Form partners in your team to coach each other as you work. Each of you make your number strips. If you have a question about how to make your number strip ask your coach. If neither of you know the answer, you check with the rest of the group. When both of you finish your strips, take turns being coaches. Check each others strips. Coaches, make any needed corrections on the number strips. Then praise your partner."

Model: it looks like, it sounds like. Have a group model how to arrange their Group Line-Up by following the directions in the next two sections. The class listens for encouraging suggestions such as: "That's almost Right." "Your number is smaller than mine." "Your close." "That's Great."

Rallyrobin: encouraging suggestions. "Talk to your partner to remember encouraging suggestions you heard the group use. Think of some other encouraging suggestions that could have been made." They discuss for a couple of minutes. Ask for the silent signal. "Now the whole group will do a Roundrobin discussion and take turns having each person share an encouraging suggestion."

Group Product Line-Up: numerical order. "Your group works together to make the Group Line-Up. Starting with the number one, each of you fastens your number strip on the Line-Up yarn where it fits in the numerical order. When the Line-Up is complete, check to see that the order is correct. Decide how to tell another group about your Line-Up and who is responsible for telling which parts."

4 **Share the Line-Ups using Teams Check/ Share, Think-And-Praise**

Assign groups who meet together to share their Line-Ups with each other. "In just a minute you will go meet with another team to share your Line-Ups with each other. Decide which team will share their Line-Up first and which team will be the audience. After the first team finishes its presentation, both teams do Team Think-And-Praise. The team who did the presentation thinks of a praiser for the audience. The team who was the audience thinks of a some praisers about the presentation and the Line-Up. Then switch jobs to share the other Line-Up."

5 **Evaluate use of praisers using Team Discussion/ Perfect Praiser Badge**

"Groups, put your heads together and decide if the team you shared with gave you praisers. If you agree that they did, have the person who made the #1 strip for your Line-Up, come and get a Perfect

Praiser Badge to give to that team. If your team received a badge, the person who made the number two strip for your group fastens the badge to your group Line-Up."

6 Debrief the lesson using *Team Discussion*

"Groups, decide on two good things about making the Line-Up together. Be sure all group members have that information so they can share it with other groups." After they discuss for three or four minutes, give the silent signal.

7 Debrief the lesson using *Two Stray*

Show the class the direction they move to find their sharing group. "The people who made the #3 and #4 strips for your Line-Up go to your sharing group and each of you shares one of your group's ideas." This same pair could move to the next group or the people who made the #5 and #6 strips could continue if these directions are given. "The people who made the #5 and #6 strips go stand next to people #3 and #4 from your group. Now people #3 and #4 come back to your group. People #5 and #6 move to the next group and share your group's ideas."

8 Share best ideas using *Roundrobin*

"Take turns around the group sharing the best ideas you heard from the other groups. See if these ideas were also things that were good for your team. See if there are any other things your group could do next time to make it even easier to make a Group Product Line-Up."

Lesson 17a Adaptation

ten rabbits K-1

L i t e r a t u r e

Ten Little Rabbits ——
by Virginia Grossman and
Sylvia Long

Students follow the same lesson sequence from Batches Of Bunnies to make another Group Line-Up for the Ten Little Rabbits. This lesson is easier for kindergarten students because it only goes from 1 to 10.

Preparation:
Students meet in groups of four. They are given the Rabbits handout (2 per team), task cards (1 per team), ten strips of paper, scissors and glue. Each member takes a task card so they know which strips to make.

Pairs Check:
Partners in the team will take turns working and coaching each other as they make their two strips. There are two strips left over that are done by students who complete their strips before the others finish.

Group Product *Line-Up:*
The team assembles the Line-Up by putting the strips in numerical order.

Teams Check:
Two teams meet and share their Line-Ups with each other.

Evaluate and debrief.

Rabbits Handout

Lorna Curran: *Lessons for Little Ones: Mathematics©*
Kagan Publishing • 1 (800) 933-2667 • www.KaganOnline.com

Batches of Bunnies Task Cards

Name _____

Numbers   1   9   17   30

Name _____

Numbers   4   11   19   28

Name _____

Numbers   3   8   15   27

Name _____

Numbers   2   10   14   29

Name _____

Numbers   6   12   18   21

Name _____

Numbers   5   16   22   24

Extra Numbers
13   20   23   26

Ten Rabbits Task Cards

Name _____

Numbers   2 and 9

Name _____

Numbers   5 and 7

Name _____

Numbers   3 and 8

Name _____

Numbers   1 and 10

Extra Numbers
4 and 6

Perfect Praiser Badges

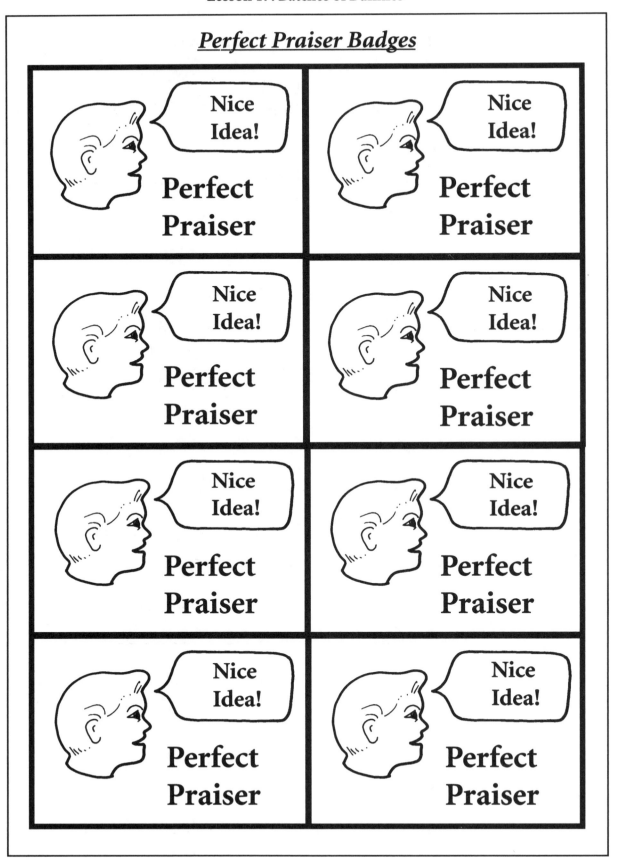

Lorna Curran: *Lessons for Little Ones: Mathematics*©
Kagan Publishing • 1 (800) 933-2667 • www.KaganOnline.com

number search
2's, 3's, & 4's

K-2 Number Value

L i t e r a t u r e

• *What Comes in
2's, 3's, & 4's?*
by Suzanne Aker

Students investigate what comes in sets of 2, 3, or 4. They teach this information to other students.

The students have practiced making sets of 2, 3, and 4. They have discussed things that would fit into these sets.

1 Provide lesson overview using *Teacher Talk*

"We have made sets of 2, 3, and 4 using blocks, unifix cubes, and counters. We talked a little bit about things we find around us that come in sets of 2, 3, or 4. Today we will meet in Expert Groups. We will look and think to find many things that come in sets of 2, 3, and 4. As we teach our groups, we will work on speaking clearly so others enjoy listening to us and can easily understand what we have to say."

2 Share ideas for speaking clearly using *Mix-Freeze-Pair*

"When I say to start, you will move around the room. Keep moving until I ask you to stop. Pair up with the nearest person. Share ideas on how to be a clear speaker who everyone enjoys listening to and can easily understand." Have the students mix and share several times, reminding them that each time they are to speak to someone they have not spoken to yet.

materials

Signs with numbers 2, 3, and 4
to label expert groups
Sets of paper, one for each
number 2, 3, and 4 (1 per team)
Crayons or pencils

Structures
Mix-Freeze-Pair
Class Discussion
Expert Groups
Roundrobin
Teams Compare
Rotating Reporters
Team Discussion

Social Skills
Speaking clearly.

**Cognitive
Skills**
Find examples of 2, 3
or 4, tell what objects
come in 2, 3 or 4.

Lorna Curran: *Lessons for Little Ones: Mathematics*©
Kagan Publishing • 1 (800) 933-2667 • www.KaganOnline.com

3 Share ideas using *Class Discussion*

"Let's share some of the ideas and put them on our Clear Speakers Chart. We will check with this chart when we evaluate at the end of the lesson."

4 Information on sets of 2, 3, 4 using *Expert Groups*

Preparation of teams. The students meet in Triads. Give each team a set of papers that has a paper for each of the numbers 2, 3, and 4. Each team member takes a paper. Display the signs with the numbers 2, 3, and 4, that let the students know where the Expert Groups Meet.

Preparation of *Expert Groups*. "Take your number paper to the area where your expert group meets." Divide the expert groups into two sub groups of three or four students.

***Roundrobin:* list of objects.** "You take turns around your group, suggesting ideas, getting agreement and recording the ideas. This is the procedure:
• The first person suggests something that comes in a set of _____.
• The team signals agree (thumbs up) or let's talk about it (thumb side ways).
• When the team agrees, each person draws or writes that idea on their paper.
• If a person cannot think of an idea, he/she can ask the group for suggestions.
• Continue the Roundrobin by having the second, third and fourth people do the same.
• Continue doing Roundrobin until time is called.

***Roundrobin:* practice the teaching.** "Read over the list of objects until everyone can read everything on the list. When time is called go back to your teams."

***Roundrobin/ Think-And-Praise:* experts teach teams.** "A team member starts by being the teacher and reading to the team his/her list of objects that come in sets of that number. The other two teammates praise the teacher. The second person reads his/her list. Teammates praise. Then the third person reads and teammates praise."

5 Evaluate clear speaking using *Teams Compare*

Let the teams know who they pair up with for Teams Compare. Read the ideas the class listed on the Clear Speakers Chart. "Discuss the things your team did to do clear speaking. Teams pair up and share information on what their teams did to do clear speaking. Discuss what ideas were the same for both teams and what ideas were used by just one team." Ask if there any additional ideas that should go on the Clear Speakers Chart.

6 Debrief the lesson using *Rotating Reporters*

"Team members, number yourselves from 1 to 3. Person #1, please stand and go to the next team on the right. Person #2, please stand and go to the second team to the right. Take a few minutes in these new groups to discuss the things that you liked about this lesson and about the things that your team did well." They can either go back to their home team or they can move a couple more times before they go back.

7 Share information using *Roundrobin/ Team Discussion*

"Take a few minutes so each of you can share what you found out from the groups you visited. Then have a discussion about the things your team did best. Think if there are any ideas from the other teams that would be helpful for your team."

Extensions

- For homework, the students look at home for things that fit in sets of 2, 3, or 4.
- Students use this information to write a team number chart. (See Lesson 30 titled Colorful Chants in *Cooperative Learning Lessons For Little Ones: Language Arts Edition* by Lorna Curran .)

Other Applications

- Students do a shape search at school and/or at home.
- Students do a pattern search around school, at home, or by looking at the illustrations of books.

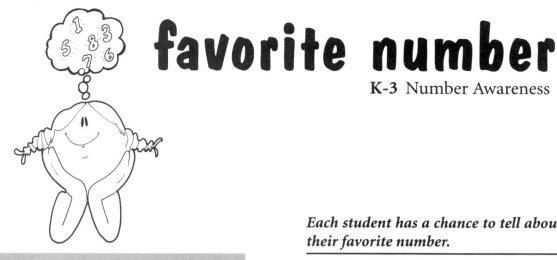

favorite number

K-3 Number Awareness

Literature

• *The Wildlife 1. 2. 3.,*
A Nature Counting Book
by Jan Thornhill

materials

None

Each student has a chance to tell about their favorite number.

This is an interesting inclusion activity where the students can get to know each other better. It is also a fun, motivating game for students to do while they are learning to count and write the numbers.

1 Provide lesson overview using *Teacher Talk*

"Today we are going to sit in a circle. Each of us will have a turn to tell about our favorite number. We will use active listening as we have a chance to share. Remember if you can't think of an answer the first time around, you may say, 'Pass.' We'll go around the circle a second time so all people who needed to pass can share their ideas at that time."

2 Review active listening chart using *Class Discussion*

Review the Active Listening Chart so the students can remember their definition of Active Listening. See if there is anything else that should be added to the chart before they start the Community Circle.

3 Share favorite numbers using *Community Circle*

The teacher and students form a circle

Structures
Class Discussion
Community Circle
Think-Pair-Share

Social Skills
Active listening.

Cognitive Skills
Tell about a favorite number.

and follow this procedure:

- The teacher says what his/her favorite number is and why it is the favorite number.
- The student on the teacher's right tells his/her favorite number and why it is the favorite number.
- The turns continue around the circle to the right until everyone has had a turn to share.
- If any students felt the need to pass, go around the circle a second time to have those students share.

4 Evaluate use of active listening using *Finger Evaluation*

When the teacher says "One, two, three, show," the students will give one of the following finger signals to show how well the students did in using Active Listening.

- Thumbs Up – all the students used active listening.
- Thumbs Sideways – most of the students used active listening but there is something to fix.

5 Validate the score using *Class Discussion*

Call on several students to tell a reason why they are giving that particular finger signal. I usually start and end with a thumbs up signal to help keep the discussion positive. Also, student names are not used, only the words someone, somebody or some of us.

6 Debrief the lesson using *Think-Pair-Share/ Class Discussion*

Ask some of the following questions to find out how the students felt about doing Community Circle. Have them first discuss with the person next to them and then share ideas they heard or said with the class.

- How did you feel while you were waiting for your turn?
- How did you feel when your turn was over?
- How did you feel about using active listening?
- How did it feel when the students used active listening while you shared?
- How did you feel about hearing others answers?

Extensions:

- Use the numbers given in the Community Circle to make a Favorite Number Graph.
- Before the lesson the students can predict which number will be the most frequent favorite number. They will write the number down on a Post-it. After the students do the Community Circle, these numbers can be made into a graph and the two graphs can be compared.
- Line-Up with favorite number.

more mittens

K-1 Addition

Literature

- *Runaway Mittens* by Jean Rogers
- *The Mitten* by Jan Brett
- *Too Many Mittens*
  by Florence and Louis Slobodkin

materials

Little mittens handout
   (1 per team)
Grandma & chest of drawers
   handouts (1 per team)
Background paper
Glue, Scissors, Crayons
Corresponding number cards
Dot cards

Partners make a picture addition problem and write the equation for their problem.

The students have heard the story *Too Many Mittens*. To reinforce the concept of addition, the first half of the story, where everyone brings mittens to Grandma and the twins, is read again. Every time more mittens are added in the story, the story is stopped. The class does an addition problem on the chalkboard and puts the correct number of mittens in a pile. When all the addition problems are done, the pile of mittens is counted to verify that the addition was correct.

1 Provide lesson overview using *Teacher Talk*

"The story *Too Many Mittens* had many addition problems in it as the twins kept getting more and more mittens. Grandma kept the mittens in the drawers until they were full. We are going to work with a partner to make a picture of Grandma with the chest of drawers full of mittens. Then you will work together to write the addition problem that goes with your picture just like we did as we read the story. As we work together we will use Happy Talk to let our partners know about the things they are doing to help get the problem done."

Structures
Pair Project
Rallyrobin
Pair Discussion
Make-A-Match
Think-Pair-Share
Corners

Social Skills
Happy talk.

Cognitive Skills
Create and record an addition problem.

Lorna Curran: *Lessons for Little Ones: Mathematics*©
Kagan Publishing • 1 (800) 933-2667 • www.KaganOnline.com

2 Evaluate ideas for happy talk using *Class Discussion*

"I will read the class Happy Talk Chart. If you think the statement I read could be used as we work together today, you will give a thumbs up signal. If you think that statement won't work for our lesson today, you give a thumbs down signal."

3 Model making and addition problem

Choose a student to be your partner to make a picture addition problem and its equation. Have the students listen for Happy Talk statements.

4 Mittens addition problem using *Pair Project*

Preparation for picture problem. Pair up the students. Give the partners a background paper, a Little Mittens Handout and a Grandma And Chest Of Drawers Handout. They also need crayons, a pencil, scissors and glue.

Make the picture addition problem. "One person colors and cuts out the chest of drawers while the other person does the same to Grandma. Both help color and cut out mittens. They glue the chest of drawers on one side of the background paper and Grandma on the other side of the paper. Decide how many mittens will be in the chest of drawers. The person who made the chest of drawers glues these mittens on the chest of drawers. At the same time decide how many mittens Grandma will carry to the chest of drawers. The person who made Grandma glues these mittens on to Grandma."

Write the addition problem. "The first partner writes the number that shows how many mittens are in the chest of drawers and writes the plus sign. The other partner writes the number that shows how many mittens Grandma is taking to the chest of drawers and the equal sign. Either partner writes the number that shows how many mittens there are in the picture. Check to see that the addition problem matches the picture. Then both sign your names on the picture."

5 Sponge activity using *Rallyrobin*

"After the problem is done, talk about details you could add to the room that Grandma is in. Share the job of adding these details to the picture."

6 Evaluate happy talk using *Pair Discussion*

"Talk together to remember some of the Happy Talk statements the two of you used. If you remember a happy talk statement that each of you used, put a happy face by each of your names. If one or both of you forgot to use happy talk, think of a happy talk statement that could have been told to your partner. Tell that statement to your partner and put a plus sign by your name." Praise or reward the class according to the number of happy faces and pluses you see.

7 Debrief the lesson using *Make-A-Match*

Preparation for *Find Someone Who...* While the students are evaluating the Happy Talk, pass out cards. On one side of the room pass out cards with dots. On the other side of the room pass out cards with the corresponding numbers.

Doing *Make-A-Match*. "In just a moment we are going to find a new partner for our discussion. I have given you some cards which you are to keep covered up until I give the signal to start. Some of you have cards with dots. Some of you have cards with numbers. When it is time to start, show your card and silently find your new partner. We may help each other find partners but only by giving signals. We will evaluate at the end to see if we did this job with only signals and no voices. Take your card and find your new partner."

Class Signal: evaluate no voices. "Those of you who heard no voices while we found our new partners give a silent cheer."

8 Debrief the lesson using *Think-Pair-Share*

"Think how you felt about working with a partner to make the addition problem. What made the job easy for you? Tell each other your ideas." After they discuss for a couple of minutes ask if there is anyone that would like to share an idea about what made the lesson easy today.

9 Share the picture problems using *Corners*

Preparation for the *Corners*. Label areas of the room from 0 - 9. "In just a minute you and your partner will go the section of the room that shows how many mittens you put in the chest of drawers. When you get there watch for the silent signal."

Go to *Corners*. If there are too many students in a corner, divide into sub groups of 4 to 6 students. "Take turns sharing your picture problems with each other. After a pair of students have shared their picture problem, give them a thumbs up if you agree with their problem. If you feel it needs correcting, give the thumbs sideways signal. Discuss what might need correcting.

Partners turn in pictures. Partners turn in their pictures to be made into a class booklet or take it back to their work space to correct before turning it in.

Extensions

- Change the amount of mittens. Partners make another picture addition problem.
- Students can bring mittens to school. A graph is made by color or by design.
- Students bring either gloves or mittens. Make a graph to record the results.

Lesson 20a Adaptation

more mice
K-1

Literature

Mouse Count
by Ellen Stoll Walsh

Partners use the procedure from the lesson More Mittens, to make an addition problem about the snakes and mice.

Materials:
More Mice for Math handout.

Preparation:
Partners are given a More Mice For Math handout and background paper.

Pair Project Picture:
One partner colors and cuts out the snake. The other partner cuts out the jar (use the jar from the lesson #30 Both Bug Jars) and draws a background. The jar is glued to the left side of the paper. The snake is glued to the right side of the paper. Both partners color and cut out mice. They decide how many mice are already in the jar and how many mice the snake is carrying to the jar. They write the addition problem as they lay out the mice.

Partners Write The Problem:
As they write the problem, one partner writes how many mice are in the jar. The other partner writes how many mice the snake is carrying to the jar.

Sponge Activity:
They could think of details to add to the background and to the mice.

Evaluate and debrief.

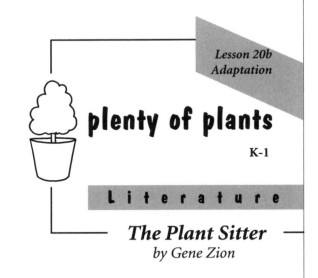

Lesson 20b Adaptation

plenty of plants
K-1

Literature

The Plant Sitter
by Gene Zion

Teams use the lesson sequence from More Mittens to do problems about the boy and his plants.

Preparation:
Partners are given the handout of plants, the handout of the boy and his wagon, and background paper.

Pair Project Picture:
One person is responsible for the wagon and one person is responsible for the boy. They both help color and cut out the plants. They make an illustration for The Plant Sitter that shows some plants in the wagon plus the number of plants out of the wagon.

Partners Write The Problem:
As they write the problem, one partner writes the number that shows the number of plants in the wagon. The other partner writes the number of plants out of the wagon.

Sponge Activity:
They draw a background for their problem.

Evaluate and debrief.

Lesson 20c
Adaptation

cat collection
K-2

Literature

—— *Millions of Cats* ——
by Wanda Zag

Teams follow the same lesson sequence from More Mittens while they create problems showing how many kittens are in different parts of the story.

Materials:
Cat Collection handout, Cat Collection Sofa and Door handout.

Sharing the Story:
As the story is read to the class, some students act out the story or lay out paper cats to demonstrate how many cats are in the story. While this is done the corresponding addition problems are written down by the teacher or students.

Preparation:
The students work in pairs to create a cat addition problem. Partners are given the Cat Collection handout, the Sofa And Door handout, and background paper.

***Pair Project* Addition Problem:**
Person #1 colors, cuts out and glues the sofa. Then he/she glues, by the sofa, the cats that already live in the house. Person #2 colors, cuts out and glues one edge of the door on to the background paper. Then he/she glues, behind the door, the cats that are coming to live at the house.

Partners Write Addition Problem:
Person #1 writes the number that tells how many cats were in the house and the plus sign. Person #2 writes the number that tells how many cats are coming and the equal sign. Either student may write the number that shows how many cats now live at the house.

Sponge Activity:
They draw things that would be in the house.

Evaluate and debrief.

Little Mittens

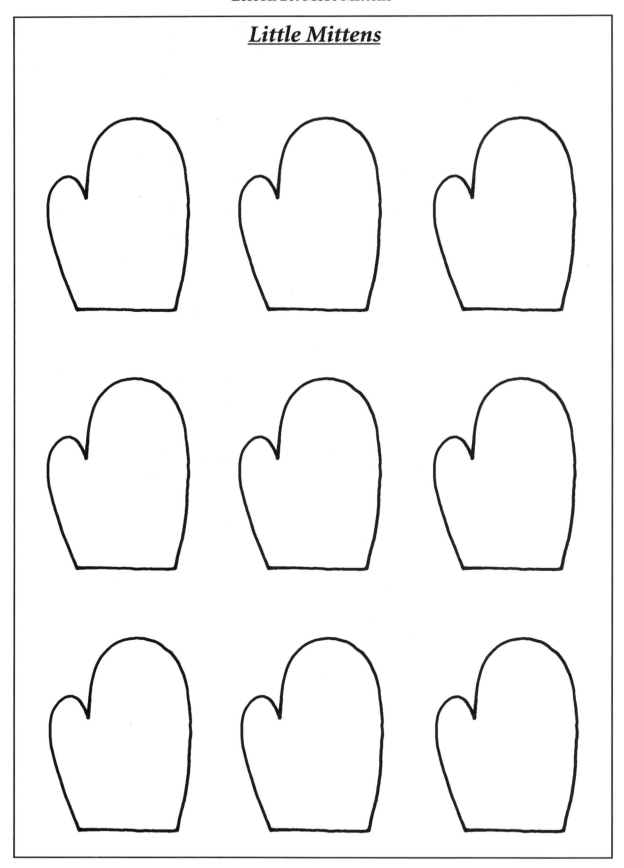

Lorna Curran: *Lessons for Little Ones: Mathematics©*
Kagan Publishing • 1 (800) 933-2667 • www.KaganOnline.com

Grandma and Chest of Drawers

More Mice for Math

Plenty of Plants

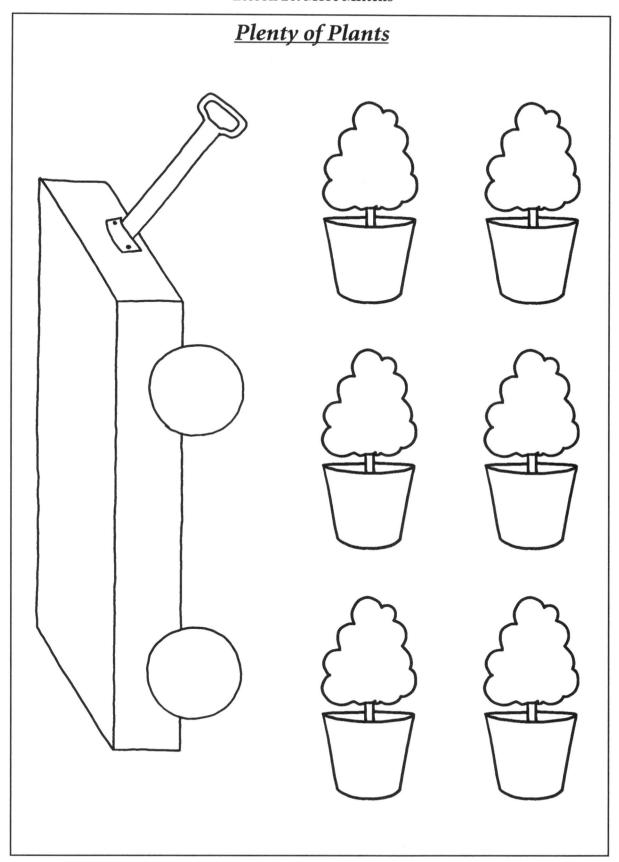

Cat Collection

Lorna Curran: *Lessons for Little Ones: Mathematics*©
Kagan Publishing • 1 (800) 933-2667 • www.KaganOnline.com

Sofa and Door

mosaic math

K-1 manipulative addition

• *Pezzettino*
by Leo Lionni

materials

A basket of 1" square
    construction paper: two colors
Mosaic math recording sheets
    (1 per team)
Mosaic math tasks sheets
    (1 per team)
Glue
Pencils
Crayons

Groups make addition problems with the sum of 8.

The class has had some practice adding two sets of objects whose sums equal eight. They also have had some practice writing addition problems.

1 Provide lesson overview using *Teacher Talk*

"Today we are going to work in groups of four to make as many addition problems as we can that have the answer of eight. We will use Roundtable so that all of you can think of problems and each of you will write some of the problems. If a problem needs to be changed, we will use the social skill of giving suggestions politely. We will also work quickly so the group has a chance to make many problems."

2 Think of polite suggestions using *Class Discussion*

"Let us take a few minutes and think of some ways to tell a person in our group that we think a problem should be corrected. We will keep a list of these ideas so we can use them anytime we want to give polite suggestions as we work together."

3 Model mosaic math problems

Students sign a task sheet so everyone knows who is person #1, 2, 3, and 4. Each

Structures
Team Praise
Team Discussion
Two Stray
Sequential
    Roundtable
Stand And Share
Signaled Sequential
    Roundtable

Social Skills
Polite suggestions,
working quickly.

Cognitive Skills
Create addition
problems with the
sum of 8.

Lorna Curran: *Lessons for Little Ones: Mathematics*©
Kagan Publishing • 1 (800) 933-2667 • www.KaganOnline.com

group is given a recording sheet, two colors of paper squares, glue and pencil.

Choose three students to join you in following steps 3 and 4 to demonstrate how the make the mosaic math problems.

4 Make mosaic math problems using *Signaled Sequential Roundtable*

Lay out the mosaic. "Person #1 will take 8 colored squares from the box and lay them in box 1 on the recording sheet. All the squares of the same color should be placed together so it makes an addition problem that is easy to record. Person #1 then reads the mosaic math problem to the group. The group gives thumbs up if they agree that is the problem that was made with the squares. Person #1 then glues the squares onto the recording sheet."

Correct a mosaic. "If any team member feels the problem is incorrect, that person would give the fix it signal which is the thumb turned sideways. Then the team needs to decide if that problem is correct, if it can be corrected, or if a new problem needs to be created. Remember to give positive suggestions on how to correct the problem.

Glue the mosaic/ change turns. "While person #1 is gluing on the squares, person #2 lays out squares for a different mosaic math problem. Then person #2 reads the problem. The group gives thumbs up if they agree with the problem and that it is a problem that has not yet been made by the group. Keep on passing the paper around the group until time is called. You probably will have time for each person to have more than one turn."

5 Evaluate working quickly using *Team Discussion, Two Stray, Team Praise*

"Count up how many problems your group got done. If your group got at least four problems done, praise each other by giving yourselves an inside high five. Discuss what you did that helped your team work quickly and what your team would like to do even better next time." Do a Two Tell by having person #3 and person #4 from each team go to a designated group to share. Person #3 shares the thing the team did best. Person #4 shares what the team would like to do better.

Curran's Comments

So that all team members are able to praise each other, I try to let the activity continue until all teams have done at least four problems. Also, I arrange the reporting so a team that had difficulty getting organized or started, hears from a reporter from a very efficient team. Then the team hears ideas that are useful to their team.

---

6 Clean Up

"Person #3 takes care of the glue. Person #4 takes care of the construction paper squares."

7 Problem Writing using *Sequential Roundtable*

"Make sure that person #1 has the paper and a pencil. The group is to reread the addition problem for the mosaic in box 1. Then person #1 writes that problem under that mosaic. The paper is passed to person #2. The group rereads the addition problem for the mosaic in box 2 and then person #2 writes that problem under mosaic #2. Keep passing the paper and pencil to the next person in your group so that person can write the problem after the group has reread the addition problem for the mosaic. When a problem has been written for all the mosaics on your paper, everyone signs his/her name and turns in the group mosaic.

8 Debrief the lesson using *Team Discussion/ Stand And Share*

Give the teams time to discuss any of the following questions. Have the teams stand. Call on a person from one team to give the team answer. That team and any other teams that had the same answer sit down. Continue until all answers have been heard.

• What made it easy to make the addition mosaics in your group?
• How did your group feel about using the agree signal in your group?
• How did you feel about writing the problems for the addition mosaics? Why?
• What was the best thing about working with your group today?

Extensions

• Have triads do this lesson where each person has a specific job for the whole lesson.
  - Person #1 lays out the mosaic
  - Person #2 glues the mosaic
  - Person #3 writes the problem
• Use objects to make the problems (seeds, crackers, leaves, etc.)
• Create problems that have larger or smaller sums.
• Use three or more colors to make mosaic representations of column addition problems.

Math Mosaic Task Sheet

Person #1 _____

Person #2 _____

Person #3 _____

Person #4 _____

Math Mosaic Task Sheet

Person #1 _____

Person #2 _____

Person #3 _____

Person #4 _____

Mosaic Math Recording Sheet

Number Problem

Number Problem

Number Problem

Number Problem

lots of ladybugs

K-2 Addition

Literature

- ***The Grouchy Ladybug*** *by Eric Carle*
- ***Ladybug, Ladybug*** *by Ruth Brown*
- ***Ladybug*** *by Emery Bernhard*
- ***Life of the Ladybug***
  by Heiderose and Andreas Fischer-Nagel

materials

Ladybug body handout
  (1 per student)
Ladybug wings handout
  (1 per student)
Lapboard
Paper
Glue
Scissors
Pencils

Pairs make and solve problems based on the number of spots on ladybugs.

The students have made ladybugs with varying numbers of spots on their wings. They also know how to write addition equations.

1 Provide lesson overview using *Teacher Talk*

"Today we are going to take the ladybugs we made and then meet up with many other people to add up ladybug spots. We will concentrate on providing a quiet working space for everyone while we work together."

2 Model *Inside-Outside Circle*

Choose four students to take their ladybugs and make a small circle facing outward. Choose four more students to take their ladybugs and sit facing these students thereby creating a larger circle that is facing inward. Each student has a lapboard, piece of paper, and a pencil. They follow the directions below to demonstrate how to do the ladybug problems with a partner using Inside-Outside Circle.

3 Write addition problems using *Inside-Outside Circle*

Preparation of partners. Assign all the students to either the inside or outside circle. They take their ladybug, a lapboard, paper and pencil.

Lorna Curran: *Lessons for Little Ones: Mathematics©*
Kagan Publishing • 1 (800) 933-2667 • www.KaganOnline.com

Structures
Inside-Outside
  Circle
Pair Discussion
Teams Check

Social Skills
Quiet voice while working.

Cognitive Skills
Create and solve problems based on the number of spots on ladybugs.

Write the ladybug problems. "Students, we use the following directions so it is easy to write ladybug addition problems and then move to a new partner. Look at the ladybug of the person who is sitting in the inside circle. Count up the dots on that ladybug. Each of you writes that number on your paper. Write the plus sign. Count up the dots on the ladybug of the person sitting in the outside circle. Write that number and the equal sign. Write the number that shows how many dots there are altogether on both of the ladybugs. Check to see if you both agree with the problem and answer."

Move to a new partner. "People in the outside circle put down your lapboards and pencils. Stand and hold your ladybug and paper. Move to the right to the next person in the inside circle. Sit down, pick up the lapboard and pencil. Face this person, and be ready to write another problem."

Continue the rotation. The students continue to write problems and rotate until they have written several problems. For simpler versions to use with young or beginning students, see the variations section at the end of this lesson.

4 Sponge Activity - Information About Bugs using *Pair Discussion*

"If you and your partner finish making your ladybug problem before I tell the class it is time to move to a new partner, you quietly discuss things you know about insects. Be sure to use very quiet voices so you will not disturb the people who are working on either side of you. We will be evaluating how well we remembered to use inside voices while we worked together and if we worked with just our partner."

5 Evaluate Quiet Working Space using *Pair Discussion*

"Students take a couple of minutes to talk to your partner and decide if you and the partners around you provided a quiet working space for everyone or if we still need a quieter working place. When I give the directions, 'One, two, three, show,' give a signal that shows your answer. If the two of you think we had a quiet working space, show a thumbs up. If both of you think we need to improve so we have a quiet working space, show the thumbs side ways fix-it sign." Ask several students to validate their score by giving a reason for their signal. Compliment or reward according to the thumb signals and what you saw and heard that can validate their signals.

6 Evaluate the Problems using *Pairs Compare*

Have the students go to their seats and meet with a partner. Pairs check to see that the problems on each others papers are correct. When they find that the problems on the partner's paper are correct, they write a happy face up in the top right corner of the paper. Compliment or reward the students according to the number of happy faces you see on the papers.

Curran's Comments

To help students develop the habits of using inside voices and working with just their partners to provide a quiet working space, an evaluation of the quiet working space can be done each time they finish working with each partner. When they are using these social skills well, evaluation can be done at the end of all the rotations.

7 Debrief the Lesson using *Inside-Outside Circle*

Have the students form an Inside-Outside Circle with the partner they had to evaluate the problems. Ask one of the questions below and have them discuss it with their partner. Have the outside circle move. Then ask the same question again or ask another one of the questions. Students continue to rotate and answer questions to find out how the students felt about working together to create the ladybug addition problems.

- What happened today to make it easy for you to make problems about the ladybugs?
- How did you feel about doing the Inside-Outside Circle?

- How did you feel about everyone having a quiet working space?
- Was there something anyone did that helped you remember to work just with your partner and to work quietly?

Extensions

- The class graphs ladybugs according to how many dots are on each ladybug wing.
- The class or groups graph the math problems they wrote to see which were written most frequently.

Variations

- Just the students in the inside circle are responsible for recording the problem. This makes it easier for the people in the outside circle because they only have to take their ladybug with them. So everyone has a turn to record, have the partners switch from the inner to the outer circle part way through the rotations.
- An easy version to use in kindergarten is to have each student make just one ladybug wing. As they meet a partner in the circle, they both lay their wings on a cut out of the ladybug's body. They write an addition problem that shows how many dots are on both wings.

adding acorns
K-2

L i t e r a t u r e

Chicken Little
by Steve Kellog

Look At A Tree
by Eileen Curran

Look At Trees
by Rena K. Kirkpatrick

—— **Chipmunk Song** ——
by Joanne Ryder

Students follow the lesson sequence from Lots Of Ladybugs to make problems about oak trees and their acorns.

Preparation:
Each team receives a background paper and the Adding Acorns handout.

Make Oak Trees:
Each person draws a large tree on his/her background paper, then colors, cuts out and glues some acorns on his/her tree.

Inside-Outside Circle:
The students then go to Inside-Outside Circle with their trees. As they meet up with a partner, they write an addition problem about the acorns on both of their trees.

Sponge Activity:
Students talk about the kinds of trees they know about or fun things that can be done because we have trees.

Evaluate Quite Working Space.

Teams Check:
Partners check each others problems to see that they are correct.

Debrief the lesson.

both bug jars
K-2

L i t e r a t u r e

Bugs
by Nancy Winslow Parker and Joan Richards Wright

The Very Busy Spider
by Eric Carle

—— **Two Bad Ants** ——
by Chris Van Allsburg

Students follow the lesson sequence from Lots of Ladybugs to make addition problems about bugs.

Preparation:
Each person receives a background paper and a bug jar.

Make Bug Jar Picture:
Each person draws some bugs in their bug jar.

Inside-Outside Circle:
The students take their jars to Inside-Outside Circle. As they meet up with a partner, they write an addition problem about the bugs in both of their jars.

Sponge Activity:

As the students finish their problems, they talk about bugs that they have seen and where they saw them.

Evaluate quiet working space.

Teams Check

Partners check the problems on their partners papers to see that they are correct.

Debrief the lesson.

Ladybug Body

Lorna Curran: *Lessons for Little Ones: Mathematics©*
Kagan Publishing • 1 (800) 933-2667 • www.KaganOnline.com

Ladybug Wings

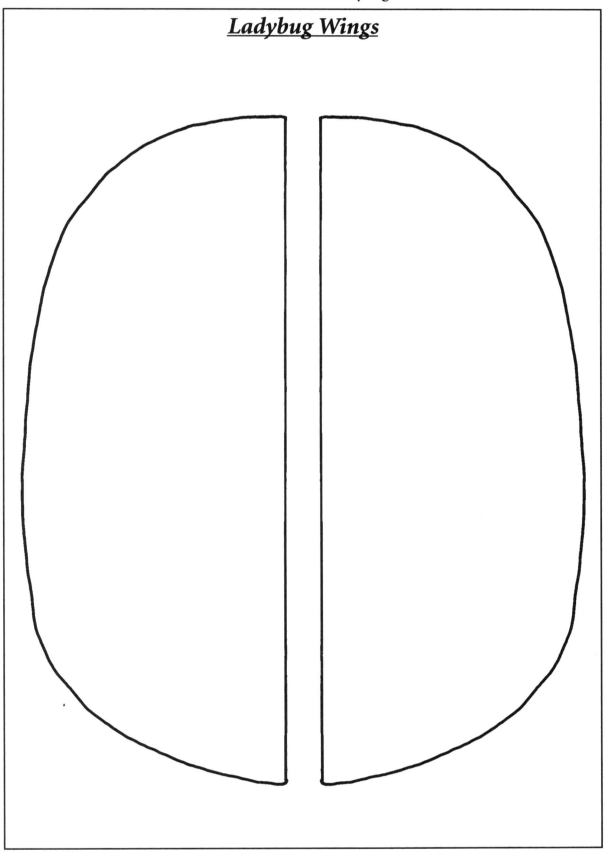

Adding Acorns

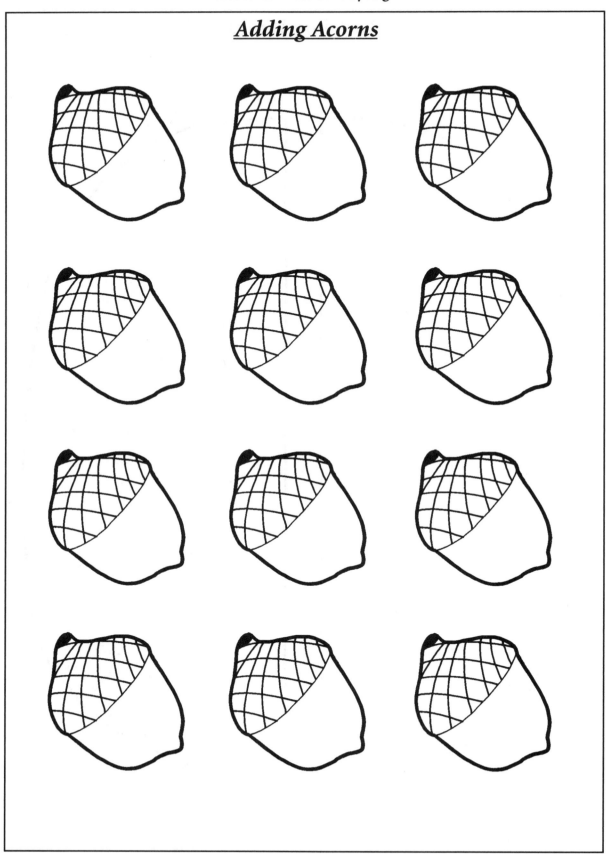

Lorna Curran: *Lessons for Little Ones: Mathematics©*
Kagan Publishing • 1 (800) 933-2667 • www.KaganOnline.com

Bug Jar

animal addition

K-1 Adding Objects

Literature

• *Marshmallow* by *Clare Turlay Newberry*

• *The April Rabbits* by *David Cleveland*

• *What Do Bunnies Do All Day*
by *Judy Mastrangelo*

• *The Bunny Book* by *Richard Scarry*

• *The Little Rabbit* by *Judy Dunn*

• *The Tale of Peter Rabbit*
by *Beatrix Potter*

• *Small Rabbit* by *Miska Miles*

• *The Baby Bunny Book*
by *Margaret Hillert*

• *The Runaway Bunny*
by *Margaret Wise Brown*

materials

Adult & Baby animals handout
   (2 per team)
Background paper
Glue
Scissors
Crayons

Partners make an addition problem by adding the adult and baby animals together.

The students have practiced acting out the type of problem that they will be working on paper. In this case two rabbit cages are outlined on the floor with yarn. One cage is for adult rabbits. One cage is for baby rabbits. Some students are tapped with the "magic rabbit maker," a yardstick with a cut out rabbit on the end. As each student is tapped with the rabbit maker, the teacher gives the student a cut out of either an adult or a baby rabbit. As each student receives a rabbit, they go either to the cage for large rabbits or the cage for small rabbits. Then the teacher writes the addition problem as the students say, "_____ large rabbits + _____ small rabbits = _____ rabbits all together." After several problems have been acted out and written, a student writes the equation while the problem is being acted out. When most students can say and/or write the addition problems, they are ready to work in partners with pictures of the rabbits.

1 Provide lesson overview using *Teacher Talk*

"For the past few days we have been using our magic rabbit maker and have written addition problems about the rabbits we put in the rabbit cages.

Structures
Think-Pair-Share
Pair Project
Pair Discussion
Team Discussion
Pairs Check

Social Skills
Use happy talk.

Cognitive Skills
Create an addition problem by adding the adult and baby animals together.

Lorna Curran: *Lessons for Little Ones: Mathematics*©
Kagan Publishing • 1 (800) 933-2667 • www.KaganOnline.com

Today you will have pictures of large and small rabbits. You will work with a partner to make a rabbit picture addition problem. While you work together remember to use Happy Talk as you tell your partner about the things he/she is doing to help get the job done well."

2 Think of ideas for happy talk using *Think-Pair-Share*

"Now that you know what we will be doing in our lesson, think of some Happy Talk you could use to tell your partner about the work both of you will be doing together." These phrases are either found on a Happy Talk Chart that was made for an earlier lesson or they are used to create a Happy Talk Chart that lists the nice things they say to their partner as they work together to make the addition problems. Some example ideas they contribute are: "I like your cutting," "You are working quickly," "You are cutting on the lines."

3 Model partner addition problems

Choose a student to join you in doing sections 4 through 5 to demonstrate how partners work together to develop animal addition problems. Ask the class to watch for things that helped get the job done quickly and easily.

4 Create animal addition problems using *Partner Project*

Preparation of partners. Pair up the students. They number themselves, partner #1 and partner #2. Give the partners handouts of large and small rabbits, background paper, scissors, glue and crayons.

Make the addition problems. Partner #1 colors and cuts out all the large rabbits while partner #2 colors and cuts out all the small rabbits. If one partner finishes early, he may ask the other partner if he would like help. Each of the partners glues on the rabbits they cut out. They both count up all the large rabbits. Partner #1 writes that number and the plus sign. They both count up the small rabbits. Partner #2 writes that number and the equal sign. After they decide on the answer, either of them writes the answer.

5 Sponge activity using *Pair Project*

When partners finish, they draw an illustration around their rabbits that shows a nice place for their rabbits to live.

6 Evaluate happy talk using *Pair Discussion*

Partners discuss Happy Talk statements that they used. If they can remember at least one Happy Talk Statement that they used, they give each other an "inside high five". Then call on some students to share the Happy Talk statements they used. Add any new Happy Talk statements to Happy Talk Chart.

7 Debrief the lesson using *Team Discussion*

Group two sets of partners together to discuss any of the following questions.
- How did your partner help make the work easy?
- How did it feel when your partner used Happy Talk?
- How did it feel when you used Happy Talk?

8 Share the picture problems using *Pairs Check*

Sets of partners share their picture problems with each other. After one set of partners has read their problem, the other partners draw a happy face on that paper to show that they think the problem is correct. If a problem needs to be corrected, the partners correct it and then receive the happy face. Then the partners switch jobs.

Extensions

- Students do Line-Up patterning using the large and small rabbits.

- Students make booklets that tell about rabbits.
- Do Corners to show the students favorite type of rabbit. Graph the results.

Other Applications

- Animal addition is done with any animals that fit the curriculum.
- One size rabbit is made in two colors for the addition or the patterning.

Lesson 23a Adaptation

cock & hen
K-1

Lesson 23b Adaptation

double dogs
K-2

L i t e r a t u r e

The Cock, The Mouse, & The Little Red Hen
by Lorinda Bryan Cauley

L i t e r a t u r e

Clifford's Pal
by Norman Bridwell

Harry, the Dirty Dog
by Gene Zion

Students use the lesson sequence from Animal Addition to make problems using the cock and hen.

Students use the lesson sequence from Animal Addition to make problems with dogs like Harry's friends or like Clifford's pals.

Preparation:
Partners are given a cock and hen handout and a background paper.

Preparation:
Partners are given a background paper and two Double Dogs handouts.

Pair Project Pattern:
One partner colors and cuts out all the cocks. The other partner colors and cuts out all the hens. They share gluing the cocks and hens on the paper and writing the addition problem.

Pair Project Pattern:
One partner colors all the dogs on one handout one color. The other partner colors all the dogs on the other handout another color. They write an addition problem that tells how many dogs there are altogether.

Sponge Activity:
Partners draw a background for cocks and hens.

Sponge Activity:
Partners draw a background for the dogs.

Evaluate and debrief.

Evaluate and debrief.

Teams Check:
Sets of partners share their problems, correct them, and give them a happy face.

Teams Check:
Sets of partners share their problems, correct them, and give them a happy face.

Adult and Baby Animals

The Cock and the Hen

Lorna Curran: *Lessons for Little Ones: Mathematics©*
Kagan Publishing • 1 (800) 933-2667 • www.KaganOnline.com

Double Dogs

minus mittens

K-2 Subtraction

Literature

- ***Run Away Mittens*** by Jean Rogers
- ***The Mitten*** by Jan Brett
- ***Too Many Mittens***
  by Florence and Louis Slobodkin

materials

Little Mittens handout
  (see Lesson 20-1 per team)
Twins and Little Girl handout
  (1 per team)
Background paper
Glue
Scissors
Crayons

Triads make a picture subtraction problem and write the equation for their problem.

The students have heard the story *Too Many Mittens*. They have done the addition problems from Lesson 20: More Mittens. Now, focus on the second half of the story where people come to take away mittens. Have the cut out mittens hung on a yarn clothes line. As characters in the story take mittens, students take turns removing one or two mittens. As mittens are removed the class figures out how to write the subtraction problem.

1 Provide lesson overview using *Teacher Talk*

"We made some subtraction problems as we pretended people came to get the extra mitten the twins had. Now, work with a partner to color and cut out characters from the story. Also, color and cut out several mittens so you can make a picture subtraction problem that shows a girl taking some of the extra mittens. Then you will work together to write the subtraction problem that goes with the picture. As we work together we will use Happy Talk.

2 Happy talk statements using *Pair Discussion*

"Reach out and touch the shoulder of the person next to you. This person will

Structures
Pair Discussion
Community Circle
Team Discussion
Team Inside-
    Outside Circle
Rotating Reporter
Team Project

Social Skills
Happy talk.

Cognitive Skills
Create a picture subtraction problem and write the equation for the problem.

Lorna Curran: *Lessons for Little Ones: Mathematics*©
Kagan Publishing • 1 (800) 933-2667 • www.KaganOnline.com

be your partner for a couple of minutes." If some students have no one near, pair them up with other students who needs a partner. With your partner, think for a couple of minutes about Happy Talk statements that we could say as we make the picture subtraction problems together."

3 Share happy talk using *Community Circle*

"Please form a circle so we can do Community Circle. You had a chance to talk about some Happy Talk statements with a partner. Now, as we go around the circle, each of us shares a Happy Talk statement we can use when making the picture subtraction problems. It is all right to say a statement that someone else has already shared, but it is nice to hear a new statement if you have thought of one."

4 Model making a subtraction problem

Choose a student to be your partner. Demonstrate making a picture subtraction problem and its equation.

5 Mittens subtraction problem using *Team Project*

Preparation for picture problem. Divide the class into groups of three. Give each triad a background paper, a Little Mittens handout, and a Twins and Little Girl handout. They also need crayons, a pencil, scissors, and glue.

Make the picture subtraction problem. "Number yourselves from 1 to 3. Person #1 colors and cuts out one of the twins. Person #2 colors and cuts out the other twin. Person #3 colors and cuts out the

little girl and draws the clothes line. All team members color and cut out the mittens. Decide where you want to glue the twins and the little girl. Everyone glues on their person."

Write the subtraction problem. "Lay all the mittens on the clothes line. Person #1 writes the number that shows how many mittens there are altogether and writes the minus sign. Decide how many mittens the girl is carrying away. Person #2 glues those mittens on to the girl, writes the number of mittens the girl carries away, and writes the equal sign. Person #3 glues the mittens that are left to the clothes line, and writes the number that tells how many mittens are still on the line. Check the picture problem to make sure it is correct and that everyone can read the problem. Then sign your names on the paper."

6 Sponge activity using *Team Project*

"Decide on matching pairs of mittens that the twins and the little girl could wear. Agree upon a design that all three of them would like to wear. Draw the pair of mittens your character would wear."

7 Use of happy talk using *Team Discussion*

"Talk together and remember some of the Happy Talk statements you used while your triad worked together. If your team forgot to use Happy Talk statements, think of some statements you could have used."

8 Share happy talk and picture problems using *Team Inside-Outside Circle*

Preparation for *Inside-Outside Circle*. "I will ask some triads to make an inside circle and some triads make an outside circle. Person #1 brings the picture problem to the circle." The class makes the Inside-Outside Circle as half of the triads form a circle facing out, and the other half of the triads form a circle facing in.

Sharing in *Team Inside-Outside Circle.* "When it is time to share, the team in the outer circle shares first. Person #1 holds the picture problem. Person #2 reads the problem. Person #3 tells a Happy Talk statement that the group used. When the outside team has finished sharing, then the inside team shares."

Sponge activity. "If you have time you may talk about the mittens you designed for the twins and little girl. If you didn't get a chance to make the mittens yet, describe the kind of mittens you would like to make. Watch for the silent signal."

Continuing the *Team Inside-Outside Circle.* "Outside circle please stand and move to the next triad on the right. Again the outside triad shares first. Then the inside triad shares. Watch for the silent signal so you know how to move the next time."

> ## *Curran's Comments*
> Sometimes the groups are asked to move more than once before they sit down to share. It adds variety, makes them listen to directions carefully, and helps move them around the circle faster.

9 Debrief the lesson using *Inside-Outside Circle/ Reporting Reporters*

Triads gather ideas. "Think about what your triad liked best about working together while you made and shared the picture problem. Have everyone in the triad practice saying those ideas."

***Rotating Reporters* Share.** "Stay in your circle. One rotating reporter from each triad goes to the triads in the circle to share how his/her group felt about the lesson. Person #1 from each triad stand. You will move clockwise to the next triad. You will have two minutes to share your information. Wait for the directions to move again." Continue until the reporter has been to all the triads in the circle.

***Team Inside-Outside Circle:* triads share.** "Now make the Inside-Outside Circle and share the ideas you heard from the reporters."

> ## *Curran's Comments*
> The reporter position can change by having person #2 go stand next to person #1. Then person #1 comes back to his/her triad. Person #2 now does the reporting. After a couple of turns person #3 can stand next to person #2. Person #2 comes back to the triad and person #3 finishes the sharing.

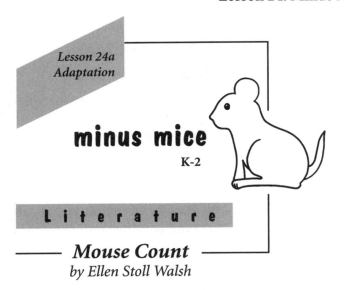

Lesson 24a Adaptation

minus mice

K-2

L i t e r a t u r e

Mouse Count

by Ellen Stoll Walsh

Triads use the same lesson sequence to make problems about the snake and the mice. They discuss what design and colors they would like on the snake and what things they would like to have in the background. One person colors and cuts out the snake. Another person cuts out the jar (use the jar from the lesson 22 Adaptation Both Bug Jars). The third person makes the background. They decide how many mice are still in the jar and how many mice have run out of the jar. They write the problem as they lay the mice on the picture. The first sponge activity could be to design and color a team snake. The second sponge activity to use during Inside-Outside Circle is to discuss all the kinds of snakes they know about and the experiences they have had with different types of snakes.

Twins and Little Girl

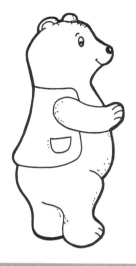

changing cherries

K-2 Subtracting Objects

L i t e r a t u r e

• *A Cake for Barney*
by Joyce Dunbar

materials

Cupcake and cherries handout
  (3 per team)
Background paper (1 per student)
Envelopes of story characters
  (1 per team)
Glue
Scissors
Crayons

Each student makes a subtraction problem that tells part of the story **A Cake for Barney.**

The students have heard the story *A Cake For Barney*. The students then color and cut out their cupcakes and cherries. As the story is told again, they take a cherry off of their cupcake each time a character in the story is given a cherry. You write the subtraction problems on the chalkboard. The story is told again. This time students write the subtraction problems on the board.

1 Provide lesson overview using *Teacher Talk*

"We will be working in groups of six to make subtraction problems that tell the story about Barney. Each of you is to make a picture subtraction problem that shows what happened when your character took a cherry from the cake. While you work together remember to use Positive Suggestions."

2 List positive suggestions using *Class Discussion*

Look at the class Happy Talk Chart to see what statements they could make while they make their booklets. Then make a chart that lists some ideas for giving positive suggestions that they use while they check each others papers and arrange them in a booklet.

Structures
Team Project
Team Discussion
Group Reporter
Stand And Share
Teams Compare

Social Skills
Giving positive suggestions to correct a problem.

Cognitive Skills
Create a subtraction problem that tells part of the story *A Cake for Barney.*

Lorna Curran: *Lessons for Little Ones: Mathematics©*
Kagan Publishing • 1 (800) 933-2667 • www.KaganOnline.com

3 Model group book making

Choose six students to make a sample booklet by following the directions in section 4. They listen for polite suggestions that are used as the students work together.

4 Make picture problem booklet using *Team Project*

Preparation for picture problems. Divide the students into groups of six. Everyone takes their cupcake and cherries and meets in the area designated for their group. Each group member is given a background paper. Each group is given an envelope which contains the pictures of the story characters.

Making the booklet pages. "Each of you takes a picture from the envelope. Color the picture of that character and cut it out. Use that character and your cupcake and cherries to make a picture problem of that part of the story. Write the subtraction problem on the page. The person who has the picture of Barney will make a cover for the book that includes the title of the book."

Sponge activity. "While you are waiting

Curran's Comments

I find it helpful to show them the pages of the book again just as soon as they know which character they are to draw. If they look at the book, they will know what colors and details to add to their pictures. Also, write the title of the book in large letters so it is easy to copy. For kindergarten students it also helps if the sample pages from the demonstration group are displayed. It helps groups get each problem correct and to get the pages in the correct order.

for the other group members to finish their pages, make a background and some interesting details for your page."

Assemble the booklet. "Check all the pages. Each person reads his/her problem to the group to be sure the subtraction problem is correct. Use positive comments as you help each other make the corrections. Put the pages in the order they happened in the story. Everyone signs his or her name on the cover of the book."

5 Evaluate positive suggestions using *Team Discussion/ Group Reporter Stand and Share*

"Discuss to find out what positive suggestions the people in your group used while you worked. Choose a person to be group reporter and share a positive suggestion that your group used." Call on the group reporters to share a positive statement from their group. Find those statements on the chart or add them to the chart.

6 Debrief the lesson using *Team Discussion/ Numbered Stand and Share*

Find out how the students felt about making the booklet as they discuss this question. What did your group do that made it easy to make the booklet together? Do a Numbered Stand and Share but instead of saying a number to designate a speaker from each group, say the name of a story character instead. The student in each group that made the picture problem for the character whose name you call will stand and share the group's answer.

7 Groups read their booklets using *Teams Compare*

Give the groups several minutes to practice using the booklet to tell the story. They then tell the story to a designated group. Put the booklets in the class library or math center.

Extensions

- Partners sequence the pictures of the story characters.
- Partners each make a cupcake with cherries on top. They make an addition problem by adding the cherries from both cupcakes.
- Read cupcake recipes. Do Corners to show their favorite cupcake and make a class graph that shows the results.

Lesson 25a
Adaptation

five little monkeys
K-1

L i t e r a t u r e

— Five Little Monkeys —

Students follow the lesson sequence from the Changing Cherries to make subtraction problems about the five little monkeys.

Preparation:

Groups of five are given a background paper and each student the Five Little Monkeys Jumping On The Bed handout.

Team Project Picture Problem Booklets:

Each person takes a section of the poem from an envelope to determine their part of the booklet. They make an illustration and write a subtraction problem about that part of the rhyme.

Evaluate and debrief.

Stand And Share:

The class can say the rhyme as each booklet is shared with the class.

Five Little Monkeys Jumping On The Bed

Five little monkeys jumping on the bed.
One fell off and bumped his head
Mama called the doctor and the doctor said,
"No more monkeys jumping on the bed."
Four little monkeys jumping on the bed.
One fell off and bumped his head.
Mama called the doctor and the doctor said,
"No more monkeys jumping on the bed."
Three little monkeys jumping on the bed.
One fell off and bumped his head.
Mama called the doctor and the doctor said,
"No more monkeys jumping on the bed."
Two little monkeys jumping on the bed.
One jumped off and bumped his head.
Mama called the doctor and the doctor said,
"No more monkeys jumping on the bed."
One little monkey jumping on the bed.
One fell off and bumped his head.
Mama called the doctor and the doctor said.
"No more monkeys jumping on the bed."

*Lesson 25b
Adaptation*

ten bears

K-2

L i t e r a t u r e

*10 Bears In My Bed,
A Goodnight
Countdown*
by Stan Mack

Students follow the lesson sequence from the Changing Cherries to make subtraction problems about the ten little bears.

Background:
Students act out the subtraction problems in the story as *10 Bears In My Bed* is read.

Preparation:
Groups of five are given a background paper, the Ten Bears handout and the bed from The Ten Little Monkeys Jumping On The Bed handout.

Team Project Subtraction Problem Booklets:
Each person makes two illustrations and writes two problems from the story. Or two groups of five combine their pages to make the complete booklet. One group makes the illustration for 10, 9, 8, 7, 6, bears in the bed. The other group makes the illustrations for 5, 4, 3, 2, 1 bears in the bed.

Evaluate and Debrief.

Stand And Share:
The class can say the rhyme as each booklet is read to the class.

Changing Cherries - Characters

Cupcake and Cherries

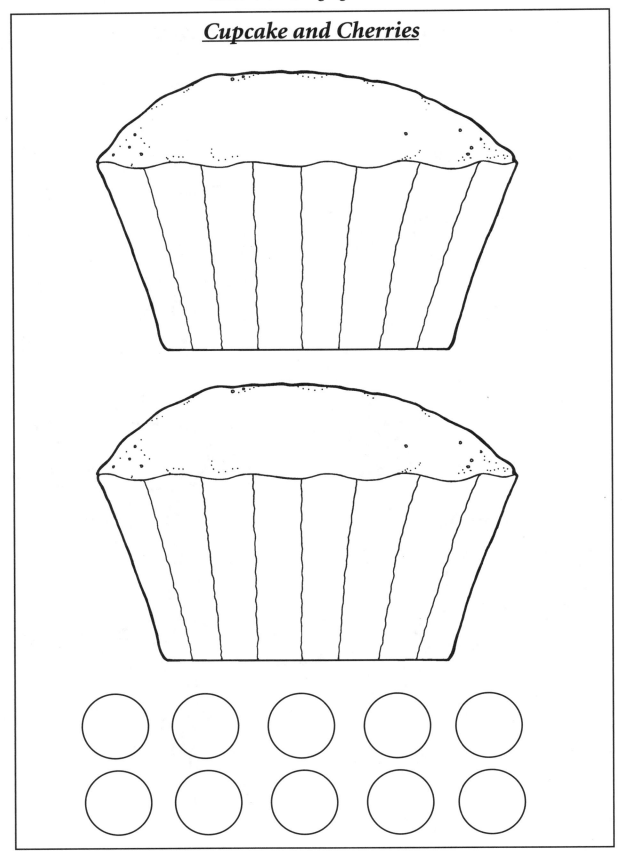

Lorna Curran: *Lessons for Little Ones: Mathematics©*
Kagan Publishing • 1 (800) 933-2667 • www.KaganOnline.com

Five Little Monkeys Jumping on the Bed

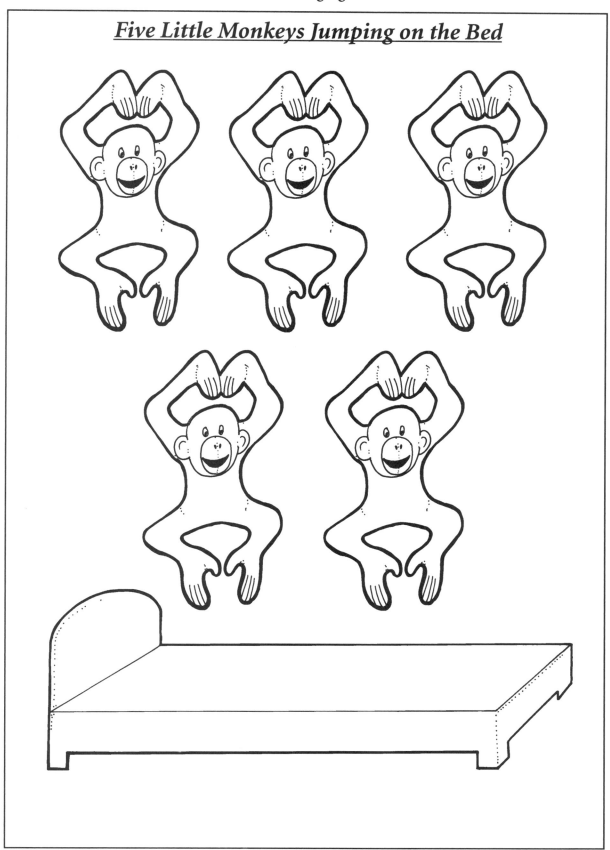

Ten Bears

Lorna Curran: *Lessons for Little Ones: Mathematics©*
Kagan Publishing • 1 (800) 933-2667 • www.KaganOnline.com

chickens here & chickens there

K-1 Subtracting Objects

Literature

• *The Cock, The Mouse and the Little Red Hen* by Lorinda Bryan Cauley
• *The Rooster, The Mouse, and the Little Red Hen* by Nova Nestrick
• *The Little Red Hen* by Paul Galdone
• *Three Baby Chicks* by Ruth Jaynes
• *Don't Count Your Chickens* by Ingri D'Aulaire
• *Chicken Little* by Steven Kellog

materials

Hen handout (1 per student)
Chick handout (1 per student)
Helping hand handout
    (1 hand per student)
Background paper
Glue
Scissors
Crayons

Partners make a pictorial subtraction problem.

The students have had practice acting out hen and chick story problems. The teacher is the hen and a few students are chosen to be the chicks. The students act out a subtraction problem by having some of the chicks disappear under the hen's wings. The students who are chicks come up to you, the hen. Some disappear under your wings, have them say the problem together "____ chicks minus ____ chicks equals ____ chicks." Then have them say the problem again as you write the numerical equation. After they find it easy to act out and say the equations to these problems, they are ready to work subtraction problems in partners using pictures of hens and chicks.

1 Provide lesson overview using *Teacher Talk*

We have been acting out stories about chicks hiding under the hen's wings. Today you and a partner will have a chance to make a picture of one of those story problems we have been acting out. We will want to use Happy Talk as we work together.

2 Think of ideas for happy talk using *Think-Pair-Share*

"Let's look at the Happy Talk Chart.

Structures
Think-Pair-Share
Pair Project
Pair Discussion
Inside-Outside
    Circle
Partner Think-
    And-Praise
Community Circle

Social Skills
Use Happy Talk.

Cognitive Skills
Create a pictorial subtraction problem.

Think if there are any statements on the chart we could use as we work together today. Pair up with the person next to you to tell each other a couple of Happy Talk statements we could use as we make the subtraction problems. Raise your hand if you would like to share a statement you heard or said." Call on several students to share their statements. Identify them on the chart or add any new statements to the chart.

3 Model partner subtraction problems

Choose a student to help you demonstrate how to make the partner subtraction problems. Ask the students to listen for Happy Talk and to watch for things that helped get the job done quickly and easily.

4 Make subtraction problems using *Pair Project*

Preparation for partners problems. Pair up the students. Give the partners one handout of a hen and a handout sheet of chicks. They decide who is partner #1 and who is partner #2.

Make the problem. Partner #1 colors and cuts out the hen and wings. Partner #2 colors and cuts out the chicks. Partner #1 glues on the hen's body. Partner #2 puts a little glue on the top of each wing and places them on the sides of the hen's body. They count up all the chicks. Partner #1 writes that number and a minus sign. They decide how many chicks should go under the hen's wings. Person #1 writes that number after the minus sign and glues those chicks under the wings. Partner #2 glues the remaining chicks on the paper and writes the equal sign and answer to the problem. Partner #2 takes care of

---

Curran's Comments

When students have their first few experiences writing math problems, they feel more comfortable if they have someone to consult with about how to write the numbers and how to write the equation. Even after they know how to do the problems well, they still like the variety of having someone to chat with and help get the work done more quickly. For these students they would enjoy each having a hen and chicks. Consult with them to see that each one makes a different problem. They can make a list of how many different problems could be made with the number of chicks they have available.

---

the scraps and equipment. They both sign their names on the paper.

5 Sponge activity - make a background using *Pairs Project*

When the partners finish they make a background that shows a nice place for their chickens to live. They discuss where their chickens will live. They decide what things they would see in that place. Then they decide who draws which items.

6 Evaluate happy talk using *Pair Discussion*

Give the partners a minute to discuss what Happy Talk statements the two of them used. If they can remember a Happy Talk statement that they used, they draw a happy face by their partner's name. Call on a few partners to share a Happy Talk statement they used. You also share some Happy Talk statements you heard. Add any new Happy Talk statements to the chart.

7 **Debrief the lesson using**
Inside-Outside Circle

Give the partners a few minutes to decide what they did as they worked together to make it fun and easy to make the hen and chick subtraction problem. The Partners form an Inside-Outside Circle. One partner stands in the inside circle. The other partner stands in the outside circle. The outside circle rotates. These new partners share with each other how their partner helped make the problem writing fun and easy. They can rotate several times, sharing information with each new partner.

8 **Give Helping Hand Badge using**
Partner Think-And-Praise

Go sit with your original partner. Think about the most helpful thing your partner did. Tell your partner a praising statement that tells your partner about this helpful thing he/she did. Give your partner a Helping Hand Badge.

9 **Share the Problems using**
Community Circle

Read the subtraction problems and then mount them in a booklet for the library or math center.

Extensions

- Partners do patterning using hens and chicks.
- Students are given an envelope of hens and chicks. They make a graph that represents the contents of the envelope.
- The partner badges can be made into necklaces by using a tab to glue them onto a piece of yarn.

Other Applications

- Do subtraction using animals or people and a location that fits the curriculum.
  bears in and out of the cave
  cookies in & out of the cookie jar
  children in and out of the house

Lorna Curran: *Lessons for Little Ones: Mathematics*©
Kagan Publishing • 1 (800) 933-2667 • www.KaganOnline.com

Lesson 26a Adaptation

rabbits & carrots
K-1

Literature

Little Rabbit's Loose Tooth
by Lucy Bate

Little Rabbit
by Judy Dunn

The Tale of Peter Rabbit
by Beatrix Potter

The Carrot Seed
by Ruth Krauss

Students follow the lesson sequence from the Chickens Here and Chicken There to make subtraction problems about rabbits eating carrots.

Preparation:
Partners are given a background paper and a Rabbit And Carrot handout.

Pair Project Subtraction Problem:
One partner colors and cuts out the rabbits. The other partner colors and cuts out the carrots. When the rabbit is glued on to the background, glue is placed only on the head and bottom of the rabbit. This leaves the top and back open so carrots can be placed behind the rabbit. Then a subtraction problem is written about the rabbit who is in the picture eating carrots. The partners share the writing of the problem.

Sponge Activity:
Partners draw a background that shows a nice place for their rabbits to live.

Evaluate and debrief.

Community Circle:
Partners share their subtraction problems.

Lesson 26b Adaptation

bears & fish
K-1

Literature

Baby Grizzly
by Beth Spanjian

Students follow the lesson sequence from the lesson Chickens Here and Chickens There to make subtraction problems about bears eating fish.

Preparation:
Partners are given a background paper and a Bear and Fish handout.

Pair Project Subtraction Problem:
One partner colors and cuts out the bear. The other partner colors and cuts out the fish. When the bear is glued onto the background, glue is placed on the head and bottom leaving a space to put in the fish that the bear eats. Partners share problem writing.

Sponge Activity:
Partners make a background that shows a place where bears would like to live.

Evaluate and debrief.

Community Circle:
Partners share their subtraction problems.

Chickens Here, Chickens There - Hen

Chickens Here, Chickens There - Chicks

Chickens Here, Chickens There - Wings

Lorna Curran: *Lessons for Little Ones: Mathematics©*
Kagan Publishing • 1 (800) 933-2667 • www.KaganOnline.com

Chickens Here, Chickens There - Hen

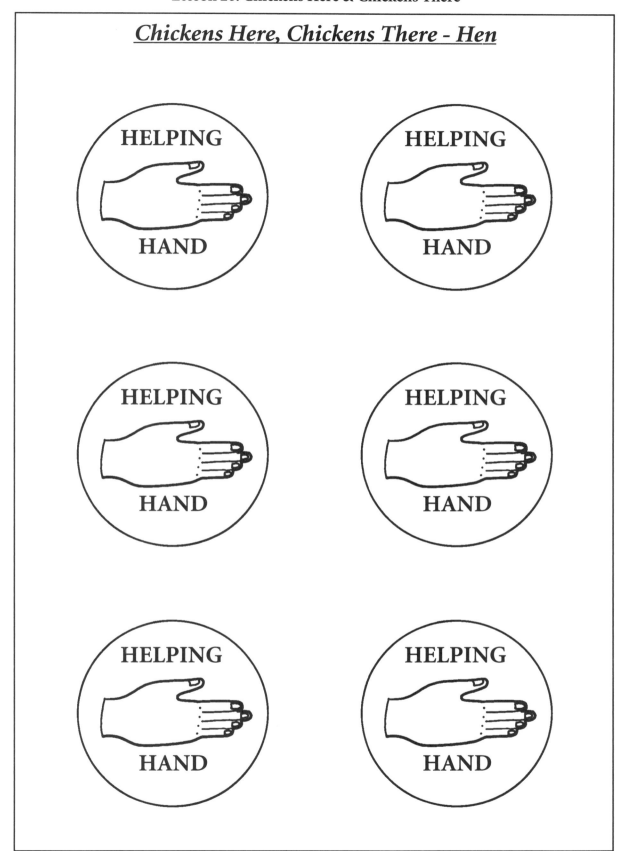

Rabbits & Carrots

Lorna Curran: *Lessons for Little Ones: Mathematics*©
Kagan Publishing • 1 (800) 933-2667 • www.KaganOnline.com

Bear and Fish

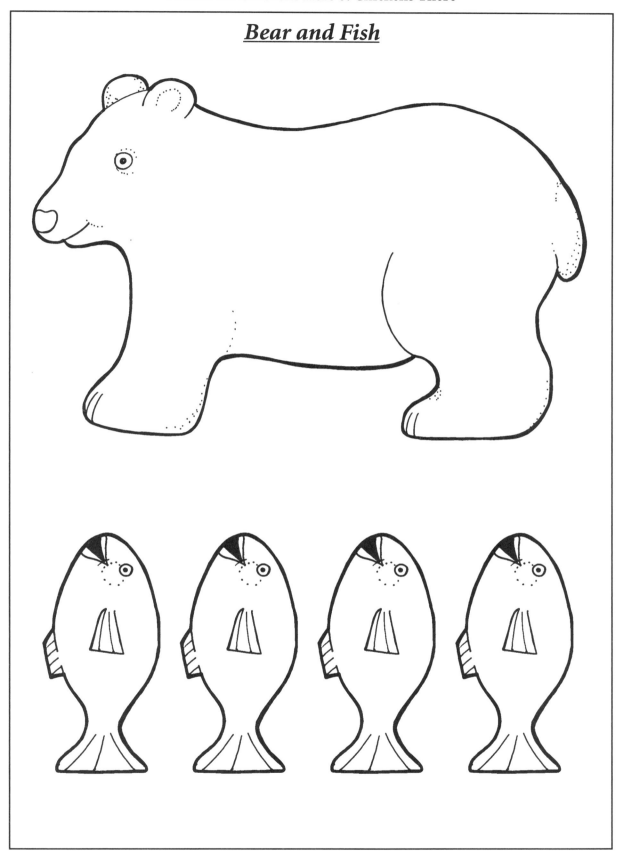

Lorna Curran: *Lessons for Little Ones: Mathematics*©
Kagan Publishing • 1 (800) 933-2667 • www.KaganOnline.com

share a problem: it makes cents

1-3 Subtraction of Money

Literature

- *Alexander, Who Used To Be Rich Last Sunday*
  by Judith Viorst

materials

Chalkboards (1 per team)
Chalk
Erasers
Task cards

Groups work subtraction problems then agree on and show the answer.

The students are able to subtract two digit numbers. The students have heard the beginning of the story *Alexander, Who Used to Be Rich Last Sunday*. As a class, they have done the first subtraction problem in the story where Alexander goes to Pearson's Drug Store and spends 15 cents of his dollar.

1 Provide lesson overview using *Teacher Talk*

As the story continues, groups of students decide how much money Alexander has left at that point in the story. The answers are shown and agreed upon by the class. Then the story continues. The students take turns writing, answering, and showing the problem.

2 Think team praisers using *Team Discussion*

"Discuss what your team can do to congratulate itself for working well to solve the problems. It can be something you do, like a team handshake, or it can be something that you all say together, like "All Right!" or "Great Job!" When you have decided on what you will do or say, practice it so you are ready to use it in the lesson."

Structures
Team Discussion
Roundtable

Social Skills
Use team praisers.

Cognitive Skills
Solve a subtraction problem.

Lorna Curran: *Lessons for Little Ones: Mathematics©*
Kagan Publishing • 1 (800) 933-2667 • www.KaganOnline.com

3 Roundtable with Rotating Roles

Preparation for problem solving. Students are in teams and number themselves from one to four. Each team is given a chalkboard, chalk and eraser. "I will continue reading the story about Alexander. Each time Alexander spends some more of his money, we will stop the story and work the problem. Write down your name on the following task cards that tells what job you will do as we start. We will be trading jobs as we go through the story.

Person #1 - Set Up Person
Person #2 - Problem Writer
Person #3 - Problem Solver
Person #4 - Reporter

Roundtable: Solve problems. "I will read some more of the story. When I get to the next place in the story where Alexander spends some money, you will do the following jobs:

- Person #1 writes the amount of money Alexander has left (It is 85 cents as the groups start.) and passes the board and chalk to Person #2.
- Person #2 writes underneath the 85 cents, the amount of money Alexander spent this time. Pass the board to Person #3.
- Person #3 writes the answer that tells how much money Alexander has left. Pass the board to Person #4.
- Person #4 stands when I say, 'Stand.' You pick up the chalkboard and hold it in front of your chest when I say, 'Show.'
- The class compares answers. If all groups have the same answer, we continue the story. If there is more than one answer, the problem is worked as

a class to determine the correct answer.
- Give the team praiser.
- Pass Task Cards to the person on your right.
- The board goes to the new person #1 who erases the board, and writes how much money Alexander has now."

4 Recognize use of team praisers using *Finger Evaluation*

"If you think you heard or saw all teams giving praisers at the end of each problem, give the thumbs up signal. All teams feel we did well. Give your team praiser for a job well done."

5 Debrief the Lesson using *Inside-Outside Circle*

Have half the class stand in a circle facing out and half the class stand in a circle facing in. The inside person and the outside person will shake hands and then share what they think was best about this lesson. The outside circle rotates a few times so they share ideas with several different people.

Extensions

- The students write Alexander's Math Book. They write story problems based on events that happened in the story. These are solved in class using the structure Send-A-Problem, or the books are sent to another class to be solved.
- In the story, Alexander was trying to find ways to earn money. The students create a story where Alexander does find ways to make a few cents here and there. Other students solve the problems in these books.

Lesson 27a Adaptation

share a problem: it's just ducky

K-1

L i t e r a t u r e

Five Little Ducks

by Jose Aruego and
Ariane Dewey

Students follow the lesson sequence from the Share A Problem: It Makes Cents to write subtraction problems as the story *Five Little Ducks* is read. This story uses the numbers 0 to 5 so it is appropriate for kindergarten and beginning first grade students.

Preparation:
Groups of four are given a chalk board and chalk.

Roundtable:
Team members share the responsibility of writing, answering, and sharing the problems that the mother duck encounters in the story. See the lesson Share-A-Problem: It Makes Cents, for each person's job.

Evaluate and debrief.

Task Cards

Set Up Person

Erases the board. Writes the amount of money left.

Problem Writer

Writes the amount of money spent.

Problem Solver

Writes the answer to the problem.

Reporter

Shows the team answer.

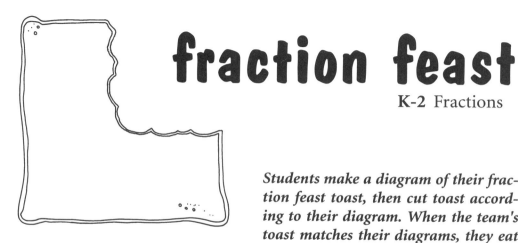

fraction feast

K-2 Fractions

Students make a diagram of their fraction feast toast, then cut toast according to their diagram. When the team's toast matches their diagrams, they eat their fraction feast toast.

The students have had some instruction on the fractions 1/2, 1/3, 1/4, 1/6, 1/8, so they understand the meaning of the numerator and denominator and understand the value of the fractions.

1 Provide lesson overview using *Teacher Talk*

"We have heard stories about fractions, have cut paper into fractions and have made pictures of fractions. Today your team members will coach each other as the team makes slices of toast into four different fractions that your team members can eat. While we coach each other we want to remember to praise our partners for the work they do. When all the groups have their fractions correct, we will have a fraction feast as we eat our fractions."

2 Model making fractions

Choose three students to join you in doing section 5 to demonstrate how to change the slices of toast into fractions.

3 Think of praising statements using *Mix-Freeze-Pair*

"Take a minute and think of a praising statement that could be used when we coach our partners. Start walking around the room. When I say stop, pair

Literature

- *Eating Fractions*
  by Bruce McMillan

materials

Fraction feast toast diagram
  (1 per student)
Adding machine tape
Square shaped bowl
Small plates of napkins
Pencils, Crayons
Cinnamon, Powdered sugar
Sifter, Knives
Toaster

Structures
Mix-Freeze-Pair
Roundrobin
Pairs Check
Team Discussion
Teams Check
Two Stray

Social Skills
Praising statements.

Cognitive Skills
Demonstrate how to draw a fraction.

Lorna Curran: *Lessons for Little Ones: Mathematics*©
Kagan Publishing • 1 (800) 933-2667 • www.KaganOnline.com

up with the person closest to you and exchange praising statements." Have them mix and share several times to collect samples of praising statements.

4 Share ideas with the team using *Roundrobin*

"Take turns around the team to share praising statements that you heard during Mix-Freeze-Pair."

5 Make toast fractions using *Pairs Check*

Preparation for fraction feast. Students meet in teams of four. Each team receives four Fraction Feast Toast Diagram Sheets, two plastic knives and four pieces of toast.

Team Discussion: **choose fractions.** "Discuss which four fractions your team would like to make. Each team member chooses one of the fractions to make."

Teams Check: **make the diagram** "Divide into partners. One partner takes a Fraction Feast Diagram Sheet and makes a diagram of how the toast will be cut to show his/her fraction. The other partner is ready to coach and praises when the fraction diagram is done correctly. The other two team members do the same thing. When all four diagrams are completed have the team check each one."

Teams Check: **make toast fractions.** "The first partner shows his/her coach how the toast will be cut so it matches the diagram. If the coach agrees, the toast is cut. If the coach doesn't agree they discuss it together or with the other

set of partners until everyone agrees on the answer. After the toast is cut, it is set aside and they switch jobs. When all four pieces of toast have been made into fractions, the team checks all four pieces."

Roundrobin: **sponge activity.** "Discuss what things we like to eat, such as crackers, that are divided into fractions."

Pairs Compare: **check diagrams and toast.** Pair the teams up to do Pairs Compare. "Teams, we are going to do Share and Check. First, both teams go to the work space of one of your teams. The first person on that team reads his/her fraction. Then check to see if the fraction on the piece of toast matches the fraction on the diagram and that both fractions are correct. The other team members read their fractions so they can be checked. After all the fractions are checked, move to the second team's work space and continue with the reading and checking."

6 Evaluate praising statements using *Two Stray*

"Teams, put your heads together to remember two praising statements your team used." After they discuss for a couple of minutes, have the first two people from each team who were the coaches go to a designated team to share praising statements. Each person shares one of the statements. When these people go back to the team, the team tells them what praising statements they heard from the visiting reporters.

7 *Fraction Feast*

"Now, we will collect the diagrams and put away our supplies. After all the teams turn in their diagrams and clean

Lesson 28a Adaptation

cookie swap

K-2

L i t e r a t u r e

The Doorbell Rang —
by Pat Hutchins

their work space, we are ready to enjoy our fraction feast."

8 Debrief the Lesson using *Mix-Freeze-Pair*

"You are to start walking around the room. Go many different directions until I say stop. When I say stop, become partners with the person who is closest to you. Share with each other how you felt about The Fraction Feast and share your reasons why you felt that way." After they talk for a couple minutes give them directions to mix again. They can continue until they have met with several partners.

9 Share Ideas from Mix-Freeze-Pair using *Roundrobin*

"Take turns around the team to share ideas telling how people felt about having a Fraction Feast." They can share some of their best ideas with the class.

Extensions

• Homework would be to find something that their family eats that is divided into sections or fractions when it is eaten.
• Read *Bread And Jam For Frances* by Russell Hoban. Have them make illustrations showing how Frances could cut her bread and jam to make different fractions.

Students follow the same lesson sequence from Fraction Feast to make diagrams showing how they to cut their favorite cookies into fractions so that each team member has the same amount of each of the cookies.

Preparation:
Each student in the team of four receives a different kind of cookie and a sheet of paper to draw a diagram of the cookie.

Team Discussion:
Team members decide what four fractions they want to do. Each person writes one of the fractions on his/her sheet of paper.

Teams Check:
The team divides into partners. First one partner, and then the other, shows how their cookies are divided into the correct number of pieces for their fractions.

Roundrobin:
Sponge Activity: students discuss favorite cookies and the best way to divide them evenly into fractions.

Teams Check:
Pairs of teams share and check the cookie diagrams.

Evaluate and Debrief.
Have the cookie feast.

Fraction Feast Toast

Lorna Curran: *Lessons for Little Ones: Mathematics©*
Kagan Publishing • 1 (800) 933-2667 • www.KaganOnline.com

coin characteristics

K-1 Coin Recognition

Literature

- *A Chair for My Mother*
  by Vera Williams
- *26 Letters and 99 Cents*
  by Tana Hoban

materials

Money Value Cards (1 per team)
Signs to label expert groups
8 nickels, dimes, quarters, and
  half dollars
Pencils

Students discover the best identifying characteristics of a coin and teach them to others.

The students would be aware that there are different types of coins with different names, but may not necessarily connect the correct name or value to the correct coin.

1 Think of ideas for helpful teacher using *Think-Pair-Share*

"In the story *A Chair For My Mother*, the family saved their coins in a big jar. When the jar was full, they counted the money in the jar to see if they had enough to buy the chair. In order to count money, we must recognize each type of coin and know how much it is worth. We will go to Expert Groups today to find some good ideas to help us remember what kinds of coins we have. Then it will be easy for us to count our money ."

2 Think of helpful teacher ideas using *Think-Pair-Share*

"Take a minute and think of the things you can do to be a helpful teacher when you teach your team about a coin. You and your partner discuss the ideas both of you thought of." After they have discussed for a couple of minutes, call on students to share an idea they heard or they said. Make a Helpful Teaching Techniques chart that lists their ideas.

Structures
Double Expert
  Groups
Partners Switch
Rotating Reporter
Roundrobin
Team Discussion
Think-And-Praise
Think-Pair-Share

Social Skills
Helpful Teacher.

Cognitive Skills
Discover the identifying characteristics of a coin, describe a coin to others.

Lorna Curran: *Lessons for Little Ones: Mathematics©*
Kagan Publishing • 1 (800) 933-2667 • www.KaganOnline.com

3 Learn coin characteristics using *Double Expert Groups*

Preparation of Teams. The students meet in teams of four. Give each team an envelope that contains a set of money value cards. Each team member takes a card from the envelope. As you display the signs that let the students know where the money value Expert Groups will meet, read the name of the coin and the number value from each sign.

Preparation of *Expert Groups*. "Take your money value card to the area where your expert group meets." Divide the expert groups into two sub-groups of three or four students each. Give each group the coin that they will be studying and remind them of the name of their coin.

***Team Discussion:* coin characteristics.** "Pass the coin so each group member has a chance to see both sides. Put the coin in the center of your group so everyone in your group can see it. Discuss the things you see on the coin that will help our class recognize that type of coin: size, color, and pictures. Decide on three or four things each of you will teach your teams so they can recognize that type of coin."

***Team Discussion:* plan the teaching.** "Put your heads together to think of the best way to teach the information to the teams. If you need to take notes or draw a picture, it can be done on the back of your money value card. Raise your hands if any special supplies are needed. You will have two minutes to teach about your coin so check to see that you can teach your part quickly."

Partners: practice teaching. "Divide into two sets of partners. Choose the partners who will practice teaching the information first. I will let you know when two minutes are up. Then the second person can teach. Think about the things each of you did to be helpful teachers. Discuss any ideas that would make the teaching easier, or would make you more helpful teachers.

***Partners Switch:* practice teaching.** "Switch partners and practice teaching the information one more time using any suggestions that were discussed as you practiced with the other partner."

***Roundrobin:* experts teach teams.** "Take turns being the teacher and teach the team about your coin. Remember, each person has two minutes to teach their part. We will do Roundrobin Think-And-Praise when the teaching is done. Think about those helpful things that the person on your right does while he/ she teaches. You can share those helpful ideas during praising time."

4 Recognize helpful teaching using *Roundrobin Think-And-Praise*

"Everyone on the team helped other team members learn something today. We will do Think-And-Praise to give our teachers the praise they deserve. Remember those helpful things the person on your right did while they taught. Take turns around the team praising the person on your right for helpful teaching."

5 Share helpful teaching ideas using *Rotating Reporter*

Tell the students which direction they move as they share. "In just a moment when we are done with directions, the person who taught about the nickel will move to the next team. Share the things your team did to be helpful teachers. When I call time, you move to the next team in the rotation order and share again." Have the reporter rotate two or three times to share the information.

6 Review ideas from the reporter using *Team Discussion*

"Team members, tell your reporter the ideas you heard. Analyze which of those ideas your team used and which of the ideas you would consider using next time."

7 Share new teaching ideas using *Class Discussion*

Invite teams to share any helpful teaching ideas that should be added to the chart.

8 Debrief the lesson using *Think-Pair-Share*

The students reach out to identify their Think-Pair-Share partner. Give the pairs time to think to themselves, discuss together, and share with the class any of the following questions to find out how the students felt about the Jigsaw lesson.
• What things made it easy to learn about the coins?
• What things made it easy to teach about the coins?
• What do you think we did best today?

Extensions

• Teams sort a jar of coins and make a graph of the results.
• Teams of students sort a jar of coins and add up how much money is in the jar.

Other Applications

• Expert groups use the same process to

teach teams about shapes and their characteristics.
• Expert groups use the same process to teach teams about fraction values.

Lesson 29a Adaptation

dollar detectives

K-3

L i t e r a t u r e

The Go-A-Round Dollar

by Barbara Johnson Adams

Students use the same lesson sequence from Coin Characteristics to find information about dollar bills instead of coins. Have the students do this lesson and the following lesson before you read the story. The story will validate and expand on the information they will teach to each other.

Preparation of Teams:

Students meet in teams of four. They choose a copy of a $1, $5, $10, or $20 dollar bill from the team envelope.

Preparations of *Expert Groups*:

Students take money and meet with the Expert Group for that type of dollar bill.

Team Discussion:

Each Expert Group finds out what is on the front and back of the bill. Then they plan the teaching and practice teaching.

Roundrobin:

Experts teach their team members.

Lesson 29b Adaptation

double the data detectives 2-3

Literature

The Go-A-Round Dollar
by Barbara Johnson Adams

The students use about the same lesson sequence as they did in the previous two lesson to find out information about dollars from the book *The-Go-Around-Dollar*. Have the students investigate and discover this information before the story is read to validate and add to the information they obtained in the lesson.

Preparation of Teams:
Students meet in teams of four. They choose a copy of a $1, $5, $10, or $20 bill from the team envelope.

Preparation of *Expert Groups:*
Students take their money and meet with the Expert Groups for that type of bill.

Team Discussion:
Each expert group is responsible for the following information from the book:

$1 Group - The weight and serial number
$5 Group - The paper and ink
$10 Group- Both sides of the seal
$20 Group - How long bills last and replacement of bills

Team Discussion:
The group members read the information about their topics from the book (Xerox just the information the group needs). They decide how to teach this information and practice teaching.

Experts teach their team members.

Coin Characteristics - Money Value Cards

Nickel = 5 cents	**Dime = 10 cents**
Quarter = 25 cents	**Half Dollar = 50 cents**

inchworm exploration

K-1 Measurement

- ***Jim and the Beanstalk***
  by Raymond Briggs
- ***Inch by Inch***
  by Leo Lionni

materials

Inchworm pattern (1 per team)
Inchworm estimation and
   recording sheet (1 per team)
Pencils
Two colors of crayons

Students estimate the length of objects and use their inchworm tape to check the accuracy of their estimates.

The students have heard the story *Inch By Inch*. After the story is read they estimate the length of the objects the inchworm measures in the story. The objects are then measured with a tape measure so the students can see the actual length of the objects. Students realize that estimation is just an educated guess and is not necessarily accurate. Most estimates are different from the real measurement. Students are familiar with the concept of measuring with a ruler or a tape measure. They have made their own inchworm tape measure.

1 Provide lesson overview using *Teacher Talk*

"We have each made an inchworm tape measure. Today we have a chance to guess the length of objects we see in the room and then work with a partner to measure those objects with our inchworm tape measures to find out exactly how long each object is. As we work, we speak to our partners politely using inside voices."

2 Model inchworm measurement

Choose another student and use the directions in section four to demonstrate how to select items around the room, estimate their length, and then work with a partner to record the length.

Structures
Pair Discussion
Pair Project
Teams Compare
Partner Switch

Social Skills
Use inside voices,
polite statements.

Cognitive Skills
Estimate and
measure the length
of an object.

Lorna Curran: *Lessons for Little Ones: Mathematics*©
Kagan Publishing • 1 (800) 933-2667 • www.KaganOnline.com

3 Ask for and receiving help politely using *Class Discussion*

"As you do the measurement with your partner you will be checking each other's measurement. Let's think of some ways we could ask our partner to check our measurement. We will put those ideas on one chart. Then we will think of how we could let them know if we agree or disagree for their measurement. We will put those ideas on another chart."

4 Do inchworm measurement using *Pair Project*

Preparation for inchworm measurement. The students take their inchworms with them as the meet with their partners. The partners are given an Inchworm Estimation and Recording Sheet. "Decide who is partner #1 and who is partner #2. Partner #1 will use a red crayon. Partner #2 will use a blue crayon."

***Pair Discussion:* objects to measure.** "Discuss what you could measure that would not be longer that your inchworm measure tapes. Each of you chooses two objects to measure. Be sure that each of you has chosen different objects to measure. When you both agree on the objects that each of you will measure, you are ready to fill in the worksheet."

Fill in the worksheet. Partner #1 uses the first two columns on the worksheet. A picture of the first item to be measured is drawn in the first box at the bottom of the sheet. The number of inches that is estimated for that object is

written on the line by the word inches. Partner #1 then does the same thing for box #2. At the same time Partner #2 is filling in the same information on his/her side of the recording sheet by using boxes #3 and #4.

***Pair Project:* measure and record.** "You will now help each other as you measure the objects on the recording sheet by following these directions.
- Person #1 uses his/her inchworm tape measure.
- Person #2 uses a pencil and recording sheet to record the measurement.
- Person #1 measures the object that was drawn in box #1 and tells Person #2 how long it is.
- Person #2 checks the measurement and gives thumbs up if he/she agrees.
- If person #2 does not agree, person#1 measures again.
- If they still disagree, they both raise their hands to signal the teacher for help.
- Starting at the bottom of the first column, person #2 uses the pencil to make an X in the correct number of boxes to record the length of the object in box #1.
- Person #1 checks the recording sheet and gives the thumbs up signal if he/she agrees. If they disagree, use the above procedure.
- Repeat the directions to record the measurement of the second object.
- Then partners switch jobs to record the objects of person #2.

The partners go back to their work space. Each partner neatly colors in with his/her color of crayon all the boxes in the columns that have been marked with an X.

Evaluate Use of Polite Statements using *Pair and Class Discussion*

Pair Discussion: **use of polite statements.** "Think about any polite statements that the two of you used as you worked together. Be ready to share these statements with other students."

Teams Compare: **share polite statements.** Two sets of partners meet. "Share with each other the polite statements you used. Decide if you have any new statements to share with the class."

Class Discussion: **new polite statements.** "Is there anyone who heard a new statement that should be put on our Asking For Help chart or our Agree and Disagree Politely chart?"

 Debrief the Lesson using *Partner Switch*

The two sets of partners now switch partners so that both #1 partners are together and both the #2 partners are together. They discuss how they felt about doing the measurement together with a partner. Some questions they can discuss are:

- What made the measurement easier with a partner?
- What was the best thing about having a partner to work with?
- Next time you work with a partner what could you do that would be helpful?

Extensions

- Partners make an inchworm collage where each partner makes leaves and inchworms of a different color for the picture.

- Students make inchworms of various lengths. They can do Inside-Outside Circle with their inchworms and create addition problems about the length of their inchworms.

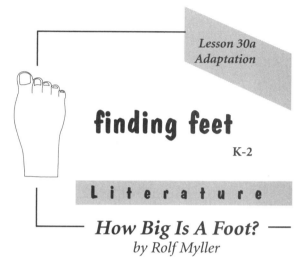

Lesson 30a Adaptation

finding feet
K-2

L i t e r a t u r e

How Big Is A Foot?
by Rolf Myller

Students use the lesson sequence from Inchworm Exploration to share the measuring and recording jobs as they use the foot to measure larger things in the classroom: like large books, the desks, the windows, or each other.

Preparation:
Partners are given a Foot Measure and a Foot Estimation Recording Sheet and two different colors of crayons.

Pair Discussion:
Decide what things to measure that are longer than the foot.

Pair Project:
Measure and record using the Foot Measure. See Inchworm lesson for the procedure.

Evaluate and debrief.

__Inchworm Pattern__

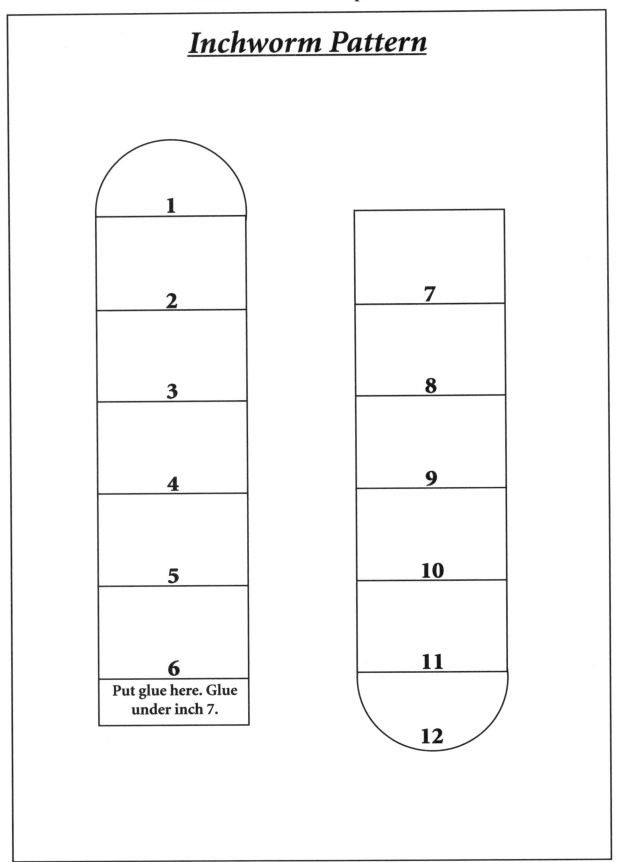

1

2

3

4

5

6

Put glue here. Glue under inch 7.

7

8

9

10

11

12

Inchworm Estimation & Recording Sheet

12			12
11			11
10			10
9			9
8			8
7			7
6			6
5			5
4			4
3			3
2			2
1			1

? ____ inches   ____ inches   ____ inches   ____ inches

Foot Measure

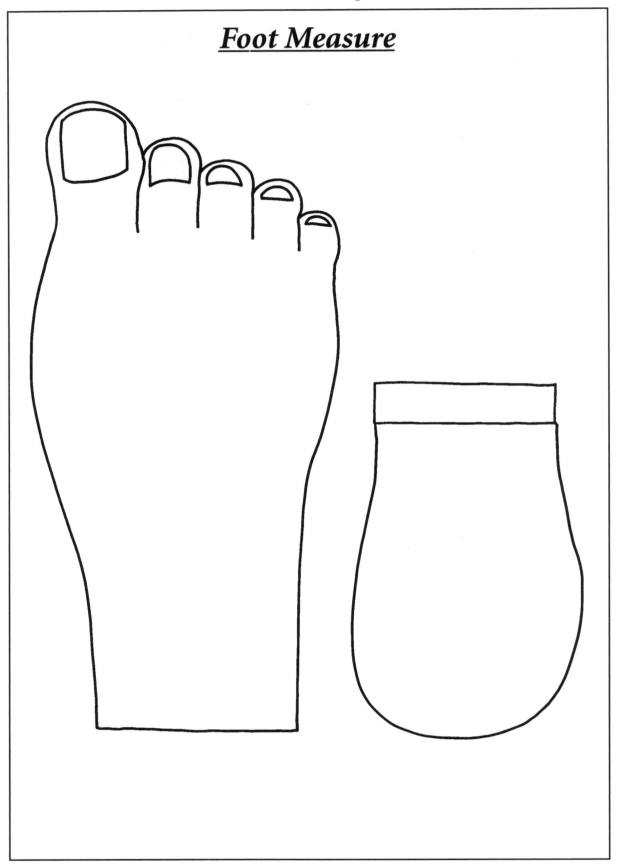

Lorna Curran: *Lessons for Little Ones: Mathematics©*
Kagan Publishing • 1 (800) 933-2667 • www.KaganOnline.com

Foot Estimation and Recording Sheet

6

5

4

3

2

1

6

5

4

3

2

1

? ____ feet ____ feet ____ feet ____ feet

big, bigger, biggest bear

K-2 Measurement

Literature

- **Richard Scarry's Big And Little Book Of Opposites** by Richard Scarry
- **A Kiss For Little Bear** by Else H. Minarik
- **Is It Large? Is It Small?** by Tana Hoban
- **Jesse Bear, What Will You Wear?** by Nancy Carlstrom
- **Deep In The Forest** by Brinton Turkle
- **The Three Bears** by Paul Galdone
- **The Biggest Bear** by Lynd Ward
- **Bears In Pairs** by Niki Yektai

materials

Adding machine tape
  (1 strip per student)
Yard, 1 yard long-1 per group
Scissors
Pencils

Students measure their bears and then arrange strips representative of the bear's height from shortest to tallest.

The class has heard the story *The Three Bears* and has experienced arranging their own teddy bears from shortest to tallest.

1 Provide lesson overview using *Teacher Talk*

"Students, after we read *The Three Bears*, we arranged some teddy bears in a Line-Up so the shortest bear was at the beginning of the line and the tallest bear was at the end of the line. Today you are going to meet in groups to make strips of paper showing how tall your bear is. The group will arrange the strips in a Line-Up from the shortest to the tallest."

2 Demonstrate the lesson

Choose five students to join you to demonstrate the lesson. Remind the students to use please and thank you as the work is being done. After the demonstration lesson, the students review how please and thank you statements were used during the lesson.

3 Measure bear using *Pairs Project*

Preparation for the measurement. Students meet in groups of six. They pair up within the group. Within the

Structures
Pairs Project
Team Line-Up
Team Discussion
Two Stray

Social Skills
Saying please and thank you.

Cognitive Skills
Measure a bear, order bears from shortest to tallest.

Lorna Curran: *Lessons for Little Ones: Mathematics©*
Kagan Publishing • 1 (800) 933-2667 • www.KaganOnline.com

pairs they decide who will be person #1 and who will be person #2. Each group is given six strips of adding machine tape, masking tape, scissors, and pencils.

Measure the bears. Person # lays his or her strip of adding machine tape and bear on the desk and asks person #2 to hold the bear on top of the tape. Person #1 then puts a mark on the tape at the top of the bears head and at the bottom of the feet. They switch jobs. Person #2 lays out the strip and puts marks for the top and bottom of his/her bear and while person #1 holds the bear. They remember to say please as they ask for help and to say thank you after they have received the help. Everyone cuts off the excess paper leaving just the part of the strip that represents the bear's height. Then each group member writes his or her name on the strip.

4 Arrange strips shortest to tallest using *Team Line-Up*

Each group is given a piece of yarn and some tape. The group arranges the strips so they go from shortest to tallest. Each person tapes his or her strip to the piece of yarn.

5 Evaluate use of please and thank you using *Team Discussion/ Finger Evaluation*

"Decide if the people in your group used please and thank you. If you heard people in your group using please and thank you, give the thumbs up signal." Praise or reward the groups according to how many thumbs were up.

6 Debrief the lesson using *Group Discussion/ Two Stray*

Agree on an answer for the following questions. Person #5 and person #6 will be the two students to do Two Stray. They go to other groups to share the team answers. Person #5 will answer one question and person #6 will answer the other question. "How did it help you to have a partner to work with while you were measuring your bear?" "Are there any things the group did to make it easy to put the Line-Up together?"

Extensions

- Students use the happy face measure strips or rulers to measure the bear strips. They find out the difference in height between the partners' or groups' bears.
- Students add up the height of all the bears in their group.
- They use yarn or string to make a Line-Up that shows the distance around all the bears in their group.

Other Applications

- Measure the group members to make a Line-Up that shows the shortest to tallest students in the group.
- Measure group members feet to make a Line-Up showing shortest to longest feet.
- Measure group members library books to make a Line-Up showing shortest to tallest books.

Happy Face Measuring Strips

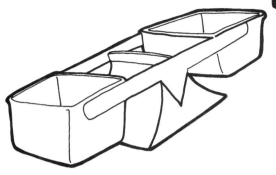

heavy or light

K-2 Weight

L i t e r a t u r e

• *Heavy Is A Hippopotamus*
  by *Miriam Schlein*

Partners weigh and record the relative weights of sets of objects.

The students have had instruction on how to use balance scales and understand the terms heavy and light. They also have an idea about relative weigh, that an object can be labeled as heavy when compared to one object and can be labeled as light when compared to another object.

1 Provide lesson overview using *Teacher Talk*

"Two of you will work together to weigh the objects from the container on the balance scales. Each time two objects are weighed, one of you will record the object that was light. One of you will record the object that was heavy. Remember this will be what we call relative weight. An object can be recorded as heavy one time and as light another time depending upon what two objects are being used in the balance scales at the same time. As you do the weighing and recording together, work on agreeing and disagreeing in a polite way."

2 Model weighing and recording

Choose a student to join you in demonstrating how to weigh and record the relative weights of sets of objects.

materials

Container of objects to weigh
   (different objects for
   each partner)
Yarn for line up
   (orange on one end, green on the other)
Heavy or light recording sheet
   (1 per team)
Crayons, Pencils, Post-Its
Plain paper
Balance scale

Structures
Line-Up–Split And
   Slide
Partners Consult
Teams Check
Pair Project
Teams Compare

Social Skills
Agreeing and
disagreeing in a
polite way.

Cognitive Skills
Weigh and record
relative weights of
sets of objects.

Lorna Curran: *Lessons for Little Ones: Mathematics©*
Kagan Publishing • 1 (800) 933-2667 • www.KaganOnline.com

3 Positive statements for agreeing and disagreeing using *Line-Up*

Preparation for the *Line-Up*.
"Think of a positive way you could tell someone that you agree or disagree with the weighing or recording we do today. Keep that statement in your head. If you thought of a statement to tell someone that you agree, draw an orange circle on your Post-it. If you thought of a positive statement to tell some one that you disagree, draw a green circle on your Post-it."

Do the *Line-Up*: categorize agree or disagree. "Put on your Post-it and stand on the Line-Up. Go to the end of the line that has the color yarn that matches your Post-it." If there are many more at the agree end of the Line-Up than at the disagree end, you may want to comment on how it is usually easier to think of positive things to say when you agree, than to think of positive ways to tell someone that you disagree.

***Split and Slide*: share statements.** Now do a Split and Slide, where the line is split in the middle and half the line moves down to form a double line. The students pair up with their partners in the other line. They share statements with each other. "In a few moments you may share statements your partner said."

***Class Discussion*: share statements from the *Line-Up*.** "Raise your hand if you would like to share your partner's positive statements for agreeing." Record these statements. Then do the same for the positive disagree statements.

4 Weighing and recording using *Partners Consult*

Preparation for weighing and recording.
Two sets of partners meet together to share a balance scale. One set of the partners becomes person #1 and the other person #2. The other set of partners becomes person #3 and person #4. Each pair needs a container of objects to weigh, a Heavy Light Recording Sheet and crayons.

Weighing and recording the objects.
"People #1 and #2 start weighing. Person #1 always records the heavy objects on the recording sheet and person #2 always records the light objects. Each of them chooses an object from the container and puts the object on the scale. Discuss which is the heavy object and which is the light object. When you agree, person #1 draws a picture of the heavy object in the first box of the column labeled heavy. Person #2 draws a picture of the light object in the first box in the column labeled heavy. While people #1 and #2 are drawing, partners #3 and #4 will weigh two objects from their container. Continue sharing the scales to weigh and record objects until you have filled the boxes on your recording sheet. Remember to use polite statements as you agree or disagree."

***Pair Discussion*: sponge activity.** "If one set of partners finishes before the other, decide which are the heaviest and the lightest objects in your container."

***Teams Check*: check recording sheet.** "In just a moment the sets of partners on your team will trade places and check the opposite pair's recording sheet. Person #1 and person #2 weigh the objects that person #3 and person #4 just weighed. Each time you weigh two objects, if you agree with the recording sheet, put a happy face by those boxes. If you don't agree, put a plus. Person #3 and person #4 do the same procedure to check the recording sheet done by person #1 and person #2. When both recording sheets have been checked, discuss and weigh again if there are pluses by any of the boxes.

Pairs Project: **continue sponge activity** "Finish deciding what your heaviest and lightest objects are. Then make a list of things in the room that would be lighter than your lightest object and heavier than your heaviest object."

5 Think of positive statements used using *Pairs Discuss*

"Think about some positive statements the two of you used as you agreed or disagreed with each other."

6 Share positive statements using *Teams Compare*

"In your team of four, share the statements you used with your partners. Then see if there were any statements you used as the four of you checked the recording sheets."

7 Share statements with class using *Numbered Stand And Share*

"When I call your number you will stand and share a positive agree or disagree statement that your team used today." Find those statements on the class chart. Add any new statements to the chart. Continue to call numbers until all the statements have been shared.

Heavy or Light Recording Sheet

Partner #1 _____   **Partner #2** _____

Heavy   **Light**

a couple of clocks

K-3 Addition

• *The Grouchy Ladybug*
  by Eric Carle

materials

Clock faces (see lesson Time
   Around-1 per student)
Drawing paper
Pencils
Crayons

Partners think something fun they like to do during two different times of day.

The students have heard the story *The Grouchy Ladybug*. They have discussed how the story could be different if it were called the Happy Ladybug. They think of some things the happy ladybug would like to do and some characters the ladybug could do these things with.

1 Provide lesson overview using *Teacher Talk*

"We have heard the story The Grouchy Ladybug. We have discussed how we could change the story around and write stories called The Happy Ladybug. We thought of some fun things the ladybug could do and who the ladybug could do them with. Now you will work with a partner to write a Happy Ladybug. You will tell your story to the class. While you work together you will use Happy Talk to let each other know how well you are working."

2 Happy talk statements using *Think-Pair-Share*

"Take a few minutes to think of Happy Talk statements we can use. Share these statements with your partner." Then invite partners to share some of the statements with the class.

Structures

Think-Pair-Share
Pair Project
Pair Discussion
Teams Compare

Social Skills

Use Happy Talk.

Cognitive Skills

Recording time.

Lorna Curran: *Lessons for Little Ones: Mathematics*©
Kagan Publishing • 1 (800) 933-2667 • www.KaganOnline.com

3 Make happy ladybug stories using *Pair Project*

Partners use the following procedure to make the Happy Ladybug Books.

1. Partners are each given a clock face and a piece of drawing paper.

2. Partners discuss two different times they could make on the clock faces, the fun things the ladybug could do at that time, and who the ladybug would talk to.

3. Each person makes a clock face that shows one of the times they agreed upon. They make an illustration for that time which shows the ladybug and another character doing the fun activity.

4. They practice telling about their clock and illustration so they are ready to tell their story to the class.

4 Evaluate happy talk using *Pair Discussion*

"Talk together and remember some Happy Talk Statements you used. If you remember a Happy Talk Statement you used or could have used, your partner can make a happy face by your name."

5 Happy talk statements using *Teams Compare*

Two sets of partners meet together. They share the Happy talk statements they used or could have used as they worked together.

6 Share stories using *Teams Compare*

The same sets of partners or new sets of partners meet. They take turns telling their stories to each other. They think of a praising statements to give the other set of partners after they have heard their story.

7 Debrief the lesson using *Teams Compare*

The same sets or new sets of students debrief the lesson by discussing the best things about making the Happy Ladybug Stories together. Provide time for a few groups to share their ideas.

Variations

- Partners decide on two things they like to do. They make a clock that shows the time that would happen and an illustration that shows that activity.

- Partners think of things they do at school. Each of them illustrates and writes the time for something done at school.

- Groups of four, five or six decide on more times and activities to include in their books.

- Kindergarten students dictate the stories to adults so the stories can be kept in the class library. First, second, and third grade students can add their own text.

roll and write the right time

K-2 Time

Literature

• *What Time Is It Jeanne-Marie?*
  by Francoice Seignobosc
• *The Grouchy Ladybug* *by Eric Carle*
• *Bear Child's Book of Hours*
  by Anne Rockwell

materials

Time recording sheets
Clock face recording sheets
Pair of dice
Glue
Pencils

Triads play the game Roll and Write to write the time indicated on a pair of dice and draw that time on a clock face.

The students are able to tell what time it is on the clocks in the story *What Time Is It Jeanne-Marie?* They have experience reading and writing time so they can help each other write time in numerals and also on a clock face. The students are also able to count up or add together the dots on a pair of dice.

1 Provide lesson overview using *Teacher Talk*

"You were telling the time on the clocks as I read the story about Jeanne-Marie. Now you will continue to have fun as you meet in triads to play the game Roundtable with Rotating Roles to tell about time. One person will roll the dice, add up the dots on the two dice, and that will tell what time to write. One person will write the numbers that tell that time. One person will draw that time on a clock face. You will switch jobs so you all get to do each job."

2 Model simultaneous Roll and Write

Choose two students to join you in demonstrating how to do Roundtable with Rotating Roles. Write different times from the story about Jeanne-Marie. Have the students watch for polite passing.

Structures
Roundtable
Team Discussion
Team Praise

Social Skills
Be a polite passer.

Cognitive Skills
Draw the time on a clock face.

Lorna Curran: *Lessons for Little Ones: Mathematics*©
Kagan Publishing • 1 (800) 933-2667 • www.KaganOnline.com

3 Writing time using *Roundtable with Rotating Roles*

Preparation for Roll and Write. The students meet in triads. Each triad is given one each of the time recording sheets, a pair of dice, two pencils and a bottle of glue. The students number themselves from 1 to 3. Person #1 is given a pair if dice. Person #2 is given the Time Writing Recording Sheet. Person #3 is given the Clock Face Recording Sheet.

Directions for Roll and Write. "Each person in the triad has a different job. Person #1 rolls the dice, add the numbers from both of the dice, and tells that number to the other two team members. They give a thumbs up signal if they agree. If they give a thumbs side ways signal, add the dots again. Person #2 writes the numbers that tell the time. Person #3 draws the time on the clock face."

Check the time. "Before you pass your things to the next person, check to see that the number of dots on the dice, the written time and the clock face all tell about the same time. Give thumbs up when you agree. Then everyone pass your materials to the person on your right."

An example of time writing with Roll and Write. "If there were three dots on one dice and two dots on the other dice, together there would be five dots. This means person #2 writes 5:00. Person #3 draws the clock hands that show 5:00 on the clock face."

Do Roll and Write. "In just a moment when we start the Roll And Write, each of you will do your job. When you have finished your job, be a polite passer as you give your supplies to the person on your right. A polite passer waits until the next person is ready before passing the materials. A polite passer also passes materials carefully so they are ready for the next person to use. After you have passed your materials, you are ready do a new job for the team, using the supplies that were just passed to you. Keep doing you jobs and passing to the right until time is called."

4 Evaluate polite passing using *Team Discussion*

"Talk it over and decide if your group worked on being good passers and how they were good passers." After they discuss for a few minutes, give the silent signal. "If your team worked on being good passers, give each other an inside high five." Call on a few of the teams that gave a high five to tell the class what their team did to be polite passers.

5 Think of best thing done using *Team Praise*

"Each of you take a minute and think of something that each person in your triad did to help get the job done. Starting with person #1 each of you tells the other two team members the best thing each of them did to help get the job done."

Extensions

- A graph is made that shows the time made by all the triads.
- Individuals or groups make booklets that show what time they do particular things.

Other Applications

- Partners play Roll and Write to make addition problems. Person #1 rolls the dice. Person #2 writes the problem. Then they switch jobs.
- Partner #1 rolls the dice and adds the numbers. That determines what number the partners will practice. Partner #2 rolls one dice and that determines how many times they practice writing the number. They both write the number the correct number of times.

Roll and Write the Right Time

Clock face showing numbers 1–12	_____
Clock face showing numbers 1–12	_____
Clock face showing numbers 1–12	_____
Clock face showing numbers 1–12	_____

Lorna Curran: *Lessons for Little Ones: Mathematics©*
Kagan Publishing • 1 (800) 933-2667 • www.KaganOnline.com

changeable clock

K-3 Time

Literature

- *Tomie dePaola's Mother Goose*
  by Tomie dePaola
- *The Little Dog Laughed and Other Nursery Rhymes*
  by Lucy Cousins
- *Leroy and the Clock*
  by Juanita Havill

materials

Changeable clock handout
  (1 per team)
Talking chips (8 chips per team)
Illustration for booklet cover
Number chart that has each
  number in written and
  numerical form
Pencils and crayons
Paper

Students work together to change the rhyme of Hickory Dickory Dock and make a clock face for the times in their rhyme.

The students have learned the nursery rhyme Hickory Dickory Dock. As they say the rhyme, they have changed the times on a clock face. They have clapped the appropriate number of times for the hour on the clock. They have had instruction on how to write the time on a clock face. They recognize the numbers and can copy them in both word and number.

1 Provide lesson overview using *Teacher Talk*

"We have had fun changing the time on our clock face as we say Hickory Dickory Dock, and then clapping the number of times the clock would chime. Today we will work in groups to write down our changeable clock rhyme so we can share it with other classes. Instead of clapping the time, we will write "Bong!", the correct number of times, like the author did in the story Leroy And The Clock.

2 Model making booklets

Choose three students to join you in following the directions in section 4 to demonstrate how the group works together to make the Changeable Clock Booklets.

Structures
Team Project
Team Discussion
Pairs Check
Teams Compare
Talking Chips

Social Skills
Giving positive suggestions, praising statements.

Cognitive Skills
Create a new Hickory Dickory Dock rhyme, draw the time on a clock face.

Lorna Curran: *Lessons for Little Ones: Mathematics*©
Kagan Publishing • 1 (800) 933-2667 • www.KaganOnline.com

3 Think of positive suggestions/ praising statements using
Think-Pair-Share

Everyone identifies who their Think-Pair-Share Partner is. "Think of a positive suggestions you can use if you partner needs to change the time on the clock you are making. In pairs, discuss the ideas you thought of." Ask students to share a positive suggestion with the class. List the ideas that are shared. Use the same process to have them think of praising statements they can use as they coach their partners during Pairs Check.

4 Make time booklets using
Team Project

Team Discussion: decide the times. Have the students meet in groups and number themselves from one to four. "Discuss what times your group would like to have in your booklet. Then each team member chooses one of those times to make for the booklet. When that decision has been made, team member #3 will get a Changeable Clock Page Handout for each of the team members.

Pairs Check: make booklet pages. "Persons #1 and #2 are partners to do Pairs Check. Person #1 tells his or her time and makes the clock face. Person #2 is the coach and watches to see if he/she agrees that the time is being written in the correct way. If they don't agree they talk to the other pair on the team. Remember to give your suggestions in a positive way. When they both agree the time has been written correctly, the coach praises his/her partner. Then person #2 draws the clock face while person #1 is the coach. At the same time persons #3 and #4 are partners and follow the same procedure."

Pairs Check: add the writing. "Look at the number chart on the wall. Spell for your partner the number word you plan on using. Tell how many times you plan on writing the word bong. If your coach agrees with the spelling of the number and the appropriate number of bongs for your clock, he/she gives the thumbs up signal. Write the number word and the word bong the correct number of times to complete your page of the booklet. Coaches, check each others page. Give any suggestions needed and the praise for the work your partner did.

Team Discussion: compile the booklet. "Discuss to decide how the pages will be arranged in your team booklet. Arrange the pages in that order. Decide on the name of your publishing company. All team members sign their names at the bottom of the booklet cover. Choose jobs to make the cover and title page of the booklet. Then Person #2 brings the completed booklet to the teacher to be fastened together."

Job #1 - Write the title of the book at the top of the cover.
Job #2 - Draw a clock to glue on cover.
Job #3 - Write the title of the book at the top of the title page.
Job #4 - Write the name of the publishing company on the title page.

5 Evaluate positive suggestions/ praising statements using
Teams Compare

"Take the next couple of minutes, to discuss with your Pairs Check partner, if you remember any positive statements or praising statements the two of you used as you worked together. Now discuss as a team to share the statements you used. Compare to see what statements were used by both partners and which were used by just one of the partners. If you have time left, discuss any other statements you could have used." Ask if there are any new statements to add to the class charts.

6 Debrief the lesson using *Team Discussion with Talking Chips*

Person #4 gives everyone on the team two talking chips. "Use your talking chips as you discuss the answers to any of these questions. What did you learn from the lesson? What was best about the lesson? What would make this job easier for you next time? Remember everyone must use all of their talking chips before they are passed out again to continue the discussion. Person #1 collects and returns the talking chips."

Variations

- Instead of writing the word bong, the students change the Hickory Dickory Dock poem so that it rhymes with the

new number. For example; "The clock struck two, he lost his shoe."

Other Applications

- Groups make shape booklets. Each team member is responsible for a particular shape. He/she draws things that are that shape or looks in magazines for pictures of objects that are that shape. Or, the whole team looks for all the shapes. One person from the team is responsible for gluing a particular shape on his/her page of the booklet.

- Groups make an Answer Booklet of problems that have an answer from 1 to 8. The team is given a page of addition or subtraction facts which they cut up into individual problems. Each team member is responsible for a couple pages of the Answer Booklet. For example, person #1 is given page 1 and 5. This person glues onto those pages any problems that have the answer of 1 or 5. Person #2 is responsible for pages 2 and 6, person #3 has pages 3 and 7, and person #4 has pages 4 and 8.

*Lesson 35a
Adaptation*

favorite times
K-3

L i t e r a t u r e

A Clock for Beany
by Lisa Bassett

Students use the lesson sequence from Changeable Clocks to show what happens at their favorite time of day.

Preparation:
Students are in teams of four. Each member has drawing paper and a piece of paper for a book page.

Pairs Check:
Partners on the team take turns writing the time and coaching to see that the time is correct. An illustration is added to each paper.

Pairs Check :
Partners take turns writing and coaching as a sentence about the favorite time is added to the illustration. They assist each other with vocabulary and spelling. For kindergarten students adults assist with the sentence writing.

Group Project:
Compile the book according to the directions in the lesson.

Evaluate and debrief.

Changeable Clocks

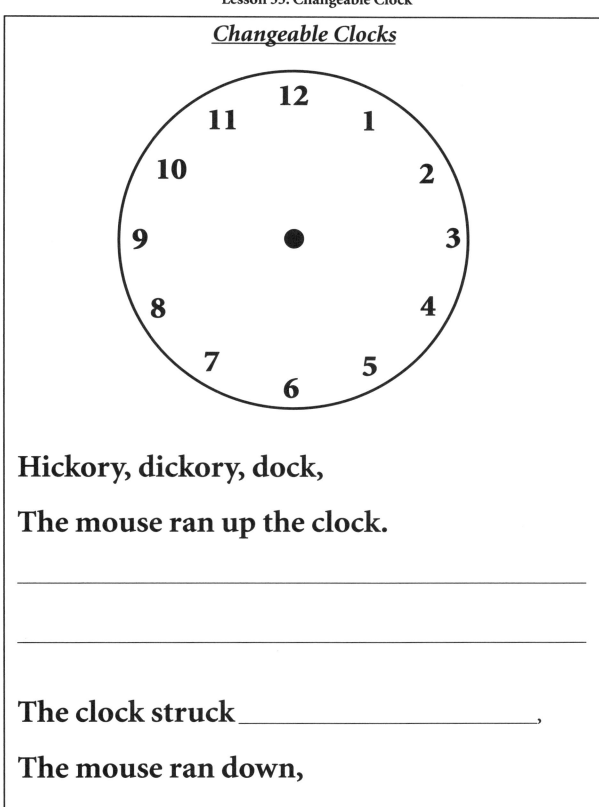

Hickory, dickory, dock,

The mouse ran up the clock.

_____

_____

The clock struck_____,

The mouse ran down,

Hickory, dickory, dock.

Talking Chips

TALKING CHIP   TALKING CHIP

TALKING CHIP   TALKING CHIP

TALKING CHIP   TALKING CHIP

TALKING CHIP   TALKING CHIP

time around

K-2 Time

Literature

• *The Grouchy Ladybug*
  by Eric Carle

Students review writing time as it appears on the clock face.

The students have had experiences reading and writing time as it appears on the face of a clock.

1 Provide lesson overview using *Teacher Talk*

"In the story *The Grouchy Ladybug*, the ladybug met an animal each hour all day long. Today we are going to play a game to remember each of the hours of the day. To help the game work well for our teams, we will use three of our social skills: paying attention to the team work, being ready for our turns and working quickly when we have our turns."

2 Time on the clocks using *Roundtable*

Preparation for *Roundtable*. Students are in teams of four. Each team is given a Roundtable Clocks handout and a pencil. The team members number themselves in order around their team so they know the rotation of the paper.

Write hours on the clocks. "In just a minute when it is time to start, person #1 writes a time on a clock face. Everyone watches so you know what time has already been used. Then the paper and pencil are passed to

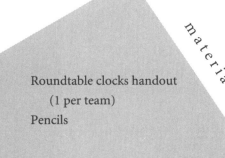

materials

Roundtable clocks handout
  (1 per team)
Pencils

Structures
Sequential
  Roundtable
Signaled Sequential
  Roundtable

Social Skills
Watch the team paper, be ready for your turn, work quickly.

Cognitive Skills
Draw the time on a clock.

person #2. Person #2 writes on the clock, a time that has not been used. Keep passing the paper and writing times that have not been used, until time is called. Remember to pay attention so you will not repeat a time that is already on the clocks. Remember to be ready for your turn by thinking about a time you can write. When the paper comes to you write the time quickly and yet neatly so it can be read at the end of the game. Then pass the paper to the next person. Continue passing and writing until I call time or the team uses all the clocks on the handout sheet."

Roundrobin: **sponge activity - favorite time.** "If your team finishes before time is called, start taking turns around your team to discuss what time of day is your favorite time and why it is your favorite time."

Signaled Roundtable: **read the times.** "Take turns around the circle reading the times on the Roundtable Clocks handout. If the team agrees with the time being read, the team members give the thumbs up signal. If they do not agree, they give the thumbs sideways signal so it can be discussed. If the team can not agree, all team members put hands up and the teacher will come to give assistance. Keep practicing until all team members can say all the times on the clocks."

3 Evaluate social skills using *Finger Evaluation/ Team Card*

"Discuss the questions on the Team Evaluation Card and come to an agreement as to how your team did. Person

#2 is the recorder. If your team did an excellent job because everyone did that social skill, then the recorder circles the face with the big smile. If your team did a good job because almost everyone did that social skill, circle the face with the smaller smile. If your team needs to improve because several team members forgot to use a social skill, circle the face with the straight mouth. Then everyone signs the card and it is turned in with your Roundtable Clocks handout.

Curran's Comments

To assist the younger students with the Team Evaluation Card, the teacher reads one question at a time, gives the team a couple of minutes to come up with consensus on the answer and the recorder circles the answer.

Other Applications

- Do Time Around again, this time writing the times in numbers as on a digital clock.
- Do an Add Around or Subtract Around by having the students write as many addition or subtraction facts as they can within the time limits of the game.
- Do a Fraction Around where the students write as many fractions as they can within the time limits and then the team illustrates the fractions.
- Do a Letter Around to review the letters in the alphabet where the team members add a letter of the alphabet on their answer sheet.
- Do a Write Around where the students add a spelling word or vocabulary word to their answer sheet.

Time Around - Roundtable Clocks

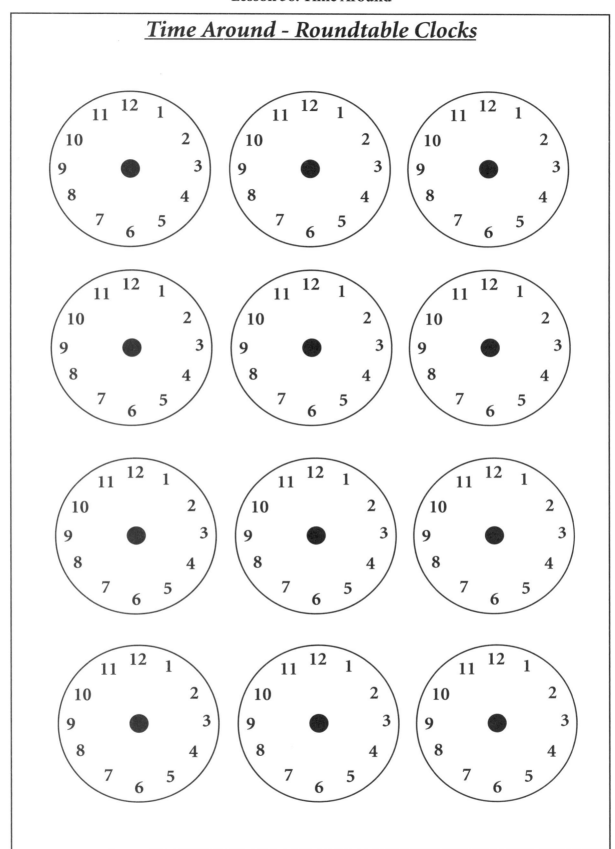

Bibliography

Adams, Barbara Johnston. *The Go-A-Round Dollar.* New York: Four Winds Press, 1992.

Aker, Suzanne. *What Comes In 2's, 3's, & 4's?* New York: Simon and Schuster, 1990.

Aruego, Jose and Dewey, Ariane. *Five Little Ducks.* New York: Crown Publishers, 1989.

Ayleworth, Jim. *One Crow A Counting Rhyme.* New York: Harper Collins, 1988.

Bang, Molly. *Ten, Nine, Eight.* Harcour Brace Jovanovich, 1989.

Bate, Lucy. *Little Rabbit's Loose Tooth.* New York: Crown Publishers, 1975.

Bassett, Lisa. *A Clock For Beany.* New York: Puffin Books, 1988.

Bernhard, Emery. *Ladybug.* New York: Holiday House, 1992.

Bishop, Claire. *Twenty-Two Bears.* New York: The Viking Press., 1967.

Brett, Jan. *The Mitten.* New York: Scholastic Inc., 1989.

Bridwell, Norman. *Clifford's Pals.* New York: Scholastic Inc. 1985.

Briggs, Raymond. *Jim and the Beanstalk.* New York: Coward – McCann Inc., 1970.

Brown, Margaret Wise. *The Runaway Bunny.* New York: Harper & Row Publishers, 1977.

Brown, Ruth. *Ladybug, Ladybug.* New York: E.P. Dutton, 1988.

Carle, Eric. *The Grouchy Ladybug.* New York: Harper & Row Publishers, 1977.

Carle, Eric. *The Very Hungry Caterpillar.* New York: Putnam Publishing, 1986.

Carlson, Nancy. *Harriet's Halloween Candy.* New York: Puffin Books, 1982.

Carlstrom, Nancy. *Jesse Bear What Will You Wear?* New York: Harcourt Brace Jovanovich, 1989.

Carroll, Kathleen Sullivan. *One Red Rooster.* Boston: Houghton Mifflin Company, 1992.

Cauley, Lorinda Bryan. *The Cock, The Mouse and The Little Red Hen.* New York: G.P. Putnam's Sons, 1982.

Cave, Kathryn. *Out For The Count.* New York: Simon & Schuster, 1991.

Charles, Donald. *Calico Cat Look At Shapes.* Chicago: Childrens Press, 1975.

Cleveland, David. *The April Rabbits.* New York: Scholastic Inc., 1978.

Cousins, Lucy. *The Little Dog Laughed And Other Nursery Rhymes.* New York: E.P. Dutton, 1990.

Bibliography

Crews, Donald. *Ten Black Dots.* New York: Greenwillow Books, 1986.

Curran, Eileen. *Look At A Tree.* Mahwan, New Jersey: Troll Associates, 1985.

Curry, Nancy. *An Apple is Red.* Glendale, CA: Bowmar Early Childhood Books, 1967.

Cutts, David. *Look...A Butterfly.* Mahwah, New Jersey: Troll Associates, 1982.

Dunbar, Joyce. *A Cake For Barney.* New York: Orchard Books, 1986.

Dunn, Judy. *The Little Rabbit.* New York: Random House, 1980.

Emberley, Ed. *The Wing On A Flea.* Boston: Little Brown & Company, 1961.

Fischer-Nagel, Heiderose and Andreas. *Life Of The Ladybug.* Minneapolis: Carolrhoda Books Inc., 1987.

Fisher, Leonard Everett. *Look Around! A Book About Shapes.* New York: Viking Penguin Inc., 1987.

Fowke, Edith. *One Little Elephant Balancing.* San Diego: Harcourt Brace Javonovich, 1989.

Freeman, Don. *Corduroy.* New York: Puffin Books, 1976.

Freeman, Don. *Dandelion.* New York: Puffin Books, 1977.

Freeman, Don. *A Pocket For Corduroy.* New York: Puffin Books, 1980.

Freeman, Mae. *Finding Out About Shapes.* New York: McGraw Hill Book Company, 1969.

Froman, Robert. *Venn Diagrams.* New York: Thomas Y, Crowell Company, 1972.

Galdone, Paul. *The Little Red Hen.* New York: Clarion Books, 1973.

Galdone, Paul. *The Three Bears.* New York: Clarion Books, 1972.

Garelick, May. *Where Does The Butterfly Go When It Rains.* New York: Young Scott Books, 1961.

Gibbons, Gail. *The Seasons of Arnold's Apple Tree.* San Diego: Harcourt Brace Jovanovich, 1984.

Giganti, Paul Jr. *Each Orange Has 8 Slices.* New York: Greenwillow Books, 1992.

Graham, Amanda. *Who Wants Arthur?* Milwaukee: Gareth Stevens Publishing, 1984.

Grossman, Virginia & Long, Sylvia. *Ten Little Rabbits.* San Francisco: Chronicle Books, 1991.

Havill, Juanita. *Leroy And The Clock.* Boston: Houghton Mifflin Company, 1988.

Hawes, Judy. *Why Frogs Are Wet.* New York: Crowell Publishers, 1968.

Herman, Gail. *Ice Cream Soup.* New York: Random House, 1990.

Heuck, Sigrid. *Who Stole the Apples?* Afred A. Knopf, 1986.

Hillert, Margaret. *The Baby Bunny Book.* Chicago: Modern Curriculum, 1981.

Hines, Anna Grossnickle. *Remember The Butterflies.* New York: Dutton Children's Books, 1991.

Hoban, Tana. *A Children's Zoo.* New York: Mulberry Books, 1987.

Hoban, Tana. *Circles, Squares & Triangles.* New York: McMillian Publishing Co. Inc., 1974.

Hoban, Tana. *Is It Large? Is It Small?* New York: Greenwillow Books, 1985.

Hoban, Tana. *Round & Round & Round.* New York: Greenwillow Books, 1983.

Hoban, Tana. *26 Letters and 99 Cents.* New York: Greenwillow Books, 1987.

Hoberman, Mary Ann And Norman. *All My Shoes Come In Twos.* Boston: Little Brown & Co., 1957.

Hutchins, Pat. *The Doorbell Rang.* New York: Greenwillow Books, 1986.

Jaynes, Ruth. *Three Baby Chicks.* Glendale, California: Bowmar Publishing Corp., 1967.

Kalin, Robert. *Jump, Frog, Jump!* New York:Scholastic Books, 1981.

Kellog, Steven. *Chicken Little.* New York: W. Morrow, 1989.

Kessler, Ethel and Leonard. *Are You Square?* New York: Doubleday & Company, Inc, 1966.

Kirkpatrick, Rena K. *Look At Trees.* Milwaukee: Raintree Childrens Books, 1978.

Krauss, Ruth. *The Carrot Seed.* New York: Harper & Collins, 1945.

Le Sieg, Theo. *Ten Apples On Top.* New York: Random House., 1961.

Lionni, Leo. *Inch By Inch.* New york: Astor-Honor, 1962.

Lionni, Leo. *Pezzettino.* New York: Pantheon, 1975.

Lobel, Arnold. *Frog and Toad are Friends.* New York: Harper Collins Publishing, 1985.

Lobel, Arnold. *Frog And Toad Together.* New York: Trophy, 1985.

Mack, Stan. *10 Bears In My Bed, A Goodnight Countdown.* New York: Pantheon Books, 1974.

Martin, Bill Jr. *Brown Bear, Brown Bear, What Do You See?* Harcourt Brace Jovanovich, 1991.

Martin, Bill Jr. *Happy Hippopotami.* New York: Holt, Rienhart, Winston, Inc., 1970.

Mastrangelo, Judy. *What Do Bunnies Do All Day.* Nashville, TN: Ideals Children's Books, 1988.

Mayer, Anne. *The Yellow Button.* New York: Knopf Books for Young Readers, 1990.

McCracken, Marlene J. and Robert A. *Some Dogs Don't.* Surrey, B.C.: McCracken, 1986.

McMillan, Bruce. *Eating Fractions.* New York: Scholastic Inc., 1991.

Miles, Miska. *Small Rabbit.* New York: Scholastic Books, 1977.

Minarik, Else. *A Kiss For Little Bear.* New York: Harper & Collins, 1968.

Myller, Rolf. *How Big Is A Foot?* New York: Dell Publishing, 1990.

Newberry, Clare Turlay. *Marshmallow.* New York: Harper & Collins, 1990.

Nestrick, Nova. *The Rooster, The Mouse and The Little Red Hen.* New York: Platt & Munk, 1961.

D'Aulaire, Ingri. *Don't Count Your Chickens.* Garden City, NY: Dell, 1993.

Parker, N.W., and Wright, J. R. *Bugs.* New York: Greenwillow Books, 1987.

dePaola, Tomie. *Tomie dePaola's Mother Goose.* New York: G.P. Putnam's Sons, 1985.

Payne, Emmy. *Katy No Pockets.* Boston: Houghton Miffin, 1944.

Pluckrose, Henry. *Butterflies And Moths.* New York: Gloucester Press, 1981.

Potter, Beatrix. *The Tale Of Peter Rabbit.* New York: Puffin Books, 1992.

Rann, Toni. *My First Look At Shapes.* New York: Random House, 1990.

Reid, Margaret. *The Button Box.* New York: Dutton Children's Books, 1990.

Reiss, John J. *Shapes.* New York: MacMillan Press, 1987.

Rey, H.A. *Don't Forget the Lion.* New York: Scholastic Books, 1970.

Rice, Eve. *Sam, Who Never Forgets.* New York: Morrow Books, 1987.

Bibliography

Rockwell, Anne. *Bear Child's Book of Hours.* New York: Dutton Childrens Books, 1989.

Rogers, Jean. *Runaway Mittens.* New York: Greenwillow Books, 1988.

Ryder, Joanne. *Chipmunk Song.* New York: Lodestar Books, E.P. Dutton, 1987.

Scarry, Richard. B*ig And Little Book of Opposites.* New York: Golden Press, 1986.

Scarry, Richard. *The Bunny Book.* Racine, WI: Western Publishing Company, 1987.

Scheer, Julian. *Rain Makes Applesauce.* New York: Holiday House, 1964.

Schlein, Miriam. *Heavy Is A Hippoptamus.* Harper Collins Childrens Books, 1954.

Seignobosc, Francoice. *What Time Is It Jeanne-Marie?* NY: Charles Schribner's Sons, 1963.

Sendak, Maurice. *One Was Johonny A Counting Book.* New York: Harper & Collins, 1962.

Serfozo, Mary. *Who Wants One.* New York: Margaret K. McElderry Books, 1989.

Seuss, Dr. *One Fish, Two Fish, Red Fish, Blue Fish.* New York: Random House, 1960.

Skorpen, Liesel Moak. *If I Had A Lion.* New York: Harper Row, Publishers, 1967.

Slobodkin, Florence and Louis. *Too Many Mittens.* New York: The Vanguard Press, 1958.

Spanjian, Beth. *Baby Grizzly.* Stamford, CT: Longmeadow Press, 1988.

Thayer, Jane. *The Puppy Who Wanted A Boy.* New York: Morrow Books, 1986.

Thornhill, Jan. *The Wildlife 1.2.3. A Nature Counting Book.* New York: Simon & Schuster, 1989.

Turkle, Briton. *Deep In The Forest.* New York: Dutton Childrens Books, 1976.

Van Allsburg, Chris. *Two Bad Ants.* Boston: Houghton Mifflin Company, 1988.

Viorst, Judith. *Alexander, Who Used to Be Rich Last Sunday.* New York: Aladdin Books, 1978.

Walsh, Ellen Stoll. *Mouse Count.* New York: Harcourt Brace Jovanovich, Publishers, 1991.

Ward, Lynd. *The Biggest Bear.* Boston: Houghton Mifflin Company, 1952.

Williams, Vera. *A Chair For My Mother.* New York: Mulberry Books, 1982.

Winthrop, Elizabeth. *Shoes.* New York: Harper & Row, 1986.

Wylie, Joanne and David. *A Fishy Shape Story.* Chicago: Children's Press, 1984.

Yektai, Niki. *Bears In Pairs.* New York: Bradbury Press, 1987.

Zion, Gene. *Harry By The Sea.* New York: Harper & Row, 1976.

Zion, Gene. *Harry The Dirty Dog.* New York: Harper & Row, 1956.

Zion, Gene. *No Roses For Harry.* New York: Harper & Collins, 1958.

Zion, Gene. *The Plant Sitter..* New York: Scholastic Books, 1959.

THE GREAT RAIDS

PEENEMUNDE

Air Commodore J Searby DSO DFC RAF (Rtd)

the nutshell press

ACKNOWLEDGEMENTS

The author gratefully acknowledges the help of the
following: Mr F. F. Lambert of the Public Record Office;
Messrs A. Williams, M. Willis and E. Hine of the Imperial
War Museum; and Group Captain E. Haslam of the Air
Historical Branch, Ministry of Defence.

He has made use of the following books in his research:
Rocket by Air Chief Marshal Sir Philip Joubert de la Ferte,
Hutchinson; *The Mare's Nest* by David Irving, Kimber;
The Strategic Bomber Offensive by Frankland and Butler;
Pathfinder by Air Vice-Marshal Bennett;
and *Bomber Squadrons of the R.A.F. and thier Aircraft*
by Philip Moyes, Macdonald.

Typeset by Chippenham Typesetting
in AM Plantin 10/12

Peenemunde by J. Searby

© Nutshell Press, 1978
© John Searby, 1978
First Published 1978
Published by The Nutshell Press
Citadel Works, Bath Road, Chippenham
Printed in Great Britain
by Picton Print, Chippenham, Wiltshire

ISBN 0902 633 473

THE GREAT RAIDS

The bomber aircraft was the supreme offensive weapon of the Second World War fulfilling the doctrine preached by Lord Trenchard, General Douhet and General Mitchell. With the release of the atomic bomb it reached its peak – and the conflict ended within hours of that catastrophe. In Europe the combination of Bomber Command and the American 8th Air Force overwhelmed the German opposition whose failure to create a similar strategic weapon capable of sustaining an all-out offensive spelt ultimate defeat. The fact that Germany ended the war with a strong fighter force capable of inflicting severe casualties could not change the march of events – even the most sophisticated fighter defence cannot achieve victory. Wars are won by offensive action only.

From the outbreak of the conflict until early 1943 Bomber Command of the Royal Air Force was virtually alone in maintaining the air offensive. The gathering strength of the United States complimented the nightly battles fought by the RAF until a point was reached where the united strength of the two strategic arms posed a threat which the enemy could no longer meet. The lessons learned by our airmen were closely studied by our American allies who lacked nothing in skill, courage and technical ability. Those of us who flew alongside the 8th Air Force will bear this out; in common with the Royal Air Force crews they fought and died bravely.

To maintain the offensive is a first principle of war: Bomber Command succeeded in doing so after the defeat of Dunkirk – continuing the fight night after night, week after week with no let-up. Lacking the electronic aids to navigation which were to come later, and using the stars and basic dead reckoning, the Wellingtons, Whitleys and Hampdens ranged far over Europe. From Stettin and Warsaw in the North to the Biscay ports in the South they gave the enemy no rest, dropping bombs on his industry and mining the estuaries and coastal waters frequented by his shipping. The pioneer crews of that era suffered great hardship – frostbite, enemy action and not infrequently dying from exposure in a frail rubber dinghy somewhere in the cold North Sea. Fourteen hours in a Hampden bomber on a winter's night was the lot of the crews who set out to destroy the oil storage depot lying outside Stettin and there are many similar stories, some of which will be recounted in this series.

With the advent of the powerful four-engined aircraft possessing a huge bomb capacity, great range and full radar equipment the pattern changed; new tactics embracing wave patterns and precise timing calculated to swamp defences plus the creation of a marker force were formulated. The main force crews following on behind the Pathfinders were relieved of the responsibility of identifying the actual aiming point and the kind of success which had for so long eluded even the most skilful and determined crews became possible: even so, the problem of seeing in the dark was not wholly solved. There were failures – a mistake by a marker crew could well wreck the night's work and make abortive the efforts of literally thousands of workers behind the scenes; the maintenance gangs, the armourers, the radar mechanics, safety workers and many more besides, to say nothing of the frustration of the hundreds of crews who, having battled their way across enemy territory suffered the frustration of knowing it had all gone for nothing when the Photo Recce Mosquito brought back the pictures the following day.

Whilst the bomber force was advancing its skills and increasing its strength so was the enemy improving and perfecting his defences. The expansion of his night-fighter force in 1943 increased our casualty rate – greater force – greater casualties – greater opposition. The illuminated target area, often a mass of searchlights and fires, became a battle ground when the engaging fighters used the fiery backdrop to silhouette the attacking bombers. Similarly, improved radar surveillance resulted in more and more interceptions both on the way in and out of the target area. Again, the equipping of the roving JU88 with search radar meant that once fed into the bombers' stream he could be sure of a kill and his upward firing twin cannon was sometimes the first warning of his presence.

We hope to bring you something of the atmosphere and the conditions familiar to the bomber boy; he has been described as somewhat dull compared with his fighter counterpart. Maybe so – but it was quite often a dull business. He needed the guts to sit it out for long hours at a time with occasional enemy attacks in the certain knowledge that at the target things would warm up and all his efforts might not save his crew. A young air gunner – on being asked what it was like modestly replied – "Oh, since you ask me, it was noisy, cold and uncomfortable!"

Contents

1   **Introduction**

7   **The Objective**

17   **Planning and Organisation**

19   **Note on Pathfinder Marking Techniques**

23   **Peenemunde**

29   **Order of Battle**

33   **The Men who Destroyed Peenemunde**

54   **Bomber Command Narrative of Operations**

79   **41 of Our Aircraft Failed to Return**

82   **Appendix 1 – Peenemunde Entry in Flight Log**

84   **Appendix 2 – Recommendation for Author's DSO**

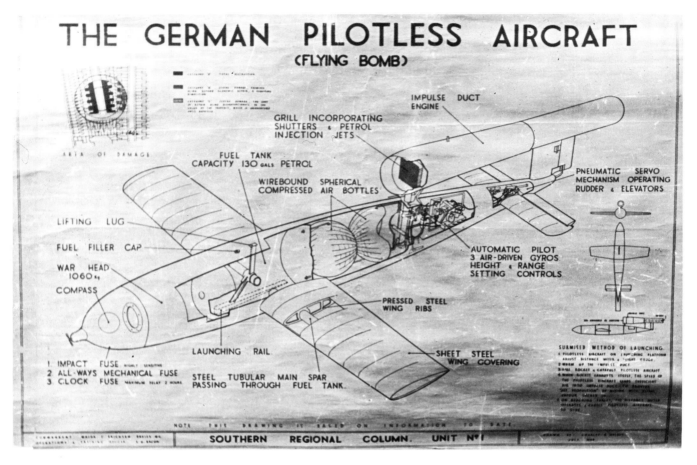

V1 Layout.

Introduction

The attack by six hundred aircraft of Bomber Command on the highly secret German Research Station of Peenemunde during the night of 17th/18th August 1943 was one of the most important and effective of the Second World War. The destruction of the laboratories, workshops and administrative complex represented a severe check to the enemy's advance in the field of rocket and pilotless aeroplane development; demolishing at a single blow his plans for a saturation onslaught calculated to destroy this country's will to continue the fight.

For those who are old enough to have witnessed the catastrophic result of the launching and strike of these weapons in the Summer of 1944 the havoc they wrought and the effect on the daily life and work of the Londoners require no emphasis. The little aeroplane approaching at high speed, some two to three thousand feet high, with its peculiar engine noise posed a savage threat: at the engine cut-off the nose would drop followed by a rapid dive and a thunderous explosion. Of the 9,000 fired against this country half were knocked down by aircraft and ground gunfire: of the remainder a large proportion fell in open country but the damage and loss of life resulting from the numbers which got through was truly grievous. Had the enemy realised his ambition of launching many thousand flying bombs daily vast areas of southern England would have been devastated and hundred of thousands killed or maimed. However, worse was to follow the V.1. programme and soon the great V.2. rockets came whistling down from the sky. They virtually came out of the blue; unheralded, plunging to earth with a shattering roar as the one ton warhead exploded on impact. Seemingly immune from all counter measures they spelt sudden and certain annihilation and became an object of terror to many.

Fortunately, the enemy did not possess any great quantity of rockets and his technique for launching was less than perfect. If he had his way both weapons would have been launched in great numbers on a specified day with a precision and timing which could have paralysed the life of the nation. He was unable to do this as a result of delay in the production schedule and uncertainties created over priorities in men and material whilst the Royal Air Force attack on his principle development station set him back by as much as six months. In a desperate attempt to wreak maximum harm with his available stocks following the D-Day landing the launchings commenced but had he been ready months earlier the whole course of the war might well have been altered.

During the build-up period preceeding Operation 'Overlord' vast numbers of men, ships, stores and weapons occupied an area of southern England stretching from Kent to Cornwall. Vulnerability to air attack was obvious but the enemy possessed no force comparable with our own Bomber Command and we enjoyed complete air supremacy by day over this sensitive terrain. However, attack by Hitler's V weapons from bases immediately across the Channel was a distinct possibility and such bases were already in course of preparation: photographic cover confirmed this, but his programme was far from complete. Many of the launching sites were only half built and the stocks of weapons totally inadequate for the task. Had it been otherwise both the build-up and launching of the invasion force would have been at risk twenty-four hours a day. With the harbours packed with troop transports and all kinds of shipping, from tank landing craft to destroyers and supply ships, the enemy was presented with juicy targets, but he was not ready and the opportunity could not be grasped. The weapons of which he had boasted so often could not be deployed and the chance was missed. D-Day came and went, the holocaust did not take place.

The story of the German V weaponry is a long one and this action, important though it proved, was but one in a series commencing with the first warning received, and we do not forget the work and sacrifice of the patriots who worked behind the enemy lines to get the vital information which set us on course. The gallant Poles who hid a V.2. assembly and finally got it away to England in the most dramatic circumstances, the secret agents who penetrated the Research Centre, the Photo Recce Spitfire and Mosquito pilots who flew over Peenemunde in broad daylight to obtain the essential cover, these and many others played a part.

The attack itself was well planned and executed. The targets lay more than six hundred miles from these shores and yet the first Pathfinder flares went down precisely on time and the show opened with a flood of light from the burning magnesium. The full moon flung the dark coast line into sharp relief and the creeping wall of smoke from the hundreds of protective canisters lining the western boundary of the airfield began to spread slowly, but it was too late. The enemy was caught with its pants down and the battle commenced. In the first phase we had it much our own way but as the minutes ticked by the bulk of the night fighter force arrived from the south, from the great city of Berlin which they had sought to protect from what they believed to be an assault of the first magnitude; but they had been tricked. Thus they arrived full of fury and determination to correct their mistake and a unique situation developed: as we watched bomber and fighter in combat set against the huge carpet of fire and explosions from the burning installations lying near the Baltic shoreline. For a full fifty minutes the bombs rained down and then the action ceased as the last wave of attackers turned for home. The show was over but it had cost us dear and the spurts of cannon fire from the pursuers continued until we were back among the many islands which occupy the Little Belt and Danish waters.

A V1 assembled from salvaged parts; these pictures were circulated to enable the public to recognise the weapon.

A V1 immediately after launching.

V1 assembly line at Nordhausen. Production planned for 50,000 first phase.

V1 storage after assembly.

Scrap!

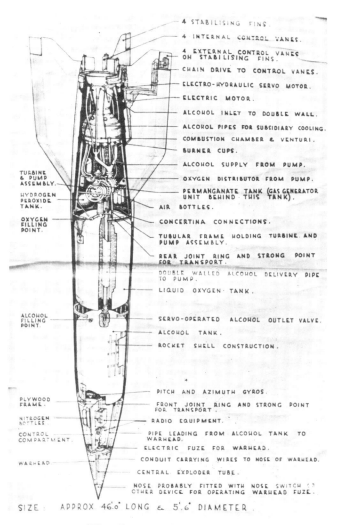

4 STABILISING FINS.
4 INTERNAL CONTROL VANES.
4 EXTERNAL CONTROL VANES ON STABILISING FINS.
CHAIN DRIVE TO CONTROL VANES.
ELECTRO-HYDRAULIC SERVO MOTOR.
ELECTRIC MOTOR.
ALCOHOL INLET TO DOUBLE WALL.
ALCOHOL PIPES FOR SUBSIDIARY COOLING.
COMBUSTION CHAMBER & VENTURI.
BURNER CUPS.
ALCOHOL SUPPLY FROM PUMP.
OXYGEN DISTRIBUTOR FROM PUMP.
PERMANGANATE TANK (GAS GENERATOR UNIT BEHIND THIS TANK).
AIR BOTTLES.
CONCERTINA CONNECTIONS.
TUBULAR FRAME HOLDING TURBINE AND PUMP ASSEMBLY.
REAR JOINT RING AND STRONG POINT FOR TRANSPORT.
DOUBLE WALLED ALCOHOL DELIVERY PIPE TO PUMP.
LIQUID OXYGEN TANK.

TURBINE & PUMP ASSEMBLY.
HYDROGEN PEROXIDE TANK.
OXYGEN FILLING POINT.

SERVO-OPERATED ALCOHOL OUTLET VALVE.
ALCOHOL TANK.
ROCKET SHELL CONSTRUCTION.

ALCOHOL FILLING POINT.

PITCH AND AZIMUTH GYROS.
FRONT JOINT RING AND STRONG POINT FOR TRANSPORT.
RADIO EQUIPMENT.
PIPE LEADING FROM ALCOHOL TANK TO WARHEAD.
ELECTRIC FUZE FOR WARHEAD.
CONDUIT CARRYING WIRES TO NOSE OF WARHEAD.
CENTRAL EXPLODER TUBE.
NOSE PROBABLY FITTED WITH NOSE SWITCH OR OTHER DEVICE FOR OPERATING WARHEAD FUZE.

PLYWOOD FRAME.
NITROGEN BOTTLES.
CONTROL COMPARTMENT.
WARHEAD.

SIZE: APPROX 46.0' LONG & 5.6' DIAMETER.

The Construction of a V2.

German test firing.

Production Line in an underground factory at Nordhausen in the Black Forest.

British Army trials – erecting a V2 on its stand prior to firing.

British Trials after capture of Peenemunde

"Lift-off"

6

The Objective

The highly secret research station of Peenemunde was set up in the mid-thirties in the sparsely populated and semi-wild coast line of Pomerania, amid pine forests and rolling sand dunes. Vast sums of money were expended in creating the best possible conditions for furthering the development of certain military projects dear to the heart of the German Staff. The star of Nazi Germany was rising fast whilst a somnolent Britain and France paid little heed to the thrusting ambitions of a people determined to wipe out the humiliation of defeat. The Treaty of Versailles, defining the size and types of equipment of the German armed forces, was rapidly becoming a mere piece of paper whilst the will and capacity of the former allies to enforce its conditions had weakened to a point where only a few voices were raised in protest. The body of scientists at Peenemunde, sponsored by highest authority and encouraged by shrewd chiefs of the three arms of the fighting services, worked with enthusiasm dedicated to the belief that their mission was vital to Germany's future. Their achievements remained a closely guarded secret and the name Peenemunde was not heard.

The study and development of rocket driven projectiles had occupied the minds of the military long before the outbreak of the Second World War and with the facilities provided by the new establishment in northern Pomerania the scientists, led by the able Werner von Braun, made considerable progress. By 1939 the development of a long range rocket was virtually complete and had the German government chosen to push forward production it is possible a useful stockpile of rockets bearing formidable war heads might have been ready after the German break through in May 1940. At this low in our fortunes the steady bombarding of these Islands from across the Channel could have been a powerful factor in reducing morale and the long-promised invasion might have got off to a good start. However, the success of German arms during the Autumn campaign in Poland had convinced the Fuhrer that final victory could be won without spending money on thousands of elaborate missiles, and the priority accorded Peenemunde in men, money, and steel was halved overnight. The delay, stemming directly from this decision, proved significant and with the man power shifted to other projects von Braun's rockets were pushed into the background.

Rivalry between the German Navy, Army and Air Force was a feature of life at the top: The Rocket programme was Army sponsored and cut across the bows of the Luftwaffe who viewed it with disfavour: their success during the Polish campaign and the advance to the Channel Ports, following the May breakthrough in 1940, had secured for them a unique position which Goering was unwilling to relinquish. Had this same success accompanied the Luftwaffe's onslaught on Britain during the fateful weeks of the air battle the rocket might well have faded entirely, but Goering failed to make good his boasts: the Luftwaffe

was beaten back and Hitler was disappointed. He looked elsewhere and the rocket offered an opportunity to restore the situation: accordingly priorities were reshuffled once again and, following a few successful launchings watched by Speer and Himmler, von Braun was back in favour with a mandate which guaranteed the necessary backing of men and materials. Despite failures the development work went forward and a production line was set up at Peenemunde and at Fredrichshafen on Lake Constance.

The German Air Force was not to be outdone. Somewhat belatedly they sponsored the development and trials of a pilotless aircraft, simple in design and far less costly to produce. This project was tested at Peenemunde and showed great promise. Unlike the rocket it relied on a petrol driven pulse engine as opposed to the costly fuels and sensitive rocket motors which hoisted the former into the sky. Carrying a similar quantity of high explosive it possessed a range of around one hundred and thirty miles; this was reckoned adequate since launchings would take place from selected sites on the French Channel Coast. It possessed certain obvious disadvantages in that a permanent ramp was necessary for launching, whilst it was capable of being intercepted and vulnerable to ground fire; radar detection was quite possible. The rocket could not be countered at that time and arrived without warning; on balance it achieved greater accuracy. Both systems continued under development and support for the rocket remained strong despite the cost; in German eyes it embraced an elegance and mystique placing it in the highest class of military weapons, symbolic of the national will to outstrip all comers. Together these two projects absorbed much of the capacity of the research station and security was well maintained until the frequency of launchings attracted attention and reports concerning the activity began to arrive in London. Gradually, in various ways and stemming from a variety of sources, the evidence began to mount and finally a series of flights by the photographic reconnaissance unit of the Royal Air Force established the facts.

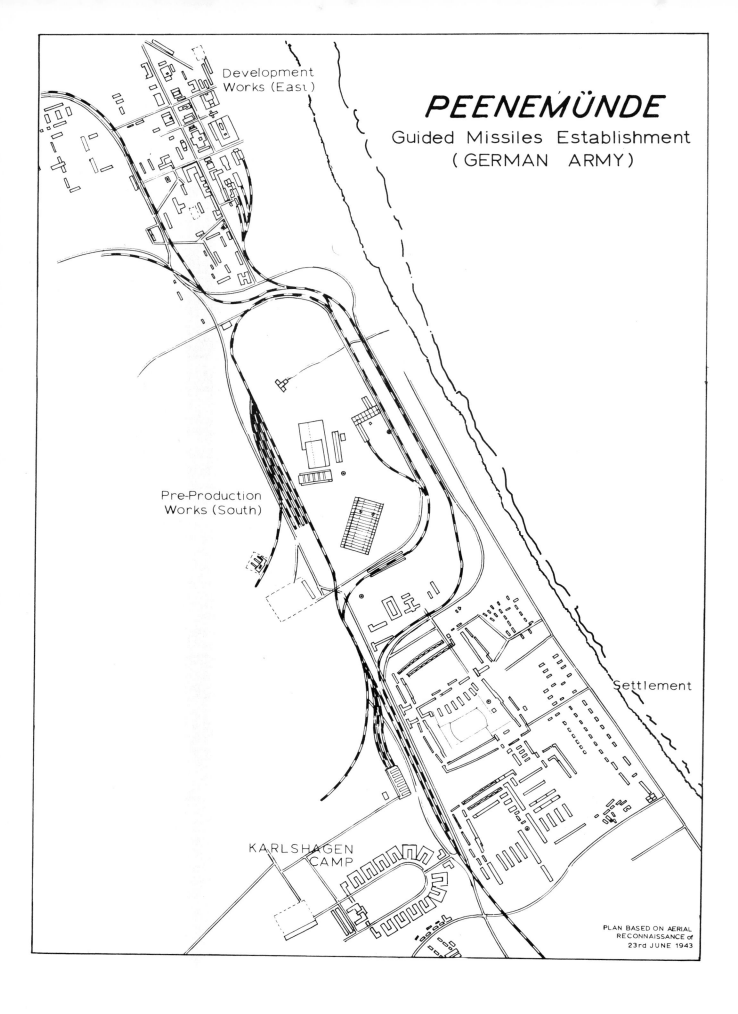

Development
Works (East)

PEENEMÜNDE
Guided Missiles Establishment
(GERMAN ARMY)

Pre-Production
Works (South)

Settlement

KARLSHAGEN
CAMP

PLAN BASED ON AERIAL
RECONNAISSANCE of
23rd JUNE 1943

8

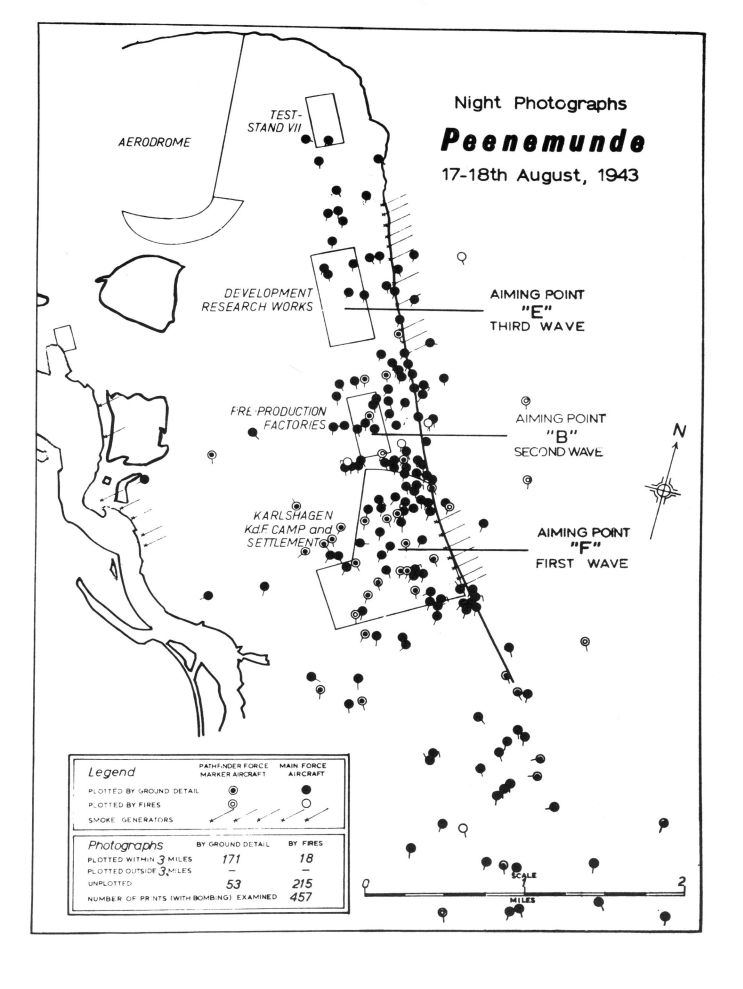

Night Photographs

Peenemunde

17–18th August, 1943

AERODROME

TEST-STAND VII

DEVELOPMENT RESEARCH WORKS

AIMING POINT "E" THIRD WAVE

FIRE-PRODUCTION FACTORIES

AIMING POINT "B" SECOND WAVE

KARLSHAGEN KdF. CAMP and SETTLEMENT

AIMING POINT "F" FIRST WAVE

N

Legend

	PATHFINDER FORCE MARKER AIRCRAFT	MAIN FORCE AIRCRAFT
PLOTTED BY GROUND DETAIL	◉	●
PLOTTED BY FIRES	◎	○
SMOKE GENERATORS	⚹ ⚹	⚹ ⚹

Photographs	BY GROUND DETAIL	BY FIRES
PLOTTED WITHIN 3 MILES	171	18
PLOTTED OUTSIDE 3 MILES	—	—
UNPLOTTED	53	215
NUMBER OF PRINTS (WITH BOMBING) EXAMINED	457	

0   SCALE   2
MILES

9

HOMES OF THE FLYING BOMBS: THE LAY-OUT C

DRAWN BY OUR

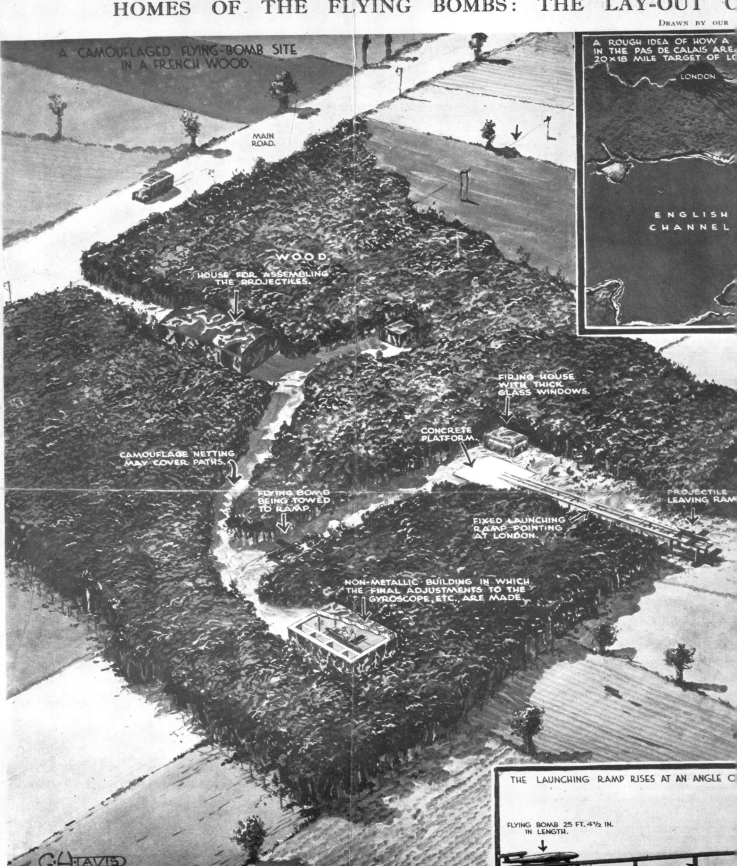

A CAMOUFLAGED FLYING-BOMB SITE IN A FRENCH WOOD.

MAIN ROAD.

WOOD.

HOUSE FOR ASSEMBLING THE PROJECTILES.

FIRING HOUSE WITH THICK GLASS WINDOWS.

CONCRETE PLATFORM.

CAMOUFLAGE NETTING MAY COVER PATHS.

FLYING BOMB BEING TOWED TO RAMP.

FIXED LAUNCHING RAMP POINTING AT LONDON.

PROJECTILE LEAVING RAMP

NON-METALLIC BUILDING IN WHICH THE FINAL ADJUSTMENTS TO THE GYROSCOPE, ETC., ARE MADE.

A ROUGH IDEA OF HOW A IN THE PAS DE CALAIS ARE 20×18 MILE TARGET OF LO

LONDON.

ENGLISH CHANNEL

THE LAUNCHING RAMP RISES AT AN ANGLE O

FLYING BOMB 25 FT. 4½ IN. IN LENGTH.

WOOD SUPPORTS CEMENTED INTO

G. H. DAVIS 1944

SOMETIMES CAMOUFLAGED AMONG WOODS, OR DISGUISED AS SMALL VILLAGES, THE LATEST LAUNCHIN

Our artist's drawing gives a general impression of the lay-out and appearance of the latest type of firing sites in Northern France from which the Germans launch their flying bombs at London. These sites are considerably more simple in design than the original heavily-built concrete installations, of which reconnaissance photographs and ground-level pictures appeared in the last two issues of "The Illustrated London News." In his survey of the new weapon, Mr. Churchill told the House of Commons on July 6 that 100 of these concrete

firing bases had been destroyed by the R.A.F. and the U.S.A.A.F. The simplified sites are usually situated in woods, where they are carefully ca flaged; and in some cases are disguised as small French villages in the ma shown in our drawing. In many instances they are designed to converg the 18-miles-by-20-miles target area presented by Greater London, the cours the flying bombs often crossing one another between launching bases and t The launching ramps, as can be seen in our drawing, are comparatively s

AUNCHING INSTALLATIONS IN NORTHERN FRANCE.

ST. G. H. DAVIS.

MBER OF LAUNCHING SITES
T POINTING AT THE GREAT

PAS DE CALAIS.

FRANCE.

A LAUNCHING RAMP CAMOUFLAGED INTO THE LAY-OUT OF A FRENCH VILLAGE.

ASSEMBLY HOUSE CAMOUFLAGED AS A FRENCH BARN.

FIRING HOUSE CAMOUFLAGED AS A FRENCH COTTAGE.

CONCRETE PLATFORM.

FINAL ADJUSTMENT BUILDING MADE TO LOOK LIKE AN ORDINARY HOUSE.

FLYING BOMB IN LAUNCHING POSITION.

LAUNCHING RAMP CAMOUFLAGED AT SIDE OF ROAD.

THE FLYING BOMB, LAUNCHED BY CATAPULT OR OTHER DEVICE, ON REACHING THE REQUIRED HEIGHT FOLLOWS A DIRECT COURSE, BEING CONTROLLED BY ITS GYROSCOPE. WINDAGE, HOWEVER, MAY DEFLECT IT FROM ITS TRUE COURSE.

ELY 7 DEGREES AND IS ABOUT 200 FT. IN LENGTH

GROUND LEVEL.

RE SIMPLIFIED VERSIONS OF THE ORIGINAL CONCRETE INSTALLATIONS DESTROYED BY ALLIED BOMBING.

construction. Built on ground level, they rise gradually at an angle of roximately 7 degrees for a distance of about 200 ft. from a concrete platform he rear to the take-off point at the front of the ramp. The buildings used assembly and control have also been simplified. They now usually consist a concrete Assembly House, to which the flying bombs are brought in sections assembly; an equally strong Final Adjustment Building, parallel with the p, to which the flying bombs are taken for the setting of the gyroscope and

other last-minute adjustments; and a concrete Firing House, with window-slits of very thick glass, from which the launching is controlled after the flying bomb has been towed from the Final Adjustment Building to the launching cradle, whence it is projected by catapult or other means. On leaving the ramp, the flying bomb (the R.A.F. permitting!) soars to a predetermined height, at which it levels off on a straight course—though strong winds may at times deflect it considerably, notwithstanding the gyro control governing its rudder and elevators.

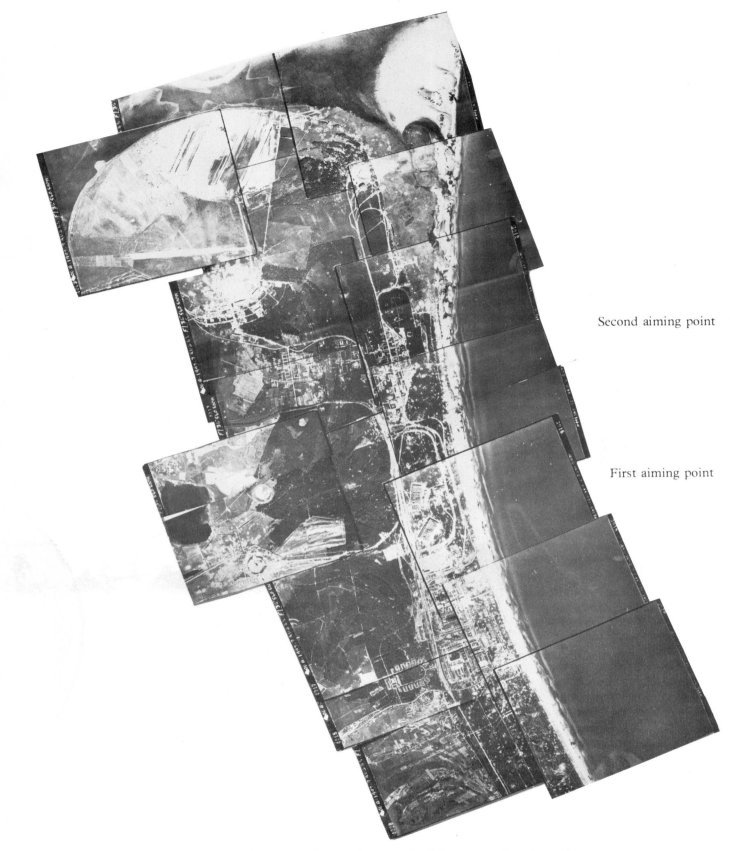

Second aiming point

First aiming point

A composite reconnaisance photograph of the target after the raid.

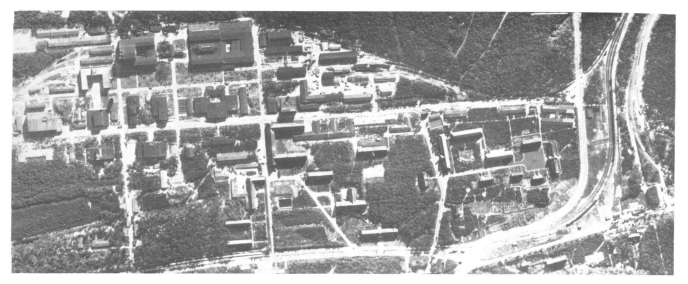

Peenemunde 17/18 August 1943. The main manufacturing and experimental section before and after the attack. A number of buildings are still on fire and throughout there is severe damage by fire and high explosive.

The small circle in the right-hand top corner is the V2 rocket launch pad. Firing trials were conducted in this area.

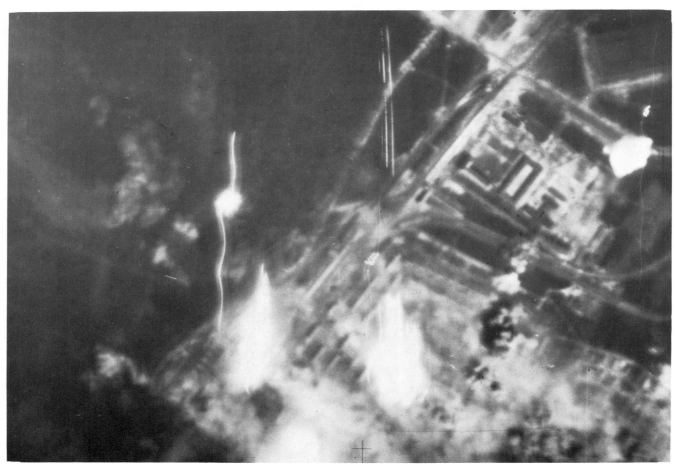

Rocket Factory . . . under attack.

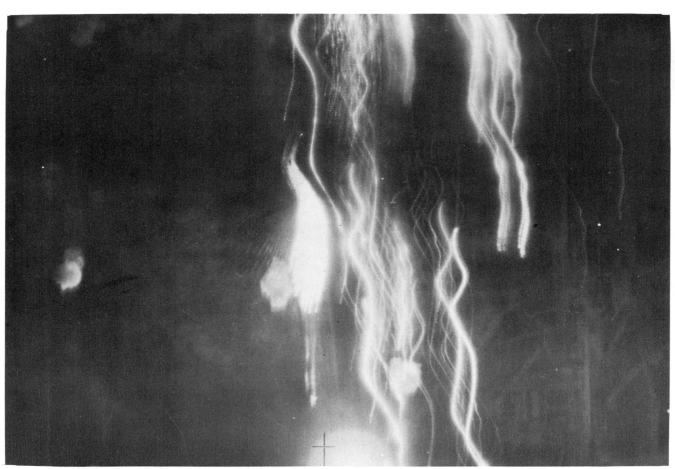

Night photo taken by a Lancaster camera with a long exposure – hence fire tracks.
Attacking bombers show up as faint shadows.

Development and Static Testing Area.

Main V2 launching area after attack. Note the high concentration of bomb craters.

This area was heavily bombed resulting in the death of many top-level scientists and engineers.

South Labour Camp – heavy destruction.

Planning and Organisation

The selection of the target for the night was the direct responsibility of the Commander in Chief, Air Chief Marshall Sir Arthur Harris, following the various directives emanating from the Chief of the Air Staff. These directives were changed from time to time as the necessity arose but in all cases the decision to launch the Bomber Force rested with Sir Arthur Harris. No bomber aircraft took off for Germany save with the authority of the Commander-in-Chief.

It was customary for the daily planning conference to take place early in the day with the C-in-C present. At this meeting he would review the priorities and the weather situation: he would be informed of the numbers of aircraft at readiness and all incidents affecting the operational capability of the Command were brought to his notice. The decision to attack a particular target was made after a careful examination of all relevant factors: weather over the target area might well be forecast as excellent but conditions for the return to the base airfields were of equal importance and it was, on occasions, no simple matter to strike a balance. Rarely was a straightforward decision possible: pressure was some times brought to bear to attack or arguments advanced as to the necessity for striking 'targets of fleeting opportunity' but Sir Arthur never wavered. Bomber Command went into battle only when he had satisfied himself that the Force could be landed safely, either on the home bases or at diversion airfields in areas of clear weather. This latter system operated most efficiently and all aircraft were informed of weather conditions for the return by means of the half hourly broadcast by W/T from the respective Group Headquarters.

Once the targets had been selected the Command Operations Staff set to work. The numbers of bombers required from each Group were determined and the route planning began taking into account all latest information concerning enemy ground defences and fighter strength. 'H' hour for the opening of the attack and the wave timing were worked out: the numbers involved necessitated careful separation between groups or waves of bombers to avoid the risk of collision. Other details such as the type of bomb load and the heights of successive 'waves' were passed via the teleprinter in coded form. The Pathfinder Force Commander was consulted as to the method of marking the target and after this had been agreed and details worked out his Staff would issue a separate notice to all main force groups acquainting them of the procedure.

Whilst the preliminary moves were under way each Group HQs was informed verbally over a secure telephone line of the nature of the target and the number of aircraft required. Confirmation in the shape of the Command 'A' form went out over the teleprinter within the hour detailing the route and bomb loads, wave timing with bombing height and any special instructions. By then the many stations involved would be aware that 'Ops' were on and commence bringing aircraft to readiness. No time was lost in getting the show going; there was much to be done before the loaded bombers arrived at the take-off point and the maintenance gangs worked like fury to get the aeroplanes fully serviceable. Later, in the course of the morning the 'B' Form, despatched from Group arrived, containing every essential piece of information necessary to the fulfilment of the task and formed the basis of the crew briefing probably set for the early afternoon.

In addition to the normal distribution of the Command orders for the night there were certain formations outside Bomber Command who needed to know what was afoot. For instance, the Royal Navy conducting coastal convoys along the East Coast had to be aware of the time and point of departure of the bomber stream as it left the English coast. Always sensitive to the possibility of air attack they took no chances and in the darkness they could not distinguish between friendly and hostile aircraft and unless they were forewarned would fire first and ask questions afterwards. Again, Fighter Command whose duty it was to guard this country from enemy attack received notice; their night fighter squadrons patrolled often from dusk to dawn and the routing-in of the homecoming bombers was essential information if accidents were not to take place. This was most unlikely but the risk could not be accepted. Coastal Command controlling the fast Air/Sea Rescue launches was alerted and their boats stood by until the operation was concluded. We had great confidence in the ASR organisation and it was a comfort to know they were at hand if necessary. The American 8th Air Force was given the information: they were spread alongside over the flat East Anglian countryside and shared our air space; there must be no possibility of a loaded bomber colliding with a Flying Fortress. There were others on the distribution list but these were among the most important.

On the bomber airfields the routine was well established. Immediately the target was made known all outgoing calls of a private nature was stopped. The identity of the target was known only by the Station Commander, the two Squadron Commanders and the Intelligence Section responsible for preparing the details concerning the enemy defences, information relating to the layout of factories, machine shops and any special features: up to the minute information on the move of enemy night fighter squadrons along the route and in the target vicinity together with reports of any new types of equipment operated by the Germans. The location of 'dummies' and similar moves by the enemy to draw the attack away from the actual target was all contained in the Intelligence brief for the night and communicated at the crew briefing before take-off.

Squadron and Flight Commanders were active. Out on the dispersal areas no effort was spared to produce the quota of bombers plus a reserve. The aircraft were surrounded by a variety of servicing vans, oxygen trailers and fuel tankers: fitters clung to the engine nacelles, radio mechanics and instrument specialists checked and rechecked for faults, armourers were servicing the gun turrets and working inside the long bomb bays examining switches and bomb crutches before starting to haul up the four thousand pounders and incendiary bombs: photographic workers fitted the night cameras, testing the operation of the small shutter beneath the belly which exposed to view the impact point of the bursting bombs: the Safety workers, responsible for the operation of the crew dinghy tucked inside the starboard mainplane, which released automatically when the bomber 'ditched', checked the hydrostatic switches and all gear relating to survival. There were others too with important tasks to perform and over all stood the technical Flight Sergeant – the key man and invariably the coolest. His job was one of providing his Flight Commander with the eight Lancasters or Halifaxes demanded and it was rare indeed for him to fail in this respect. Occasionally, there were serious problems and fingers were kept crossed until one looked out of the window to see eight Lancasters on the line; fully serviced, bombed-up and ready with a full hour to go before take-off. 'Chiefy' had pulled it off once again. Winter and Summer, in fair weather and foul, the maintenance staffs slogged away, never in the limelight and content to see their own particular crews taxying back along the perimeter track after a successful sortie over enemy country.

A quick meeting between the Squadron Commander and his two Flight Commanders results in the Squadron Battle Order for the night. Sometimes it is not a matter of choosing – if casualties have been heavy – and the muster can be made up without discussion. Again, if the Squadron is 'fat' certain crews may be rested following a succession of seven and eight hour sorties over the past few days. They will be called the next time – maybe within twenty-four hours but until then they may take the day off. Curiously, this was not a popular move: irritation, frustration and wondering what the hell was happening to the others overrode any feeling of pleasure and one saw young officers,

who might well have taken the opportunity to leave the Station sitting in the Mess Ante Room – moody and staring our of the windows unable to make up their minds as to how to spend the free time. The old hands virtually refused to be left out, preferring to go into battle with the rest and unwilling to break the continuity – when the luck was running for them.

In winter a six o'clock take-off was common and briefing took place immediately after lunch – some times with no more than two hours to go before take-off. In the Summer months with the short nights take-off was late – usually around nine or even ten o'clock – so that briefing was held back until the evening. This could be agonising for those who dwelt on the possibility of this or that happening though no one ever suspected and the attitude of most was casual – even indifferent–playing cricket to while away the time or reading in their rooms. It was their own affair and privacy was respected. Knowing the show was on, since early morning, it was a long long wait to get into the air and on with the job: The harsh voice on the Tannoy, calling all crews to report to Flights, came as a relief. After take-off one was too busy to think of anything but the immediate task.

On the day of the Peenemunde attack briefing was late. Crews were not permitted to leave the Station or communicate with any one via the telephone box near the Guardroom – security was tight: they were in possession of the target details and there could be no leaks. For some this was a miserable wait for action; for others an opportunity to read and write letters. After a time one became used to it and it must be borne in mind that in some instances bomber crews were out over Germany four and even five nights a week. The contrast between the relative comfort of the home airfield and the battle over the target, with a two or three hour slog back to the coast, was sharp yet we reckoned ourselves better placed than our countrymen in the other two services and no one would have changed places.

Marshal of the Royal Air Force Lord Trenchard (right) visits Wyton after the destruction of Peenemunde, with him in the picture are Group Captain Searby (centre) and the Group Doctor Wing Commander John McGown who flew many sorties with the group.

18

Note on Pathfinder Marking Techniques

From early 1943 onwards the Pathfinder Force adopted standard marking techniques designed to exploit fully the potential of the new radar systems – notably, the ground-controlled 'Oboe' marking and the airborne H2S scanning equipment. The former was more accurate and freed the aircrew from set-manipulation since the actual release point was signalled to the aircraft by the ground operator: in this fashion a distinctive target marker bomb was placed with great precision on the planned objective. The following main force aircraft aimed directly at the mark resulting in a bomb pattern which virtually swamped the target. By this means the vast Krupps complex of machine shops, foundrys, asembly plants and loading bays was destroyed: the genius of British Scientists had triumphed over the old old problem of 'seeing in the dark' and, one by one, the Ruhr cities were flattened and production ground to a halt.

It is rare for any method to achieve absolute perfection and there were attendant disadvantages to the use of this weapon: only a small number of Mosquitoes could be accepted by the equipment and it was essential for a number of 'Backers-Up' to be on hand to keep the pot boiling by showering down large numbers of additional markers, thus maintaining the marking until the next Mosquito arrived when the whole process was repeated. It should be noted that with the arrival of each fresh 'Oboe'-controlled aircraft the marking was brought back to the same precise spot and in theory no accumulated error developed.

Since the projection of the radio wave lay tangential to the earth's curvature range was limited: 'Oboe' was good for the Ruhr targets but useless at greater distances from the transmitting stations in Southern England. Nevertheless, it filled an important role in the bomber offensive and the high flying Mosquito Squadrons of the Pathfinder Force rendered great service over the two and a half years during which it was employed. They received little publicity since the nature of their work was one of the most closely guarded secrets of the whole war yet in all attacks on these relatively close (and very hotly defended) targets such as Essen they were in the forefront of the battle. So much for 'Oboe'.

In the early days of the P.F.F. when endeavouring to mark targets at long distances from this country we were equipped with nothing more than the traditional basic means for establishing the aircrafts position namely, deduced reckoning based on vectors or, in simple terms, the solving of the triangle of velocities: to this we added the refinement of celestial navigation measuring the star's altitude through the eye piece of the 'bubble-sextant'. Under good conditions of level flight and a clear sky the resulting 'sight' could establish a position within a few miles of the correct location. On the broad Atlantic, when ferrying aircraft from Newfoundland to Prestwick, it worked very well – given fair weather and in those days of few radio aids it was part of the drill. Careful preparation before take off, a sound understanding of the method and confidence in oneself made for a three star 'fix' within the limits of accuracy defined above. The high degree of accuracy achieved by the Marine navigator measuring the altitude with a brass sextant sighted on the sea horizon and with a stable platform under his feet was beyond the reach of the air navigator. Quite apart from the miserable conditions – cold, discomfort, cramped space and an unstable aircraft – the limitations of the bubble for obtaining a true level – and the wallowing motion, however slight but inherent in all aeroplanes, increased the size of the problem. Add to all this the undesirability of maintaining straight and level flight over enemy territory, whilst the navigator held the elusive star in the bubble chamber for the prescribed two minutes, and his difficulties may be understood. Even so, we made use of the stars on the long sorties to the Baltic and on those deep penetrations to southern Germany and Italy which provided plenty of time and opportunity for an improvident navigator to lose himself. Few did so, and in the Pathfinder Force, provided at the outset with some of the best crews in the command very high standards were maintained. Later, when due to a reluctance of some of the Main Force Groups to send us similar material we had to accept second best, the possession of the new radars partly compensated for lack of skill and experience in some of the crews.

Having arrived in the target area using these basic methods, identification of the objective could only be achieved by the naked eye. In this situation the release of powerful magnesium flares, hanging pendulous in the night sky for two minutes or more, enabled the Aiming Point Marker Crew to identify and mark. These latter crews were the creme de la creme of the P.F.F. and though not always successful gained great credit. After identifying the mark it was necessary to pull off and make a steady run-in to drop the Aiming Point Flare: the whole procedure demanding precision, skill and patience of a high order. The enemy would not be idle, meantime, and his searchlights and heavy anti aircraft guns would do their level best to knock one out of the sky. The strength of the wind at altitude would carry the parachute flares quickly away from the target area so that the persevering Pathfinder crew would need to work fast in their struggle to mark the objective: the knowledge that maybe hundreds of main force bombers were hard on their tails gave an extra fillip to the exercise.

The airborne H2S radar greatly reduced the time and effort described above though this did not happen overnight; there were periods of doubt and no lack of arm chair critics but Bennett, who had great faith in the equipment, encouraged his crews to use every minute of their spare time on the ground in attempting to master the techniques of matching the positive outline of the photograph with the bewildering mish-mash of reflected signals on the H2S screen. Coast lines showed up clearly, and many similar features, where contrast assisted identification, but to separate out the desired objective from the apparent confusion presented by scanning a large city drove some to fury. Like most things the difficulties were surmounted and subsequent improvements in the design of this 'black box' rewarded the faith and patience of the operators.

At the time of the Peenemunde operation we had made great strides, the fact that the area was to be illuminated by 'blind markers' proves the point. Their function was one of releasing yellow flares solely on the authority of the H2S picture – as being more reliable method than trusting the human eye – and the little peninsula on which the targets were situated had a pronounced shape – 'sticks out like a sore thumb' was the general comment.

We believed at the time that Peenemunde was the ideal target in terms of radar echoes, not only is the peninsula itself quite distinctive, providing good contrast between land and water, but the small islet of Ruden lay almost due north of the run of targets; a precisely timed run from the moment the aircraft crossed it to the first aiming point would give us a degree of insurance rarely encountered in other work. The radar experts assured us somewhat gleefully that this pimple set in the sea would stand out well on the screen and thus we should have both 'belt and braces' to secure a precision attack. Alas, the returning echoes were weak and some crews failed altogether to pick up the datum on their sets. This was an example of the vagaries of radar, and it happened occasionally in near-perfect conditions. During the first phase of the attack it certainly

contributed to a displacement of the bombing pattern.

In the light of the flares and yellow markers dropped by the first arrivals the Visual Markers went to work, aided by the full moon and the presence of the clearly discernible coast line. Their red markers were steadily 'backed up' by a team of Pathfinders dropping green target indicators and bombs: this was always the rule and no bomb hook remained empty. Thus, the attack built-up until the allotted time for the first target had expired when a new category of marker arrived on the scene – the aiming point shifter – who bore the responsibility for switching the full weight of the onslaught to the next objective. He did this by means of a special setting on his Mark XIV bombsight and it worked like a charm. A similar procedure was enacted for the third objective.

It is apparent that the marking sequence discussed above demanded precise timing. In the Pathfinder Force of Bomber Command a tolerance of ten seconds was the maximum permitted! Considering the distances we flew to some of these far flung objectives in those days this may seem a little tight but the combination of Blind Illuminators, Visual Markers, Backers up and Aiming Point Shifters demanded the highest precision if the Flight Plan and Marking Procedure for the night was to be successful. In the last month of the war more than a thousand heavy aircraft were led successfully by the P.F.F. to distant targets previously immune from attack: the steady pounding of heavily defended centres of industry was made possible through the skill and devotion of the crews, working out their sixty sorties and obeying the unofficial Pathfinder motto – *Press on Regardless*.

F/L Frank Forster, DFC, DFM, RAAF, flight engineer. This officer was responsible, together with Ross the bomb aimer for correcting mistakes in the marking procedure.

F/L George Ross, DFC bomb aimer whose experience and skill contributed greatly to the success of the operation (he was subsequently killed during the Battle of Berlin).

No 83 Pathfinder Squadron, RAF Wyton, August 1943.

No 83 Pathfinder Squadron.

Master Bomber Crew.   (F/L G. Coley absent)

| F/L Forster, | F/L Davies, | S/L N. Scrivener, | G/C Searby, | F/L Ross, | F/O Preece, |
| DFC, DFM | DFC | DSO, DFC | DSO, DFC | DFC | CGM, DFM |

S/L John Manton, G/C Searby DSO, DFC, S/L Ambrose-Smith DSO, DFC

Peenemunde *Written by* Air Commodore J. H. Searby, DSO, DFC, RAF (Rtd).

"If you don't knock out this important target tonight it will be laid on again tomorrow and every night until the job is done". The significance of these words were not lost on the Pathfinder Crews assembled in No. 83 Squadron briefing room on the afternoon of 17th August 1943. To return to a target on successive nights meant stiffer defences and heavier casualties. Once the element of surprise was gone no one could say how much effort and how many lives might be required to take out Peenemunde: we know now that the Germans would have gone to extraordinary lengths to protect this great Research and Development Station on the Baltic Coast. Having shown our hands with a first abortive attempt the Nazis would take steps to move out much vital equipment together with the Scientists and Technicians. In short, the moment would have passed and might never occur again.

The Pathfinder Crews could not know the nature of this target for the secret had been well kept. Don Bennett, our Air Vice Marshal, may have known but certainly Mr. Duncan Sandys, standing at the back of the briefing room knew a great deal since he had been given the task of uncovering the German plans for rocket attacks on this Country: hence his appearance at the Squadron briefing that evening.

From the low dais in front of the large map of Europe, with its coloured tapes and pins which marked the heavily defended areas of occupied territory, I watched the faces of my crews. They were impressed by the urgency, but not worried, for the job would be done to the best of their ability. I caught the eye of Brian Slade, veteran Pathfinder Captain at Twenty-one years of age, and he grinned; he was all for it. Against the background of Essen, Berlin, Hamburg, Munich, Cologne and similar bloodbaths Peenemunde did not, at this stage, make much impression. In fact, the reactions of the crews was one of relief at the prospect of a sortie to Northern Germany. The only real hazard lay in the long penetration under conditions of full moonlight with the possible increased fighter activity. No one had heard of this insignificant pimple sticking out of Pomerania and there was nothing humdrum about the operation. Hence Brian's smile. Alas, he would be lost over the Big City (Berlin) in five short days time. A most courageous young Officer in all he undertook, only a few days earlier he had had occasion to 'feather' one engine soon after take off for Germany but had continued to the target, marked it, and returned, on his remaining three engines.

Over the past weeks No. 83 Pathfinder Squadron had been fortunate and our losses had been light. The crews were mostly experienced Pathfinders and on this particular afternoon the Squadron Battle Order listed some exceptional men. The average age was around twenty-five although one or two were in their early thirties. Guy Sells, graduate of two Universities in England and Germany – quiet of speech and with a marked aversion to anything in the nature of drama – was one of the most experienced. Squadron Leader Ambrose Smith and Wing Commander John Manton with Norman Hildyard would lead the early marking: Maurice Chick, Archie Cochrane, Norman Scrivener, King, Mason, Turp, Finding, Thompson with young Reid and Shipway completed the list of Captains. Norman Scrivener, small of stature and with more than a hundred heavy bomber sorties behind him had been my navigator for some time: his role tonight was a vital one for he had to get the aircraft to the target alone and ahead of all the others with precisely five minutes in hand. We would need this to complete our survey of the aiming points before the real show started. Of these men, Turp, Manton, Cochrane and Reid would disappear with their crews in the next few weeks to lose their lives over Germany. The gentle and brave Archie Cochrane had been my friend for many years: he displayed the utmost in loyalty and determination to get his bomber to the target when he might, with honour, have turned back. King, a fine Australian boy would be killed before the end of the year taking with him my own Bomb Aimer, George Ross – the same who would be with me tonight for this assault on Peenemunde. The Gunnery Leader S/Ldr 'Johhny' Johnson was flying: he was to survive a hundred sorties. These were some of the men and the passing of years has not dimmed their image.

On the previous day, together with my crew, I had studied a model of the target together with Don Bennett and his Staff. This model, beautifully constructed, was the result of taking photographs from our Reconnaissance aircraft some time earlier. We endeavoured to memorise certain features which lay near the three aiming points and discussed with Bennett the essential features. We did not know any more than that this was an experimental station. Bennett gave good advice: his reputation for thoroughness, his record and intimate knowledge of our work more than qualified him. Envy of Bennett's rapid rise was never justified, in my opinion; his drive and enthusiasm coupled with his outstanding knowledge of all aspects of navigation made him the right man for the job. Men will always follow a leader who is able instantly to step into the aircraft and do the job as well and better than they. He was not alone, the Royal Air Force possessed many war leaders of similar calibre.

The plan for the night's operations was well conceived and in the course of the briefing I acquainted the crews of the fact that Mosquitoes of No. 139 Squadron would make a 'spoof' attack on Berlin with the object of holding the German night fighters in that region, or at least a proportion of them. By the time the ruse was discovered many fighters would require to refuel before proceeding to the scene of the actual attack. Clearly, we could not hope for this plan to do more than delay the opposition but if it worked long enough to enable the Pathfinders and following waves of heavy bombers to make an effective start on the destruction of the target much would have been accomplished. The full moon was at once a friend and an enemy. It would help the bombers initially but on balance it would serve the cause of the German night fighters even more: with so much light there would be scope for the free lance or 'catseye' fighter and this would greatly increase the strength of the opposition.

Our route lay across the North Sea to Denmark and we would fly at a low altitude to avoid alerting the German radar system. Nearing Denmark the Bombers would climb quickly to a medium altitude and pass the narrow land mass North of the Island of Sylt into the confined waters of the Little Belt; then across Kiel Bay into the Baltic. In the early stages the main threat would come from the fighter defences in the Hamburg – Kiel – Lubeck areas. If early warning of our approach were received from the big Freyas, or radar screens, these fighters would rise like a cloud of hornets and tear into the mass of heavily laden bombers. Similarly those fighters based on Berlin would, once our objective was confirmed, speed northwards. Between the two something approaching a massacre might take place in the moonlight. Around Kiel and some of the cities on the coast there would be heavy flak defences and searchlights and the usual spread of light anti-aircraft guns on headlands and islands. One thing more, the Germans would already know that a large force was going to the Continent from their excellent wireless intelligence which collected and analysed every scrap of information. Much activity necessarily takes place on bomber bases during the time before an operation is launched; from radio testing and other sources it would be possible to estimate the size of the attack in preparation. The Germans would not, however, know the time or the place at which it would strike.

The briefing over, all crews returned to their Messes for a meal and at eight o'clock were dressed and ready to go out to the dispersal points where the Lancasters stood ready. This was the final moment in the long programme of preparation. This was a time for something to go wrong – an aircraft unserviceable perhaps: ground crews had toiled to haul the bombs from the fusing points to load them in the long bomb bays: radio, radar and electrical circuits had been checked and rechecked. Petrol, oil and oxygen had been fed into the wings and fuselages, magnesium flares placed in the flare chutes, hydraulic systems release mechanisms and safety devices examined, guns loaded and turrets swung, bombsights and controls checked, flight rations put aboard and many more essential services performed. It was a matter of personal pride with our ground airmen that the Lancasters were supremely fit to go into battle and as spotless as time and circumstances would permit.

I saw my crews away and then climbed into the vehicle with my own crew to go out to Lancaster William. I can remember Chick and his merry men departing, laughing as usual because with Chick around nothing could be serious for long. They were clutching the odds and ends of their various trades, the two gunners huge in their padded suits. I waved to Chick and set out. 'W' William stood on the far side of 'B' Flight dispersal area. It was a fine evening, warm and pleasant, the sun about to set and the long twilight beginning: a time for the river pub down at the Ferry where No. 83 Squadron foregathered. I suppose there will never again be gatherings quite like that and to

recapture the atmosphere is impossible: all was warmth and friendliness with much laughter. Tommy Blair, doyen of Pathfinder Navigators, red faced and of powerful build, waving his tankard in time to the singing – a striking personality and in his own way a tremendous factor for morale – but this was no evening for the Ferryboat Inn.

'W' William was ready – we were ready. Our part to control the bombing over the full forty-five minutes of the Bomber Command attack and stay with it. Two Deputy Master Bombers had been appointed and in the event of our being shot down they would take over in turn. Johnny Fauquier of No. 405 Squadron was first Deputy and John White of No. 156 Squadron the other; both very experienced Bomber Captains. Fauquier, a tough Canadian was an old friend and a fine leader. Our pre-flights checks completed we prepared for take-off. At the prearranged hour Frank Forster pressed the starter buttons and the four Merlins came to life. We would set out five minutes ahead of the others in order to have time to make a run across the targets and verify the landmarks we had noted the day previously.

We taxied past the Squadron dispersals and got a wave from the crews, then turned into wind at the runway threshold. A quick brake check, flaps to take off setting; and Frank moved the four throttle levers slowly forward: the Merlins thundered out their full power and Lancaster William moved easily at increasing speed up the wide runway. This was the moment, when one forgot the worry, the anxieties and stress of the day's pressing sequence – keep her straight – tail coming up – airspeed building up and suddenly the jarring and roughness ceases: easily, beautifully, the great Lancaster leaves the ground with her burden of men, bombs and equipment. "Wheels up" – "Wheels up Skipper" and the Flight Engineer moves the undercarriage lever. Now the drag is less and she gathers speed, being held in level flight for a few seconds until the far runway lights flash past and we fly out into the twilight. "Flap in" – "Flap in Skipper".

"Climbing power" – "Climbing power Skipper" and Frank sets the throttles to plus six boost and the revs to twenty six fifty. For a moment he balances out the pitch controls until all four propellers are running evenly – checking pressures and temperatures.

"Navigator to Captain – course 0 six five degrees" and at one thousand feet we level out, reducing power to cruising revs. The time is 9 p.m. precisely. Behind me as we head for the Norfolk coast six hundred bombers are leaving the ground in grand procession, bound for Peenemunde. In eight hours time we hope to return. Already, the full moon is rimming the Eastern horizon. The North sea is calm below and after one hour and twenty minutes we alter course to due East to make a landfall on the Island of Romo just off the mainland.

Height is reduced to two hundred feet for the next thirty minutes to give the watchful Germans no radar warning of our approach. We look out sharply for the German fishing craft which are equipped with radio, and the gunners maintain unceasing watch from the rear and dorsal turrets. This kind of vigilance will be needed whatever we are doing for the full time we are away from the English coast – the Bomb Aimer looking ahead from his nose position, Frank and I watching above the nose and on the beam – the radio operator looking through the astro hatch when he can get away from his set and the gunners covering all the sky astern above and below on the beam. We are weaving the aircraft gently so that as she swings the gunners can see directly below, and once we are up to the higher altitude I shall increase the swing into a full blooded corkscrewing movement calculated to confuse the radar equipped night fighter as he searches for us with his electronic eye. This corkscrew is sickmaking after long periods and calls for considerable effort at the controls if done properly but it has stood No. 83 Squadron in very good stead and all my Captains swear by it. We think this tactic is, in part, responsible for our low losses and although we have our critics outside the Pathfinder force – the "George In to the target boys" I am not disturbed. Norman our Navigator sees nothing outside the aircraft because he is working away behind his curtains – behind his blackout in fact. His task is an onerous one and he leaves his cubby hole only at intervals to take a sight with his sextant through the perspex Astro hatch. Over the defended areas he has a bad time – hearing everything but bound to concentrate on his essential duties. ('Scriv' can be very bad tempered sometimes if asked what he deems to be an unnecessary question which breaks his thought processes). This is a different world from that of the marine navigator – discomfort, cramped and often bitterly cold the air navigator in a Bomber Command aircraft must work swiftly and accurately because in a matter of minutes the aircraft travels so far that we may be heading into a heavily defended area: and, of course, we are doing the sick-making corkscrewing all the time. In the Pathfinder force tolerances are small and after flying for just under four hours with no outside aids to navigation we must mark the target within seconds of the planned 'H' hour: bearing in mind that there are hundreds of aircraft behind in a great mass which leaves no room for manoeuvre or delay.

More than two hours after leaving Wyton we see the shadowy outline of Romo and the mainland; Sylt with its fighters lies just to the South of us. Here and there we see small points of light but the blackout in Denmark is rigidly enforced and these lights are burned deliberately – often as markers for German fighter aircraft. The aircraft is at four thousand feet and slightly nose down to increase speed over the enemy held mainland. The moon is now very bright and Ross is down in the nose checking on the coast line. He is always the first to see the A.A. guns open up and will give immediate warning so that I can 'jink' the aircraft to avoid the bursting shells. During the time it takes for the shell to travel to our altitude we can get out of the way. George Ross was a school teacher in civilian life and he wears large spectacles; at first I found him very shy but he rapidly overcame this and has proved an outstanding bomb aimer. He is to lose his life after sixty heavy bomber sorties over Germany.

The enemy is well and truly alerted by this time and all over North Germany the night fighters will be scrambling off their airfields. A big raid is on its way, but it appears to them that this is not the main attack for the night, which seems to be Berlin. In fact the Mosquito Spoof raid began crossing Denmark more than an hour ago and has already convinced the enemy that the German capital is about to take another pasting. Everything is ordered to Berlin to defend the city but all this information is not known to us as we fly over the sea and commence to alter course to starboard for the final leg which will take us to the Island of Rugen, lying to the North West of Peenemunde. In the moonlight I can see the whitewashed cottages on the Southern tip of Langeland. The exhaust stubs of the Merlins glow redly and we feel pretty well naked: many eyes are now watching us – enemy eyes – and our aircraft must stick out like a sore thumb since we are ahead of the main body by several minutes.

"Navigator to Captain – five minutes to Rugen Island when we alter course to one seven 0 degrees".

To my disappointment I observe a sheet of cloud ahead but on closer inspection it proves to be higher than at first estimated and I can fly beneath it easily, keeping the Island in sight. Shortly after this we are over the tip of Usedom on which Peenemunde is located. In the bright moonlight we fly close to the objective, and Ross, Forster, Scrivener and I take a close look at that which so far we have only seen as a model. It is all there – the airfield at the tip and the Development Station spreading along the coast on the East side. We run directly down the line of buildings and check off one by one the important features. Hundreds of smoke canisters are commencing to belch out fumes and the wind from off the sea is carrying the smoke across the target area. This could be serious. In succession we pass over the three aiming points – the development factory – the rocket assembly plant and the large living site where the German workers and technical staffs are housed. "Light flak opening up Skipper" from Ross. The green and red shells shoot past the aircraft and we turn out to sea where in the moonlight I observe two ships anchored. As we near them they open up with both light and heavy flak but the shooting is poor and the aircraft is in no danger at present. We pull away to the North and stand off a short distance from the coast. With two minutes to go before 'H' hour, when the heavy bombing would commence, we waited for the preliminary marking of the target to begin. The method selected for the night was one of first illuminating the whole area with powerful flares dropped by the first Pathfinders using their radar equipment; they would use the tiny Island of Ruden as a datum point from which to start their timed run and from previous experience we knew this to be the best way of ensuring accuracy. By the aid of the strong white light thrown out from the magnesium flares the target would be marked visually by the most expert crews in the Pathfinder Force using a yellow marker which would burn for several minutes as it scattered over the ground. This was a most exacting task and all depended on the skill of these men. The time was short and allowed little correction of the bombing run once the datum point had been left behind: two minutes only in which to line up, identify and drop the vital target indicator. When this was done other Pathfinders coming along behind would drop green markers on the yellow to keep the pot boiling. The main force of heavy bombers would bomb either green or yellow ground markers unless ordered to do otherwise by the Master Bomber aircraft which would stay over the target and maintain a constant watch on the proceedings. This was our task. Since there were no less than three separate aiming points the target would be changed every fifteen minutes until the whole area of the Research and Development Station was destroyed. A complicated operation and one which demanded the utmost in accuracy and timing from the Pathfinder crews. No rehearsal was possible beforehand and for obvious reasons and it had to succeed. My own aircraft was equipped with yellow markers which, if needs be, I would employ to correct the marking should it go astray for any reason. Thus the scene was set for one of the most complicated bombing operations of the war.

So far all was relatively quiet save for the firing of the ground defences and the play of the few searchlights. The moon was reflected in the calm waters of the Baltic sea below us and the coast line stood out stark and clear.

Suddenly, the area was lit up by brilliant light from the flares as the first wave of Pathfinders passed over and red target indicators dropped in dazzling cascade to the ground. Ross, my bomb aimer had his eyes glued to the aiming point and startled us all with a shout that these first markers had fallen to the South by more than a mile but in the same instant another clutch of red markers fell almost an equal distance to the North and a yellow marker, most important of all, fell between the two; virtually on the mark. This splendid effort was achieved by Wing Commander John White of No. 156 Pathfinder Squadron, backed up at once by the green target indicators. Immediately, I broadcast to the bombers approaching the target and instructed them to bomb the green markers which we judged to be accurate. We made another turn out to sea and the flak ships had another go at us but it was not their night and we passed round in a circle for another run across the aiming point.

By now the area was beginning to assume the familiar spectacle of a target under massive attack; bursting bombs; masses of billowing smoke through which the sliding beams of the searchlights crossed and recrossed: the red burst from the heavy anti-aircraft mingled with it all and yet we could not say that the defences were anything but light in character. This happy situation continued for some twenty minutes until the second aiming point, the actual rocket factory, was under heavy bombardment.

Because the target area was rapidly becoming a veritable inferno in which it became increasingly difficult to identify the various features we flew lower on our next orbit and to my horror the gunners informed me that they had seen large four thousand pound bombs falling past our aircraft: this was most alarming but was to be expected since many bombers were flying well above the height at which we were orbiting. Curiously enough, this simple fact had quite escaped notice when considering how best to do our job and yet it was the most obvious one. The possibility of our being walloped by a passing 'block buster' was more frightening than anything the enemy could do.

After fifteen minutes the attack shifted to the next aiming point and it was apparent immediately that the green marker bombs were falling to the South once again – overshooting the mark. I broadcast to the main force and warned them of this error and successive backers up brought the marking back again to the correct spot. Some stray greens fell along the coast and I broadcast again to stop the waste of bombs. It was about this time that Ross called me over the Intercomm. "Bomb Aimer to Captain – look out for fighters – a Lanc. has just blown up over the target". I saw it almost at the same moment. So, the fighters had arrived, and from now on things were likely to be difficult. Silhouetted against the flame and smoke of the burning Research Station the bombers presented a clear mark and in the next twenty minutes we were able to see many of our aircraft destroyed. The moon was high and in short the odds were now against us but we were grateful for the respite gained for us by the gallant efforts of the

Mosquitoes of No. 139 Squadron in simulating an attack on Berlin. As for ourselves much remained to be done,. The second mark, Aiming Point 'B' was well and truly covered and a mass of fire and smoke. The third aiming point was difficult to mark and for several minutes we remained in ignorance of the fact that bombs were falling to the South once more. This phase did not last long owing to the action of a single Pathfinder aircraft in placing his green markers on the Development works but many aircraft continued to overshoot the mark. This is not hard to understand since little could now be identified and in the event much damage was, in fact, done by relatively few bombs correctly aimed. We were hard put to it to discern anything at this stage but continued as before to orbit out to sea and return back along the line of targets.

The German fighters were now right in amongst the bombers and one after another was shot down around us, exploding before our eyes and falling in burning fragments. Twin and single engined fighters flew through the bomber stream and the bright tracer shells were all too plain to see. This was our seventh orbit of the target and the final scene in one of the most impressive bombing attacks we had witnessed. Enormous destruction lay below us. It is not possible to find words which will convey accurately the true picture. Only a bomber crew can appreciate the truth of these words and the awful fascination in watching an assault of this magnitude taken to a wide target area. It was one o'clock in the morning; nothing more remained to be done at Peenemunde. These fifty minutes of time would remain long after other and similar experiences had been forgotten. We turned for home.

Lancaster William was now at the tail end of a long stream of bombers all heading back over the Baltic and our best chance of survival lay in losing our identity amongst them. After our last pass across the target we turned to starboard instead of port and said farewell to the persevering gunners on the flak ships off the coast. We did not feel cocky, only thankful and if we could survive the attentions of the night fighters during the next hour or so all would be well. Alas, our hopes were short lived for within a matter of minutes of leaving Peenemunde the battle was on again: "Rear Gunner to Captain – fighter attacking from astern and below" and I heard the rattle of the four machine guns in the same instant. Heaving on the controls violently I brought the Lancaster in a sharp turn to starboard – nose down – a manoeuvre which strained every rivet in her frame – and red tracers streamed past without finding us. The fighter was attacking in a climb and the nose down altitude proved more effective than the turn though the combination made the evasive action complete.

"Captain to Gunners – watch for him returning" and there was complete silence amongst the crew. Every man took a point of vantage from which he could observe the night sky. Classically, I expected the enemy to attack from the dark side with the Lancaster silhouetted against the moon and the rear turret was watching this flank – the dorsal gunner taking the starboard side. Suddenly, "Mid Upper to Captain – fighter coming in starboard quarter Down" – and the Lancaster heaved over in a smart turn towards the attacking fighter. Both turrets opened fire and I saw the enemy's tracer bullets pass a little behind the tail. An excited shout from Flight Lieutenant Coley, our Mid Upper informed me that he had got in a burst and hit the fighter and we claimed this German as damaged since we did not see him crash. Certainly, this was no time in which to stay and look for him. We sped on into the night. The fires of burning Peenemunde made an impressive glow behind us as we left Stralsund on our right and lost height over the Baltic Sea. Any elation we may have felt over the apparent success of the operation was tempered by the knowledge that the German Night Fighters were taking a fearful toll of our returning bomber stream.

My crew were tired but for the next hour and a half unremitting vigilance would be needed. Fighter aircraft from all over Northern Germany were concentrating on the Lancasters and Halifaxes and in the bright moonlight conditions were perfect for interception. By flying at a low altitude over the sea we might hope to escape attention for a while since the majority of the combats we witnessed were taking place around eight to ten thousand feet. The chief danger for us lay in the distribution of light flak guns along the coast and on the many small islands in the Little Belt.

"Mid Upper to Captain" . . . Lanc. on fire to port. I looked to the left of the aircraft and watched a small point of bright light grow rapidly until the aircraft was entirely visible – illuminated by its own burning fuselage. The fighter struck again and his tracer bullets ploughed through the flaming mass which quickly broke apart and plunged into the sea below. In a moment or two we observed another bomber shot down a few miles ahead of us and this one exploded in mid air. Combats took place the whole way across the sea to the Danish mainland where the leading wave of the bomber stream was now located. Below me I saw a strip of white sand with a white washed cottage and a fishing boat drawn up from the waters edge – a peaceful spot and in marked contrast to the events which were taking place around us. I was wrong, however, for a light flak gun emplacement opened up at us immediately and the tracers snaked their way towards 'W' William shooting over the starboard mainplane. We turned quickly out to sea again. The tip of the island of Langeland loomed ahead. Frank Forster, my Flight Engineer, cool and methodical as usual paused for a moment from his sky watching task to make his periodical check of our fuel tanks, oil pressures, boost gauges and other instruments. His oxygen mask hung loosely from his helmet since we were not using oxygen at this low altitude and in the dim light I saw the hint of a grin as our eyes met: steady as a rock and thoroughly capable, he had demonstrated these qualities often enough – as when we were 'coned' over the Ruhr and the searchlights held us: his task was then to lean out into the perspex blister and watch the anti aircraft fire from the guns below giving me the necessary information when taking avoiding action. The searchlight cone could hold the aircraft long enough for the gunners to fire visually at their target and this technique had been successful in destroying many a bomber. Frank was trained to fill any role in the aircraft except those of Navigator and Wireless Operator: in the event of a gunner being injured he could take over his post and he knew sufficient about handling the aircraft to fly it home should I be wounded or taken ill in the air.

"Danish Coast coming up Skipper" – the voice of George Ross came over the inter-comm and I pulled the nose of the Lancaster up to climb rapidly to four thousand feet. Without a load of bombs and with most of her petrol gone the lancaster handled like a fighter.

"Captain to Flight Engineer – Climbing Power" and Forster instantly moved the throttle and pitch controls forward. Ross was peering forward and down from his position in the nose to note the exact point at which we crossed the enemy held coast line. Only a little longer and we should have the North Sea below us once again. More than five hours had elapsed since setting out and at least another two must pass before returning to Wyton, our home airfield.

"Crossing the Coast Skipper" – from the Bomb Aimer – and immediately one felt relieved. How many times had one heard this simple but significant phrase – the feeling of escape from danger and things which go bang in the night. One felt as if this were the last time but I knew that tomorrow we were likely to be called again – maybe the Ruhr. If we were lucky we might enjoy a free evening. Ours was a strange war – the heavy brigade of the Royal Air Force. There was no glamour in what we did – a long cold ride spending eight or nine hours in the darkness, shot at and bound to a rigid schedule – the flight plan. The nature of our task induced crushing fatigue and it is truly remarkable how very few ever cracked up. Staying power was a prime requirement if one flew under Air Marshall Harris's orders.

Ahead of us the bomber stream wound its way home. We were certainly the last. Sharp eyes continued to search the sky and the surface below. A convoy of German ships making its way down the coast could strike us down in a moment at the low height we were flying. The full moon cast cloud shadows on the sea below – our faithfull Rolls Merlins drummed on a fine even note as we continued our course to the West. I eased my straps a little to take some of the ache away. I felt grubby, and the rubber lining of my face mask was sticky against my cheeks, the familiar stench of the aircraft – oil, body odours and the strange indefinable smell given off by the heated radar and electrical equipment – all combined to make one think of getting clean again. I thought about the Gunners – Coley and Preece, – cramped in their turrets, staring into the dark hour after hour, hands always on the gun controls, flung madly against their straps when the aircraft took evasive action.

"Captain to Mid Upper – can you see anything?"

"Mid Upper to Captain – all quiet".

"Rear Gunner to Captain – nothing to report".

Nothing to report, and the likelihood of interception was decreasing every second as we flew towards England. Coley and Preece were both young: the former a popular figure – liking a scrape, and always successful in getting out of it. Preece had come with me from my previous Squadron volunteering for Pathfinder Duty, tall and fair haired with looks which made the W.A.A.F. gasp. He wore the ribbons of the Conspicuous Gallantry and the Distinguished Flying Medals. At twenty-one he had a long combat record.

"Captain to Navigator – are we in Gee range yet?"

"Navigator to Captain – Eastern chain is strong".

"Gee" was our radar aid to navigation and, in my opinion the best of all devices devised by our British Scientists for helping the bombers. The reliability and accuracy was such that we relied almost entirely upon it when leaving and returning to this country. The boffins gave us many excellent 'Black boxes' but this was the best.

After seven and a half hours in the air we picked up the Wyton flashing beacon and landed, to be driven immediately to the Interrogation Room. Mr. Sandys was waiting. He had already gathered much information from the crew reports but wanted final confirmation from me. I could only say that from what I had seen this had been a successful operation but I could not confirm the destruction of Peenemunde. We must await the photo recconnaissance aircraft with its detailed survey of the area. Mr. Sandys was very pressing and this was understandable but he appreciated the necessity for caution, and, in any event, he had heard enough to convince him that the job was well done. This operation was a major disaster for the enemy and Sandys congratulated the crews on their efforts. Even had we known what lay behind it all I don't think it would have made the slightest difference: the determination and "press on" spirit of the bomber crews never varied regardless of the character of defences of the target.

Our losses were heavy. Forty four-engined bombers and one Mosquito; more than two hundred and eighty Officers and N.C.O.s failed to return from Peenemunde and we might well have faced worse but for the splendid achievements of 139 Squadron Mosquito crews over Berlin. Their attack delayed the arrival of the enemy fighters over the main target area and at this commencing phase casulties were light.

The names of those who did not come home from Peenemunde on the night of the 17/18th August are recorded in the Rolls of Honour in the Bomber Command Chapels of York, Lincoln and Ely Cathedrals.

Typical of the crews who flew the raid on Peenemunde, 103 Squadron's DV 221.
Left to right, standing: Ground Crew; Bomb aimer, Sgt 'Jock' Aitken; Engineer Sgt C. D. Hornby; Navigator, W/O Dave Groome; Captain, W/O Ernie Presland; Rear-gunner, F/S E. E. Piper; Wireless operator, Sgt Stan Staplehurst; Kneeling: Ground crew; Mid upper gunner, F/S E. R. Foster.

Lancaster

Order of Battle

Pathfinder Force – *Target Marking*

4 Blind illuminator markers
1 Visual marker
2 Aiming point shifters
4 Backers up
6 Non markers

No 7 Squadron–Lancasters

2 Aiming point shifters
7 Backers up
1 Non marker

No 35 Squadron–Halifaxes

Master of ceremonies
7 Blind illuminator markers
3 Visual markers
2 Aiming point shifters
2 Backers up

No 83 Squadron–Lancasters

1 Blind illuminator marker
2 Aiming point shifters
13 Backers up
4 Non markers

No 97 Squadron–Lancasters

2nd Deputy master of
     ceremonies
4 Blind illuminator markers
2 Visual markers
2 Aiming point shifters
10 Backers up
3 Non markers

No 156 Squadron–Lancasters

Deputy master of Ceremonies
2 Aiming point shifters
4 Backers up
5 Non markers

No 405 (Vancouver) Squadron
Royal Canadian Air Force
     Halifaxes

Diversionary attack on Berlin
8 Mosquitoes

No 139 Squadron

Note the Function of the various Pathfinder Crews is explained in a separate note. The Master Bomber or M.C. was given two Deputies : in the event of his being shot down the first and second Deputy would take over in that order if still in the vicinity.

Main Force Squadrons

No 1 Bomber Group

No 460 R.A.A.F. Sqdn.
24 Lancasters

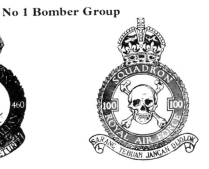

No 100 Squadron
21 Lancasters

No 214 Squadron
8 Stirlings

No 620 Squadron
7 Stirlings

No 101 Squadron
22 Lancasters

No 103 Squadron
24 Lancasters

No 75 Squadron
13 Stirlings

No 218 Squadron
5 Stirlings

No 12 Squadron
24 Lancasters

No 149 Squadron
2 Stirlings

No 199 Squadron
8 Stirlings Special Radio
Countermeasures duties

No 3 Bomber Group

No 15 Squadron
5 Stirlings

No 90 Squadron
6 Stirlings

No 622 Squadron
2 Stirlings

No 115 Squadron
12 Lancasters

No 4 Bomber Group

No 158 Squadron
24 Halifaxes

No 76 Squadron
21 Halifaxes

No 78 Squadron
22 Halifaxes

No 102 Squadron
18 Halifaxes

No 10 Squadron
19 Halifaxes

No 77 Squadron
22 Halifaxes

No 51 Squadron
24 Halifaxes

No 5 Bomber Group

No 9 Squadron
12 Lancasters

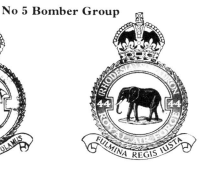

No 44 Squadron
13 Lancasters

No 49 Squadron
12 Lancasters

No 50 Squadron
12 Lancasters

No 61 Squadron
13 Lancasters

No 57 Squadron
16 Lancasters

No 106 Squadron
9 Lancasters

No 207 Squadron
9 Lancasters

**No
Badge
Authorised**

**No
Badge
Authorised**

No 619 Squadron
12 Lancasters

No 467 R.A.A.F. Sqdn
10 Lancasters

No 6 Bomber Group Royal Canadian Air Force

No 427 Squadron
12 Halifaxes

No 434 Squadron
10 Halifaxes

No 428 Squadron
14 Halifaxes

No 419 Squadron
17 Halifaxes

No 426 Squadron
9 Halifaxes

A Mosquito similar to those of No 139 Squadron which made the diversionary raid on Berlin

Lancaster of No 467 Squadron

The Men who Destroyed Peenemunde

No 1 Bomber Group *No 12 Squadron – Lancasters*

DV187
F/L J. Burkhardt
Sgt H. M. Hoey
Sgt J. Morley
Sgt A. Washbrook
Sgt P. Smith
P/O Walker J. A.
Sgt W. E. Jones

DV168
S/Ldr F. B. Slade
P/O G. R. Carpenter
P/O P. H. Phillips
P/O J. F. McIntyre
P/O C. W. Manning
Sgt S. Chapman
Sgt L. Myers

DV 158
F/O H. Ashbourne
P/O V. C. Bye
P/O H. Laverick
Sgt T. J. Gleeson
Sgt D. Barras
Sgt D. W. Fraser
Sgt W. T. Peace

JA 864
F/S Smithergale
F/O L. Kingman
Sgt H. E. Muge
Sgt W. Hall
Sgt R. J. Brewer
Sgt G. D. Milton
W/O A. S. Lancaster

DV 225
F/O M. Lloyd
Sgt G. E. Parkes
Sgt W. G. Smith
Sgt K. E. McDonald
Sgt I. Ellis
Sgt A. J. Baker
Sgt W. J. Edwards

W 4370
F/O Leader-Williams
P/O R. W. Gard
Sgt J. McNab
Sgt S. W. Frost
Sgt K. J. Wilson
Sgt J. Pollard
Sgt J. Harding

W 4881
F/S F. R. Joy
Sgt H. C. Maynard
Sgt J. M. McCormack
P/O W. J. Lake
Sgt A. D. Duffy
Agt G. H. Harmer
Sgt J. Short

ED 993
Sgt R.P. Rabbett
Agt J. O'Reilly
Sgt R. Davies
Sgt R. E. Gratwick
Sgt T. Roberts
Sgt E. W. Croxon
Sgt L. D. Davidson

DV 17
F/S G. R. Kremer
Sgt T. P. Bishop
Sgt D. Tibbs
Sgt J. O'Brien
Sgt T. Clarke
Sgt W. M. Cloutman
Sgt F. T. Rees

JA 922
F/S J. P. Hutchinson
Sgt L. E. Goodkey
Sgt G. R. Gabriel
Sgt D. J. Bemrose
Sgt K. A. Stapely
Sgt R. Burr
Sgt A. F. Relshaw

ED 392
Sgt G. W. Fordyce
Sgt L. J. Collins
Sgt A. E. Egan
Sgt R. Harries
Sgt C. Johnson
Sgt R. H. Hodges
Sgt J. Minogue

DV 222
Sgt J. A. L. Currie
F/O J. Cassidy
Sgt C. Fairbearn
W/O H. E. Myring
Sgt G. Walker
Sgt V. G. Protheroe
Sgt C. W. Lanham

JA 865
P/O M. G. Brown
P/O M. Pritchett
Sgt E. Brookes
P/O F. G. Kauter
Sgt A. J. Evans
Sgt H. F. Binder
F/S S. M. Dunshea

W 4991
W/O W. R. Sharpe
Sgt H. A. Oldmixon
Sgt W. Gaskin
Sgt W. J. Hollis
Sgt A. Hodgson
Sgt H. Hooper
Sgt C. H. Forward

W 4994
F/S W. Patterson
Sgt J. Aldritt
Sgt T. H. Franklin
Sgt T. F. Carney
Sgt J. A. Dodds
Sgt. F. Arthur
F/S J. A. Seaton

EE 133
Sgt D. E. Tribe
F/O M. C. Furnell
Sgt J. E. Thompson
Sgt G. D. B. Moore
Sgt Collier G. T.
Sgt H. W. Hildebrand
Sgt J. Hill

ED 424
S/Ldr C. A. Roden
F/Sgt B. Weller
Sgt G. H. Brittle
Sgt T. R. Jackson
Sgt S. P. George
Sgt H. Whitemore
Sgt H. H. Alcock

LM 321
F/L F. J. Wood
P/O L. H. Kirkby
Sgt W. Cruickshank
Sgt G. H. Wood
Sgt C. G. Davies
Sgt J. R. Wilkins
Sgt R. B. Coll

DV 171
F/S H. H. Adams
Sgt T. H. Kinmett
Sgt C. F. Solly
P/O F. L. Lake
Sgt F. A. Atwood
Sgt D. Cameron
Sgt N. A. P. Chew

W 4990
F/L J. N. Rowland
Sgt D. J. Parry
Sgt E. F. Stainer
Sgt B. J. Kennedy
W/O C. O. Edwards
Sgt K. B. Robinson
Sgt P. J. Lyons

ED 972
F/L A. Booth
F/S Brown S. Y.
Sgt A. R. Bish
F/S J. M. Short
Sgt N. Stacey
Sgt R. Wildbore
F/S C. W. Frazer

ED 995
F/O F. J. Wright
F/O E. V. Saunders
Sgt D. T. Hone
Sgt D. R. Tattersall
Sgt W. Smith
Sgt B. S. Heath
Sgt G. W. Shrimpton

LM 301
F/O D. G. Lighton
Sgt I. M. Ward
Sgt F. Foreman
Sgt G. T. Lindsay
Sgt F. Wadsworth
Sgt A. C. Farmer
P/O D. A. Hickman

DV 218
F/O W. P. Snell
Sgt D. H. Russell
Sgt I. J. Copping
P/O D. E. Braybrook
Sgt L. W. Heath
Sgt R. J. Bennett
Sgt T. Matthews

DV 200
F/L D. G. R. Weeks
Sgt W. R. Mitchell
P/O H. Drew
Sgt A. H. Baines
Sgt F. Rigley
Sgt G. W. Vicker
Sgt J. W. Swan

No 1 Bomber Group *No 100 Squadron – Lancasters*

DV 176
W/O D. G. Edwards
Sgt J. C. Scott
F/O B. R. Mallinger
Sgt W. K. Hynham
Sgt W. L. Malthouse
Sgt T. Harrison
Sgt J. D. Brocklebank

ED 652
F/S D. G. Phillips
Sgt W. Snow
Sgt Wood L.
Sgt K. P. Osmund
Sgt V. D. Burrell
Sgt R. P. Kinsella

JA 934
F/O C. A. Wilson
Sgt F. G. Pataky
Sgt H. Lievesley
Sgt J. C. Cornhill
Sgt D. Craigie
Sgt J. W. A. Peters
Sgt A. J. Muir

ED 835
P/O F. G. Cracknell
Sgt O. B. Dowdall
Sgt J. Freckleton
Sgt A. W. Cooke
Sgt G. Harvey
Sgt W. S. Stericker
Sgt N. P. Reilly

ED 991
W/O C. H. Harris
Sgt J. Jennings
Sgt R. D. McClure
Sgt C. R. Gordon
Sgt P. Arch
Sgt F. Campbell
Sgt H. Moran

DV 192
F/L A. Gersekowski
Sgt T. Pearce
F/O J. J. Berg
Sgt W. Peake
Sgt I. Levene
Sgt O. Steinberg
Sgt F. G. Roberts

DV 162
F/S D. Close
Sgt A. B. Frost
Sgt J. L. Whitlock
Sgt H. Jennings
Sgt B. G. Winzar
Sgt E. Brennan
Sgt I. W. Nash

EE 139
W/O J. R. Clarke
Sgt H. Bennett
Sgt J. H. Siddell
Sgt D. Wheeler
Sgt L. Y. Easby
F/O K. J. Wilson
Sgt W. G. Green

JA 699
W/O L. H. Wright
Sgt Henderson
F/O W. Bentley
Sgt T. J. O'Dea
Sgt T. S. McCleod
Sgt S. O. Hodges
Sgt J. McKean

LM 317
F/S R. G. Bowden
Sgt A. A. Pearce
Sgt S. N. Cunnington
Sgt J. N. Mather
Sgt R. Brockbank
Sgt E. Watton
Sgt A. Farr

JA 969
F/S K. L. Needs
Sgt P. A. Whitter
Sgt R. G. Reay
Sgt H. J. Hahn
Sgt W. B. Jamieson
Sgt A. Stansfield
Sgt W. S. Fletton

JA 930
Sgt D. Baker
Sgt C. Robinson
Sgt J. W. Jeffs
Sgt W. H. Pallett
F/S G. H. Adams
Sgt R. H. Pitman
Sgt K. Watmough

ED 555
F/O R. L. Proudfoot
Sgt S. D. Viggers
Sgt J. Noyes
Sgt J. Bamford
Sgt B. Heaton
Sgt B. Phillips
Sgt F. H. Taylor

DV 189
Sgt C. C. Goff
Sgt F. Hindley
Sgt W. E. Haslam
Sgt J. G. Smith
Sgt E. C. Burnett
Sgt J. Sutherland
Sgt P. E. Duckers

EE 180
F/S D. C. Dripps
Sgt H. Jones
P/O J. Stewart
Sgt W. T. Sibley
Sgt T. Campbell
Sgt R. Gillies
Sgt A. F. W. Croft

LM 319
W/O J. H. Berry
Sgt W. T. Roberts
Sgt L. C. Howell
Sgt F. Bradbury
Sgt F. Johns
Sgt A. L. Evans
Sgt J. A. Orr

ED 583
Sgt L. J. Stow
Sgt J. E. Lumb
Sgt A. D. Walker
Sgt D. R. Tapper
Sgt K. A. Grainger
Sgt M. R. Sheer
Sgt D. J. Devlin

DV 159
Sgt G. W. Brook
Sgt E. V. Condell
Sgt E. G. Paterson
Sgt A. Ferdinando
Sgt J. J. McAnaney
Sgt J. Godsave
Sgt J. Flynn

ED 647
F/O H. I. Spiers
Sgt C. W. Torbett
P/O J. Weaver
Sgt K. F. Goode
Sgt S. J. Cassell
Sgt O. M. Atkins
Sgt W. Francis

ED 536
Sgt C. W. J. Boone
Sgt D. Bick
Sgt E. A. Pack
Sgt F. Warhurst
Sgt R. Davis
Sgt I. P. Nyland
Sgt G. R. Smith

No 1 Bomber Group *101 Squadron - Lancasters*

W 5009
F/L R. L. McCulloch
Sgt R. L. Marshall
F/O T. W. Fagg
Sgt C. Middleton
F/O C. S. Hodgeson
Sgt F. J. Burton
F/S E. Parker

E 370
F/S D. H. McConnell
Sgt C. Thompson
Sgt D. Hall
Sgt R. R. Clarke
Sgt R. G. Brookes
Sgt W. E. Whitfield
Sgt L. Young

W 4993
W/O T. Cunningham
Sgt F. E. Hill
Sgt J. B. Wright
Sgt J. Hartley
Sgt G. Williams
Sgt C. Scaife
Sgt G. E. G. Foster

JA 926
F/S Sexton
Sgt T. C. Marchant
Sgt E. W. Batten
Sgt T. Tilley
Sgt F. C. Osborne
Sgt G. W. Wright
Sgt J. C. K. Platts

W 4997
F/S E. H. Shattock
Sgt G. Rowlinson
Sgt R. L. Jacobs
Sgt R. J. A. Houseden
Sgt E. H. Blank
Sgt C. R. Anthony
Sgt C. W. Gibb

DV194
F/S N. A. Marsh
Sgt de Brock F. C. G.
Sgt C. G. Kaye
Sgt D. W. Ince
P/O K. R. Middleton
T/Sgt E. Jones
Sgt G. J. Watson

ED 372
F/L D. W. Mackay
Sgt P. M. Wilks
Sgt R. Halperin
F/S H. T. Shewan
Sgt R. B. Hooper
Sgt C. Gibson
F/O R. Matthews

ED 382
F/O T. W. Rowlands
Sgt S. Deedle
P/O D. G. J. Higgs
Sgt P. H. Lamprey
Sgt W. H. Yuill
Sgt R. Bateman
Sgt H. G. Clements

W 4966
F/S F. M. Rays
Sgt W. A. Lyneham
F/O S. K. Smith
Sgt N. Winterburn
Sgt D. R. Booker
Sgt K. Wood
Sgt A. S. W. Orchard

EE 192
F/O I. Robertson
Sgt T. Calvert
P/O S. I. Kennedy
Sgt R. J. Gosling
Sgt T. C. Williams
Sgt I. J. Minguy
Sgt K. Lydall

ED 422
P/O R. R. Leeder
Sgt G. F. Smith
P/O J. A. Turner
Sgt B. G. Lyall
Sgt P. J. Drought
Sgt E. N. Bickley

W 4995
F/L S. Wedderburn
Sgt R. Schofield
Sgt R. Sidwell
Sgt L. H. I. King
F/S R. B. Reid
Sgt R. F. Booth
F/S R. S. Cradock

W 4923
W/O G. P. R. Bond
Sgt C. E. Blanchette
Sgt A. Morassi
Sgt G. Barry
P/O A. R. Bolsover
Sgt M. Stein,
Sgt L. Underwood

ED 317
Sgt G. R. Fawcett
Sgt F. R. Greig
Sgt J. N. Lawrence
Sgt L. Wild
P/O L. W. Moore
Sgt D. W. Andrews
Bgt R. J. Griffiths

EE 137
F/L J. C. Day
Sgt J. Saker
P/O P.J. Slingsby
Sgt E. P. Coyle
Sgt J. A. E. Stevens
Sgt J. F. Crowley
Sgt L. J. Nash

ED 809
Sgt D. W. Skipper
Sgt P. Hands
Sgt T. C. Kerr
Sgt R. Meredith
Sgt J. D. Gulliver
Sgt W. J. Phillips
Sgt S. Harris

ED 328
F/O D. J. Carpenter
Sgt C. H. A. Warner
P/O J. F. Waterman
Sgt J. Billington
Sgt J. D. M. Flett
Sgt D. R. Browne
Sgt H. McQuade

Sgt R. G. Naffin
Sgt D. M. Ellis
F/S N. V. Bullen
Sgt J. A. Currey
F/S D. J. Tressider
Sgt J. H. Phillips
F/S E. J. Phillips

ED 659
F/S D. D. Tucker
Sgt L. Hobson
Sgt J. S. K. Dalziel
Sgt G. Cheadle
Sgt D. Hopkins
Sgt J. Clarke
F/S J. L. Stubbins

ED 951
W/O A. J. S. Walker
Sgt S. Mayer
Sgt G. G. Whittle
F/S S. T. Player
P/O A. W. Gadd
Sgt R. Stott
Sgt K. N. Hicklin

No 1 Bomber Group *103 Squadron – Lancasters*

LM 343
S/Ldr C. S. F. Wood
F/O C. L. Grisdale
F/S J. E. Craig
Sgt A. R. Wilson
Sgt J. W. Lowrie
Sgt C. Kershaw
Sgt W. Brown

ED 767
F/L D. W. Finlay
Sgt J. A. McFarlane
Sgt H. S. Wheeler
F/S R. J. E. Vivers
Sgt I. D. Fletcher
Sgt R. H. Rowe
F/S W. C. C. Gillespie

ED 646
F/O J. F. Marshal
P/O F. J. Dempsey
Sgt C. K. Mann
Sgt F. C. Bence
Sgt I. F. Gray
Sgt G. F. Potts
Sgt J. H. Marston

LM 332
S/L T. O. Prickett
F/L W. G. Langstaff
Sgt S. Blakely
F/S W. J. Miller
F/S J. Torrans
P/O L. Pulfrey
P/O D. J. Montgomery

DV 221
W/O E. J. Presland
W/O L. D. Groome
Sgt S. G. Staplehurst
F/S E. R. Foster
Sgt G. Aitken
Sgt C. D. Hornby
F/S E. E. Piper

JA 951
P/O F. J. Hopps
Sgt F. J. Roberts
Sgt R. Thomas
Sgt N. James
P/O N. Olsberg
Sgt R. S. Imeson
F/S R. E. Black

ED 713
W/O R. J. Edie
F/S E. H. Suarez
F/S Greenhalgh
Sgt E. C. Benham
P/O J. C. Maxwell
Sgt E. S. Boorman
F/S J. May

ED 905
F/L F. Van-Rolleghem
Sgt G. A. Agar
Sgt J. Proctor
Sgt R. White
Sgt W. Carlin
Sgt P. O. Vickers
P/O R. K. McLeod

ED 731
1st Lieut J. C. Drew
P/O H. Ellis
Sgt S. A. Pett
F/O H. G. Cook
Sgt P. W. Lees
Sgt K. S. Lewis
Sgt D. Lowe

LM 335
W/O J. D. Warren
W/O J. R. Evans
Sgt F. P. Smith
Sgt W. H. Bolt
Sgt M. N. Greenwell
Sgt J. Nunn
F/S W. C. Russell

ED 904
F/O J. A. Day
Sgt R. Tandy
Sgt J. W. Colbourne
Sgt J. M. Woodburn
Sgt J. E. Grown
Sgt S. I. Miller

W/O S. E. Gage
F/S J. M. Stewart
Sgt R. J. Westwood
P/O F. J. A. Beiber
F/S H. L. Dawson
Sgt D. Major
F/S V. G. Heath

ED 725
Sgt P. J. O'Donnell
Sgt C. P. Williams
F/S M. G. Medhurst
F/S P. J. Capon
Sgt W. H. Greaves
Sgt C. N. Lee
F/S E. R. Biggs

LM 314
F/O L. Kilvington
F/O F. C. W. Healey
Sgt B. H. Heasman
P/O T. R. Thomson
F/O A. Muggeridge
Sgt L. Rogers
Sgt S. Galley

JA 808
Sgt J. E. Thomas
Sgt W. G. Bell
Sgt E. M. L. Davies
Sgt A. V. Collins
Sgt D. J. Edwards
Sgt J. J. Robshaw
Sgt W. N. O'Malley

EE 196
P/O R. Atkinson
Sgt G. F. Price
Sgt A. L. Norman
Sgt W. Campbell
Sgt R. J. H. Littleton
Sgt H. K. Garewal
Sgt R. L. Taggart

ED701
F/S A. W. Buxton
Sgt N. Kidd
Sgt G. Sweeney
Sgt A. Davidson
Sgt W. S. Whalley
Sgt J. Leeming
Sgt G. A. G. Daldy

ED 492
F/S A. H. Pargeter
Sgt H. E. Thompson
Sgt H. Sykes
Sgt J. C. McLean
Sgt L. Cross
Sgt W. G. Cane
Sgt J. P. Neville

DV 180
F/S C. E. Phelps
F/S E. D. Nesbitt
Sgt R. Winder
Sgt W. H. Clarke
F/S W. W. Mitchell
Sgt E. P. Hillyard
Sgt H. R. Gibbon

W 4337
F/S J. E. Rule
Sgt C. W. Reaves
Sgt P. Coyne
Sgt A. G. A. Race
Sgt F. J. Pulfrey
Sgt E. A. Shorter
Sgt J. J. Sloan

W 4364
F/S C. W. Annis
W/O J. W. Renwick
Sgt S. McDonald
Sgt R. L. Oldershaw
P/O J. T. Birkbeck
Sgt N. W. H. Turrell
Sgt E. B. Edwards

ED 751
W/O P. F. Chesterton
Sgt E. Milling
Sgt J. Bullock
Sgt A. H. Robson
Sgt K. Cave
Sgt H. Ackroyd
Sgt C. R. Jackson

W 4323
Sgt E. T. Townsend
F/O G. H. Palin
Sgt J. W. Bateman
Sgt C. R. Greenwell
Sgt A. J. Darby
Sgt H. A. Joint
Sgt G. R. Creber

No 1 Bomber Group *460 Squadron R.A.A.F. – Lancasters*

DV 175
F/O F. A. Randall
F/S N. J. Conway
P/O L. G. Greenaway
Sgt H. H. Peterson
Sgt A. E. Johns
Sgt H. Bell
F/S H. K. Ward

W 4988
F/S G. J. Sharpe
F/S W. C. Gordon
Sgt C. W. Hudson
Sgt J. Wilson
Sgt C. H. Veitch
F/S L. J. Brown
F/S M. E. Hamilton

LM 316
F/S Gardner J. R.
F/O A. Flett
F/S M. R. Nash
Sgt R. M. Stratford
Sgt L. E. Flatt
Sgt D. H. Roberts
Sgt J. H. Marsh

LM 315
F/S F. H. Magnus
F/O K. L. Shepherd
Sgt B. Walters
F/S A. N. Robinson
Sgt J. Robinson
F/S W. H. T. Robinson
F/S C. N. Robinson

JA 680
W/C C. E. Martin
F/O G. A. Hadley
P/O T. E. Osborne
F/S H. A. Pender
Sgt E. G. Sutton
F/O C. P. Prentice
F/S W. Osmotherly

DV 193
P/O E. R. Greenacre
Sgt J. McCorkindale
F/S C. M. Manning
Sgt H. E. Hall
Sgt G. Cairns
F/S S. G. Webster
F/S W. F. Thorburn

W 4301
S/Ldr K. D. Baird
W/O A. E. Cox
Sgt A. L. Jackson
F/O J. Liddle
F/S W. F. H. McIntyre
F/S Q. A. Richardson
F/S P. D. Borcherds

JA 681
F/S C. R. Smith
F/S K. R. Galt
F/S E. M. Sibbit
F/S A.A. Cranfield
Sgt E. C. Clayton
Sgt R. T. Hampton
F/S H. K. Lucy

EE 138
F/O G. J. Oakshott
F/O W. J. Cameron
F/S W. P. Brannelly
F/S B. M. Treacy
Sgt B. J. Wisby
Sgt N. C. Dorriant
F/S F. R. Goldsworthy

JA 856
F/S F. L. R. Lloyd
Sgt R. Hurrell
Sgt R. N. Wilton
Sgt R. E. Woodford
Sgt G. Douglas
F/S Sheehan
Sgt L. A. Sim

JA 861	**W 4783**	**JA 689**	**W 4927**	**JA 862**
F/O F. N. Robinson	P/O D. B. Moodie	Sgt A. M. Marshall	F/S J. Turnbull	F/S J. H. J. English
F/O T. V. Watts	F/S A. L. Aitken	F/S J. R. Penny	F/O L. T. Carter	F/S N. T. Anderson
F/S A. T. Mitchell	F/S S. J. Bethel	F/S I. G. Kernaghan	F/O C. J. White	F/S A. N. Calty
Sgt N. Dodd	Sgt J. Dawson	F/S A. J. O'Brien	Sgt E. Graham	Sgt A. G. Cole
Sgt F. G. Kitson	F/S K. W. Miller	Sgt A. D. West	Sgt R. W. Spencer	Sgt W. L. Miller
Sgt J. T. Egan	P/O C. T. Crooks	F/O J. M. David	Sgt A. B. Brunton	F/S T. Rodin
Sgt W. T. Hollings	F/S H. J. McWaters	Sgt R. M. Edmonds	F/S D. C. Lake	F/S A. E. Kan

W 4987	**DV 173**	**DV 174**	**ED 421**	**ED 730**
F/S J. Goulevitch	W/O W. C. H. Munsch	F/S N. M. Peters	F/S Richards	Sgt R. R. Wicks
Sgt R. J. Garbett	F/S Reid	F/S A. E. Llewellyn	F/S K. Gay	Sgt N. McDonald
F/S A. G. Elwing	F/S Harper	F/O E. G. Roser	F/S T. G. Munro	W/O R. K. Thomas
Sgt H. Gorell	Sgt Moore	F/S E. C. Patten	Sgt W. A. Finlay	Sgt K. Edmonds
Sgt E. F. Groom	Sgt T. L. Walkley	Sgt H. K. Cheslin	Sgt T. Smale	Sgt P. E. Wells
P/O E. Anderson	Sgt T. C. Heath	F/S C. J. Slouch	F/S J. March	F/S K. A. Wood
Sgt S. C. Williams	F/S G. S. Jordan	F/S H. J. Britton	F/S Collins	F/S R. E. Inglis

ED 985	**JA 859**	**JA 860**	**ED 986**
F/S D. Rees	F/S H. G. Carter	F/S T. L. Hills	F/S J. D. Hocking
F/S L. T. Quaife	P/O G. Peters	F/O T. E. C. Radcliffe	F/O H. F. Symons
F/S J. F. Parker	F/S H. K. Harris	F/O C. E. Agg	F/S W. R. Ingram
Sgt R. Townsend	F/S R. C. Coveny	F/S J. H. Graham	Sgt T. J. Wood
Sgt S. A. Rolfe	Sgt L. T. A. Regan	Sgt A. Cleverly	F/S L. T. Haymes
Sgt C. W. Harris	F/S H. D. F. Hodge	Sgt H. Hartwell	F/S W. H. Fitzgerald
F/S J. Venning	F/S F. G. Brown	F/S A. R. Duel	F/S T. J. Jones

No 3 Bomber Group *15 Squadron – Stirlings*

EE 912	**EE 940**	**EE 908**	**EE929**	**EE 954**
W/C J. Stephens	W/O A. Niall	Sgt R. Grundy	F/O R. Lown	F/S N. Thomas
P/O G. Baker	F/O L. Glenday	Sgt C. Hudson	Sgt A. Ramsay	P/O D. Mann
Sgt E. Court	P/O E. Stevenson	Sgt C. Carter	F/O R. Horner	Sgt R. Mackay
F/S W. Combs	Sgt O. Robinson	Sgt L. Wood	F/O D. M-Pleydell	Sgt K. Baker
Sgt Ferguson	Sgt T. Peters	Sgt R. Taylor	Sgt J. Bolduc	Sgt J. Chamberlain
Sgt Copeland	Sgt W. Green	Sgt J. Scandrett	Sgt J. Pullen	F/S G. Farrell
Sgt Wiseman	Sgt G. Iddison	Sgt E. Honeybill	Sgt D. Day	Sgt D. Brock

No 3 Bomber Group *115 Squadron – Lancasters*

667	**691**	**720**	**678**	**683**
F/S F. Tinn	F/O R. Seddon	F/L J. B. Starky	W/O H. Hicks	W/O E. Boutillier
Sgt D. Bigg	P/O R. Sullivan	Sgt E. Ferrell	P/O I. G. Barham	Sgt D. Franklin
Sgt W. Kilmurray	Sgt R. Chappell	F/O A. Beer	Sgt C. Farquarson	Sgt W. Rogers
Sgt G. Adamson	P/O T. Sweeting	Sgt K. Tugwell	Sgt A. Todd	Sgt A. Horton
Sgt W. Roberts	Sgt R. Rock	Sgt J. Willis	Sgt J. McLaughlin	Sgt G. Mooney
Sgt R. Hawkins	Sgt J. Chabot	Sgt W. Moll	Sgt H. Bean	Sgt S. Allen
Sgt E. Ross	Sgt J. Anderson	Sgt M. Irwin	Sgt A. Elms	Sgt J. McCabe

653	**631**	**659**	**664**	**626**
F/L J. H. Christianson	F/S W. Townsend	F/O R. L. Barnes	F/S F. Wolfson	F/L L. K. Eggleston
F/S E. Webb	Sgt D. McDonald	Sgt J. McLachlan	Sgt R. Bates	F/S T. Graham
F/O A. B. Braithwaite	Sgt F. Abell	Sgt R. Bett	Sgt J. Deacon	Sgt G. Lee
P/O C. H. Wright	Sgt R. Gardham	Sgt L. Karwood	Sgt J. Gregory	Sgt H. Smith
Sgt A. Kewin	Sgt A. Line	Sgt E. Marshal	P/O M. Gladwell	Sgt E. Back
F/S Boswell-Kitching	Sgt E. Morgans	Sgt E. Campbell	Sgt A. Summers	Sgt L. Fradgeley
Sgt R. Rodhouse	Sgt Coulthart	Sgt J. Dalziel	Sgt K. Pearson	Sgt E. Albone

722	**630**
P/O A. S. Cade	F/O Pusey
F/O W. C. Lewitt	F/O C. G. Bruton
Sgt D. Davis	Sgt L. Howard
P/O W. Pryde	P/O J. D Cable
Sgt W. Nethersole	Sgt M. McKibbon
Sgt S. Rice	Sgt J. Corbett
Sgt A. Rogers	Sgt T. Leonard

No 3 Bomber Group *214 Squadron – Stirlings*

EE 914
F/S A. Beever
F/S T. Curtle
Sgt E. H. Maughan
Sgt R. K. Hansen
Sgt R. Nicholson
Sgt C. R. Wale
Sgt E. A. Wood

EF 385
F/L H. C. Lee
Sgt J. Robertson
Sgt A. Wright
Sgt R. Rae
Sgt T. E. Eldred
Sgt T. L. Salter

EE 405
F/O F. Henderson
F/O K. E. W. Evans
Sgt L. H. Kinsett
Sgt D. McGilchrist
Sgt R. O. Connolly
Sgt T. Smyth
Sgt G. D. T. Cann

EE 956
F/S N. J. Tutt
Sgt A. Bell
Sgt P. W. Upton
Sgt R. Foggin
Sgt H. J. Dahle
T. G. Kilfoyle
Sgt R. A. Bannister

EF 404
P/O Verrall
F/O D. J. Furner
F/S A. Boyd
Sgt A. C. Shankland
Sgt C. Wilkes
Sgt N. Beswarwick
Sgt J. S. McDonald
F/S K. J. Simpson

EF 405
Sgt G. A. Welch
Sgt Marshall
Sgt O. J. Singer
Sgt P. A. Tansley
Sgt C. W. Walmsley
Sgt L. E. Cox
Sgt R. L. Wensley

EH 895
F/S H. Thriplow
F/O G. H. Hart
Sgt W. Jeffcott
Sgt E. Wolk
Sgt L. Lapensee
Sgt V. Nagle
Sgt C. Houlgrave

No 3 Bomber Group *No 218 Squadron – Stirlings*

EE 888
S/L I. R. Ryall
F/O M. J. Morel
P/O A. C. Murgatroyd
F/S J. C. Allan
Sgt A. Howe
F/S J. W. Hughes
Sgt W. W. Kett

BK 700
W/O S. R. Grant
F/O H. D. Thomas
F/S G. W. Sivall
Sgt A. T. McPhee
Sgt L. Clay
Sgt F. W. Lambert
Sgt H. Bossick

BF 522
W/C W. G. Oldbury
P/O D. Taylor
Sgt I. Segal
Sgt J. A. Taylor
Sgt D. E. Twining
Sgt M. R. Bell
Sgt W. Lamont

BK 650
F/S H. Adams
P/O W. Hunter
Sgt W. Fisher
Sgt W. Bullen
Sgt J. Symes
Sgt F. W. Cornwell
Sgt A. Weller

EH 923
F/L L. C. Kingsbury
F/O D. W. Souchen
Sgt P. N. Mills
Sgt D. M. T. Ingram
Sgt E. Parr
Sgt F. E. Somers
Sgt A. W. King

No 3 Bomber Group *90 Squadron – Stirlings*

BK 781
P/O K. T. Kinsella
P/O N. B. Blakey
Sgt E. M. Inkpen
Sgt R. D. Clarkson
Sgt W. D. Hope
Sgt W. A. Heaney
Sgt R. Blair

EF 426
Sgt G. R. Hilton
Sgt W. J. Pollard
Sgt D. W. Meikle
Sgt J. F. Bickley
Sgt L. Langley
Sgt J. L. Moran
Sgt R. Whitford

BK 723
F/S A. Lowe
F/S D. Allen
Sgt V. Warren
Sgt P. Donovan
Sgt R. Young
Sgt C. Sharpe
Sgt S. Watkins

EF 443
P/O E. G. Appleby
Sgt L. W. Howell
Sgt A. J. Hitchcock
Sgt S. Guyan
Sgt J. P. Crisp
Sgt J. V. J. Higgins
Sgt G. D. Brierly

BK 811
F/L W. H. Cheek
P/O V. G. Gerrard
P/O J. R. Jeffrey
Sgt C. F. Whitehead
Sgt E. J. Harris
P/O E. R. Evans
Sgt R. J. S. Brace

EE 952
F/L C. G. Crew
P/O L. E. Jordan
F/O G. W. Ingram
Sgt G. Hudson
Sgt J. Kennedy
Sgt D. J. Dimond
Sgt J. McFarlane
F/S K. Longmore

EE 951
F/S F. E. Sheppard
Sgt G. D. Geddes
Sgt R. Spencer
Sgt R. Coates
Sgt T. D. Gregory
Sgt G. F. Millar
Sgt K. Forest
F/S F. Langford

EE 896
P/O D. A. McInnes
Sgt A. R. Clarke
Sgt W. D. Dickson
Sgt E. Cautherly
Sgt j. H. Nolan
Sgt K. J. Hawkins
Sgt J. Williams

MZ 262
F/O K. R. Yates
P/O R. Greaves
P/O A. E. Wyton
Sgt G. A. Hayes
Sgt D. G. Davies
Sgt B. Thorpe
Sgt S. T. Kettlety

EH 944
S/L M. I. Freeman
Sgt J. Hudson
Sgt C. H. A. Clarke
F/O P. P. S. Cunningham
Sgt W. J. Hoar
P/O S. T. Smith
Sgt D. G. Robertshaw

EH 937
Sgt S. A. Luyk
P/O E. Thompson
Sgt A. S. Robertson
Sgt J. Dowding
P/O J. Keyes
Sgt W. McPherson
Sgt F. Eggo

BF 566
W/O C. P. Wood
F/O J. G. Brewster
Sgt H. J. Burgess
Sgt D. C. Pittman
Sgt P. Foolkes
Sgt C. Cipparrone
Sgt E. Armstrong

BK 655
Sgt F. Mason
Sgt A. M. Watson
P/O S. R. Grafton
Sgt E. Young
Sgt B. R. Cantera
Sgt B. J. Lucking
Sgt B. F. Kington

EF 446
F/S S. C. Brayshaw
Sgt W. T. Cooper
Sgt R. E. M. Clarke
Sgt H. Morrison
Sgt W. T. Winslett
Sgt J. G. Mudge
Sgt L. J. Seager

EH 908
F/O W. Day
Sgt J. Morris
P/O B. Beaton
Sgt Fenn
Sgt R. A. James
F/S C. A. Mitchinson
Sgt T. Fitzsimmonds

No 3 Bomber Group   *75 Squadron – Stirlings*

EH 949
P/O A. Burley
F/S F. Lundon
F/S R. Hill
F/S E. Elmslie
Sgt A. Wilson
Sgt R. Risbridger
Sgt J. Hubbock
Sgt A. Peters

BF 564
P/O A. Sedunary
Sgt Kirk
Sgt A. Lens
Sgt C. Parish
W/O D. Moss
Sgt F. Alcock
Sgt J. Nicholson
Sgt F. Gratton

EH 880
Sgt J. Joll
F/O T. Graham
Sgt W. Kane
F/S E. Gray
Sgt G. Falloon
F/S L. Sorenson
F/S W. Reid

EH 454
W/O P. Hartstein
Sgt R. Reeves
Sgt E. Kempson
Sgt R. Woodward
Sgt T. Silcock
Sgt T. O'Sullivan
Sgt W. Eaton

EH 905
F/S H. Batger
F/S G. Reade
F/S F. Stewart
F/S T. Nation
F/S R. Dalkins
F/S C. Billington
F/S J. Manns

EE 893
P/O C. Logan
F/S W. Masters
F/S G. Sowerby
F/O J. Ingham
Sgt T. Hegarty
Sgt T. Stewart
Sgt F. Crowther
F/S A. Knox

EF 435
F/S O. White
F/S J. Rogerson
F/O J. Murray
Sgt A. Smith
Sgt C. Worledge
Sgt T. Collins
Sgt J. Poole

EF 454
F/S K. K. McGregor
F/O J. Lovelock
Sgt W. Kilby
F/S J. Baker
Sgt G. Bond
Sgt G. Dummett
Sgt T. Grange

EF 465
F/O A. Wilson
F/O T. Lodge
P/O A. Dance
Sgt G. Cross
Sgt R. Stratton
Sgt L. Gaskins
Sgt A Fawcett

BK 809
W/O P. Moseley
Sgt G. Bates
Sgt E. Taylor
Sgt V. Farningham
Sgt C. Hughes
Sgt C. Middleton
Sgt A. North

BF 938
F/O A. Alexander
F/S M. Anderson
F/S P. Pullyn
F/S T. Mayhew
F/S A. Lyon
Sgt W. Macdonald
Sgt E. Howard

BK 778
F/S A. Mayfield
Sgt G. Tyler
P/O J. Jarmy
Sgt R. Somerville
F/S W. Lake
Sgt A. Warburton
Sgt T. Darbyshire
Sgt J. Hullena

EH 901
F/S F. Higham
Sgt J. Culshaw
Sgt M. Bailey
Sgt C. Bridger
Sgt R. Renfrew
Sgt H. Jennings
Sgt H. Clarke

No 3 Bomber Group   *199 Squadron – Stirlings* Electronic Countermeasures. Function to black out enemy radar detection

LJ 510
P/O E. McNamara
Sgt A. Marshall
F/S J. F. Lowry
F/O J. T. Hodgson
Sgt D. McNicol
Sgt A. W. Fraser
Sgt W. T. Cleghorn
Sgt R. A. Norton

LJ 582
F/S J. F. Reidy
Sgt G. W. T. Goss
F/S G. R. Shaw
F/O R. Delaroche
F/S H. Buchan
P/O M. Byers
Sgt F. E. Burton
Sgt F. A. Wingrove

LJ 569
F/O F. S. G. Robbins
F/O F. Hartwright
P/O J. R. Sergeant
F/O D. H. Halliwell
F/O L. Francis
F/S G. N. Tye
F/S J. R. Phipp
F/L E. C. Borley

LJ 544
F/L K. Eady
P/O F. J. Goulding
F/S K. Hallbrookes
W/O S. H. Voce
F/O L. E. McKenzie
F/S B. E. Challis
F/S K. W. Wilkinson
Sgt D. E. Lambert

LJ 525
F/L G. A. Noble
P/O R. Smith
F/O G. Cubby
F/O D. G. McIlroy
F/L P. J. Banahan
P/O L. J. Davies
F/S H. W. Chessell
P/O S. McGarriggle

LJ 536
F/L W. Hancock
F/O A. E. Wood
F/S B. G. Riggs
F/O T. S. L. Burr
F/O W. C. Pacholka
Sgt E. Harvey
Sgt C. W. Cooper
Sgt O. J. Pask

LJ 580
F/O F. I. Briggs
W/C N. A. N. Bray
F/O F. Barter
F/O H. Tomlinson
F/O J. P. Parridis
F/O R. Laird
Sgt H. M. Dammarell
Sgt L. B. Champion
Sgt T. D. Wake

LJ 531
F/S A. D. Hegginson
F/S M. Kesselman
Sgt J. Sowden
W/O D. T. Hughes
Sgt L. G. Langley
Sgt J. D. Campbell
Sgt G. J. Dennison
Sgt S. C. Rennie

No 3 Bomber Group   *149 Squadron – Stirlings*

EE 872
F/S R. L. L. Smith
Sgt M. M. Cross
F/S R. A. Sharrock
Sgt E. F. L. Crow
Sgt K. K. Muir
Sgt D. G. Keay
Sgt C. L. R. Gilman

BK 798
P/O B. E. C. McPherson
P/O S. B. Richards
Sgt M. G. Smallridge
Sgt T. R. Spencer
Sgt E. A. Printon
Sgt F. R. Brine
Sgt G. Christianson

No 3 Bomber Group   *622 Squadron – Stirlings*

EE461
F/S J. Young
Sgt S. Marks
Sgt D. Barnes
Sgt N. Hugill
Sgt J. Nicol
Sgt H. Napier
Sgt H. Huckman

No 3 Bomber Group *620 Squadron – Stirlings*

EP 457
S/L A. P. Lambert
F/O L. G. Kennett
Sgt E. W. Evans
Sgt R. I. Cooper
Sgt D. J. Carrington
Sgt E. F. Leeming
Sgt V. Enders

EF 440
P/O J. Griffiths
Sgt D. F. Arnaldi
Sgt M. Manashe
Sgt H. K. Hunter
F/S T. G. Black
Sgt R. A. Jones
Sgt W. E. Malley

EE 945
P/O F. C. McDonald
Sgt B. F. Bunce
P/O P. S. Hobbs
Sgt H. W. Hill
Sgt J. Martin
Sgt A. P. Gamble
Sgt R. Lambert

BK 802
F/S J. F. Nicholls
Sgt S. G. Bond
P/O N. S. Mitchell
Sgt M. Meakin
Sgt J. P. Donnelly
Sgt G. C. Burton
Sgt S. G. Coyne

No 4 Bomber Group *158 Squadron – Halifaxes*

JD 260
F/S W. D. Caldwell
F/O W. R. Schmehl
Sgt R. H. Reay
Sgt J. E. Pearson
Sgt M. Czajkowski
Sgt A. Tice

HR 941
F/S H. G. A. Fisher
Sgt S. J. Muldoon
P/O G. U. Smith
F/S R. E. Hughes
Sgt P. W. Cramb
Sgt H. Reddy
Sgt A. S. Soutar

HR 937
W/C C. C. Calder
P/O P. Crawley
Sgt J. L. Hindle
F/O B. C. Sandall
P/O D. Weatherill
F/O E. W. Bristow
Sgt D. Brookes

JD 255
F/S D. Nicholls
Sgt H. Marsden
P/O G. W. Hailstone
P/O D. A. Ross
Sgt A. W. Simpson
Sgt L. G. Raymend
Sgt L A. L. Gregory

JN 887
Sgt H. Mottershead
Sgt D. A. Jones
Sgt A. Glendinning
Sgt C. McKinnon
P/O J. Handley
Sgt W. C. Martin
Sgt D. S. Hawkes

HR 942
Sgt J. S. Knox
Sgt C. R. A. Challis
Sgt C. E. Berry
Sgt L. Fenwick
Sgt J. Pringle
Sgt W. Cornwall
Sgt T. Kennedy

JD 298
F/O J. Y. Clarke
Sgt H. Robinson
Sgt J. H. J. Dix
Sgt E. W. Brearley
Sgt G. H. Hurst
Sgt J. Thomas
Sgt G. Rippingale
P/O R. G. W. Richards

HR 978
Sgt J. A. V. Denton
F/O J. D. Cazes
Sgt J. R. V. Morgan
Sgt N. H. Stimson
Sgt E. Furness
Sgt R. G. Richards

JD 300
P/O D. C. Cameron
Sgt J. F. G. Lane
F/O G. J. Wallace
Sgt H. Booth
P/O A. K. Young
Sgt H. Hulme

JN 886
Sgt A. E. Winn
Sgt A. P. Royse
Sgt L. J. Powell
Sgt T. Grundy
Sgt R. Bennett
Sgt J. J. Lovett
Sgt E. Heweston

HR 725
P/O H. Frisby
Sgt D. De Lanrier
Sgt H. Selman
Sgt D. A. Riches
P/O B. P. Allan
Sgt G. G. Heyes
Sgt A. W. Kyle

H 945
Sgt J. D. Colter
Sgt V. C. Hicks
P/O M. Hawkridge
Sgt H. R. S. Reid
Sgt W. Griffiths
Sgt W. Lomax
Sgt R. Rooney

HR 739
F/S B. N. Allsop
P/O A. T. Hennessy
Sgt W. Spooner
Sgt D. J. Jones
Sgt R. P. Dean
Sgt M. G. Aubin
Sgt A. Girdler

HR 715
P/O E. James
F/O W. A. Lennard
P/O R. McInnes
Sgt A. W. Davies
F/L W. A. Gorton
Sgt S. W. Evans
Sgt G. W. Stokes

HR 944
Sgt J. R. M. Atkins
Sgt L. Buckley
Sgt K. C. Sutton
Sgt D. J. Every
Sgt B. C. Anderson
Sgt R. Prince

HR 977
F/L J. Reynolds
F/O T. Smart
Sgt T. Lincoln
Sgt E. Grace
Sgt D. R. Courage
Sgt B. A. Faulkner
Sgt K. C. Diment

JN 903
F/O K. T. Holmes
Sgt H. J. W. Smith
P/O K. A. Leonard
Sgt B. O. Savage
Sgt H. Phillips
Sgt L. V. Moran
Sgt M. Anderson

HR 755
Sgt S. W. Emms
Sgt E. Ameraskera
P/O P. H. Ackling
Sgt G. S. Almond
Sgt D. G. Cree
Sgt J. McGuire
Sgt W. H. Strong

JD 265
F/S C. F. Penfold
F/O B. R. Robinson
Sgt S. R. Chafer
P/O H. B. Briscoe
Sgt L. J. McPhee
Sgt H. Barrett
Sgt E. C. Duffy

HR 943
Sgt T. C. Edwards
Sgt F. G. Field
Sgt D. E. Slack
Sgt D. E. Whitfield
Sgt P. C. Chapman
Sgt E. L. Cole
Sgt R. Goddard

HR 738
F/S W. A. Burgum
Sgt P. L. Buck
Sgt D. R. Hempstock
Sgt J. Batty
Sgt G. R. Harrison
Sgt H. C. Harber
Sgt R. Hill

HR 858
Sgt T. C. Mattey
Sgt M. T. Airey
Sgt R. J. Woolton
Sgt A. W. Steen
Sgt R. A. Duck
Sgt B. C. Anderson
Sgt G. V. Harris

HR 979
F/L H. Hornibrook
P/O R. W. Chaston
P/O A. E. Bryett
Sgt J. E. Hanks
Sgt L. G. Chesson
F/S G. A. G. McLeod
Sgt G. E. Scott

JD 246
Sgt K. Ward
Sgt P. H. Payne
Sgt J. Stubbings
Sgt A. P. Arnott
Sgt R. A. Thurston
Sgt T. Craven
Sgt W. N. Avery
Sgt H. Simister

No 4 Bomber Group *102 Squadron – Halifaxes*

DT 703
F/S W. A. Rooney
F/S S. A. Weekes
Sgt E. A. Church
Sgt H. W. Jarvis
P/O J. A. Henderson
Sgt M. Beerbaum
Sgt W. M. Mauser

W 7912
Sgt S. W. Templar
F/S A. C. Fraser
Sgt G. S. Spicer
Sgt E. Clarke
P/O A. A. Joseph
W/O J. L. Hirst
Sgt T. S. Strong
Sgt P. T. Pragnell

JD 165
F/S B. R. Moss
P/O S. Whittingham
Sgt W. J. T. Hayden
Sgt E. J. Pearce
Sgt K. Page
Sgt L. Todd
Sgt D. Copeland

JD 366
Sgt A. Kularatne
Sgt W. F. Johnson
Sgt J. A. Downs
Sgt A. J. Stapleton
P/O J. M. Filmer
Sgt R. Gillespie
Sgt D. Kneeshaw

DT 702
P/O T. H. Dargavel
F/O H. P. Jeffreys
Sgt A. J. Harris
P/O E. P. J. Behiels
F/S J. R. S. Power
Sgt H. Walton
P/O W. A. T. Brewer
Sgt A. R. Banks

JD 128
Sgt J. A. Chappell
Sgt G. Lee
F/O E. I. Smallfield
Sgt D. Zander
Sgt L. G. Smart
Sgt J. Harris
Sgt J. J. Jones

JD 111
P/O J. Bowman
F/S D. Galbraith
F/S L. C. Parry
Sgt F. G. Tregunno
F/S J. J. Prinsloo
Sgt R. H. Mock
S/L A. Ables
Sgt C. E. Hall

JD 307
F/O J. W. Ward
F/O H. J. Plank
Sgt W. A. Murray
Sgt L. Milne
P/O R. A. H. Dube
Sgt H. Williams
Sgt J. Burns

JD 407
Sgt K. Mountney
F/S R. Ingram
Sgt R. G. Pharo
Sgt H. Bartlett
Sgt R. Learmond
Sgt E. L. Dalton
Sgt H. D. Proctor
Sgt D. Cullen

JD 127
S/L J. W. H. Marshall
Sgt J. C. Fell
P/O G. B. Mitchell
P/O G. P. Clarke
P/O J. Bell
F/S A. Pickard
Sgt P. O'Grady
P/O W. H. A. Dick

DT 485
Sgt W. Hughes
Sgt W. W. Cottle
Sgt R. A. Dabnor
Sgt R. B. Bainbridge
Sgt D. Willington
Sgt J. Boxall
Sgt F. Dunn

JD 415
Sgt P. Sayer
Sgt P. P. Greene
F/S H. Bilborough
F/S D. J. Reels
Sgt L. J. Jones
Sgt J. Muldoon
Sgt J. Kidd
Sgt L. H. Hancock

BB 383
F/L J. L. Causton
F/O D. H. Phillips
F/O G. G. Russell
Sgt G. Ollerhead
F/O K. G. Harris
F/S R. B. Valvasori
Sgt J. S. Rowland
F/O V. W. Armitage

JD 176
Sgt G. S. Roadley
Sgt D. M. E. Pugh
Sgt W. G. Jennings
Sgt J. Chalkey
Sgt N. G. Webb
Sgt E. Kirk
Sgt B. E. Woodrow
Sgt R. F. Roberts

JD 296
F/S W. R. Lambert
F/O W. L. Cook
Sgt W. A. Rice
Sgt H. E. Bentley
Sgt J. Hope
Sgt E. J. Dyke
Sgt L. H. Thomas

JD 378
Sgt K. G. McAlpine
Sgt E. W. Traylor
Sgt A. A. J. Myers
Sgt D. Sinclair
Sgt E. A. Baverstock
Sgt R. G. Twine
Sgt L. Chant

JB 365
W/C S. J. Marchbanks
P/O W. A. Corbett
Sgt E. G. Clarke
Sgt S. Corner
Sgt J. J. Duncan
Sgt E. R. Crane
P/O H. J. Pullen

No 4 Bomber Group *78 Squadron – Halifaxes*

JD 305
W/O T. Wilson
Sgt S. Mills
Sgt A. Coresby
Sgt S. Warriner
Sgt H. Kirkham
Sgt D. Nicholls
Sgt H. Groom

JB 784
F/L G. Carver
Sgt S. Woods
Sgt E. Allen
Sgt R. Saiger
Sgt A. Wiltshire
Sgt J. Hyde
Sgt H. Clarke

JD 328
W/O R. Martin
Sgt E. Salmon
Sgt A. Landon
Sgt A. Parlour
Sgt S. Bird
Sgt R. Taylor
Sgt J. Thompson

HR 748
P/O A. Ferguson
F/O A. Beales
P/O H. Hamley
Sgt A. Fleming
Sgt R. Davies
Sgt F. O'Dwyer
Sgt H. Greet

JD 118
F/S F. Pool
Sgt F. Scott
Sgt A. Sturgeon
Sgt J. McDonald
Sgt K. Rabbage
Sgt P. Stroud
Sgt G. Gibson

JD 173
W/C G. Lawrence
W/C Hutchings
F/L A. Dowden
F/O J. Kelt
Sgt G. Simpson
F/S D. Petrie
F/S D. Booth
Sgt J. Flood

JD 170
W/O W. Smith
P/O A. Paul
Sgt A. Cocking
Sgt J. Norman
Sgt G. Hickling
Sgt R. Smith
F/S J. Wilkins

JD 377
F/S G. Rowlands
Sgt P. Terry
Sgt A. Robinson
Sgt J. Marshall
Sgt G. Bloomfield
Sgt D. Wade
Sgt H. Entwhistle

HR 874
F/S Watson
Sgt E. Burgess
Sgt W. McKenzie
Sgt Harrington
Sgt H. Clayton
Sgt A. Woodward
Sgt L. Hannay

JD 414
F/S S. Norris
P/O T. Tabberer
Sgt McTergaugham
Sgt D. Crompton
Sgt D. Purcell
Sgt D. Sanderson
Sgt Payne

JB 874
W/O E. Kitchen
P/O D. Polmah
Sgt D. Sharpe
Sgt H. Watson
Sgt R. Cherry
Sgt H. Wobick
Sgt G. Gibney

JD 248
Sgt B. Bolsworth
Sgt W. Gray
Sgt D. Hynes
Sgt A. Hampton
Sgt E. Gosling
Sgt G. Coggans
Sgt A. Thorne

BB 373
Sgt G. Bell
P/O E. Platt
Sgt W. Clarke
Sgt A. Lee
Sgt A. Lester
Sgt G. Walton
Sgt R. Fletcher

JB 926
Sgt H. Ferne
Sgt G. Preston
Sgt F. Hicker
Sgt T. Dorn
Sgt E. Bream
Sgt H. Gill
Sgt Drinkwater

JD 406
F/S B. Rudge
Sgt Dynock J.
Sgt H. Hearsurn
Sgt Chesswass
Sgt A. Beswick
Sgt R. Peters
Sgt W. Dunleavy

JB 872
F/S F. Ebeling
Sgt G. Milligan
Sgt H. Salter
Sgt G. Groom
Sgt Sheffield
Sgt H. Pratt
Sgt W. Huntley

JD 306
F/L R. Hunter
P/O M. Walsh
Sgt R. Caldwell
Sgt J. Miles
Sgt J. Buchanan
Sgt J. Gibney
Sgt J. Mein

JD 201
F/O A. Short
F/O F. Street
F/O T. Boyle
P/O M. Davies
Sgt W. Onion
Sgt L. Cotton
Sgt D. White

JD 310
F/S K. King
Sgt A. Bishop
P/O W. Patterson
Sgt E. Davies
Sgt J. Oliver
Sgt F. Lambert
Sgt F. Tolan

No 4 Bomber Group   *77 Squadron – Halifaxes*

JD 418
F/S R. O. Rochester
Sgt J. Marsden
Sgt S. R. Tattersall
Sgt F. D. Rix
Sgt J. J. Knight
Sgt E. W. Dredge
Sgt H. J. McAdam

BB 284
F/S R. J. Caseley
P/O F. G. Shaw
Sgt C. R. Boyd
Sgt W. H. J. Webb
W/O W. Wright
Sgt W. R. Farrell
Sgt K. E. Lees

JD 385
Sgt E. A. Brown
Sgt P. Davidson
Sgt N. E. Rudge
Sgt M. Tarpey
Sgt F. G. Dilnatt
Sgt A. Welham
Sgt R. A. Greene

JD 162
F/L T. Rowe
Sgt R. Tailford
F/S A. E. Harvey
F/O A. Grant
Sgt O. E. Burger
Sgt A. Knapp
F/O C. G. Bellhouse
Sgt E. W. Thompson

JD 413
S/L E. C. Badcoe
P/O E. Lowry
Sgt F. J. Chell
F/S B. W. Folkes
P/O W. D. Rees
Sgt D. Rickett
Sgt J. B. Mannix
F/S S. Downes

JD 383
Sgt J. Byrne
Sgt G. Graham
Sgt R. E. Olive
Sgt V. H. Bradley
Sgt A. G. Willis
Sgt S. J. Wilson
Sgt E. K. Sears

JB 851
Sgt H. V. Gawler
Sgt A. Cotterall
P/O J. R. Randall
F/S C. Langston
Sgt A. Burgess
Sgt P. W. Kitchen
Sgt T. Todd

JB 839
F/S S. Richardson
Sgt J. S. Stephens
F/S J. Swallow
Sgt D. McF. Boyd
Sgt H. Taylor
Sgt L. A. Foster
Sgt F. K. Smith
F/S T. Robinson

JD 301
S/L D. H. Duder
Sgt B. J. Kearley
Sgt R. W. Pendergrest
Sgt T. F. Bolter
Sgt R. F. Walter
Sgt A. G. McCulloch
Sgt W. H. Hagen
Sgt E. E. Lincoln

JD 379
F/S A. Massie
Sgt R. Crofts
F/Sgt W. Plunkett
Sgt W. A. Peers
F/O P. A. Stiff
Sgt C. W. Brister
F/O C. Rollings

JB 788
F/S J. K. Ellis
Sgt A. R. Downes
Sgt D. H. J. Mackie
P/O R. D. Sullivan
Sgt H. F. Payne
Sgt L. Letts
F/S D. Fletcher

JD 371
Sgt C. T. Manson
Sgt J. F. Shirley
Sgt C. C. Smith
Sgt A. S. Jackson
Sgt J. H. Diffley
Sgt R. Hunter
Sgt G. E. L. Angel

JD 123
F/S A. Gay
F/S G. Ibbotson
P/O J. Lockhart
P/O H. J. Pointer
P/O T. G. Stammers
P/O G. R. Bird
P/O B. Graham

JB 963
F/S R. Daffey
Sgt J. Henderson
F/O J. Naylor
F/O T. C. Treadwell
Sgt B. J. Keynes
Sgt F. A. Sparkes
F/O D. S. Smart
Sgt F. Crowther

DT 807
Sgt R. J. Jones
Sgt R. V. Woods
Sgt R. Walton
Sgt G. M. Wade
Sgt W. Shaw
Sgt T. R. Oxley
F/S G. F. McKinnon

JD 313
Sgt D. C. Hamblyn
Sgt E. Hollamby
Sgt G. Perkins
F/O D. F. Frodham
Sgt S. Hall
Sgt R. D. Collis
Sgt D. C. Elliott

JD 342
Sgt F. E. Shefford
Sgt F. J. Lane
Sgt G. Wood
Sgt J. R. Vint
Sgt H. F. Roza
Sgt A. W. Ready
Sgt J. B. S. Smith

DT 643
F/O G. W. Warren
Sgt D. G. E. Brookes
Sgt D. Taunton
Sgt C. D. Gibbons
Sgt A. H. Griffin
Sgt E. R. William
Sgt L. G. Preece

JB 911
F/L V. H. Surplice
Sgt A. A. Timpson
Sgt J. L. Duffy
Sgt H. P. Hopkins
Sgt T. King
Sgt K. Emeny
P/O D. M. Clarke

BB 328
Sgt A. R. Baxter
Sgt A. L. Thomas
P/O J. Saxon
Sgt E. G. Classen
Sgt D. W. Wood
Sgt A. Lane
Sgt V. G. Greene

JD 405
Sgt T. W. Hill
Sgt W. McCulloch
Sgt V. M. Hanks
Sgt C. Lawes
Sgt S. G. Murrell
Sgt S. R. Danniels
Sgt R. C. Bailey

No 4 Bomber Group   *76 Squadron – Halifaxes*

DK 231
Cpt J. M. Stene
P/O J. B. Grady
Sgt G. E. A. Hudson
Sgt J. Clarke
Sgt W. A. Lindo
Sgt J. M. Walde
Sgt S. E. Pursglove

DK 167
Lt G. Hoverstad
Sgt S. Brazier
Sgt E. Murphy
Sgt A. C. Briggs
Sgt W. J. Cooke
Sgt A. Storm
Sgt H. S. Slatter

DK 203
W/O K. A. Myers
Sgt E. L. Bauman
Sgt D. K. Williams
Sgt R. A. Mcleod
Sgt R. F. Hughes
Sgt L. I. Brown
Sgt C. B. Wood

EB 253
F/S E. Holmes
Sgt R. W. Pape
Sgt J. V. Kent
F/S T. H. Warren
F/S J. M. College
Sgt F. R. H-Smith
Sgt J. A. Van Marle

LK 903
Sgt G. C. Dunn
Sgt A. Maitland
F/O R. G. McCadden
Sgt A. D. Todd
P/O A. Scrivener
Sgt F. A. Newton
Sgt H. D. Weaver

LK 902
Sgt S. J. Troake
F/O T. G. Paton
Sgt R. J. Fayers
Sgt P. I. Weeks
P/O G. H. P. Potter
Sgt L. H. Barnes
Sgt R. S. Orr

DK 241
F/L J. E. Sanderson
P/O A. E. Robbins
S/L N. J. Bennett
F/L H. G. M. Robinson
Sgt R. G. Morgan
Sgt A. Shilcock
P/O W. W. Wanless

DK 204
F/L A. J. S. Hodson
Sgt W. F. Banks
P/O W. C. Wright
Sgt E. G. White
Sgt J. A. Fawcett
Sgt E. W. Hughes
S/S B. W. Flewell

EB 245
F/S H. R. W. Whittle
Sgt V. A. Thompson
P/O R. C. Saunders
Sgt W. Coates
Sgt W. J. Hyndman
Sgt V. T. Bradley
Sgt J. R. Rogers

DK 266
P/O S. W. Hickman
Sgt Whitehead
Sgt A. S. Pring
F/O G. W. Keene
Sgt L. C. A. Walters
Sgt J. Emerson
F/L W. F. Readhead
Sgt G. Scott

DK 223
F/S L. Falgate
Sgt F. S. Francis
Sgt A. D. Wallis
F/O I. G. Evans
Sgt G. J. E. Jennings
Sgt R. S. Demey
Sgt N. G. Day

EB 240
Sgt A. Thorpe
Sgt G. D. Barrell
P/O J. E. Suzor
Sgt J. F. Perry
Sgt J. T. Zuidmulder
Sgt E. Luder
Sgt E. P. Marvin

DK 269
Sgt C. Kirkham
Sgt A. B. Ward
Sgt H. G. Foster
Sgt C. Wicks
Sgt J. Whitter
Sgt M. A. Manser
Sgt E. N. Maville

LK 890
F/O D. E. Hicks
Sgt D. Morrison
Sgt S. W. Lucyk
Sgt A. E. Bristow
Sgt R. W. Elder
Sgt R. Clough
Sgt T. W. Davis

DK 194
P/O K. Hewson
Sgt T. Isaacs
Sgt K. R. Parry
Sgt C. W. Taylor
Sgt A. W. Davis
Sgt G. W. Jones
Sgt A. H. Atkinson

DK 236
F/S E. G. Little
Sgt B. A. Phillis
P/O E. Farrington
Sgt E. Naylor
Sgt R. E. Lewis
Sgt J. Arnold
Sgt G. W. Broadbent

EB 250
Sgt E. N. Wright
Sgt G. Duthie
F/L E. A. Strange
Sgt H. Jones
Sgt G. B. Halbert
Sgt A. C. Everett
Sgt J. L. Barton

DK 247
Sgt G. C. Greenacre
Sgt A. S. Arnell
Sgt A. Thorpe
Sgt J. A. Henthorn
Sgt A. D. A. Maw
Sgt A. Monk
Sgt A. H. Death

LK 891
Sgt D. G. Griffiths
P/O K. A. Barber
Sgt A. E. Holmes
Sgt R. Freeman
Sgt L. Glentworth
Sgt C. R. Walker
Sgt A. B. Entwhistle

DK 193
Sgt F. S. Giortz
Sgt D. F. Roberts
Sgt A. Poenter
Sgt W. Iverson
Sgt D. H. Stocker
Sgt S. J. Cancea
Sgt G. C. Harris

No 4 Bomber Group   *51 Squadron – Halifaxes*

JN 900
Sgt T. J. Bishop
Sgt J. A. Neve
Sgt K. H. Isaac
Sgt J. L. Boulter
Sgt A. G. Wales
Sgt H. Turnham
Sgt A. J. S. Holder

JD 309
F/L T. R. Dobson
Sgt L. R. Merrick
Sgt A. McGregor
Sgt H. F. Maughan
Sgt D. W. Kemp
F/S D. I. Cameron
P/O R. M. Lorenzo

HR 948
Sgt D. W. Hearsey
Sgt W. Morton
Sgt C. Izzard
Sgt F. Stevens
Sgt S. H. Jenkins
F/S W. L. Gaul
Sgt W. H. F. Alexander

JN 883
F/L E. P. Herrald
Sgt P. E. T. Jones
Sgt A. Kell
P/O S. Gibbon
Sgt W. H. Higgs
Sgt J. F. O'Dowda
Sgt M. F. Sibley

JN 901
F/S W. H. Addison
Sgt P. H. Spindler
F/O F. P. C. Garland
Sgt W. Goldstraw
Sgt J. C. Clarke
Sgt D. Goldstein
F/S W. J. Simpson

HR 726
Sgt D. M. Thompson
Sgt H. S. Russell
Sgt A. S. Sharpe
Sgt D. Pay
Sgt J. Harris-Ward
Sgt K. D. Murray
Sgt G. Jones

HR 936
Sgt R. J. Cribb
F/O W. J. A. Nicholson
Sgt G. E. Lloyd
Sgt D. Samuels
Sgt D. J. Whyte
Sgt P. E. M. Gosling
Sgt J. L. Wright

JN 899
Sgt J. B. Morris
Sgt E. Storey
P/O J. Binham
P/O A. Hebblethwaite
Sgt J. Russell
Sgt R. S. Kennedy
Sgt A. Massey

JN 885
Sgt A. W. James
Sgt W. J. Preece
P/O E. D. Porter
Sgt R. Crofts
Sgt F. Davies
Sgt D. N. Hadlow
Sgt E. Hickmott

HR 950
F/S H. M. George
Sgt F. R. Rohrer
Sgt F. R. Chadwick
Sgt G. Davies
Sgt J. H. Lanaghan
Sgt R. H. W. Cook
W/O K. R. Brooks

HR 783
Sgt S. C. Turner
Sgt D. Leslie
Sgt A. J. East
F/S E. Blanchard
Sgt T. G. Stevens
Sgt E. M. Evans
Sgt E. J. Liptrott

HR 946
Sgt S. A. Durrant
Sgt A. Jordan
Sgt C. Packham
Sgt G. Hart
Sgt W. Kingham
Sgt A. R. Brace
Sgt R. S. Kift

HR 732
P/O G. Richards
Sgt E. H. Fenning
P/O J. H. Barnicott
P/O A. K. Dean
Sgt A. G. Holland
Sgt R. Stow
P/O A. F. Tidmarsh
Sgt R. W. Grisdale

HR 782
Sgt H. H. Sherer
Sgt W. H. Craig
Sgt D. D. Dempster
Sgt T. J. Jackson
Sgt J. Hendry
Sgt L. W. Ball
Sgt S. F. Whitehead

JD 203
Sgt W. E. Bruce
P/O D. J. White
Sgt D. R. Slann
Sgt J. Hepburn
Sgt S. Tait
Sgt E. Richardson
Sgt K. S. Batten

HR 951
F/S R. Levy
Sgt H. G. Phillips
Sgt J. C. Collins
Sgt H. Graham
Sgt W. Fox
Sgt R. W. Birch
Sgt T. B. Walker

JD 264
Sgt J. McGregor
F/S G. C. Stephens
Agt C. L. Alliker
Sgt A. W. Burnett
Sgt D. Barker
Sgt G. McFadden

HR 939
Sgt A. J. Salvage
Sgt F. J. Baker
Sgt T. McCarthy
Sgt M. Hampson
Sgt W. B. Hamilton
Sgt R. J. Edwards
Sgt D. W. Milliken

HR 868
F/L A. D. Andrew
F/O W. Auld
Sgt T. Kidger
Sgt G. J. McMillan
Sgt R. E. Lewis
P/O A. E. Thomas
Sgt A. M. Davidson
F/L A. Hart-Lovelace

JD 266
Sgt F. W. Lerl
Sgt J. L. R. Coleman
Sgt K. G. Redford
Sgt C. E. White
Sgt S. Hayes
Sgt J. M. Davis
Sgt W. W. Hall

JN 906
F/S M. C. Foster
F/S G. B. Page
Sgt E. A. Hughes
Sgt W. Willetts
Sgt J. G. Service
Sgt W. Tewrt

HR 728
Sgt H. F. Farley
P/O F. H. Moyniham
P/O H. C. Hetterley
P/O A. Springett
P/O S. Godfrey
P/O E. H. G. Dyer
P/O J. A. J. Darvall

HR 946
Sgt J. Brooks
Sgt D. P. McCormack
F/O C. K. King
Sgt G. W. West
Sgt T. S. Connell
Sgt D. A. Churchill
Sgt S. Glass

JN 891
F/L T. W. A. Hutton
F/O W. H. L. S. Way
F/O P. Barber
P/O D. R. Perrin
P/O R. J. Child
P/O W. Inverarity
F/L T. Bayfield
Sgt D. Jackson

No 4 Bomber Group *10 Squadron – Halifaxes*

JD 120
Sgt W. Still
Sgt R. C. Clarke
Sgt Stanbridge
Sgt W. Sander
Sgt J. Holmwood
Sgt C. Talby
F/S E. Deveson
Sgt J. J. Rolfe

JB 910
Sgt H. Stinson
Sgt D. Richardson
Sgt M. J. Day
Sgt G. W. Allso
Sgt R. Wells
Sgt F. M. Smith
Sgt F. McCubbin

JB 899
F/S N. D. Wardman
Sgt C. L. Cox
Sgt G. Holmes
Sgt Warrell
F/S J. M. McIntosh
Sgt Matthews
Sgt E. M. Wood
Sgt I. M. Lowe

JD 315
F/S J. W. Heppell
Sgt W. Booth
Sgt S. Adams
Sgt G. W. Varley
Sgt A. M. Grainger
Sgt J. Shaw
Sgt R. Wingate
F/O R. G. West

JD 273
Sgt F. J. Walker
Sgt W. Brock
Sgt L. Slaughter
Sgt J. McNeill
Sgt L. Miles
Sgt D. Hudson
Sgt F. Selby
Sgt R. Fiddes

JD 368
Sgt G. Baker
Sgt V. Davies
Sgt M. Pearce
P/O F. Lawrence
Sgt G. M. Darvill
Sgt H. Bridge
Sgt W. Cooper

JD 146
Sgt C. R. Glover
Sgt J. Whitton
Sgt H. Mogridge
Sgt C. Jenkins
Sgt E. A. Jones
Sgt D. Gerrard
Sgt T. Hammett
Sgt A. Lindsey

JD 119
F/S N. W. Kilsby
F/S Columbell
F/S G. F. Woods
Sgt S. Daggett
Sgt F. B. Capper
Sgt W. R. Davies
Sgt D. F. Shipley

DT 786
Sgt B. Holdsworth
Sgt C. Telfer
F/O Pottier
Sgt R. Downs
Sgt C. E. Smith
Sgt D. T. Hand
Sgt J. Harper

JD 272
F/S H. E. Plant
Sgt S. Blandford
Sgt T. A. Bird
Sgt Burton
Sgt L. S. Smith
Sgt L. W. Noton
F/S R. J. Paull

JD 166
W/O R. J. Kennedy
F/O R. A. Rath
P/O R. G. Skinner
Sgt J. W. Capstick
Sgt N. Round
Sgt F. N. Payne
Sgt K. C. Beard

HR 691
P/O G. K. Hewlett
Sgt D. McClelland
F/S J. R. Hulley
F/O L. C. Williams
Sgt R. S. Minnet
Sgt T. L. Thackeray
Sgt C. McFarlane
F/O G. E. Farquharson

JD 367
F/S J. Clarke
Sgt Whiteman
Sgt L. Mabbs
Sgt L. Harvey
Sgt D. Johnson
Sgt W. Walker
F/S Girardua

JB 314
F/L D. W. Cox
F/O D. E. Tranter
F/O J. Burnell
Sgt E. Wakeford
Sgt D. Chisholm
Sgt L. Hopkins
Sgt R. J. Burton

JD 364
P/O C. D. Belcher
Sgt J. Poynter
Sgt K. Dempster
Sgt J. Harper
Sgt Mowatt
Sgt H. Lomas
Sgt G. Kenny

BB 427
Sgt P. S. Davies
Sgt P. Murphy
Sgt S. H. Hill
Sgt B. Fear
Sgt T. Holmes
Sgt B. E. Tate
Sgt W. G. Nolan

JD 202
F/S H. Cockrem
Sgt E. G. Marsh
Sgt C. Roe
Sgt H. W. Nash
Sgt R. Barker
Sgt A. Stanworth
Sgt P. Panes

JD 200
F/S A. J. E. Long
F/S J. Heal
F/S J. Cooper
F/S L. Sefton
F/S D. M. Goulden
F/S D. Galloway
F/S Willetts
F/O C. L. Berbezat

No 5 Bomber Group *9 Squadron – Lancasters*

EE 188	ED 836	R 5744	ED 666	W 4964
Sgt I. C. B. Black	F/O R. Wells	P/O J. Billing	Sgt T. H. Gill	P/O C. P. Newton
Sgt E. Button	Sgt D. J. Nutman	Sgt F. Hope	Sgt M. McPherson	Sgt J. Turner
F/O G. E. McTaggart	Sgt A. Duncan	Sgt K. E. Moriarty	Sgt R. V. Gough	Sgt P. Hall
Sgt G. Brothers	F/S K. Garnett	F/O K. N. Gibson	F/S B. P. Devine	Sgt E. J. Duck
Sgt A. E. Bauman	Sgt F. Smith	F/S J. M. Campbell	F/S W. A. Morton	Sgt J. Ryan
Sgt D. T. Gordon	Sgt W. Gough	Sgt J. B. Findlay	Sgt K. McDomagh	Sgt R. McFerran
Sgt W. H. A. Cardwell	F/S S. Moss	Sgt R. D. Curtis	Sgt R. McKee	Sgt W. J. Wilkinson

ED 551	ED 700	EE 136	DV 198	ED 656
F/S G. E. Hall	S/L R. H. Bunker	F/S J. H. S. Lyon	P/O G. E. Stout	F/S N. J. Robinson
Sgt L. J. G. Field	Sgt W. Possee	Sgt K. Pack	Sgt J. Gurney	Sgt R. Taylor
Sgt W. D. Evans	Sgt W. A. Gall	Sgt R. W. Corkhill	F/S J. H. Bryant	Sgt T. R. Davis
Sgt E. Colbert	F/O J. Prior	Sgt H. W. Jeffrey	Sgt K. Gavin	Sgt P. J. Pitman
Sgt O. J. Overington	Sgt L. Lever	Sgt A. Fielding	Sgt H. Nuttall	Sgt W. E. Jones
Sgt R. A. Chorley	Sgt R. G. Thomas	Sgt A. G. Denyer	Sgt D. Burden	Sgt L. E. Mitchell
Sgt H. G. Williams	Sgt F. G. Hayler	Sgt G. Clegg	W/O R. Smith	Sgt J. Casey

ED 499	W 5011
F/L C. J. Brain	F/S J. Livingstone
Sgt C. E. Bower	Sgt F. Parsons
P/O F. E. Foreshew	F/S F. T. Watson
Sgt H. T. Jolliffe	Sgt H. C. Brewer
P/O A. H. Millward	Sgt J. Prendergast
Sgt N. E. Adams	F/S C. J. Houbert
Sgt D. A. Powey	Sgt T. C. Taylor

No 5 Bomber Group *49 Squadron – Lancasters*

ED 702	ED 999	JA 894	JA 691	JA 690
W/C P. W. Johnson	S/L J. G. Day	F/S A. R. Hales	F/O Randall	F/L R. Munro
P/O B. B. Gottwalty	Sgt A. McCracken	Sgt W. Hutchinson	Sgt L. J. Henley	Sgt J. Reddish
F/L P. Kelly	Sgt V. Pitcher	Sgt J. Warwick	Sgt L. F. Freeman	P/O J. Harris
Sgt J. W. Hudson	Sgt Bickle	Sgt A. E. Every	Sgt R. Fowlston	F/O Schaunberg C. L.
Sgt C. W. Morley	Sgt H. McKay	Sgt A. Amos	Sgt N. J. Buchanan	F/S Vaughan
F/L S. H. Mansbridge	Sgt Jeffrey	Sgt J. Patterson	Sgt W. J. Stiles	F/S H. Wilkinson
F/O E. B. Chandler	Sgt H. Kennedy	Sgt H. S. Fraser	Sgt R. W. Slaughter	P/O T. S. Cooke

LM 306	ED 805	ED 438	JA 851	JA 892
F/S B. Kirton	S/L R. G. Todd-White	F/L T. D. Taylor	P/O T. E. Tomlin	Sgt C. Robinson
Sgt F. Wilby	Sgt A. Purrington	Sgt E. Winstanley	F/S K. E. Watson	Sgt W. Boyd
F/O N. Perry	P/O A. Batchelor	F/S J. Costello	F/S W. Rooke	F/O Duckham
Sgt J. O. Davies	P/O R. James	Sgt R. Stopani	Sgt Stancliffe	Sgt A. E. Anderson
Sgt W. T. Batty	Sgt G. Humble	Sgt A. Boag	Sgt W. Davies	Sgt D. Parkin
Sgt W. Mathison	P/O F. Plant	Sgt R. Seddon	F/S F. Tonkin	P/O W. J. Lowe
Sgt D. Burdett	Sgt Brocklehurst	P/O S. Sherman	Sgt Sylvester	Sgt J. Wallner

ED 426	ED 428
F/S E. B. Oglesby	W/O J. O. McCabe
Sgt G. Leggott	Sgt G. Hazeltine
Sgt T. Taylor	Sgt G. Sergcer
Sgt E. Howard	Sgt T. Thompson
Sgt K. Swinchatt	Sgt A. E. Falck
Sgt J. Turnbull	Sgt W. Moore
Sgt D. Dawson	Sgt L. Ford

No 5 Bomber Group *44 Squadron – Lancasters*

ED 611	EE 158	W 4935	DV 202	DV 155
P/O D. H. Aldridge	P/O H. Rogers	Sgt R. M. Campbell	P/O R. C. Harding	W/C R. L. Bowes
Sgt T. Phillips	Sgt J. R. Sutton	Sgt J. G. Watkins	Sgt T. N. Weston	Sgt K. E. Blundell
F/O D. B. E. Heslop	F/O C. R. Savage	P/O L. G. Poperwell	F/S L. Prendergast	Sgt A. Holden
Sgt T. S. Dellow	F/S H. E. Palmer	Sgt A. H. Thompson	F/S P. Pynisky	Sgt J. A. McCullum
Sgt R. W. West	F/S T. S. Carter	Sgt T. Graham	Sgt Quanee W. H.	P/O P. F. Roberts
F/S D. L. Welensky	Sgt G. E. Abel	Sgt H. G. McCannich	F/S S. Shaw	Sgt E. D. Pratt
Sgt T. S. Holmes	F/S F. C. Holmes	Sgt W. Phillip	Sgt L. F. McDermott	F/S G. A. Wilkie

W 4831
F/S Holms-a-Court
Sgt S. J. Bristow
Sgt J. W. Woods
Sgt K. L. Sumner
Sgt R. A. Kidleys
Sgt R. B. Groves
Sgt N. A. Norton

JA 897
Sgt W. J. Drew
Sgt J. B. Reid
Sgt S. Rudkin
Sgt W. Sparkes
Sgt J. F. Jopling
G. G. Jones
Sgt J. H. Bassett

W 4961
S/L R. G. Watson
Sgt C. H. Edwards
Sgt N. A. Tyreman
Sgt K. Gilbey
Sgt A. Corrie
Sgt C. G. James
Sgt N. J. Smith

JA 700
F/S R. L. Ash
Sgt G. F. Ives
Sgt C. G. Whitehead
Sgt H. Cushon
Sgt N. D. Deeble
Sgt J. Murphy
Sgt C. Knox

ED 433
F/O L. W. Pilgrim
Sgt J. A. Skilton
P/O E. J. Benner
Sgt L. C. Williams
F/S G. Fanning
Sgt G. T. Short
F/S R. M. Kethro

JA 703
F/O C. G. Hill
Sgt E. G. Wright
F/S J. Marsden
F/O G. W. Nunn
Sgt A. Yates
Sgt R. Ledsham
Sgt F. B. Kirwan

ED 665
F/S C. R. Snell
Sgt L. T. Harman
P/O L. Lintott
F/S E. J. Smith
Sgt J. Grieve
Sgt C. J. Green
Sgt E. Wood

JA 684
Sgt G. I. Ransome
Sgt G. S. McKinnon
Sgt C. P. Plumb
Sgt F. T. West
Sgt R. W. Coote
Sgt A. E. Millard
Sgt P. V. B. Vickers

No 5 Bomber Group *50 Squadron – Lancasters*

DV 227
F/S J. W. Thompson
Sgt R. W. Laws
Sgt S. Chapman
Sgt C. R. Corbett
Sgt A. E. Nicholson
Sgt A. E. Conlon
Sgt F. A. Wylie

W 5004
F/S R. M. Code
Sgt A. E. Langford
Sgt B. Ridsale
Sgt A. Noble
Sgt H. J. Boyton
Sgt E. F. Coling
Sgt C. R. Moad

JA 961
F/L W. F. Parks
Sgt R. E. Pearson
Sgt J. M. Laing
Sgt S. O. Smith
Sgt N. Jackson
F/O W. Boden
Sgt S. J. Proctor

DV 217
P/O J. H. Mason
Sgt W. T. Tildesley
F/S N. Stott
Sgt D. Grant
Sgt F. Tweedale
Sgt L. R. Cook
Sgt J. R. Pollock

LE 189
S/L W. Abercromby
P/O R. G. Huton
F/L C. H. Conway
W/O R. Frazer
F/S J. D. Halbert
F/O Boswell
F/L G. Hipkin

EE 124
F/S W. G. Smith
Sgt W. V. Ward
Sgt V. M. Munro
Sgt R. Baines
F/S H. M. Humphrey
Sgt J. R. Scott
Sgt H. Brown

ED 415
F/S W. G. Nelson
Sgt J. B. Atkinson
Sgt V. A. Darkin
Sgt H. L. Heason
Sgt W. A. Heale
Sgt S. E. Shepherd
Sgt L. M. Jeffery

ED 393
Sgt E. D. Weatherstone
Sgt D. Gregory
Sgt P. E. Thompson
Sgt A. D. Spruce
Sgt H. J. Lineham
Sgt P. H. Lane
Sgt R. A. Collingwood

ED 470
F/S S. J. Thompson
Sgt J. A. Winterford
Sgt P. C. Davies
Sgt J. M. Hydes
Sgt G. Clewlow
Sgt W. H. Wyer
Sgt S. Loseby

ED 588
P/O D. A. Duncan
Sgt E. Poulter
F/S W. J. Evans
Sgt R. L. Hayter
Sgt I. C. Dooley
Sgt J. Fulton
Sgt K. D. White

ED 755
F/L D. H. Chopping
Sgt R. A. Wooding
P/O E. Parsons
F/O D. M. Webster
Sgt Twitchett
F/S A. J. Thomas
Sgt J. C. Ruppert

ED 470
F/S M. J. Banks
Sgt W. T. Smith
Sgt I. N. F. Cameron
Sgt L. C. Jordan
Sgt A. H. Simpkin
Sgt H. W. F. Cooke
Sgt R. C. Tonkin

No 5 Bomber Group *57 Squadron – Lancasters*

ED 989
W/C W. R. Haskell
F/S C. Butterworth
Sgt R. Stringer
F/O J. Jones
Sgt J. Harkness
Sgt D. E. Nye
Sgt J. E. John
Sgt J. Lamb

ED 827
S/L R. E. S. Smith
F/O R. V. Munday
Sgt L. W. J. King
W/O J. Brown
F/S F. R. Farr
F/O P. Robins
Sgt C. Wood
Sgt J. Smith

JA 910
F/L A. R. Dunn
Sgt T. E. Eddowes
Sgt F. Mycoe
Sgt E. Fortune
Sgt E. G. King
Sgt Nightingale
Sgt D. Pinckhard

ED 920
F/O D. West
Sgt W. F. Neil
P/O N. F. Buggey
F/O J. Elliott
Sgt H. McKernin
Sgt F. P. Heaton
Sgt J. Edmunds

ED 946
F/L A. F. Gobbie
Sgt J. Hemmings
F/O A. E. Gardner
Sgt I. R. B. Jackson
F/O T. Scott
Sgt T. Sherborne
Sgt F. Lamble

ED 777
F/O P. L. Levy
Sgt W. Lynn
Sgt W. McKillop
Sgt R. May
Sgt W. C. Thomas
Sgt J. C. Perry
Sgt T. Crowther

ED 758
F/O F. L. Perrers
Sgt C. H. Pell
Sgt J. Clapperton
Sgt J. F. White
Sgt R. B. Mutam
Sgt Cruickshank
Sgt F. C. Crowe

ED 197
F/O P. Whittam
Sgt H. Siddons
F/O D. Brown
F/O B. McGonagle
F/O E. F. Belcher
Sgt R. C. Wallace
Sgt T. A. Marden

W 4822
F/O E. Hodgkinson
Sgt G. Martin
F/O P. N. Rolfe
F/O F. Butler
Sgt W. A. Hallam
Sgt R. Young
F/S W. Pryde

J 872
F/S T. G. Irwin
Sgt W. F. Griffiths
Sgt A. R. Knowles
F/O R. McRobbie
Sgt K. Sanderson
Sgt W. C. Dawkins
Sgt A. Heap

JA 875	DV 201	W 5008	ED 655
F/S H. S. Gifford	Sgt A. H. Moores	Sgt K. H. Ryrie	Sgt E. H. Tansley
Sgt C. W. Luke	Sgt A. J. Tompkin	Sgt G. Johnson	Sgt D. Griffiths
Sgt J. F. Agnew	Sgt R. F. Jowett	Sgt T. Ledingham	Sgt D. Park
Sgt A. Harrison	Sgt J. D. Cushing	F/O G. Pow	Sgt E. H. Patrick
Sgt L. R. Tanner	Sgt F. Northcliffe	Sgt K. M. McGrath	Sgt I. Groves
Sgt R. Campbell	Sgt W. H. Golding	Sgt V. R. Hawking	Sgt R. A. Lewis
Sgt H. E. Morris	F/S J. B. Hughes	Sgt A. Conway	Sgt H. A. Moad

No 5 Bomber Group *61 Squadron – Lancasters*

ED 718	DV 228	JA 874	ED 661	DV 232
W/C W. M. Penman	F/L D. C. Thomas	F/O N. D. Webb	P/O H. R. Madgett	P/O W. H. Eager
W/C Palmer	Sgt P. H. Todd	Sgt J. W. Brown	Sgt Lewis	Sgt L. Lawrence
F/O W. H. McDowell	Sgt G. Burrell	Sgt P. S. Watkins	Sgt H. Robinson	Sgt E. T. Petts
P/O D. J. Thompson	F/O C. H. Cleveland	Sgt J. Bailey	Sgt S. C. Palk	F/O F. L. Hewish
P/O D. I. Wilkinson	F/S R. M. Watford	Sgt C. J. Collingwood	F/O F. D. Norton	Sgt E. R. Stone
F/L W. C. Ingram	Sgt Webb	Sgt L. J. Prucell	P/O R. Bradley	Sgt F. R. Sharrard
P/O L. Healey	Sgt J. J. Little	Sgt D. J. Chapman	Sgt A. W. Souter	Sgt L. S. Vanner
	Sgt L. G. Davis		Sgt J. J. Wakefield	

W 4198	ED 630	W 4766	W 4934	JA 900
F/S A. E. Wilson	Sgt M. C. Lowe	F/L T. A. Stewart	F/O W. Hughes	F/S R. J. Docker
Sgt E. H. Buckley	Sgt C. R. Moffitt	Sgt Bradey	Sgt T. Graham	F/S Vidler
Sgt F. Melling	F/O R. J. Clarke	P/O F. Barker	Sgt L. H. Scholey	Sgt L. Lucas
Sgt H. P-Roberts	Sgt M. W. McPhail	Sgt J. F. Trotter	Sgt R. J. Brown	Sgt R. Laughton
Sgt R. M. Morris	Sgt D. A. Turner	Sgt Clarke	Sgt D. Easton	Sgt E. G. Francis
Sgt P. J. Pyle	Sgt A. W. Dearden	Sgt L. H. Thompson	Sgt R. C. Walton	Sgt S. W. James
Sgt P. Toole	Sgt A. Atkins	F/S R. K. Buxton	Sgt W. B. Ness	Sgt P. W. Mitchell
		Sgt A. E. Harris		Sgt R. R. Urquhart

W 4729	ED 314	W 4900
Sgt A. P. Strange	Sgt F. J. Roberts	Sgt E. Willsher
Sgt C. Cogdell	F/S S. R. Arter	Sgt T. J. Hardiss
F/S J. Toombs	Sgt R. Dudley	Sgt J. E. Grippon
F/O D. N. Calman	Sgt G. Young	Sgt J. S. Cooke
Sgt E. Smith	Sgt H. T. Blower	Sgt B. W. Bell
Sgt K. F. Johnson	F/S P. A. Marsh	Sgt R. E. Salter
F/O J. A. Stephens	Sgt W. A. Parsley	Sgt H. A. White

No 5 Bomber Group *106 Squadron – Lancasters*

ED 819	ED 191	JA 871	W 4922	R 5609
W/C R. E. Baxter	F/L G. H. Hartley	F/S J. G. Barker	F/O H. D. Ham	P/O A. Whetter
F/S J. Coulton	P/O J. Liston	Sgt W. Rawlinson	Sgt N. Gale	Sgt S. Gray
Sgt L. G. Berry	F/O McIver	Sgt A. G. Mearns	F/O L. C. Pitman	Sgt G. A. Johnson
F/L R. Lodge	Sgt L. D. Cromb	Sgt R. C. Curtis	Sgt J. E. Jones	Sgt J. A. Worsdale
F/L R. W. Moore	Sgt T. E. Sillitoe	Sgt V. Lynch	Sgt J. Weight	Sgt N. D. Cameron
F/O H. S. Nicholson	P/O G. W. Roberts	Sgt J. Withington	Sgt N. D. Higman	F/S T. J. Price
F/O J. Horobin	Sgt G. S. Miles	Sgt A. E. Elworthy	Sgt T. Waller	Sgt G. Smith

ED 409	JA 876	JA 973	ED 593
F/S J. L. Hendry	P/O F. W. Yackman	Sgt C. H. Storer	F/O J. R. T. Hoboken
Sgt L. Woods	Sgt S. Warsop	Sgt J. Cunliffe	Sgt G. E. Lucas
F/O H. L. Ashley	P/O H. Williams	Sgt E. G. Grundy	P/O J. P. Jenkins
Sgt S. Trevett	P/O G. L. Morey	Sgt R. E. Hackett	F/O J. C. Graham
Sgt J. Thomas	Sgt J. Gibson	Sgt F. W. Kite	P/O A. W. Read
Sgt T. R. Collins	Sgt A. E. Evans	Sgt C. Frankish	Sgt Williamson
Sgt W. Bruce	F/S R. J. Talbot	Sgt M. J. Martin	Sgt G. S. Broome

No 5 Bomber Group   *207 Squadron – Lancasters*

ED 832
S/L I. Huntley-Wood
Sgt J. G. Myerscough
F/O J. A. Waterman
F/O J. L. Young
F/S A. J. C. Whitehead
F/O J. G. Spanner
F/L J. G. Moore

DV 191
P/O W. H. Baker
Sgt D. H. Peppal
Sgt T. Gedling
Sgt G. H. Castell
Sgt E. M. Bunn
Sgt E. H. Shimeild
Sgt J. Skelton

LM 326
P/O G. H. Weeden
Sgt A. W. Richardson
F/S A. W. Jones
Sgt R. G. Howell
Sgt E. J. Walters
Sgt L. Robinson
Sgt E. Cummings

W 5006
S/L D. M. Balms
Sgt G. J. E. Bashford
F/S C. M. Lawes
Sgt H. Thomas
Sgt R. L. Rumgay
Sgt A. Cordon
Sgt S. Mitchell

ED 550
P/O J. A. G. Stevens
Sgt N. R. Bury
Sgt J. N. Love
Sgt A. J. C. Pegrum
Sgt K. Bate
Sgt A. Barfoot
Sgt A. T. McDevitt

ED 627
Sgt G. L. Caxon
Sgt A. W. Marsh
Sgt F. C. Shergold
Sgt K. Saville
Sgt J. L. Holding
Sgt H. A. Freeman

W 4185
P/O J. Kirkwood
Sgt E. G. Hubbard
Sgt R. G. Stewart
Sgt Johnson
P/O G. A. Wigley
Sgt L. Madley
Sgt J. Killen

W 4120
P/O R. M. Fitzgerald
Sgt S. Mitchell
Sgt C. H. Pratt
Sgt W. W. Addison
Sgt H. A. Toomey
Sgt S. Preston
Sgt J. Goodwin

EE 126
P/O J. McIntosh
Sgt R. C. Sooley
F/S M. Nicholson
F/S D. A. J. W. Ball
F/S J. Hyde
F/S J. Simmons
F/S R. Middleton

No 5 Bomber Group   *467 Squadron (R.A.A.F.) – Lancasters*

ED 949
F/S G. F. Tillotson
Sgt A. L. Winston
Sgt J. L. Harden
Sgt C. E. H. Graham
Sgt J. A. Steele
Sgt K. W. G. Mantock
Sgt W. P. Pankhurst

JA 902
F/O W. A. Forbes
Sgt F. G. Miller
Sgt W. J. O. Grime
Sgt J. Robertson
Sgt W. McLeod
Sgt J. D. Garth
Sgt J. A. Norman

ED 547
P/O J. H. Whiting
Sgt H. J. Pyke
Sgt J. G. Simpson
F/O W. S. Close
Sgt G. Self
F/S G. G. Blair
Sgt F. Fowler

ED 539
P/O K. A. McIver
Sgt A. B. McClelland
Sgt M. E. McGrath
Sgt J. K. Gale
Sgt G. McLean
Sgt R. Short
Sgt F. W. Shaw
F/O H. C. Ricketts

ED 545
W/O W. L. Wilson
Sgt S. A. Cawthorne
F/O C. N. Campbell
Sgt W. P. Crumplin
Sgt D. Booth
Sgt G. W. Oliver
Sgt P. G. Barry

LM 338
S/L W. J. Lewis
Sgt C. E. Stead
Sgt A. J. Scott
Sgt K. Garvey
Sgt R. C. Morley
Sgt G. P. Bayliss
Sgt J. H. Mallan
F/S D. C. Dunn

ED 541
Sgt D. B. Claxton
Sgt J. S. Wilson
Sgt D. Evans
Sgt A. E. Dishington
Sgt G. E. Fitt
Sgt T. B. Williams
Sgt R. M. Clarke

LM 340
F/L H. Blucke
Sgt A. M. Finch
Sgt E. F. Townsend
Sgt H. Hassall
Sgt L. Butler
Sgt R. G. Wellington
Sgt T. Munro

LM 342
S/L A. S. Raphael
Sgt V. Smith
Sgt F. Gray
F/O R. G. Carter
F/S D. Fielden
Sgt A. C. Brand
F/S F. B. Garrett
F/L M. H. Parry

ED 764
P/O F. W. Dixon
Sgt L. Hayward
Sgt C. A. Bicknell
Sgt E. W. Dickson
Sgt P. Lowe
Sgt R. Hughes
Sgt R. Garnett

No 5 Bomber Group   *619 Squadron – Lancasters*

EE 110
F/O A. H. Tomlin
Sgt E. G. Cass
Sgt T. A. Peatfield
Sgt J. Simkin
Sgt R. W. Thompson
Sgt A. W. Hobbs
Sgt P. R. Mitchell

EE 116
Sgt R. T. Hughes
Sgt G. Clarke
P/O G. W. Brake
Sgt R. Hume
Sgt R. N. Spratt
Sgt R. Atkinson
Sgt J. B. Crisp

JA 848
F/O D. M. Joss
Sgt T. Monoghan
P/O B. W. Hulse
P/O F. Anderson
Sgt P. Engel
Sgt J. Lowe
Sgt K. G. Mortlock

EE 111
F/L R. Aytoun
F/S S. Bremer
Sgt L. R. Lovitt
Sgt E. Brunt
Sgt F. A. Wilshire
Sgt D. R. Jones
Sgt R. Watts

JA 847
F/O T. O'Shaughnessy
Sgt D. G. Stewart
P/O A. D. Holding
P/O G. A. Kendrick
F/S A. G. Ward
F/S G. G. Turnbull
F/S J. Hutton

ED 977
P/O C. Firth
Sgt G. M. Weighell
Sgt C. N. Wright
Sgt D. Demaine
Sgt D. W. Dillnutt
Sgt M. Jones
Sgt A. G. Osborne

ED 109
F/L F. Pullen
Sgt G. Bradley
P/O T. W. E. Hughes
Sgt W. L. Ford
P/O J. R. Ferguson
F/S F. Amey
Sgt K. A. Humphries

EE 106
F/L S. E. Jones
Sgt A. E. Brookes
F/S A. C. E. Lance
Sgt E. Deschaine
Sgt R. G. Faux
Sgt G. S. Cook
P/O E. Cartwright
P/O E. K. Williams

EE 115
F/S F. G. Metcalfe
Sgt W. G. Mycock
F/S R. W. S. Gollogy
Sgt H. E. Kilburn
Sgt F. G. Dryden
Sgt R. W. Measor
Sgt H. D. Watkins

EE 117
W/C I. J. McGhie
F/S P. J. Horsham
F/O E. G. Prest
F/S P. M. Goldsmith
Sgt F. A. Thompson
Sgt W. Mitchell
Sgt A. Chapman
F/S V. G. Stabell

EE 982	EE 147
Sgt A. J. Pearce	P/O O. A. O'Leary
Sgt W. Humphrey	Sgt T. Underdown
F/O J. M. Warren	F/S R. Crossley
Sgt L. G. Davis	Sgt J. T. Hubbard
Sgt T. B. Barrie	Sgt J. H. Shaw
Sgt R. D. Deugard	Sgt D. G. Cox
Sgt D. B. Francis	F/S L. F. English

No 6 Bomber Group   *419 (Moose) Squadron R.C.A.F. – Halifaxes*

JD 382	JD 456	JD 458	JD 158	JD 457
F/L B. J. Corcoran	F/S T. Douhassoff	F/S S. Pekin	F/O S. M. Heard	F/S D. T. Cooke
W/O A. J. McKenzie	Sgt E. Gargett	F/O P. J. Sparkes	Sgt C. S. Walter	P/O O. W. Fonger
F/S A. C. Harris	Sgt J. Davie	Sgt J. K. Gilvary	Sgt P. O. McSween	Sgt H. H. Campbell
W/O H. d'Aperng	Sgt H. Marshall	Sgt H. Price	Sgt J. J. Newbon	Sgt R. J. Packer
Sgt J. G. Allen	Sgt D. A. West	Sgt F. P. Davis	Sgt G. Blyth	Sgt A. Simpson
Sgt J. T. Venier	Sgt R. Murie	Sgt S. C. Ramm	Sgt D. Thornton	Sgt R. W. G. Sullivan
F/O D. E. Larlee	Sgt J. Pilon		Sgt J. W. Dally	Sgt D. W. Robertson
			Sgt D. M. McPherson	

BB 376	JB 929	JD 204	DT 731	JD 163
F/L W. N. Keddie	F/O H. A. Hewitt	F/O W. H. Hamilton	W/O J. R. Morrison	Sgt J. M. Batterton
P/O F. S. Hair	F/O F. T. Judah	P/O E. L. Riley	F/O M. C. Andrews	Sgt G. F. Parker
P/O A. D. Winskill	F/O H. A. Lee	P/O J. R. Dale	P/O E. A. Hieland	Sgt O. Jerome
Sgt T. J. Bright	Sgt J. J. Salaba	Sgt T. Reay	Sgt W. R. Touchie	Sgt Lloyd D. A.
Sgt E. R. Kirkham	Sgt J. Edmondson	Sgt T. McEwen	Sgt H. Looney	Sgt K. Dixon
Sgt G. A. Hurst	Sgt F. W. Griffiths	Sgt E. Griffin	Sgt A. E. Johnson	Sgt L. Powers
Sgt R. J. Wagner	Sgt J. Broadhurst	Sgt A. Bartollussi	Sgt J. H. Lynk	Sgt H. V. Morris
F/O H. T. Brown				

JD 114	JD 270	JD 459	JD 459	JD 420
Sgt J. McIntosh	Sgt W. D. L. Cameron	F/S R. Stewart	F/L A. N. Quaile	F/O J. A. Westland
F/S W. L. White	Sgt G. E. Birtch	P/O E. E. James	P/O L. E. Aspinall	P/O J. B. Hall
Sgt R. M. Keary	Sgt V. J. Wintzer	Sgt D. A. Cleveland	P/O G. T. Graham	P/O J. W. Galvin
Sgt A. D. Runsam	Sgt L. H. Duggan	Sgt A. Embley	Sgt K. I. J. Deane	Sgt W. Beer
Sgt E. S. Mulholland	Sgt J. T. Mullany	Sgt H. R. Tenny	Sgt L. F. Martin	Sgt H. G. Davies
T/Sgt M. S. Braniff	Sgt B. W. Scharf	Sgt L. Northcliffe	Sgt L. J. Lemire	Sgt W. S. Atkinson
Sgt K. N. Doe	Sgt R. E. Boos	Sgt A. E. Garland	P/O H. F. Smith	T/Sgt B. Blount

JB 965	JD 325
Sgt R. K. Metherall	Sgt C. M. Coutlee
Sgt A. D. Cheswell	F/O W. S. Hendry
Sgt R. Edwards	Sgt W. E. Hay
Sgt A. B. Kelsall	Sgt J. A. Norman
Sgt C. H. Pollard	Sgt R. A. Booth
Sgt J. L. Mercier	Sgt W. H. Barnes
Sgt R. M. Marritt	Sgt G. H. Marjoram

No 6 Bomber Group   *426 –(Thunderbird) Squadron R.C.A.F. – Lancaster Mk II's*

DS 681	DS 676	DS 619	DS 677	DS 708
W/C L. Crooks	S/L W. H. Swetman	Lt S. Gaunt	F/L W. L. Shaw	Sgt M. B. Summers
F/S A. J. Howes	F/O R. E. D. Radcliffe	F/O A. McCormich	Sgt E. G. Farr	F/O J. J. Beaton
F/L F. P. Marsh	F/S I. N. Peterson	Sgt J. H. Jones	Sgt J. Williams	F/S G. Davies
Sgt K. W. Reading	F/L M. Roach	Sgt J. Salisbury	F/O A. J. Gibson	F/S J. Wilde
Sgt J. C. Hislop	P/O J. J. Devan	Sgt R. W. Elliott	Sgt A. Lucas	Sgt C. J. Bettesworth
P/O T. Dos Santos	Sgt C. F. Jelley	Sgt T. H. Hastings	P/O D. D. du Boulay	Sgt G. E. Aldous
Sgt H. M. Smith	P/O H. J. Thomas	Sgt F. E. Fox	Sgt L. G. E. Burnett	Sgt D. E. Newland

DS 688	DS 713	DS674
Sgt C. A. Griffiths	F/L R. F. Epps	F/L D. D. Shuttleworth
F/S R. Allwell	F/O D. W. Simpson	F/O G. C. Robinson
Sgt R. H. Filbey	F/S M. W. Warren	Sgt K. G. Gawthrop
F/S G. Sparkes	Sgt W. F. Woodley	Sgt J. M. L. Bouvier
Sgt G. Jowett	Sgt K. Beeley	Sgt S. Barnes
Sgt R. G. Gridland	Sgt E. C. G. Jones	F/O G. W. Scammell
Sgt J. S. Morton	Sgt J. T. McLaughlin	Sgt G. Bentley

No 6 Bomber Group *427 (Lion) Squadron R.C.A.F. – Halifaxes*

DK 184
F/O G. R. Baum
P/O R. C. Day
P/O W. Bray
Sgt P. Murphy
Sgt G. F. Painter
Sgt M. R. Singer
Sgt D. C. Davies

LK 900
Sgt N. E. Fletcher
Sgt F. P. C. Walters
Sgt G. C. Tew
Sgt R. S. Johnson
Sgt L. S. Stemmler
Sgt T. R. Fox
Sgt G. S. Wood

DK 243
Sgt F. J. D. Brady
Sgt R. W. Charman
Sgt R. I. Johnson
Sgt J. L. Troman
Sgt O. M. McIntyre
Sgt J. L. Fletcher
Sgt I. W. Pugh

DK 253
F/S W. Champion
F/O T. J. Thomas
Sgt J. E. Paquette
Sgt R. Ranger
Sgt G. B. Squair
Sgt J. L. Perrin
Sgt G. J. King

EB 247
Capt C. A. Taylor
F/O G. A. Martin
P/O D. Mortimer
Sgt W. F. Baker
Sgt G. J. Chaput
Sgt W. Lumsden
Sgt T. C. Jones

DK 227
Sgt W. H. Schmitt
P/O A. H. Fernand
P/O G. L. Vogan
Sgt S. Fahner
Sgt L. S. Gray
Sgt R. McNamara
Sgt N. W. Wood

EB 251
Sgt D. O. Olsvik
Sgt J. P. McKenzie
Sgt R. L. Warren
Sgt D. Jonassen
Sgt W. R. Tobin
Sgt A. G. Taillon
Sgt J. P. Richards

DK 234
Sgt G. Wolton
F/O G. M. Walls
F/O D. F. Wilson
F/O S. M. Byrne
F/O O. J. Moller
F/O R. Potentier
F/O J. R. Brown

EB 246
F/S J. R. G. Milton
P/O A. W. Shirley
P/O E. Atkins
Sgt E. A. Perdue
Sgt A. V. Humphries
F/S A. C. Middleton
Sgt F. C. Barker

EB 241
F/O B. Arnot
Sgt L. W. Jones
F/O W. Thom
Sgt R. Dawson
Sgt L. C. Benier
Sgt R. O. Nickerson
Sgt R. A. Rondelet

EB 243
F/L B. G. Crew
F/S R. L. Skillen
F/S H. W. Campbell
Sgt W. F. Suter
Sgt L. H. Smith
F/S H. Nelson
Sgt W. E. Powell

DK255
F/L J. A. Morton
P/O S. S. Schellenberg
Sgt P. H. J. Elsee
Sgt J. Pennack
Sgt J. G. Roberts
Sgt R. F. Shortidge
Sgt J. A. McClune

No 6 Bomber Group *428 (Ghost) Squadron R.C.A.F. – Halifaxes*

EB 205
F/O K. W. Jones
P/O W. C. Ingram
Sgt L. Pelmear
Sgt C. F. Fox
Sgt G. W. E. Palmer
Sgt V. Moore
Sgt E. C. Bartram

EB 210
P/O W. A. Hadden
Sgt A. F. Morris
Sgt S. A. Whitby
Sgt J. Curran
Sgt P. J. Flower
Sgt G. W. Renwick
Sgt A. Yuill

EB 211
Sgt J. Sheridan
Sgt H. E. Murphy
Sgt T. B. Lifman
Sgt D. Kennedy
Sgt W. E. Cogger
Sgt N. R. Mitchell
Sgt E. R. Marks

EB 274
F/S H. A. Reade
Sgt L. S. Bates
F/O J. J. McQuade
Sgt S. W. Patterson
Sgt S. E. Crampton
Sgt J. Taylor
Sgt J. A. Kerr

DK 238
Sgt W. W. Blackmore
Sgt N. F. Oliver
Sgt W. S. E. Wood
Sgt F. S. Williams
Sgt C. F. Richard
Sgt G. F. Hobson
Sgt G. C. Seaborn

DK 235
F/L A. V. Retlander
F/O B. W. Foskett
Sgt J. W. Fisher
Sgt A. F. Dowding
Sgt F. Janes
Sgt S. Lucas
Sgt F. W. Barthy
Sgt N. W. Neilson

DK 252
F/O G. R. Drimmie
F/S J. K. Evans
F/O J. Gilbey
Sgt E. A. Lane
F/S A. Haslehurst
Sgt R. F. Peterson
Sgt D. Smith

EB 252
F/S W. J. Armour
Sgt J. P. McMaster
Sgt L. P. Coupe
Sgt S. P. Page
Sgt B. C. Dumbrill
Sgt J. J. Moon
Sgt F. G. Clucas

EB 214
Sgt J. Harkins
Sgt D. J. Richard
Sgt S. A. Baldwin
Sgt A. Scott
Sgt A. Parkinson
Sgt G. F. Columbus
Sgt N. Lee

EB 215
P/O L. F. Williamson
P/O W. M. Watkins
P/O H. B. Parker
Sgt J. H. R. Oakley
Sgt J. Powey
Sgt E. Chamberlain
P/O D. H. Christie
Sgt J. B. A. Este

DK 230
F/L G. W. Fanson
F/O D. H. Orr
Sgt D. J. McNeill
Sgt R. A. Lewis
Sgt L. M. Banks
Sgt M. C. McCullum
Sgt J. A. Leighton

DK 233
Sgt K. O. Fry
Sgt P. S. McGowran
P/O J. G. Taylor
Sgt A. E. Moss
Sgt W. Poston
Sgt D. A. Crossan
Sgt J. J. McNeil
Sgt W. M. Brown

EB 206
W/O A. Harrison
P/O N. M. Bush
Sgt A. R. Brock
Sgt A. C. Yule
Sgt E. F. Freeman
Sgt P. P. Bentley
Sgt G. J. North

DK 196
Sgt R. L. Borrowes
Sgt J. Mitchell
Sgt A. B. Leslie
Sgt R. L. Squires
Sgt F. J. Montgomery
Sgt G. J. Spearman
Sgt B. F. Pothier

No 6 Bomber Group *434 (Bluenose) Squadron R.C.A.F. – Halifaxes*

DK 259	EB 258	EB 256	EB 255	DK 260
F/L Thompson	F/S Piper	Sgt Austin	F/O Lord	F/O Colquhoun
Sgt Purdy	P/O Wetter	P/O McKay	P/O Jones	Sgt Dobie
Sgt Miller	Sgt Jordan	Sgt Scott	P/O Sinclair	F/S Fitzpatrick
Sgt Bellingham	Sgt Connor	Sgt Barrette	Sgt O'Hara	F/O Beswick
Sgt Plouffe	Sgt Brown	Sgt Dixon	Sgt Wallis	Sgt Young
Sgt Reynolds	Sgt Renaud	Sgt McConnell	Sgt Desieyes	F/S Lapointe
Sgt Malcolm	Sgt Irving	Sgt Foster	Sgt Walters	Sgt Crees

EB 254	EB 255	EB 276	DK 248
Sgt Snelgrove	Sgt Harrison	Sgt Johnston	Lieut Clary
F/O Smith	Sgt Ledford	Sgt Gibbs	Sgt Pollard
P/O Hunt	Sgt Ford	P/O McPherson	F/O Dodge
Sgt Dane	Sgt Walshaw	F/S Christmas	Sgt Bellinger
Sgt Holmes	Sgt Climie	F/S Labelle	F/S Lockhart
Sgt Hoffman	Sgt Morgan	Sgt Rowe	Sgt Stuart
Sgt Mitton	Sgt Ebbers		P/O Hovey
			Sgt Hayes

No 8 (Pathfinder) Group *156 Squadron – Lancasters*

JA 702	JA 921	EE 926	JA 858	JA 915
P/O J. L. Sloper	P/O L. W. Overton	F/O A. M. Lutz	F/O J. E. Prichard	F/L A. S. Cook
Sgt H. C. Thorn	P/O D. P. Clements	P/O D. D. Curtis	F/O T. D. Ferres	P/O H. J. Wright
Sgt R. J. Woolmer	Sgt J. A. M. Arcari	W/O J. Hurst	Sgt W. Friend	F/O W. L. Bagg
Sgt S. Gibbs	Sgt T. Cable	P/O R. E. Manvell	Sgt T. Hoyle	F/S D. A. Cartwright
Sgt S. D. Coy	Sgt N. H. Denyer	P/O G. B. Clements	F/O C. R. Norton	P/O C. B. T. McSweeney
Sgt G. Wilson	Sgt F. Sunderland	Sgt K. Pearson	Sgt A. Grout	Sgt W. C. Marriage
Sgt G. Milburn	Sgt A. Barnett	Sgt J. Fletcher	Sgt H. J. Simpson	Sgt L. A. J. Lockley

ED 952	ED 969	JA 909	JA 698	JA 674
P/O P. A. Coldham	W/C J. H. White	F/O J. L. Wright	F/L P. R. Vincent	S/L R. E. Young
F/O A. P. Stevens	F/L R. Roberts	F/O A. S. Drew	S/L H. R. Hall	F/L T. Burger
Sgt A. A. P. Bland	F/S M. J. E. Stonely	F/O M. A. Carter	Sgt A. Swinney	Sgt H. G. Murley
Sgt T. E. Rees	F/S W. Wilkinson	Sgt H. A. C. Hammond	Sgt C. W. Hodges	Sgt J. K. Calton
F/S G. R. Robinson	F/S J. C. Otter	P/O C. W. B. Kelly	Sgt S. W. Hatwell	Sgt T. H. Evans
F/S N. Warwick	F/O E. M. Thompson	P/O M. J. Reynolds	Sgt A. J. Clarke	Sgt J. S. Goodman
F/S G. H. Pascoe	F/S D.M.G.Silverman	P/O K. A. Crankshaw	Sgt C. E. Morgan	Sgt J. W. Boynton

ED 856	JA 941	JA 861	JA 694	ED 859
P/O R. G. F. Stewart	F/L G. L. Mandeno	W/O Rose	F/L J. F. Thompson	F/L D. C. Anset
F/S D. A. S. Hanard	F/L H. G. Innes	Sgt J. E. Foley	Sgt J. E. Farnell	F/O S. C. P. Godfrey
F/S C. H. Handley	W/O A. P. Fast	Sgt J. B. Sullivan	Sgt L. W. Lapthorne	P/O J. H. Wright
F/S F. Thorington	Sgt J. C. Champan	Sgt Anderson	P/O C. F. Hamilton	Sgt J. Walker
F/S R. J. Hudson	P/O D. C. A. Saunders	F/S M. M. Patrick	F/S J. C. Baxter	Sgt H. Stokes
F/S D. A. Mills	Sgt G. G. Forbes	Sgt R. J. Longmore	P/O D. Moffat	Sgt R. Watson
F/O C. F. Horner	F/S T. H. Knight	F/S R. H. Gee	P/O F. J. Wilkin	Sgt G. A. Davis
		F/S D. H. Royle		

JA 925	JA 697	EE 177	JA 714	ED 883
F/L R. E. Fawcett	F/S Stimpson	S/L N. R. Manfield	F/S H. F. Slade	F/L A. L. McGrath
Sgt D. R. Lydford	Sgt H. N. Jackson	F/O E. S. Alexander	F/L J. Geoghegan	F/O R. P. Wright
Sgt J. Bell	Sgt R. A. C. Robinson	P/O C. R. Swinney	F/O R. H. McDonald	F/O J. Facey
Sgt R. J. Bowen	Sgt W. J. Catchpole	F/S C. H. Lawrance	Sgt B. Johnson	Sgt D. L. Wilkie
Sgt G. Vickers	Sgt J. L. Gurton	F/S Trott	Sgt H. E. Jones	F/O G. R. Johnson
Sgt G. Headley	Sgt W. H. Smith	F/S Waterhouse	Sgt R. Andrews	Sgt Prochera
Sgt D. C. Hinks	Sgt T. R. Dalton	P/O D. MacKie	Sgt H. Toon	Sgt G. D. Aitken

ED 841
F/S T. G. Stephens
Sgt A. C. Clegg
Sgt T. Stocks
Sgt S. J. Ryan
Sgt H. Trusctott
Sgt L. R. Wright
Sgt V. E. Attree

JA 673
F/S F. J. Fry
F/O W. A. Kerry
Sgt Dalton
Sgt D. H. Evans
F/O N. H. Carter
Sgt W. E. Chambers
Sgt L. Ducat

No 8 (Pathfinder) Group *35 Squadron – Halifaxes*

HR 897
F/L A. J. F. Davidson
F/L G. R. Whitten
F/L S. R. Green
F/S R. J. Bloom
F/S E. J. Simpson
P/O D. H. Stanley
P/O D. W. Craig

JB 786
F/O J. J. Jagger
F/O P. McGarry
F/L J. Baker
Sgt V. Smedley
Sgt E. Hie
Sgt N. G. Raperi
Sgt W. Percival

HR 926
S/L A. P. Cranswick
W/O W. McRobbie
F/L H. A. Hulme
F/S D. McKenzie
P/O I. I Howard
Sgt M. Arnot
F/S R. Johnson

HR 907
F/S N. J. Matiche
Sgt R. Tully
F/O C. A. Hewlett
F/S F. R. Dolling
P/O H. E. Tuck
F/S A. W. Forsythe
Sgt Mather

HR 855
P/O R. R. G. Appleby
Sgt Nixon
F/L D. P. P. Archer
Sgt E. V. Redfearn
Sgt D. S. James
Sgt H. M. Bromham
Sgt T. I. Robinson

HR 913
F/S T. R. Skerrett
Sgt R. M. Dando
Sgt J. T. Strachan
W/O F. G. Murphy
Sgt M. E. Weighall
Sgt R. N. Telfer
Sgt R. Fox

HR 802
F/S A. V. Hardy
Sgt B. C. Brooker
Sgt S. J. Walters
Sgt M. R. Bates
Sgt E. M. Davis
Sgt R. H. Gill
Sgt A. G. Page

HR 862
F/S P. R. Raggett
F/O S. A. Baldwin
P/O A. J. Perkins
Sgt Roberts
Sgt P. H. Palmer
Sgt D. S. Woods
Sgt Webster

HR 777
S/L E. W. Deacon
Sgt C. Hogg
F/L J. H. N. Carter
Sgt P. Wright
Sgt F. Poynton
Sgt W. McCormick
Sgt G. Foreman

HR 925
P/O L. E. N. Lahey
F/L J. W. Annetts
F/L D. F. Bland
F/S D. D. Cleary
Sgt R. Hogg
Sgt L. A. Such
Sgt W. Sutton

No 8 (Pathfinder) Group *97 Squadron – Lancasters*

JA 846
F/L Eaton-Clarke
Sgt F. Dunning
W/C R. C. Alabaster
P/O A. E. Carlton
F/S C. K. Smith
Sgt E. Hambling
Sgt P. Walder

JA 908
S/L J. H. Sauvage
Sgt W. G. Waller
F/O H. A. Hitchcock
F/O F. Burbridge
F/S Wheeler
F/L J. E. Blair
Sgt C. W. Wood

JA 958
F/L C. B. Robertson
Sgt W. C. Peel
F/L G. C. Crockett
F/S P. Scott
F/O J. C. Frizzell
Sgt W. Wilkes
F/S W. St C Hebb

ED 938
P/O J. F. Munro
P/O Swetman
P/O A. Spencer
P/O A. J. Suswain
Sgt Campbell
Sgt Underwood
Sgt K. S. Bennett
F/S W. Hill

EE 107
P/O K. Brown
Sgt M. Hogg
P/O F. N. Alexander
Sgt Graham
F/S K. W. Knight
Sgt J. Curry
Sgt J. T. Sullivan
Sgt W. T. Saunders

ED 869
F/O R. A. Fletcher
Sgt J. Nelson
F/S J. Dunn
Sgt J. Beesley
F/S W. M. Layne
Sgt Laing
Sgt Page

ED 839
S/L E. E. Rodley
Sgt K. J. Bell
S/L K. J. Foster
S/L E. H. Parrott
Sgt C. T. Ambrose
F/O L. J. Williams
Sgt A. J. Croll

ED 814
F/L R. F. Clayton
Sgt A. S. Palmer
F/L F. W. Chandler
Sgt A. C. Newbigin
F/S Halsey
Sgt R. C. Haviland
F/S P. O. Bone

JA 711
F/O B. H. Berridge
Sgt O. Ramsay
W/O L. Brenner
F/O Griffith
F/S W. Parker
F/S A. R. Flowerday
F/S W. Lochrie
F/S Pearce

ED 950
P/O K. Fairlie
Sgt C. E. Addison
Sgt W. G. Clutterbuck
Sgt K. Prouten
Sgt F. Ball
Sgt A. J. Coossin
Sgt O. Coombs

ED 875
P/O D. A. Montgomery
Sgt G. C. Grainger
P/O E. L. Cohn
Sgt J. N. Gardner
F/S J. Baker
Sgt S. N. Neill
F/S C. P. Baggs

ED 868
F/S L. Stevenson
Sgt Roberts
Sgt J. Brett
Sgt R. G. Christie
Sgt J. D. Bradford
Sgt H. G. Mitchell
Sgt J. Mallaber
Sgt T. G. Pugh

ED 179
F/O G. de Wesselow
Sgt Bamblett
Sgt S. Caryle
F/O W. G. Cooper
Sgt F. White
Sgt Harris
Sgt Press

ED 870
Sgt J. H. Saxton
Sgt P. H. Fryer
Sgt F. H. Baker
Sgt J. C. Rees
Sgt C. Watson
Sgt C. J. Zunti
Sgt W. E. Coates

JA 707
F/S H. A. Pond
Sgt E. J. Gillman
Sgt S. B. Stevenson
F/O V. C. Peters
Sgt T. M. Kenny
Sgt O. Ramsden
Sgt T. N. McGrath

EE 105	ED 176
S/L J. M. Garlick	F/O W. Riches
Sgt J. M. Anderson	Sgt G. Winter
Sgt A. G. Boyd	Sgt H. W. Watts
Sgt E. O. Carlson	Sgt E. H. Pack
Sgt Cohen	Sgt J. Wrigley
F/S T. M. Ward	Sgt R. W. Lowe
Sgt M. Edwards	Sgt F. C. Nordhoff

No 8 (Pathfinder) Group *83 Squadron – Lancasters*

JA 686	ED 984	ED 602	JA 677	ED 876
P/O A. C. Shipway	F/L I. C. B. Slade	S/L G. D. Sells	S/L R. J. Manton	F/O M. R. Chick
Sgt E. Cummings	F/S V. C. Lewis	Sgt R. L. Taylor	Sgt F. J. Chadwick	Sgt A. W. Hicks
P/O B. Moorcroft	F/L A. N. McPherson	S/L A. S. Johnson	S/L A. G. A. Cochrane	Sgt J. W. Slaughter
Sgt R. W. Silk	Sgt Robinson	F/L C. Webb	Sgt A. E. Evans	Sgt B. Turner
Sgt W. D. G. Wilkes	W/O Baker	F/S A. Drinkell	Sgt S. A. R. Taylor	F/O C. A. S. Drew
Sgt P. L. T. Lewis	W/O H. Allen	Sgt G. J. Horton	F/S Rutter	Sgt L. R. Howell
Sgt B. Denoon	F/L R. F. Turner	F/S A. Dickenson	F/O A. J. Ellis	Sgt Ellwood
		Sgt S. J. Davis		

JA 927	JA 705	JA 913	JA 940	ED 984
P/O J. A. Reid	S/L A. B. Smith	S/L N. F. Hildyard	F/O W. R. Thompson	P/O R. King
Sgt D. Lawes	F/S Rathbone	F/S E. Sutton	Sgt A. W. Belton	Sgt K. E. L. Farmiloe
P/O A. J. E. Brown	F/S J. H. Wright	P/O J. F. Hacking	F/O C. F. Bedell	F/O E. D. Gallagher
W/O H. Kitto	F/O C. H. Wilson	F/S J. Endean	Sgt A. Wilkes	Sgt D. J. Phelan
P/O W. Wardrop	F/L R. F. Tinkler	F/L S. J. Coleman	Sgt R. P. Hanratty	P/O R. M. Smalley
F/S S. Hatton	Sgt S. W. Gray	F/S J. P. Meddings	Sgt R. B. Hicks	Sgt E. D. McPherson
Sgt A. Cousens	Sgt R. W. Roberts	W/O J. Goldie	Sgt J. H. Tolman	Sgt R. A. Adams
	F/S P. Menzies			

AJ 701	JA 712	JA 928	EE 175	W 4959
F/L Mason	F/S K. C. Turp	G/Cpt J. H. Searby	P/O F. C. Allcroft	W/O J. Finding
W/O Goodwin	Sgt D. Bailey	P/O F. A. Forster	Sgt H. Coles	Sgt T. C. Evans
P/O A. Feeley	F/O H. A. Clarke	S/L N. H. Scrivener	P/O H. Readman	Sgt H. E. Borrow
P/O W. G. Williams	Sgt J. W. Pimm	F/O L. G. Davies	P/O R. H. C. Reynolds	Sgt W. Bainbridge
F/S H. C. Highet	F/S W. E. Freeze	F/O W. G. Ross	P/O F. C. Pemberton	Sgt D. Wilson
W/O J. N. Papworth	F/S C. H. Silvester	F/O J. H. Coley	Sgt A. McDonald	Sgt C. R. B. Everard
F/L D. Johnson	Sgt T. P. Shelmerdine	P/O I. W. Preece	Sgt S. O. Hargreaves	Sgt J. H. Lyons

No 8 (Pathfinder) Group *7 Squadron – Lancasters*

JA 717	A 685	JA 710	JA 706	EE 119
F/L B. H. D. Foster	F/L J. A. Zee	P/O A. C. Harding	F/O K. McIntyre	F/L S. Baker
F/O J. Perfect	F/L E. F. Leevin	F/S E. J. Clement	F/L D. A. Brown	S/L J. A. Sinclair
F/S C. J. Stokes	F/S W. H. Swain	F/S T. J. Walsh	Sgt D. Gainford	W/O W. H. Cutts
Sgt W. Wilson	F/S D. C. Johnston	F/O J. Hough	Sgt E. H. Barron	Sgt F. Lashford
F/O F. S. Whittlestone	Lieut. W. M. Bradford	Sgt E. C. Millidge	Sgt G. Harris	F/L P. H. Cutchey
F/O G. J. B. Neil	F/S F. A. Darlington	F/S W. C. O'Connor	Sgt J. F. Reed	W/O C. Thornhill
F/S D. Jones	W/O W. Hindmarsh	Sgt F. A. G. Parker	F/S A. C. Turner	W/O J. E. Robbins

JA 907	JA 853	EE 200	JA 933	JA 678
F/L V. Harcourt	P/O P. Wilby	F/S J. R. Petrie	F/O Philipson-Stowe	S/L C. J. Lofthouse
Sgt W. V. J. Gould	F/O M. B. Whitbread	F/O P. K. B. Williams	F/O R. V. Coutts	F/L B. D. Cayford
F/S G. A. Inverarity	Sgt T. Hayward	F/L L. A. Gibson	P/O D. N. Rowe	W/O J. Pane
Sgt G. M. Welsh	Sgt G. W. D. Drew	Sgt E. E. Edmonds	Sgt A. S. Simpson	Sgt L. G. Cooper
Sgt N. Kaye	F/S S. E. Launchbury	Sgt A. W. Osborne	Sgt P. J. Aldridge	Sgt J. S. Caton
Sgt A. R. G. Rouse	Sgt J. R. Dickenson	Sgt S. R. Rose	Sgt R. L. Jones	F/S A. J. Dart
Sgt J. G. Miles	Sgt L. H. Standley	Sgt A. H. Hartshorn	Sgt C. S. Goodman	F/S A. Davidson
		F/S C. J. Seery		

JA 854
F/L R. O. French
F/O F. E. Lewis
F/S G. E. Weber
Sgt J. K. S. Williams
Sgt A. R. Fraser
F/S B. E. Lindsay
F/S R. Lawson

JA 964
F/O R. D. Campling
P/O R. J. H. Clayton
Sgt G. E. Combe
Sgt C. H. L. Wright
F/O D. F. Langham
Sgt B. S. Cubbage
F/S G. W. Pride

JA 932
F/S C. A. Negus
Sgt W. Currie
Sgt L. Wimshurst
Sgt R. J. Wheway
Sgt M. Davies
Sgt S. W. Rayner
Sgt J. J. Davenport

JA 936
S/L C. Anakstein
P/O G. A. Beaumont
F/O H. Smith
Sgt S. Thorogood
Sgt J. W. C. Ganney
F/O G. A. Atkinson
P/O W. H. Cross
Sgt V. T. Perdue

JA 935
F/O O. J. Wells
Sgt F. A. G. Clarke
Sgt W. D. J. Stevenson
Sgt B. J. W. Balster
F/O W. J. Watts
Sgt T. E. Barton
Sgt H. R. McKay

JA 917
F/S J. Sutherst
F/S C. G. Baker
Sgt A. Harris
Sgt R. H. Nash
E. N. N. Beldon
Sgt H. S. Hayward
Sgt W. N. Kinsey

JA 713
W/C K. Rampling
P/O R. Crease
F/S R. Hayward
Sgt W. A. Clegg
F/O R. G. Layley
Sgt D. G. Pooley
Sgt L. C. Hartman

No. 8 P.F.F. Group *No 405 Squadron R.C.A.F – Halifaxes*

J
W/C J. E. Fauquier
S/Ldr P. G. Powell
F/L E. H. Anthony
F/O J. C. Lowther
P/O J. R. Sipple
S/L J. F. Clarke
P/O L. R. King

V
F/O W. Weiser
F/O G. B. Elwood
P/O P. J. Magson
Sgt G. F. Mayon
F/O H. C. Banks
F/S L. Coburn
Sgt T. H. Geary
W/O H. Smith

D
P/O J. A. Weber
F/L I. Hewitt
P/O W. J. Lawrence
F/S P. Ricard
P/O B. A. Craddock
F/S S. H. Nutting
P/O R. S. Mclean
F/O F. A. Harman

L
P/O G. S. McMenemy
P/O H. W. Fenton
P/O L. M. Holtby
Sgt R. G. Williams
F/S J. Roderick
F/S H. R. Welch
Sgt A. C. Sondergard

T
F/O M. Sattler
F/S H. Fawcett
F/S H. C. Card
Sgt H. F. Watson
Sgt G. S. Read
Sgt I. McEwen
Sgt D. B James

A
P/O H. Cowan
Sgt B. W. Culpin
F/S R. O. Milne
Sgt D. J. Langley
Sgt D. G. Hirschfeld
Sgt C. F. Mace
Sgt H. R. Hurst

R
P/O B. F. McSorley
Sgt A. Livesey
F/S G. L. Watts
Sgt J. Holden
Sgt W. M. Gorman
Sgt W. D. Ridgeway
Sgt F. C. Bolter
P/O G. T. South

C
F/O H. S. McIntyre
Sgt D. C. Angus
Sgt W. E. Gimby
Sgt T. J. Bowling
Sgt W. Haugen
Sgt T. A. Pargeter
Sgt H. Cooke

H
Sgt R. H. Larson
F/O J. M. Pedersen
Sgt R. D. Mutch
Sgt J. B. Errington
Sgt E. F. Wren
Sgt J. P. Dube
Sgt T. Thompson

X
P/O K. R. Wood
P/O J. N. R. Redpath
Sgt F. W. Bunday
Sgt W. H. Hedley
F/S O. O. Johnson
Sgt E. C. Brunet
Sgt J. H. Lovelock

K
Sgt A. C. Branton
Sgt R. Thompson
Sgt L. J. Broderick
Sgt G. W. Acorn
Sgt G. E. Agate
Sgt M. A. Menzies
Sgt C. Hewitson

N
Sgt C. Nielson
Sgt D. M. Awrey
Sgt L. V. Milward
Sgt H. Cooper
Sgt J. J. Wells
Sgt J. C. McLaughlan
Sgt C. W. Panton

No 8 P. F. F. Group *No 139 (Jamaica) Squadron – Mosquitoes*

DZ 478
G/C L. C. Slee
F/L G. F. Hodder

DZ 373
F/O H. Swan
Sgt D. C. Boa

DZ 337
P/O C. H. Guest
Sgt J. Fox

DZ 465
F/L R. A. V. Crampton
F/O P. L. U. Cross

DZ 519
F/L M. W. College
F/O G. L. Marshall

DZ 348
Sgt H. M. Prince
Sgt C. R. T. Mottershead

DZ 379
F/O A. S. Cooke
Sgt D. A. Dixon

DZ 521
W/O V. J. C. Miles
Sgt E. R. Perry

Bomber Command Narrative of Operations

```
STAND BY FOR B/CAST        71
  SRL 805
    WTN B48   OAK B71   GRY B88 WBS B26   GSD B13 BOU B19   MAR B88   UPW B97
    NR GPH   2/22
WTN PASS TO SELF AND 83 SQDN = 139 SQDN
  GRY PASS TO SELF = 35 SQDN
  OAK PADD TO SELF = 7 SQDN
  BOU PASS TO 97 SQDN
  GSD PASS TO SELF = 405 SQDN
  MAR PASS TO 105  AND   109 SQDNS
  WBS PASS TO 156 SQDN

UPW PASS TO N.T.U.


TO WYTON, GRAVELEY, OAKINGTON, GRANSDEN,
7, 35, 83, 97, 105, 109, 139, 156, 405 SQDNS. N.T.U.
FROM PATHFINDERS

            PATHFINDER NARRATIVE OF OPERATIONS NO 74
              NIGHT 17TH/18TH AUGUST 1943
                    PEENEMUNDE
              ------------------------
```

```
1. DETAILED :-
   --------
   7  SQUADRON  - LANCASTERS  - 4 BLIND ILLUMINATOR - MARKERS
                                1 VISUAL MARKER
                                  2 AIMING - POINT SHIFTERS
                                4 BACKERS -UP
                                  6- NON- MARKERS.
  35      ' '         HALIFAXES - 2 AIMING - POINT SHIFTERS
                                  7  BACKERS - UP
                                W  NON-MARKERS
  83      ' '         LANCASTERS-  MASTER OF CEREMONIES
                                  7  BLIND ILLUMINATOR-MARKERS
                                  3 VISUAL   MARKERS
                                  2 AIMING-POINT SHIFTERS
                                  2 BACKERS -UP
  97      ' '             ' '    -  1 BLIND ILLUMINATOR - MARKER
                                   2  AIMING POINT  SHIFTERS
                                 13 BACKERS -UP
                                  4 NON-MARKERS
  156     ' '             ' '    - 2ND DEPUTY  MASTER OF EREMONIES
VH                               4 BLIND ILLUMINATOR - MARKERS
                                 2 VISUAL MARKERS
                                  2AIMING -POINT SHIFTERS
```

```
                         10  BACKERS-UP
                          3  NON-MARKERS.
405  ' '           HALIFAXES - DEPUTY  MASTER OF CEREMONIES
                          2  AIMING-POINT SHIFTERS
                          4  BACKERS-UP
                          5  NON-MARKERS
```

2. PLAN OF ATTACK

----------- - NEWHAVEN GROUNDMARKING WITH AIMING-OINT SHIFTING TWICE DURING THE ATTACK. THIS WAS TO BE ACHIEVED BY FALSE SETTINGS ON THE BOMB-SIGHT. SPECIAL BOMBING INSTRUCTIONS TO BE GIVEN AS REQUIRED BY THE MASTER OF CEREMONIES.

3. WEATHER ETC.

---------- PATCHES OF THIN CLOUD AT ABOUT 8,OOO FT. VISIBILITY, APART FROM THIS CLOUD. WAS GOOD. BRIGHT MOONLIGHT.

4. PATHFINDER RESULTS.

(A) TIMING - VERY GOOD THE ATTACK OPENED ON TIME AND THE AIMING POINT WAS TWICE MOVED EFFECTIVELY, AND THE MARKING WAS WELL MAINTAINED THROUGHOUT THE ATTACK.

(B) ACCURACY- THE ATTACK STARTED CORRECTLY ON THE 1ST AIMING POINT, BUT WITHIN ABOUT THREE MINUTES SEVERAL CREWS, FIVE OF WHOM OBTAINED PHOTOGRAPHS, AND INCLUDING ONE VISUAL MARKER, OVERSHOT AND DROPPED THEIR MARKERS ABOUT WM. S.E. OF THE AIMING POINT. THIS COULD NOT HAVE OCCURRED HAD CREWS CHECKED THE TIME OF THEIR RUN FROM RUDEN ISLAND WHICH WAS MARKED, AS 2M. REPRESENTS AN ERROR IN TIME OF ABOUT HALF A MINUTE. THE CREWS CONCERNED ARE DOUBLY BLAMEWORTHY AS THE ATTACK UNDOUBTEDLY OPENED ON THE RIGHT SPOT AND THE AIMING POINT WAS ACCURATELY MARKED BY THE 1ST VISUAL MARKER (W/C WHITE (15). HOWEVER, THIS PHASE WAS SHORT-LIED, THANKS LARGELY TO THE INSTRUCTIONS OF THE MASTER OF CEREMONIES, AND TO THE SUBSEQUENT MARKERS HAVING THEIR FINGERS OUT, AND FROM ABOUT Z+5 ONWARDS THE MARKING WAS OF HIGH QUALITY GENERALLY. THE AIMING POINT SHIFTING WAS ACCURATELY DONE AND ON TIME. THERE IS A GOOD CROP OF PHOTOGRAPHS, AND EXCEPT FOR THE BUNCH OF OVERSHOOTS, DISCUSSED ABOVE, THEY ARE NEARLY ALL OF THE CORRECT AIMING-POINT.

5. SUCCESS OF RAID.

-------------- - THE MAIN FORCE BOMBING, AS EVIDENCED BY NIGHT PHOTOGRAPHS, WAS PROBABLY THE MOST ACCURATE EVER ACHIEVED. OUT OF THE WHOLTE OF THE COMMAND (APART FROM THE P.F.F.) ONLY SIX PHOTOS. ARE SO FAR PLOTTED MORE THAN 1.M FROM THE TARGET. DAMAGE IS PROVED BY P.R.U. PHOTOGRAPHS TO BE VERY SEVERE INDEED ON ALL THE AIMING POINTS ATTACKED, AND NIL ON THOSE NOT DETAILED, AND THE RAID WAS UNDOUBTEDLY A GREAT SUCCESS. THAT THIS SHOULD HAVE BEEN ACHIEVED IN SPITE OF THE MOST EFFECTIVE SMOKE-SCREEN EVER ENCOUNTERED, DOES GREAT CREDIT TO THE COOL-HEADEDNESS OF THE MAJORITY OF CREWS, AND IS EXCELLENT TESTIMONY TO THEVERY FINE JOB DONE BY THE MASTER OF CEREMONIES. A FURTHER POINT IS THAT THERE WERE PRACTICALLY NO GROUND DEFENCES, ALTHOUGH THERE WERE NUMEROUS FIGHTERS OPERATING IN THE TARGET AREA. THIS SHOWS THAT, WHILE IT MAY BE MAINLY FIGHTERS WHICH CAUSE LOSSES, IT IS FLAK AND SEARCH-LIGHTS WHICH SPOIL BOMBING.

6. DEFENCES
   -------   -   NEGIBIGIBLE OPPOSITION FROM THE GROUND, EXCEPT
                 FOR A VERY EFFECTIVE SMOKE-SCREEN. MANY FIGHTERS
                 IN TARGET AREA AND EN ROUTE.
7. SORTIE DETAILS.
   -----------   DETAILED 97, WITHDRAWN 3, RETURNED EARLY 3.
                 ATTACKED PRIMARY 89, MISSING 2.

T.O.O. 0945
 HOLD
P JW TOD 1041 ++

Operational Record Book

Following are excerpts from O.R.B. 83 Sqdn.

17th-18th August 1943, Night Operation. Bombing PEENEMUNDE.

(Complete Extract, some crew names omitted)

Aircraft	Crew	Bombload and duty	Time up.	Time down.	Details of Sirtie or Flight.
===	===	===	===	===	===
Lanc 'K' JA.686	P/O A.C. Shipway Sgt. E. Cummings P/O B. Moorcroft	4 x 4 Flares white 1 x T.I. red 3 x T.I. red spots 1 x 4,000 3 x 1,000 MARKER	20.58	03.36	Target bombed 00.11 hrs, 16,300', 161°N 140 kts; thin layer cloud visibility poor. Bombs dropped on yellow T.I. which was between two reds surrounded by greens. On arrival no T.I.'s seen. As our aircraft released flares, another aircraft's flares went down and we were unable to see our aiming point "F". On 2nd run, two yellows with green around 2nd yellow, so bombed 2nd yellow, which was more in T.I. concentration.
Lanc 'A' ED.984	F/L A.C.B. Slade F/S Lewis, V.C. F/L A.N. McPherson	"	20.56	04.20	Bombed 00.10 hours, 16,000', 165°M 140 knots. Very efficient smoke screen T.I. red and flares undershot A/P "F" and fell in sea 200 yards from shore. Bombed on 'Y'. Few fires seen.
Lanc 'F' ED.602	S/L Sells G.D. Sgt Taylor R.L. S/L A.S. Johnson, DFM	"	21.04	03.49	Bombed 00.11 hours, 16,000', 164°M, 140 knots, dropping four flares white and one T.I. red. At 00.17 hours 1 x 4,000 and 3 x 1,000 on second run; low haze. T.I. reds cascading on run in, and appeared rather scattered. On 2nd run greens and yellows seen in good concentration. Small fires gaining on leaving. Bombed on 'Y'.

83 Squadron O.R.B.)

Aircraft	Crew	Bomb Load			Remarks
Lanc 'U' JA.677	S/L Manton, R.J. Sgt Chadwick, F.J. S/L A.G.A. Cochrane, DFC	"	20.59	03.59	Bombed 00.11 hours 16,000' 154°M 140 knots 4 x 4 white flares, one T.I. red; 00.20 15,000' 160°M 140 kts, 1 x 4,000 and 3 x 1,000 on second run. Own T.I. appeared to cascade inthe sea. Bombed estimated centre of greens. Smoke obscured buildings so made dummy run after dropping bombs. Excellent concentration of T.I.'s large explosion observed, and fires seen 80 miles away.
Lanc 'V' ED.876	F/O M.R. Chick Sgt Hicks A.W. Sgt Slaughter J.W.	4 x 4 Flares white 1 x T.I. red 3 x T.I. red spots 1 x 4,000 3 x 1,000	20.57	03.17	Bombed dropped (sic) 54°08'N-03°15'E 22.00 hours 13,000'. Starboard outer oil pressure zero, temperature 50° at 21.50 At 21.55 hours was down to zero. Starboard outer feathered, returned on three. EARLY RETURN.
Lanc 'O' JA.927	P/O J.A. Reid Sgt Lawes, D. P/O A.H.E. Brown	"	20.54	03.55	Bombed 16,000', 00.13 hours, 162°M, 140 knots, 1 x 4,000 and 3 x 1,000; 00.23 hours 16,000', 110°M 150 knots; 4 x 4 flareswwhite one T.I. red. Good visual identification of A/P "F" easy by light of flares on 1st tun (sic) on 2nd run out red seen covered by yellow. Some greens N of one red, and yellow T.I.'s well positioned to coastline and stretched for 1½ miles.
Lanc 'M' JA.705	S/Ldr A.B.Smith F/S Rathbone F/S Wright	"	20.53	04.03	Bombed 00.12 hours 16,000' 225°M 150 knots 4 x 4 flares white, one T.I. red. 00.17 hours 15,000' 162°M 150 knots, 1 x 4,000 and 3 x 1,000. On first run A/P "E" seen quite clearly in moonlight. On leaving some flares and T.I.'s seen going down. On 2nd run some reds and yellows seen to N of A/P "F". Greens which we bombed were according to position on or near A/P "F".

58

83 Squadron O.R.B.)

Lanc 'T' JA.940
F/O W.R. Thompson
Sgt Belton A.W.
F/O C.F. Bedell
21.03 — 04.07
2 x T.I. red LB
2 x T.I. red
1 x 4,000
7 x 500

Bombed 00.26 hours 12,000' 154°M 140 knots Hazy smoke:generators in operation. Our reds seen to go down on greens. Run in 1st, red spots seen at 00.10 hours. Good concentration but no visual identification. A red and green seen slightly to S.W. of pattern of T.I.'s. One green well to S.W. believed dummy. No fires seen.

Lanc 'Y'
P/O R. King
Sgt Farmelo
F/O E.D. Gallagher
21.16 — 04.26
2 x T.I. red LB
2 x T.I. red
1 x 4,000
8 x 500

Bombed 00.39 hours 12,000' 167°M 140 knots Low cloud, visibility good. Large explosion to west of target area, followed by reds and greens at regular intervals.

Lanc 'G' JA.913
S/L N.F. Hildyard
F/S Sutton E.
P/O J.F. Hacking
21.12 — 03.44
2 x T.I. yellow LB
2 x T.I. yellow
1 x 4,000
8 x 500

Bombed 00.17 11,000' 241°M 160 knots 2 T.I. yellow LB and 2 T.I. yellow. 00.22 hours 11,000' 040°, 160 knots 8 x 500 lbs. Thin wispy cloud. Identified visually. One yellow T.I. seen to fall across living quarters. One very large explosions to W of target amongst buildings. On 2nd run bombs seen to fall across buildings. General impression: a well concentrated action.

Lanc 'E' JA.701
F/L Mason
W/O Goodwin
P/O A. Feeley
21.00 — 04.15
"
"

Bombed 00.13 hours, 12,350', 200°M135 knots, 4 T.I. yellow. 00.22 hours 12,300' 170°M 130 knots 1 x 4,000lbs and 8 x 500 lbs Hazy, visibility good. Aiming point "F" visual identification by flares. On first run all aiming points visual in light of moon. Fires getting on as a/c left. Blue and mauve explosion to N of A/P "F".

83 Squadron O.R.B.)

Lanc 'B'
JA.712
F/S Turp K.C.
Sgt Bailey D
F/O H.A. Clark

"

20.55   04.19

Bombed 00.15 hours, 14,000', 140°M, 138 knots, 2 yellow LB and 2 yellow TI. 00.20 hours, 12,000', 101°M, 1 x 4,000 and 8 x 500. Visually by light of flares "F". Yellow seen to cascade in centre of point "F". 1 x 4,000 seen to explode in S portion of "F". Bombed estimated centre of area between beach and parallel road.

Lanc 'W'
JA.928
G/C J.H. Searby DFC
P/O F.A. Forster, DFM
S/L N.H. Scrivener, DFC
F/O L.G. Davies
F/O W.G. Ross DFM
F/O J.H. Coley
P/O I.W. Preece CGM

2 x T.I. red
2 x T.I. green
2 x T.I. yellow
4 x 12 x 20 G.P.
4 x 8 x 40 G.P.
MASTER OF CEREMONIES

20.52   04.31

Bombed 00.24 hours 14,000' 276°M 150 knots 4 x 12 x 20 G.P. and 4 x 8 x 40 G.P. dropped on searchlights and ground defences. 1st reds overshot, but following yellow well-placed and a green fell near. Some T.I.'s fell in sea, but main force were warned. 2nd phase was not as well marked as expected, this being due to confused nature of the 1st G.P. at this stage. After attack had been going 30 minutes it became one mass of fires. Fighters much in evidence and fight took place between our gunners and T/E aircraft, our gunners doing damage.

Lanc 'C'
EE.175
P/O F.C. Allcroft
Sgt Coles H
P/O H. Readman

2 x T.I. green LB
2 x TI green
1 x 4,000
5 x 500

20.51   04.11

Bombed 00.13,5 hours, 13,000' 164°M 160 knots, 1 x 4,000, 2 x T.I. green LB 2 x T.I. green. 00.18 hours 13,000' 174°M 160 knots 5 x 500. Green fell N of A/P "F". 1 x 4,000 on Southern part of buildings; and explosions among buildings of A/P's "B" and "F". Fires seen 60 miles away. 3 x 500 hung up and jettisoned live.

Lanc 'X'
W.4959
W/O Finding J
Sgt Evans T.S.
Sgt. Borrow H.E.

"

21.01   03.52

Bombed 00.17,5 hours, 12,000', 150 knots; 4 greens T.I.; 00.23 13,000' 126°M 145 knots 1 x 4,000 and 8 x 500. Three-fifths thin stratus Bombed between 3 yellow, one of which was cascading. The circular unidentified apparatus to N.W. of A/P was clearly seen. Smoke generator

83 Squadron O.R.B.)   (7/8.8.1943

7th - 8th August 1943. Nigh Operations. Bombing Turin.

Lanc 'A'	C/C J.H. Searby DFC	8 x S.B.C. x 20 lb F	21.25	04.48	Acted as Raid Commentator. Throughout
ED.984	P/O F.A. Forster D.F.M.	3 x S.B.C. x Flares			attack an R/T broadcast was made directing
	S/L N.H. Scrivener DFC				crews to good T.I.'s, exhorting the Main
	F/O A.N. McPherson DFM				Force to press on, and generally binding
	F/L R.F. Tinkler				the effort into one consolidated force.
	F/O W.B. Ross DFM				Results achieved were excellent, anticipate
	F/O J.H. Coley				that this will be an important feature
	P/O I.W. Preece CGM				in each subsequent attack.

(One crew referred to the radio commentary, from 83 Squadron)

Lanc 'T'	F/O W.R. Thompson	8 x T.I. green	21.44	05.22	Turin bombed from 16,000' at 01.03.
ED.601	Sgt Melton A.W.	5 x 500 MC			Commentator clearly heard. Reds and
	F/O F.C. Bedell	2 x Flares Int			green very well concentrated in the town;
					large and small fires seen on return from
					Genoa, which was bombed at 01.25 hrs from
					17,500'. T.I.'s all in town area, but not
					quite as concentrated as those in Turin.

Extract from 83 Squadron O.R.B. Section headed, August 1943. SUMMARY OF EVENTS. (Incomplete)

7th August 1943.   Operations on. Fourteen Aircraft on Turin and Milan. This raid was laid on for political rather than military reasons, in an effort to persuade the Badoglio regime that peace was a far far better thing; not only was a precedent set by two targets being attacked on the same night, but also by the fact that this was the first operation carried out on a large scale with R/T control. Wing Commander Searby acted as Raid Commentator, and throughout the attack directed crews to well-placed T.I.'s, exhorted the main force to press on, and generally binding the effort into one consolidated force. The results achieved were excellent, and it is anticipated that this will be an important feature in each subsequent attack. The general impression of the effort was that Turin was good, but that Genoa was a trifle scattered. ...

15th August 1943.   Crews were resting after the previous night's operations. There was no training during the day. At night 13 crews paid a return visit to Milan, and all returned, safe and sound.

16th August 1943.   'Y' training and practice bombing were proceeded with, but the Squadron activity was slight.

61

83 Squadron O.R.B.)   (16.8.1943 &c

16th August 1943 (cont'd).
Stand down from operations.

17th August 1943. A fine with day with normal work up to about 10.00 hours, when the target came through, that even the route and the details were withheld from all but the C.O. Details were late through, the armourers had to wait until after lunch; loads and suspense grew apace. The attack was on Peenemunde, and the following Captains were detailed to attack:- 'W' Group Captain Searby, was M.C. and controlled the raid throughout. He was attacked by night fighters, but stayed them off, through good crew drill and co-operation. (There follows a list of aircraft and their Captains, detailed to attack; see preceeding O.R.B. extract) The crews were unanimous in their opinion that the raid was a great success. The following is a special report by Group Captain Searby:-

"On the approach to the target, across the Danish Islands, the weather was clear, and no difficulty was experienced in map-reading. Thus it was hoped that the same conditions would prevail over the target. Rugen Island was clear apart from one or two small patches of cloud, and on approaching Rudem Island a layer of very thin cloud sheet, estimated to be between two and three thousand feet was seen to cover the small promontary. On reaching the target area, and before any markers had been dropped, we made a run across and were able to discern the target reasonably well through the thin cloud layer. After turning left across the sea, and flying parallel to the shore, the first reds were seen to fall at Zero - 5, and it was considered that they had slightly overshot the aiming point. A second bunch of reds fell a few minutes later, and then a yellow was seen to fall between the two, and as near as could be judged, this yellow marker was very well placed. Green markers fell almost immediately on the yellow, and instructions were broadcast to the main force aircraft to bomb these green markers. More reds were dropped, and some of these were observed to fall into the sea, and backers up were warned by broadcast of this fact. Backing-up continued, and greens were observed to fall into the sea. A third broadcast informed the main force that this was so, and they were to bomb the greens which lay to the right, as it was estimated these were on the target. Two more runs across the target by our own aircraft confirmed this, and whilst we were over the target, more greens overshot. A fourth broadcast informed the backersup that they had overshot, and other backers up were instructed to watch their bombing runs, and not to overshot. The sixth broadcast to the main force instructed them to ignore the southerly greens which had overshot, and bomb those lying to the north. This was repeated. Another run across showed that the second aiming point was well covered, but some reds were still falling into the sea, and backers up were warned of this. At 00.42 hours, another broadcast informed backers up that they must endeavour to avoid any green markers falling into the sea; another run across showed that those aiming points were still being bombed, and fires were seen breaking out, and in the case of the large target to be going well. There is no doubt that the woods were burning, and it was difficult to differentiate. First instructions were given to the main force to carry on bombing greens, and a broadcast informed them that the attack was going well despite the smoke screens. These smoke screens were put into operation very soon after the attack started and were very effective. They were located to the East and North East of the target area, and the generators could be plainly seen. One more broadcast was made, urging the main force to watch their bombing and to make steady runs and to carry on bombing greens. During the whole of the time our aircraft was over the target area, seven runs were made across the target and many aircraft were seen shot down. Fighter activity was intense,

62

83 Squadron O.R.B.)   (17/18.8.43 &c

number of heavy flak guns, the most troublesome to us being located approximately one mile out to sea due East of the promontary. This gun fire insistently at us as we circled left away from the target to make another run. Other heavy flak guns were seen to be firing from the western shore in the neighbourhood of the aerodrome; after making the last broadcast we circled right with the main string and a few miles from the target were engaged by a twin engined fighter. This fighter was first seen below, when the rear gunner fired four bursts directly at him. He then attacked from the starboard side when a sharp turn was made in the direction of the attack, and the M.U. gunner got in a burst as he passed below. His own fire was inaccurate, the aircraft was claimed as damaged. A large mass of fire was observed in the target area which did not seem to be consistent with the size of the target, and these fires were observed until well past Langeland on the way home. In this particular area there was much fighter activity, several more aircraft were seen to go down. Light flak guns too were very much in evidence and there can be no doubt that some aircraft were employing very bad tactics indeed in flying low across these islands."

<u>18th August 1943.</u> Operations stood down. Training for crews not operating on previous night. ...

<u>19th August 1943.</u> Operations laid on in morning with a special target for u/t blindmarkers. It came as a complete surprise when the operation was cancelled, at briefing. The C.O. paid special tribute to the crews partaking in the Peenemunde raid which from recent reports to hand was an outstanding success. ...

<u>25th August 1943.</u> Stood down. ... Intensive training. Our C.O., Group Captain Searby was awarded the Distinguished Service Order (Immediate) for his particularly magnificent leadership on the Peenemunde raid.

540 Squadron O.R.B.) (1943

Selected Extracts from the Operational Record Book of 540 Squadron (Photographic Reconnaissance)

23rd June 1943.

| Mosquito DZ 473 | F/Sgt E.P.H. Peek
F/Sgt J. Williams | Photo-recco | 06.05 | 12.41 | Photo-recco of Stettin, Swinemunde, etc. Photos taken of Rugen (Job 87/AM) Peenemunde Swinemunde, Garz Usedon Airfield, Stettin (Job 300/152) Stargard airfield and shipping Took off from Leuchars. Ref: N.860 |

22nd July 1943

| Mosquito DZ 404 | P/O P.J. Hugo
F/O M.L.H. Rose | Photo-recco | 06.20 | 11.25 | Photo-recco of Peenemunde. Job 158/AM, and 168/AM + 2 Photos taken of Kosser, Greisswald Airfield, Peenemunde,airfield, Bug auf Rugem, S.P.B., Bug Wittow L/G, Jobs 158 and 168/1 part cover through cloud Ref: N.885 |

16th August 1943

| Mosquito LR 413 | F/O Hosking
P/O H.A. Sowerbutts | Photo-recco | 07.00 | 11.15 | Photo-recco of Swinemunde, Stettin; no photo taken owing to cloud cover. |

18th August 1943

| Mosquito LR 413 | S/L G.E. Hughes DFC & Bar
Sgt J. Kime | Photo-recco | 07.35 | 13.00 | Photo-recco of Swinemunde, Stettin. Photos taken of Swinemunde, Stettin, Warnemunde, Flensburg, Rostock and Peenemunde and Airfield, Lek Airfield, Greifswald Airfield, Flensburg A/F, Westerland Sylt A/F; aircraft landed at Benson. Ref: N.902 |

6th September 1943 There was a P.R. of Stettin and Peenemunde and Rostock - no photos taken because of 10/10 cloud. 0735-1140.

30th September 1943

| Mosquito LR 429 | F/K A.C. Graham
F/Sgt T. Osborn | Photo-recco | 08.35 | 13.30 | Photos of Kolberg A/F, Kamp A/F, and S.P.B. Peenemunde A/F and Dievenow S.P.B. (Oblique). Ref: 945 |

102 Squadron O.R.B.)   (17/18.8.1943)

Selected, condensed extracts from the Operational Record Book of No. 102 Squadron (4 Group).

17th-18th August 1943. Bombing Peenemunde.

Halifax

Aircraft			Remarks
'F'	21.00	04.23	Attacked from 8,000', 170°M. Green TI's at target
'H'	21.01	04.12	5,000', 160°M Yellow and green T.I.'s.
'G'	20.59	04.15	18,000', 158°M Yellow and green T.I.'s.
'J'	21.03	04.16	8,000' 290° Bombed greens
'K'	21.02	04.34	8,000 165°M 2/10 cloud green T.I.
'M'	21.00	05.20	8,500' 155°M red track markers and green T.I.'s at target. Centre of greens in bombsight.
'P' JD 111	21.04	04.20	Attacked primary at 6,100', heading 176°M 170 117S 10310 over target - good visibility saw all P.F.F. markers. Green in bombsight. Smoke from fires hampered results.
'Q'	21.07	04.55	8,000' 155° 10/10 at target, greens in bombsight.
'R'	21.11	04.03	6,000' 174° target identified visually and green T.I.'s bombed on centre of greens.
'U'	21.13	05.01	7,000' 180°M No cloud Green T.I. Green bombed.
'W'	21.09	05.00	8,000' 163°M 6/10 cloud, heavy smoke screen green ground markers in bomb sight.
'Y'	21.10	04.29	10,000' 204°M Green T.I. seen and bombed
'Z'	21.14	04.55	8,000' 162°M No cloud Green T.I.'s.
'B'	21.23	05.30	6,000' 164°M 8/10 stratus cloud. Green markers. (Bomb doors manually operated, etc).
'C'	21.24	05.07	8,000' 155°M Green T.I. and coastline seen
'E'	21.18	05.05	7,500' 165°M 6/10 broken cloud. Green T.I. in bombsight.

'P' JD 111 crew:
P/O J. Bowman (Pilot)
F/S D. Galbraith (Navigator)
F/S L.C. Parry (W/Operator)
S/L A. Ables (Bomb-aimer)

139 Squadron O.R.B.)

Selected, condensed extracts from the Operational Record Book of 139 (Jamaica) Squadron P.F.F.

12th-13th August 1943.

Seven Mosquitoes were detailed to attack Berlin. Those marked (*) were hit by accurate and intense flak. The Mosquito of F/Sgt Valentine failed to return; R.A.F. Coltishall obtained a fix on it on the return 40 miles from Lowestoft. Nothing more was heard or seen of it afterwards. All others, except for that of Sgt Mellor which returned early, obtained pinpoints in area of target and bombed either visually or on D.R. from pin-points.

Time up:	Time Down:
21.49	2.35
21.47*	2.24
21.50*	----
21.48	23.58 (returned early)
21.52	2.21
21.53	2.44
21.51	2.41

14th-15th August 1943.

Seven Mosquitoes were detailed to attack Berlin. Aircraft (1) was attacked by enemy aircraft, took evasive action, dropping from 27,000 to 20,000 feet. Late, so abondoned operation. Aircraft (2) had engine trouble, so returned early. Aircraft (3) also returned early, reporting cloud 10/10 up to 27,500 feet. The remainder reached target by Gee and D.R., lakes on way and to S.W. being visible. F/O Denny saw two bombs burst in target area. Another pilot saw small glow in centre of the city.

Time Up:		Time Down:
00.26	(2)	02.35
00.20	(3)	02.29
00.25	(1)	02.15
00.24		05.12
00.19		05.04
00.21		05.17
00.25		04.59

15th-16th August 1943.

Eight Mosquitoes were detailed to attack Berlin. Aircraft (1) returned early, Gee being out of action; aircraft (2)

139 Squadron O.R.B.)   (August 1943)

returned early, its navigator being sick; aircraft (3) returned early with radiator trouble. The remainder reached the target and found it easily, identifiable in bright moonlight.

Time Up:		Time Down:
21.17	(1)	22.28
21.16	(2)	23.06
21.18		01.50
21.15		01.58
21.15		02.17
21.20		02.09
21.19		02.15
21.22	(3)	22.10

17th-18th August 1943.

Eight Mosquitoes were detailed to attack Berlin, as a diversion for the main attack on Peenemunde. One Mosquito, DZ.379, crewed by F/O A.S. Cooke and Sgt D.A.H. Dixon, failed to return. The remainder reached the target, getting excellent pinpoints on the lakes north of the target, also those adjoining the target S.W. There was no cloud and visibility was good. Windows were dropped. Cameras and T.I. flashes were taken in three aircraft, but the results were not satisfactory. Air dispatched as follows:-

Time Up:	Time Down:
20.49	02.12
20.47	02.04
20.48	01.51
20.54	02.00
20.52	-----
20.46	01.55
20.50	01.46
20.51	01.41

GRP-K

A.H.B. Papers)   (copy

MOST SECRET

<u>NIGHT RAID REPORT NO.404.   COPY NO.:16</u>

BOMBER COMMAND NIGHT OPERATIONS REPORT
ON OPERATIONS 17th-18th AUGUST, 1943:-

<u>PEENEMUNDE : BERLIN</u>
Summary.

<u>PEENEMUNDE</u>

1.   597 aircraft were detailed to attack the research and experimental
station at Peenemunde, a small target of the highest priority. The force
attacked in three waves, each wave having a separate aiming point.
A Master Bomber remained over the target throughout the raid issuing instructions to aircraft as they arrived; he was greatly responsible for
the success of the operation. Much of the station was devastated, and a
number of highly important buildings were destroyed. Forty bombers were
          lost in conditions especially favourable to the night fighter.

<u>BERLIN</u>

2.   Eight Mosquitoes were dispatched on a harassing raid against the
German capital; they dropped their bombs an hour before the attack began
on Peenemunde, and succeeded in diverting at least two Groups of fighters
from the main target. One Mosquito was lost without trace; another crashed
on return, but without injury to the crew.

<u>Weather Forecast.</u>

3.   Midnight Frontal Positions:
(i) Warm from Stornaway to Aberdeen to Rotterdam to 49°N10°E,
becoming cold to Vienna and Eastwards;
Bases:
     Risk of isolated thunderstorms in later part of night; otherwise
bases should everywhere hold fit, with cloud base nowhere below 1,500'.
Moderate visibility;
Germany:
     Multi-layered cloud on warm front, a little cloud north east of
the front, possibly thinkstrato-cumulus. Fine weather south of the
front.
Swinemunde:
     Probably less than five-tenths alto-cumulus and little or no
cloud; chance of clear sky: at worst, seven to eight-tenths medium
cloud. Moderate visibility.
Route:
     Some thin medium cloud especially on first half of route; con-
trails may be troublesome above 16,000'.
North Italy:
     Fine
Winds to Swinemunde:

	750 mbs	500 mbs	300 mbs
Bases to 2°E	200°/30mph	310°/35mph	230°/40mph
2° to 7°E	240°/25mph	270°/35mph	280°/40mph
7°E to target	290°/35mph	290°/45mph	290°/70mph

Plan of Attack.

4.   Routes: 1,3,4,5,6 Groups: 55°10'N/07°00'E - 55°20'N/08°29'E -
       54041/13°26'E - RUDEN ISLAND - TARGET - MANDO - 51°10N/07°00'E

       8 Group: 55°00'N/05°00'E - 55°20'N/08°29'E - 54°41'N/
       13°20'E - RUDEN ISLAND - TARGET - MANDO - 55°00N/05°00E

5.   Marking Technique:

(i) "Datum Line Red Spot Fires" were to be dropped on the Northern edge of Ruden Island by all Blind Markers and 15 of the Backers-Up.

AIMING-POINT "F"

(ii) Blind Markers were to mark the aiming point with T.I. red and strings of flares. They were not to drop their bombs on this run but were to make a second run and drop them after the visual markers

(iii) Visual Markers were to mark the exact A/P with T.I. yellow, but only after certain identification.

(iv) Backers up were to aim T.I. green in order of preference at:-

          (a) T.I. Yellow
          (b) Centre of all T.I. green
          (c) Centre of all T.I. red with 3-second overshoot.

AIMING-POINT "B"

(v) Shifters were to aim their T.I. red at the centre of all T.I. green and were to approach exactly over RUDEN ISLAND with their bombsights on the following false settings:

          Target Height: 5,000'
          T.V.:12,000 feet per second.

T.I. to be released on single and salvo; they were then to wait ten seconds before releasing their stick of bombs. Other settings were to be normal. Attack to be made at 12,000 feet. This would result in the T.I. dropping on the second aiming point, when aimed at the first.

(vi) Backers Up to aim T.I. green at:-

          (a) Centre of T.I. green
          (b) Centre of T.I. green;

AIMING-POINT "E"

(Vii) Shifters were to aim red T.I. at the centre of T.I. green as in (v), thereby marking the third aiming point, while aiming at the second.

(viii) Backers up were to proceed as in (vi). Main force were to aim their bombs at the centre of T.I. green or as directed by the Master Bomber. They were to igmore T.I. red and T.I. yellow.

Nt. Raid Report (ORS)   (A.H.B. Papers)

6.   Timing.

        Zero hour: 00.15 hours.   T.O.T.: 00.11 - 00.55 hours.

AIMING-POINT "F"

Blind Markers
16 a/c at (Z - 4)
No T.I. after zero
but flares might be dropped
after this time

Visual Markers
6 a/c at (Z - 2)
No a/c after (Z-2)

Backers Up
3 a/c at zero
2 a/c at (Z + 1)
10 a/c (1 per minute)
from (Z + 2) to (Z + 11)

Main Force
(Z + 2) to
(Z + 15):   143 Hals
             59 Stirls
             25 Lancs
            227 a/c

AIMING-POINT "B"

Shifters
6 a/c (Z + 12)

Backers Up
3 a/c at (Z + 14)
9 a/c (1 per minute) from
(Z + 15) to (Z + 23)

Main Force
115 Lancs at
(Z + 16) to (Z + 27)

AIMING POINT "E"

Shifters
6 a/c at (Z + 24)

Backers Up
3 a/c at (Z + 26)
10 a/c (1 per minute)
from (Z + 27) to (Z + 36)

Main Force
(Z + 28) to
(Z + 40)
126 Lancs
 54
180 a/c

7.   Total number of a/c planned: Blind Markers, 16; Visual Markers, 6;
Shifters, 12; Backers-up, 50; Main Force, 522; TOTAL: 606 a/c.

8.   Markers to be carried:
        (i) Blind Markers: 16 Lancs (4 x 4 flares white) and 1 T.I. red
     LB, and 3 T.I. red spot.
        (ii) Visual Markers: 6 Lancs; 2 x T.I. yellow LB, and 2 x T.I. yellow.
        (iii) Backers up: 23 Lancs and 4 Hals: 2 x T.I. green LB and 2 x
     T.I. green. 13 Lancs: 2 x T.I. green LB and 2 x T.I. green and
     3 x T.I. red spot.
        (iv) Shifters: 8 Lancs and 4 H ls: 2 x T.I. red LB and 2 x T.I. red.
        (v) Master Bombers: 3 Lancs: 2 T.I. red and 2 T.I. green and 2
     T.I. yellow.

Nt. Raid Report (ORS)   (A.H.B. Papers

9.   Tactics:

(i) WINDOW: Continuously from 08° East to target and back to
08°East at the rate of one bundle per minute, except between
08°East and 10°East where the rate was to be doubled.

(ii) Master Bomber: A Master Bomber with two deputies was to
give a commentary on the raid.

(iii) Importance of target: The vital importance of this target was
to be stressed to all crews.

(iv) Bombing winds: Bombing winds would be broadcast as previously.

(v) Bombing height: 1 and 6 Groups were to bomb as low as possible
between 6,000 and 10,000 feet. No aircraft below 4,000 feet.

(vi) Bomb loads: H.E. loads would be carried by all 4 Group and
non-marking P.F.F. and by 75 per cent of 1,3,5 and 6 Groups; those
aircraft carrying incendiaries were to bomb at the end of the
attacks on each aiming point in order to interfere as little as
possible with the marking technique.

(vii) Defences: Non-marking P.F.F. and Master Bomber were to carry
anti-personnel bombs for use on flak defences in the target area.

(viii) "Red Spot Fires" were to be used for the first time. These
markers consist of a two-hundred and fifty pound case filled with
cotton wool soaked in liquid; they burst and ignite at 3,000 feet
and burn on the ground like vivid crimson fire, for about ten minutes.

10.   Sorties:

(a) Number of aircraft despatched 597
(b) Number of aircraft reporting attack on primary area 531 (89.0%)
(c) Number of aircraft reporting attack on alternative area 3* (0.5%)
(d) Number of abortive sorties (technical defect of
       manipulative error) ....18).....................18
              (Sickness of crew ....3).....................23   (3.9%)
              (Late take-off ....1)
              (Bomb hung up ....1)
(e) Number of aircraft missing 40   (6.7%)

* Plus three aircraft which also attacked the primary.

11.   Weather experienced:

Bases:
     Lincolnshire, fit all night. East Anglia, fit apart from local
thunderstorms, from 01.00 to 04.00 hours. Yorkshire, low stratus
affected coastal districts by 23.00 to 24.00 hours and the whole of
South Yorkshire by 03.00 hours. Local thunderstorms from 04.00 to
05.00 hours - then generally fit.
Route:
     Variable layer cloud, tops at 4,000 feet, over North Sea generally
five-tenths or less. No cloud over Denmark. Batches of ten-tenths
layer cloud over Baltic to 14°East, thence cloudless to target.
Return similar, but ten-tenths medium cloud in layers from 2 to 3°
East to English coast at 10 to 17,000 feet, with isolated thunderstorms.
Visibility good.

71

Nt. Raid Report (ORS)   (A.H.B. Papers

    <u>Peenemunde:</u>
       Small amounts of layer cloud at 3,000 feet. Moon nearly full.
Visibility good, but smoke screen in target area. Surface wind
W/10 mph.
    <u>Winds:</u>
       Base - Danish coast at 18,000': 250°/45 mph decreasing to 30mph.
From Danish coast to 11°East and veering slowly to 290°, then increasing
towards target to 290°/40 mph.
    <u>Enemy Airfields:</u>
       Little cloud, moderate visibility.

12.   <u>Night photographic statistics.</u>

       Number of photographs examined 457
       Number of photographs showing ground detail
           (plotted within 3 miles .... 171)
           (plotted outside 3 miles ......0)........... 224
           (unplotted ....53)
       Number of photographs showing fire tracks only
           (plotted within 3 miles ......18)
           (plotted outside 3 miles ......0)........... 233
           (unplotted ....215)

    It is probable that nearly all the aircraft bombed within three
miles and the majority within one mile, of the aiming point.
The presence of a smoke screen over the target makes an exact
assessment impossible.

13.   <u>Narrative of attack.</u>

    The Blind Markers opened the attack well on time, but not accurately.
Most of their T.I.'s fell 1½ to 2 miles beyond their correct aiming point,
"F". This seems to have been due to Ruden Island, their release point,
registering poorly on the 'Y' apparatus; many aircraft carried on, and
mistakenly released their markers on the image of the Northern tip of the
Peenemunde penisula. Some crews tried to confirm their position visually,
but were misled by the similarity of the Karlshagen Labour Camp with the
buildings around their aiming point. Fortunately, however, one aircraft
(156/O) dropped its markers really accurately, and was supported by the
Master Bomber and five visual markers between Zero - 3 and Zero + 2.
At least four of these six salvoes of yellow were placed near Aiming Point
"F", and although a very effective smoke screen, started soon after the
first markers were dropped, hampered visual identification. Only one visual
marker dropped his yellow near the inaccurate concentration of reds.
The backers up supported the good work of the visual markers; of the
eight plotted by photographs, six are shown in the immediate vicinity of "F"
the aiming point. The first wave of the main force attacked soon after
the first group of the Backers Up had fallen, and about two thirds of
the aircraft bombed the correct concentration, the remainder being diverted
to the encampment.

14.   The first wave of "Shifters" attacked punctually between zero + 10
and zero + 12. Four of the five were plotted and only one showed Aiming
Point "B", the others overshooting to Aiming Point "F" The second wave
of Backers Up naturally tended to support the incorrect markers of the
shifters, but were warned of their inaccuracy by the Master Bomber, with
the result that this phase of the attack came to be fairly well centred
on Aiming Point "B", although slightly to the seaward side of the factory.

72

Nt Raid Report (ORS)   (A.H.B. Papers

15.   The transfer from Aiming Point "B" to "E" was less successful
than that from "F" to "B". Five of the six shifters in the next wave
were plotted, three between "E" and "B", and two the other side of "F".
Because of this overshooting, most of the third wave of backers up
also bombed 1 - 1½ miles beyond the correct position, so that much more
of this wave was centred on "B" instead of "E" The Master Bomber was
apparently under the impression that this was the correct Aiming Point
and continually broadcast that the greens were well placed, exhorting
the M in Force to support them. No T.I. were photographed on Aiming
Point "E" until Zero + 33, and even then comparatively few aircraft bombed
them. Those which did so employed visual identification, or else a
time and distance run from Ruden Island.

Bay Reconnaissance.

16.   Photographs taken twelve hours after the attack showed many buildings
still burning in the Experimental Station at Peenemunde. Damage to
factories and houses for personnel was extremely severe. In the Northern
Manufacturing Area (Experimental Establishment - A/P "E") 27 buildings
of medium size including the Senior Officers' Mess were completely
destroyed, and 9 others, including some of the largest and most important
badly damaged. In the Southern Manufacturing Area (Factory Workshops -
A/P "B") another large building was partly demolished by two direct hits,
and another of equal size seriously affected. A medium sized building was
damaged by a direct hit, and another by blast. Many hits were recorded
on the railway tracks in this part of the Station, and one on a stationery
train. The steam pipe which skirts the foreshore on the Eastern side was
disrupted in at least ten places, the target area was full of craters.

17.   In the living and sleeping quarters (Karlshagen K.D.F. Camp) - A/P
"F") forty small detached huts were completely flattened, and fifty more
gutted by fire or shattered by H.E., as well as three large barrack
type blocks in the central section. West of the camp, a large carriage
shed was half demolished, and a coal dump was still on fire at the time
of photography. In the nearby labour camp to the south, at least 23 out
of 45 large huts for personnel were completely destroyed, and others
damaged. A few detached houses suffered badly from high explosive.

Alternative Targets.

18.   Three aircraft resorted to alternative targets: Two bombed Sylt and
a third an island East of Rostock. Three other aircraft which had already
attacked the primary dropped bombs on Ruden Island (2) and Stralsund.

Special Equipment.

19.   H2S: 67 'Y' aircraft were despatched - 16 blind markers and 51
Main Force aircraft, carrying H2E for navigational purposes only.
15 of the blind markers reported attack, twelve dropping flares and
T.I. on H2S and the other three retaining their markers as their sets
were unserviceable. 39 Main Force aircraft found their sets in working
order over the target, but none used them for bombing. Two 'Y' aircraft
were lost.

20.   GEE: The Norther Chain operated on the Utah frequency, and the
Eastern chain on the Wyoming frequency, throughout the raid. The
Eastern chain also operated on the Arizona frequency from 23.15 to 01.45
hours. Average ranges of 315 and 340 miles were obtained and the maximum
range was 524 miles. Many types of jamming were reported and this was

73

the limiting factor on the Wyoming frequency. The weakness of the
Utah transmission limited the ranges on the Northern chain. But relatively
free fixes were obtained on the Arizona frequency whcih was mainly
jammed by "noise". The use of various transmissions forced the enemy
to spread his jamming so that fixes were obtained on the normal
frequency beyond the usual range, several being over 400 miles, and
one 524 miles.

Defences.

21. Flak and Searchlights:- Light flak was active in the target area
against low flying aircraft. Heavy flak was reported as slight in
the form of barrage at ten thousand feet. There were few searchlights
near the target. Active opposition was encountered off the track at
Flensburg, Kiel and Abenraa. Fourteen aircraft were damaged.

22.   Fighters:- Little was overheard of individually controlled fighters
but one patrol was intercepted on VHF. Other VHF traffic may not
have been heard because of the distance of all the overland part of
the route from our intercepting stations. A running commentary was
however heard in operation from 22.20 hours until 02.24 hours, announcing
the probable targets for the approaching force consecutively as Kiel,
Berlin, Rostock, Swinemunde and Stettin. At least two Groups of
fighters were directed to the German capital after the diversionary
Mosquitoes had dropped their bombs. From aircraft heard landing on
W/T, it is estimated that the total fighter effort was about 100
aircraft. R/T gave no indication of the success achieved apart from
one fighter which claimed the destruction of three bombers as it
was about to land at Sylt, 92 interceptions were reported including
26 attacks, not an excessive number for so long a route in bright
moonlight. Fighter activity was marked on the whole journey especially
along the first part of the homeward journey. Seven returning bombers
were damaged by enemy aircraft.

Casualties:

23.   Number of aircraft missing 40 (6.7%)
      Number of aircraft damaged
              (flak ....14)
              (fighter ....7).......... 30 (5.2%)
              (non-enemy action ......11)

     The aircraft attacked in three waves - 231 Lancasters, Stirlings,
and Halifaxes from Zero + 2, to Zero + 12; 113 Lancasters from Zero + 16,
to Zero + 24; and 180 Lancasters and Halifaxes from Zero + 28, to
Zero + 40. Six aircraft were lost in the first wave (2.5%), three
(2.7%) in the second wave, and twenty-nine (6.1%) in the third wave.
The reasons for the heavy losses in the last wave are probably:-
      (i) The fighters sent to Berlin had probably returned;
      (ii) More than half these aircraft bombed from less than 8,000 feet;
      (iii) The last wave straggled, and thirty five aircraft bombed
      in the fifteen minutes after the planned end of the attack.

24. Thirty four losses have been located: 11 in the target area (four
to fighters and seven to flak), 9 outbound (one to fighter, four to flak
over Flensburg, Sylt, Mando and Abenraa, and four to unknown causes); 13
homebound (four to fighter, four to flak, and five to unknown causes), and
1 en route, the direction of which is uncertain. Fighters were probably
                                        responsible for

Nt. Raid Report (ORS)

most of the unknown losses.

BERLIN

25.   8 P.F.F. Mosquitoes were ordered to make a diversionary raid on Berlin an hour before the start of the main attack. Seven bombed the capital from a clear sky. One aircraft overshot on landing and was destroyed, but the crew escaped unhurt. One aircraft was lost without trace. All carried WINDOW

MLM/PVD
BC/S26342/2/ORS
20th October 1943.

STATISTICAL APPENDIX TO O.R.S. REPORT

TARGET	GROUP	TYPE	SORTIES	A/C REPORTING ATTACK on PEENEMUNDE	ALT'VE TGT	ABORTIVE Over enemy territ.	ABORTIVE At home	MISSING	DAMAGE Flak	DAMAGE Fighter	DAMAGE N.E/A	INTERCEPTIONS Attacked	Not Attacked
PEENEMUNDE	8 PFF	Hal II&V	1	1									
		Hal IA	14	13				1					
		Lanc I	1	1									
		Lanc III	58	55	1*	3							6
	8 Main Force	Hal IA	6	5									
		Lanc III	14	14	2*			1					
	1	Lanc I	20	18		2			1		1AC	1	2
		Lanc III	93	86	2	2		3	2	1AC+1		5	14
	3	Stirl I	1	4				2					5
		Stirl III	53	47		4		1	1	1	1B	5	
	4	Lanc II	12	11		3				1AC+5	1B+1	4	10
		Hal II&V	87	80	1	2		3		1	1		9
		Hal IA	58	55			1				1	2	
	5	Lanc I	23	18		1		4		1AC+1		1	2
		Lanc III	84	79		2		13	6	2AC	1AC+2	9	8
	6	Hal II&V	37	29		2		6		1	1	2	7
		Hal IA	16	16		1		4		1AC	1AC		1
		Lanc II	9	6				2					2
PEENEMUNDE TOTAL			597	531	3+3*	22	1	40	1AC+13	4Ac+3	2B+3AC	26	66
BERLIN	8 PFF	Mosquito IV	8	7				1	1E				
BERLIN total			8	7				1	1E				
TOTAL			605	538	3+3*	22	1	41	1E+1AC +13	4AC+3	2B+3AC	26 +6	66

RESULTS

	H.E.	Incend.
P.	1518.0	270.0
A.	9.3	2.1
M.	122.7	26.6

HEAVY BOMBS 4,000-pound
P. 227
A. 2
M. 14

TONS OF BOMBS H.E.
P. 5.2
H. 8

* = Also attacked primary.

Appendix to O.R.S. (B.C.) Night Raid Report on attack on Peenemunde of 17/18th August 1943.

Nt. Raid Report (ORS)

(A.H.B. Papers

Extract from Operational Night Raid Report 386, 27/28.7.43

HAMBURG

***

Defences

22. <u>Flak and searchlights</u>: The general opinion of crews indicated that enemy ground defences at Hamburg had been increased since the previous attack. The usual decrease in intensity during the attack was reported, but the number of a/c damaged by flak was fairly constant throughout the raid. Much of the flak was considered to be of barrage form. Some reported instances of aircraft held in seachlight cones but not engaged by flak suggest searchlight co-operation with fighters. ...

23. <u>Fighters</u>: The R/T traffic intercepted on this night was from some areas of a different nature from that which is usually heard. Instead of the usual brief instructions as to course and height, ground stations were heard to give something of a running commentary regarding the course and height of the British aircraft, and information about their being held in searchlights. The conclusion to be drawn is that the enemy have decided to use a system of much looser control of his fighters when interference from window made it necessary. In the traffic heard there were several direct references to the fighters flying without ground control.

24. Some remarks indicate that the enemy was placing considerable reliance on the use of A.I. It would appear therefore that Window was not having as serious an effect on the enemy A.I. as had been hoped. The number of night fighters heard by Wireless Intelligence on this night were 80, in the traffic of 26 of which British aircraft were mentioned. The total number is somewhat less than on the first Hamburg raid, but the number in whose traffic British aircraft were mentioned is about the same.   (ORS Report dated 11 Oct 1943)

Extract from Operational Night Raid Report No. 387.28/29.7.43

HAMBURG

***

Enemy Defences.

7. Controlled fighters were active in North West Germany and Holland, but only one was sighted by our bombers, a Ju.88 over Terschelling. At both Hamburg and Duesselfordmoderate heavy flak was accurately predicted at heights above 20,000 feet. Aircraft were held in searchlight cones at both targets, one for four minutes over Duesseldorf at 29,000 feet. ...   (ORS Report dated 28 Sept 1943)

Extract from Operational Night Raid Report No.397 28/29.7.43

HAMBURG

***

Defences.

20. <u>Flak and searchlights.</u> Flak was more intense over Hamburg than on 27th-28th July, starting strongly in co-operation with searchlights, but then easing off noticeably. It was mostly fired in barrage, but

Nt Raid Reports (ORS)   (A.H.B. Papers

sometimes predicted and sometimes against illuminated targets. The
number of searchlights had been greatly increased both en route and
in the target area; an outer belt stretched in a semi-circle round
the town, from the North East to the south-west, and inside this,
other searchlights apparently acted as fighter guides, sometimes
exposing horizontally for track indicating and to silhouette attacking
bombers. ...

Fighters.
   24 interceptions by enemy fighters were reported, including
22 attacks. Most of the fighters operated in the height band from
17,000 to 20,000 feet, in which seventy per cent of the interceptions
occurred. This explained why the new technique of limited ground
control which the enemy has been forced to adopt. Fighters were given
general instructions regarding the course and height of the British
aircraft, rather than specific instructions to enable them to inter-
cept particilar aircraft. Some seem to have landed, refuelled, and
taken off again - an unusual procedure, but one which would be
encouraged in a freelance system.   (ORS Report dated 28 Sept 43)

Extract from Operation Night Raid Report No. 389 30/31.7.43

REMSCHEID

***

Fighters
        Intercepted wireless traffic revealed eleven or twelve
fighters operating on the same frequency in the target area; the
terms and call-signs used indicate that these were day fighters.
They also appeared to be co-operating with searchlights when landing.
There was little evidence of the system of freelance fighters with
the running commentary by the ground control on the general direction
and height of the bombers was in general use, although a few references
to height and direction were overheard. 130 fighters were heard
operating, but only 45 of these mentioned British Aircraft.

Extract from Operational Night Raid Report No.396. 7/8.8.43

TURIN AND GENOA

***

Turin and Genoa: Method as for Milan.

8.   Tactics: WINDOW was to be used only when within fifty miles
of the target; rate of dropping one packet per minute; one P.F.F.
Lancaster on Turin was to carry the Raid Commentator, who was to
broadcast on "Darky" frequency to aid and advise. All crews were
to listen on this frequency while over the target area. It was
emphasised that very careful co-operation between pilot and bomb-
aimer would be necessary to make full use of the commentary. Brief
reports on its effectiveness were to be rendered in each Raid Report.
One blind marker was to carry a reserve commentator.
                              (ORS Report dated 4 October 43)

41 of Our Aircraft Failed to Return

Pathfinder Force

No 139 (Jamaica) Squadron
F/O A. S. Cooke
Sgt D. A. Dixon

No 35 Squadron
F/S P. R. Raggett
F/O S. A. Baldwin
P/O A. J. Perkins
Sgt Roberts
Sgt P. H. Palmer
St D. S. Woods
Sgt Webster

Pathfinder Force

No 405 R.C.A.F. Squadron
F/O H. S. McIntyre
Sgt D. C. Angus
Sgt W. E. Gimby
Sgt T. J. Bowling
Sgt W. Haugen
Sgt T. A. Pargeter
Sgt H. Cooke

No 1 Bomber Group

No 12 Squadron R.A.F.
S/L F. B. Slade
P/O G. R. Carpenter
P/O J. F. McIntyre
P/O C. W. Manning
Sgt S. Chapman
P/O P. H. Phillips
Sgt L. Myers

No 100 Squadron R.A.F.
F/O H. I. Spiers
Sgt T. W. Torbett
P/O J. Weaver
Sgt K. F. Goode
Sgt S. J. Cassell
Sgt O. M. Atkins
Sgt W. Francis

No 103 Squadron R.A.F.
Sgt P. J. O'Donnell
Sgt C. P. Williams
F/S M. G. Medhurst
F/S P. J. Capon
Sgt W. H. Greaves
Sgt C. N. Lee
F/S E. R. Biggs

No 3 Bomber Group

No 15 Squadron R.A.F.
Sgt R. Grundy
Sgt C. Hudson
Sgt C. Carter
Sgt L. Wood
Sgt R. Taylor
Sgt J. Scandrett
Sgt E. Honeybill

No 620 Squadron R.A.F.
S/L A. P. Lambert
F/O L. G. Kennett
Sgt W. W. Evans
Sgt R. I. Cooper
Sgt D. J. Carrington
Sgt E. F. Leeming
Sgt V. Enders

No 115 Squadron R.A.F.
F/O R. Pusey
F/O C. G. Bruton
Sgt L. Howard
P/O J. Cable
Sgt M. McKibbon
Sgt J. Corbett
Sgt T. Leonard

No 4 Bomber Group

No 10 Squadron R.A.F.
F/S A. J. E. Long
F/S J. Heal
F/S J. Cooper
F/S L. Sefton
F/S D. M. Goulden
F/S D. Galloway
F/S Willetts
F/O C. L. Berbezat

No 77 Squadron R.A.F.
Sgt F. E. Shefford
Sgt F. J. Lane
Sgt G. Wood
Sgt J. R. Vint
Sgt H. F. Roza
Sgt A. W. Ready
Sgt J. B. S. Smith

No 158 Squadron R.A.F.
F/S W. D. Caldwell
F/O W. R. Schmehl
Sgt R. H. Reay
Sgt J. E. Pearson
Sgt M. Czajkowski
Sgt A. Tice

No 5 Bomber Group

No 467 R.A.A.F. Squadron
S/L A. D. Raphael
Sgt V. Smith
Sgt F. Gray
F/O R. G. Carter
F/S D. Fielden
Sgt A. C. Brand
F/S F. B. Garrett
F/L M. H. Parry

No 467 R.A.A.F. Squadron
P/O F. W. Dixon
Sgt L. Hayward
Sgt C. A. Bicknell
Sgt E. W. Dickson
Sgt P. Lowe
Sgt R. Hughes
Sgt R. Garnett

No 619 R.A.F. Squadron
Sgt A. J. Pearce
Sgt W. Humphrey
F/O J. M. Warren
F/O L. G. Davis
Sgt T. B. Barrie
Sgt R. D. Deugard
Sgt D. B. Francis

No 619 Squadron R.A.F.
W/C I. J. McGhie
F/S P. J. Horsham
F/O E. G. Prest
F/S P. M. Goldsmith
Sgt F. A. Thompson
Sgt W. Mitchell
Sgt A. Chapman
F/S V. G. Stabell

No 619 Squadron R.A.F.
P/O O. A. O'Leary
Sgt T. Underdown
F/S R. Crossley
Sgt J. T. Hubbard
Sgt J. H. Shaw
Sgt D. J. Cox
F/S L. F. English

No 61 Squadron R.A.F.
P/O H. R. Madgett
Sgt Lewis
Sgt H. Robinson
Sgt S. C. Palk
F/O F. D. Norton
P/O R. Bradley
Sgt A. W. Souter
Sgt J. J. Wakefield

No 61 Squadron R.A.F.
F/L T. A. Stewart
Sgt Bradey
P/O F. Barker
Sgt J. F. Trotter
Sgt Clarke
Sgt L. H. Thompson
F/S R. K. Buxton
Sgt A. E. Harris

No 61 Squadron R.A.F.
F/O W. Hughes
Sgt T. Graham
Sgt L. H. Scholey
Sgt B. J. Brown
Sgt D. Easton
Sgt R. C. Walton
Sgt W. B. Ness

No 61 Squadron R.A.F.
F/S R. J. Docker
F/S Vidler
Sgt L. Lucas
Sgt R. Laughton
Sgt E. G. Francis
Sgt S. W. James
Sgt P. W. Mitchell
Sgt R. R. Urquhart

No 57 Squadron R.A.F.
W/C W. R. Haskell
F/S C. Butterworth
Sgt R. Stringer
F/O J. Jones
Sgt J. Harkness
Sgt D. E. Nye
Sgt J. E. John
Sgt J. Lamb

No 49 Squadron R.A.F.
F/O Randall
Sgt L. J. Henley
Sgt L. F. Freeman
Sgt R. Fowlston
Sgt J. Buchanan
Sgt W. J. Stiles
Sgt L. W. Slaughter

No 49 Squadron R.A.F.
S/L R. G. Todd-White
Sgt A. Purrington
P/O A. Batchelor
P/O R. James
Sgt G. Humble
P/O F. Plant
Sgt Brocklehurst

No 49 Squadron R.A.F.
P/O T. E. Tomlin
F/S K. E. Watson
F/S W. Rooke
Sgt Stancliffe
Sgt W. Davies
F/S F. Tonkin
Sgt Sylvester

No 49 Squadron R.A.F.
Sgt C. Robinson
Sgt W. Boyd
F/O Duckham
Sgt A. E. Anderson
Sgt D. Parkin
P/O W. J. Lowe
Sgt J. Wallner

No 44 Squadron R.A.F.
Sgt R. M. Campbell
Sgt J. G. Watkins
P/O L. G. Poperwell
Sgt A. H. Thompson
Sgt T. Graham
Sgt H. G. Macannich
Sgt W. Phillip

No 44 Squadron R.A.F.
P/O R. C. Harding
Sgt T. N. Weston
F/S L. Prendergast
F/S P. Pynisky
Sgt Quanee W. H.
F/S S. Shaw
Sgt L. F. McDermott

No 44 Squadron R.A.F.
Sgt W. J. Drew
Sgt J. B. Reid
Sgt S. I. Rudkin
Sgt W. Sparkes
Sgt J. T. Jopling
Sgt C. G. Jones
Sgt J. H. Bassett

No 6 R.C.A.F. Group

No 428 R.C.A.F. Squadron
Sgt J. Sheridan
Sgt H. E. Murphy
Sgt T. B. Lifman
Sgt D. Kennedy
Sgt W. E. Cogger
Sgt N. R. Mitchell
Sgt E. R. Marks

No 428 R.C.A.F. Squadron
Sgt W. W. Blackmore
Sgt N. F. Oliver
Sgt W. S. E. Wood
Sgt F. S Williams
Sgt C. F. Richard
Sgt G. F. Hobson
Sgt G. C. Seaborn

No 428 R.C.A.F. Squadron
F/L G. W. Fanson
F/O D. H. Orr
Sgt D. J. McNeill
Sgt R. A. Lewis
Sgt L. M. Banks
Sgt M. C. McCullum
Sgt J. A. Leighton

No 419 R.C.A.F. Squadron
F/S S. Pekin
F/O P. J. Sparkes
Sgt J. K. Gilvary
Sgt H. Price
Sgt F. P. Davis
Sgt S. C. Ramm

No 419 R.C.A.F. Squadron
F/O S. M. Heard
Sgt C. S. Walter
Sgt P. O. McSween
Sgt J. J. Newbon
Sgt G. Blyth
Sgt D. Thornton
Sgt J. W. Dally
Sgt D. M. McPherson

No 419 R.C.A.F. Squadron
Sgt J. M. Batterton
Sgt G. F. Parker
Sgt O. Jerome
Sgt D. A. Lloyd
Sgt K. Dixon
Sgt L. Powers
Sgt H. V. Morris

No 426 R.C.A.F. Squadron
W/C L. Crooks
F/S A. J. Howes
F/L F. P. Marsh
Sgt K. W. Reading
Sgt J. C. Hislop
P/O T. Dos Santos
Sgt H. M. Smith

No 426 R.C.A.F. Squadron
F/L D. D. Shuttleworth
F/O G. C. Robinson
Sgt K. G. Gawthrop
Sgt J. M. L. Bouvier
Sgt S. Barnes
F/O G. W. Scammell
Sgt G. Bentley

No 427 R.C.A.F. Squadron
Sgt F. J. D. Brady
Sgt R. W. Charman
Sgt R. I. Johnson
Sgt J. L. Troman
Sgt O. M. McIntyre
Sgt J. L. Fletcher
Sgt I. W. Pugh

No 434 R.C.A.F. Squadron
F/S Piper
P/O Wetter
Sgt Jordan
Sgt Connor
Sgt Renaud
Sgt Irving
Sgt Brown

No 434 R.C.A.F. Squadron
F/O Colquhoun
Sgt Dobie
F/S Fitzpatrick
F/O Beswick
Sgt Young
F/S Lapointe
Sgt Crees

No 434 R.C.A.F. Squadron
Sgt Johnston
Sgt Gibbs
P/O McPherson
F/S Chistmas
F/S Labelle
Sgt Rowe

King George VI
Distinguished Service Order

The Awards

Distinguished Flying Cross

King George VI
Distinguished Flying Medal

Appendix 1   Peenemunde Entry in Flight Log

YEAR 1943. MONTH | DATE	AIRCRAFT Type	No.	PILOT, OR 1ST PILOT	2ND PILOT, PUPIL OR PASSENGER	DUTY (INCLUDING RESULTS AND REMARK
—	—	—	—	—	TOTALS BROUGHT FORWAR
August.					
17/18.	Lancaster	W.	Self.	S/L Scrivener F/o Forster F/o Ross F/o Davies F/o Tober. F/o Price.	Operations Peenemunde. (Baltic)
20	Lanc.	F.	Self.	Crew.	Air Test.
25	Lanc.	B.	Self.	Crew.	S. Harcourt + return
September					
6.	Lanc.	B.	Self.	S/L Scrivener F/o Ross F/o Forster F/o Davies S/L Johnson F/o Price.	Operations Munich.
8.	Lanc	B.	Self	Crew	to Steddington + return
13.	Lanc.	B.	Self.	Crew	to Stanton Harcourt + return.
14.	Lanc	S.	Self	Crew	To Wellfield (Border) + Training. Return

GRAND TOTAL [Cols. (1) to (10)]
1801 ....Hrs 55 ....Mins.

TOTALS CARRIED FORWAR

82

"Master of Ceremonies". Night Fighters accounted for   2·00
many of our aircraft in bright moonlight. A good
attack and resulted in the destruction of the Experimental
Establishment. Attacked by T.E. fighter and we claimed
it as "damaged."   7.45.

Awarded immediate D.S.O.
                          1·00.

                          1·00.

Fair attack — but cloud rather spoiled the show — it
was about 8/10 thin St. cu.   2·00
                              8·00.

                          ·50

                          ·50

                          3.15.

| 475.55 | | | | 824.40 | | | 296·25 | | | | | |
| (1) | (2) | (3) | (4) | (5) | (6) | (7) | (8) | (9) | (10) | (11) | (12) | (13) |

HMS 30/175/169

Most Humbly submitted to Your Majesty
by Your Majesty's Most Humble
and Most Devoted Servant,

appd GR

THAT Your Majesty may be graciously pleased to approve the following immediate awards which have been made by the Air Officer Commanding-in-Chief, Bomber Command, in recognition of gallantry displayed in flying operations against the enemy:-

Distinguished Service Order

Acting Group Captain John Henry SEARBY, D.F.C., Royal Air Force, No.83 Squadron.

Distinguished Flying Cross

Flying Officer Alfred HAGAN (135880), Royal Air Force Volunteer Reserve, No.77 Squadron.

Flying Officer Robert TAYLOR (130843), Royal Air Force Volunteer Reserve, No.1409 Flight.

Pilot Officer Granville WILSON, D.F.M., (141094), Royal Air Force Volunteer Reserve, No.7 Squadron.

Warrant Officer Warren Leonard WILSON, (Aus.403972), Royal Australian Air Force, No.467 (R.A.A.F.) Squadron.

Conspicuous Gallantry Medal (Flying)

618877, Sergeant George William OLIVER, Royal Air Force, No.467 (R.A.A.F.) Squadron.

/continued overleaf

Archibald Sinclair

Air Ministry

30th August, 1943.

Air Commodore John Searby, DSO, DFC, RAF (Rtd)

Air Commodore Searby commanded two Lancaster Squadrons during the Second World War. After six months as a Flight Commander serving under Wing Commander Guy Gibson V.C. he succeeded to the command of No 106 Bomber Squadron at Syerston. This was the period when the Command was building up strength for the furious battles of The Ruhr, Hamburg and Berlin and the Pathfinder Force; a most logical solution to what had long been a serious problem, was beginning to achieve results in the face of every kind of difficulty. Although tour-expired in terms of sorties flown Air Commodore Searby accepted an invitation from Air Vice-Marshal Bennett to assume command of No 83 Pathfinder

Squadron immediately following his departure from Syerston on conclusion of his tour of duty as Commanding Officer of No 106 and he embarked on a succession of Pathfinder operations lasting to the end of the year. Previous experience and a lifetime interest in every aspect of air navigation lay behind his decision and No 83 Squadron enjoyed a period of highly successful operation coupled with a relatively low casualty rate. Included in these attacks was the mounting of the assault by six hundred aircraft on the German Research Station at Peenemunde in August 1943 when he played the part of Master Bomber remaining over the target for forty-five minutes until the last main force bomber had made its attack.